EPITOME OF BIBLIOGRAPHY OF AMERICAN LITERATURE

Compiled by
Michael Winship

with Philip B. Eppard and Rachel J. Howarth

North American Press
a division of Fulcrum Publishing
Golden, Colorado

1995

Library of Congress Cataloging-in-Publication Data

Winship, Michael.
        Epitome of Bibliography of American literature / compiled by
    Michael Winship, with Philip B. Eppard and Rachel J. Howarth.
            p.   cm.
        ISBN 1-55591-950-2 :
            1. American literature—Bibliography. I. Eppard, Philip B.
    II. Howarth, Rachel J. III. Blanck, Jacob, 1906–1974. Bibliography
    of American literature. IV. Title.
    Z1225.W74   1995
    [PS88]
    016.81—dc20   94-36955
                                                                        CIP

Printed in the United States of America

0   9   8   7   6   5   4   3   2   1

North American Press
a division of Fulcrum Publishing
350 Indiana Street, Suite 350
Golden, Colorado 80401–5093
(800) 992-2908

TABLE OF CONTENTS

INTRODUCTION

This is an Epitome of *Bibliography of American Literature* (New Haven: Yale University Press, 1955–91), compiled by Jacob Blanck for the Bibliographical Society of America, and is designed to make the information contained in that standard reference work more readily accessible. It contains concise and accurate information about a large number of books important to American literature described there with references by entry number. We hope that it will prove useful to all who are interested in reading and studying our national literary culture.

According to booktrade lore, Jacob Blanck was introduced to Merle Johnson in 1930 by I. R. Brussel (L.O.G.S.). Brussel insisted that Johnson hire the promising young bookman at twenty-five dollars a week, and Johnson set Blanck to work revising and correcting his compilation of checklists of the works of American authors, *American First Editions*, first published in 1929. Blanck contributed substantially to the expanded second edition of that work published in 1932 and was chiefly responsible for the third and fourth editions of 1936 and 1942. This and other bibliographical work established Blanck as one of the foremost bibliographers of American books, and in 1943 he convinced J. K. Lilly, Jr.—an Indianapolis businessman, book collector and philanthropist—to support the preparation of Blanck's greatest accomplishment, *Bibliography of American Literature* (BAL). This nine-volume analytical bibliography of the works of 281 significant American literary authors from the late 18th to the early 20th centuries is now a standard reference source, regularly consulted by scholars, librarians, booksellers and collectors as the best source of detailed and accurate bibliographical information about American authors and their books. Blanck lived to see only six volumes through to publication; the final three volumes were completed and edited after his death in 1974 by Virginia L. Smyers and Michael Winship.

From the very beginning of his work on that project, Blanck recognized the need for a condensed or abridged version which would serve the same uses as *Merle Johnson's American First Editions* by providing a summary checklist of the publications of American literary authors in a form that is both portable and affordable. This epitome is our attempt to realize that vision and to provide the academic, library and booktrade communities with increased and easier access to the core information in the nine volumes of BAL.

Our goal has been to provide a useful complement to the full BAL rather than a replacement for it. We have followed the scope and style as set forth in Blanck's "Preface" in the first volume of BAL and have limited ourselves to information contained in the published volumes. In particular we have not included editions of an author's works that have appeared since the publication of that author's list in BAL, nor have we incorporated the few corrections or additions that have been discovered since publication of the original volumes. Because we have not been able to reexamine original copies of works listed in BAL, it has not always been possible to use such terms as "edition" or "reprint" in strict accordance to modern bibliographical usage. In producing the epitome, we have made every attempt to present information in a clear and useful manner even when this has required us to adapt or ignore our general guidelines.

Every author in the BAL has been included in the epitome, but each author's list has been reduced to include only primary works in separately published books, those items that are generally given full entries in BAL. As in BAL, British editions of titles published in the United States are only given separate entries when they precede the American edition. Generally omitted from the epitome are sheet music, broadsides, leaflets and ephemeral pamphlets, as well as special copyright and (especially posthumous) private printings of an author's works. We have also generally omitted off-subject or non-literary works (especially of a political, religious, medical or educational nature), translations and compilations, as well as occasional addresses, orations and sermons. Reprints (including first separate editions of individual works and collections of short pieces that are made up of a majority of reprinted material) are ignored. Where it seemed useful, however, we have made exceptions to these guidelines and have included important or well-known secondary or ephemeral works (especially an author's first or early publications), compilations or translations, private printings of dramatic texts for acting, and standard collected editions (even if chiefly made up of reprinted material).

Although we have been consciously selective in creating the epitome, we have included in the epitome many references to BAL entries for publications that have not been given separate entries. In this way, the epitome accounts for earlier private or copyright printings of a work, separate printings of an important piece, revised and extended editions of reprints published under changed titles. In such references the BAL entry numbers are always placed within parentheses to indicate that the entry will not be found in the epitome.

Each epitome entry begins with the BAL entry number on which it is based. A star "*" before the BAL number in the epitome entry indicates that significant additional information will be found in the full BAL entry. Typically, this indicates that the BAL entry distinguishes and identifies multiple editions, printings, issues or states. Variant bindings have not, however, been signaled in this way. Users of the epitome will also need to consult the BAL for additional information such as signature collation, publication information and location of copies, though ample margins have been provided to encourage individual users to transfer such information as may prove useful to their needs.

A short title follows the BAL entry number in the epitome entry. Titles are transcribed exactly from the BAL but may be shortened. Omissions from the beginning or end of a title are not noted, but omissions within the title are indicated by marks of omission ("...") Where appropriate, a statement from the title page that explains the facts of a work's creation or publication is given in a separate paragraph of comments.

Any pseudonym which appears on the title page follows the title in upper and lower case letters, as does the title page statement of the author for works published under an author's initials or name before marriage. Minor misspellings of an author's name are not noted nor are such fictitious claims as that a work was "edited" by the author from the memoirs or papers of another, though this or other relevant information about the author or pseudonym may appear in the comments. In BAL works published as "by the author of" an earlier work are treated as if pseudonymous, but in the epitome we have simply labeled these works as anonymous in the comments. Pseudonyms have not been transcribed in those few instances where authors regularly published their works under a single pseudonym, e.g. Gail Hamilton, Charles Egbert Craddock, Mark Twain.

Imprint information is regularized in the epitome entry with all supplied information not taken from the title page placed within angle brackets. The primary city of publication is given first, often abbreviated, followed by secondary places of publication given on the title page. No more than two cities are given, however; the style followed is "NY & Lon" or "NY, Lon, &c." Next, the primary publisher is named, again shortened or regularized, though initials are included if needed to distinguish between publishers with the same or similar names. Secondary publishers and their places of business are not usually listed, even when the primary and secondary publishers are closely linked (as in the case of Macmillan & Co., New York, and Macmillan Company, Ltd., London; or, Wiley & Putnam, New York, and Wiley's London Agency). If the printer and no publisher is named in the title page imprint, the printer is noted. If the author is the publisher, the publisher is given as "The Author"; if a society is the publisher and named in the title, the publisher is given as "The Society." Dates are regularized and given in arabic numerals. For multivolume works with multiple imprint dates, the style is "1883–86".

Comments or references follow in a separate paragraph. These begin with a statement of the number of volumes or parts, if more than one, followed by information on the author or editor. Series titles or other title information are given next, taken from the title page and placed within quotation marks if appropriate. References to other relevant BAL entries or other information complete this paragraph.

This is in every sense a collaborative work. Philip B. Eppard carefully selected and checked entries from four volumes of BAL, helped with the planning and reviewed the drafts of the entire work. His contributions are everywhere apparent. Rachel J. Howarth worked two long summers as an assistant on the project: without her care, common sense and good humor it would not have been completed. Her work was funded in part by a grant from the University Research Institute at the University of Texas at Austin. We have been advised and encouraged in the preparation of this work by W. H. Bond, V. L. Smyers and R. E. Stoddard. But the work owes its greatest debt to the vision of Jacob Blanck. As he well understood, a work such as this requires judgment and understanding, as well as attention to detail and dedication to accuracy. To whatever extent we have succeeded here, he stands as our inspiration.

LIST OF AUTHORS IN
BIBLIOGRAPHY OF AMERICAN LITERATURE

VOLUME 8

VOLUME 9

ABBREVIATIONS

A star "*" before the BAL number at the beginning of an epitome entry indicates that significant additional information will be found in BAL. In addition to common abbreviations, the following have been used:

Assn	Association
BAL	*Bibliography of American Literature* (1955–91)
Bos	Boston
Chi	Chicago
Evans	Charles Evans, *American Bibliography* (1903–59)
Hts	Heights
Lon	London
NY	New York
Phila	Philadelphia
PR	Press
Ptd	Printed
Ptg	Printing
Ptr(s)	Printer(s)
Pub.	Publishing or Publisher
Pub'd	Published
SF	San Francisco
Soc'y	Society
Spgs	Springs
U	University
Wash DC	Washington, D.C.

Henry Brooks Adams
1838–1918

1. CIVIL-SERVICE REFORM. Bos: Fields, Osgood, 1869.
"From the North American Review for October, 1869."

2. CHAPTERS OF ERIE, AND OTHER ESSAYS. Bos: Osgood, 1871.
With Charles F. Adams, Jr.

9. THE LIFE OF ALBERT GALLATIN. Phila & Lon: Lippincott, 1879.

11. DEMOCRACY AN AMERICAN NOVEL. NY: Holt, 1880.
Anon. *Leisure-Hour Series*, No. 112 <i.e. 111>.

14. JOHN RANDOLPH. Bos & NY: Houghton, Mifflin, 1882.
American Statesmen Series. Revised edition published in 1883 (No. 15).

16. ESTHER A NOVEL. By Frances Snow Compton. NY: Holt, 1884.
American Novel Series, No. 3.

19. HISTORY OF THE UNITED STATES OF AMERICA DURING THE FIRST AD-
MINISTRATION OF THOMAS JEFFERSON. NY: Scribner's Sons, 1889.
2v.

*20. HISTORY OF THE UNITED STATES OF AMERICA DURING THE SECOND
ADMINISTRATION OF THOMAS JEFFERSON. NY: Scribner's Sons, 1890.
2v. Also privately printed in 1885 (No. 17).

*21. HISTORY OF THE UNITED STATES OF AMERICA DURING THE FIRST AD-
MINISTRATION OF JAMES MADISON. NY: Scribner's Sons, 1890.
2v. Also privately printed in 1888 (No. 18).

22. HISTORY OF THE UNITED STATES OF AMERICA DURING THE SECOND
ADMINISTRATION OF JAMES MADISON. NY: Scribner's Sons, 1891.
3v.

23. HISTORICAL ESSAYS. NY: Scribner's Sons, 1891.

25. MEMOIRS OF MARAU TAAROA LAST QUEEN OF TAHITI. <n.p.>, 1893.
Privately printed. A revised edition was privately printed in 1901 (No. 29).

31. MONT SAINT MICHEL AND CHARTRES. Wash DC, 1904.
Anon. Privately printed. A revised edition was privately printed in 1912 (No. 37).
For published edition see No. 38.

32. THE EDUCATION OF HENRY ADAMS. Wash DC, 1907.
Privately printed. For published edition see No. 39.

34. A LETTER TO AMERICAN TEACHERS OF HISTORY. Wash DC, 1910.

36. THE LIFE OF GEORGE CABOT LODGE. Bos & NY: Houghton Mifflin,
1911.

38. MONT-SAINT-MICHEL AND CHARTRES. Bos & NY: Houghton Mifflin,
1913.

39. THE EDUCATION OF HENRY ADAMS AN AUTOBIOGRAPHY. Bos & NY:
Houghton Mifflin, 1918.

40. THE DEGRADATION OF THE DEMOCRATIC DOGMA. NY: Macmillan,
1919.

HENRY ADAMS (cont.)

43.   LETTERS TO A NIECE AND PRAYER TO THE VIRGIN OF CHARTRES. Bos & NY: Houghton Mifflin, 1920.

*47.   LETTERS OF HENRY ADAMS (1858–1891). Bos & NY: Houghton Mifflin, 1930.
Ed. Worthington Chauncey Ford.

*49.   LETTERS OF HENRY ADAMS (1892–1918). Bos & NY: Houghton Mifflin, 1938.
Ed. Worthington Chauncey Ford.

52.   HENRY ADAMS AND HIS FRIENDS A COLLECTION OF HIS UNPUBLISHED LETTERS. Bos: Houghton Mifflin, 1947.
Ed. Harold Dean Cater.

Oscar Fay Adams
1855–1919

54.   A BRIEF HANDBOOK OF ENGLISH AUTHORS. Bos & NY: Houghton, Mifflin, 1884.

55.   A BRIEF HANDBOOK OF AMERICAN AUTHORS. Bos & NY: Houghton, Mifflin, 1884.

70.   POST-LAUREATE IDYLS AND OTHER POEMS. Bos: Lothrop, <1886>.

78.   DEAR OLD STORY-TELLERS. Bos: Lothrop, <1889>.

83.   THE STORY OF JANE AUSTEN'S LIFE. Chi: McClurg, 1891.

86.   THE PRESUMPTION OF SEX AND OTHER PAPERS. Bos: Lee & Shepard, 1892.

91.   A DICTIONARY OF AMERICAN AUTHORS. Bos & NY: Houghton, Mifflin, 1897.

*92.   THE ARCHBISHOP'S UNGUARDED MOMENT AND OTHER STORIES. Bos: Page, 1899.

*95.   SOME FAMOUS AMERICAN SCHOOLS. Bos: Estes, <1903>.

97.   SICUT PATRIBUS AND OTHER VERSE. <Bos>: The Author, <1906>.

100.   A MOTLEY JEST SHAKESPEAREAN DIVERSIONS. Bos: Sherman, French, 1909.

Amos Bronson Alcott
1799–1888

105.   RECORD OF CONVERSATIONS ON THE GOSPELS, HELD IN MR. ALCOTT'S SCHOOL. Bos: Munroe, 1836–37.
2v. Ed. Elizabeth Palmer Peabody.

112.   TABLETS. Bos: Roberts Bros., 1868.

114.   CONCORD DAYS. Bos: Roberts Bros., 1872.

*117.   TABLE-TALK. Bos: Roberts Bros., 1877.

A. BRONSON ALCOTT (cont.)

124. SONNETS AND CANZONETS. Bos: Roberts Bros., 1882.

127. RALPH WALDO EMERSON AN ESTIMATE OF HIS CHARACTER AND GENIUS IN PROSE AND VERSE. Bos: A. Williams, 1882.
Also privately printed in 1865 (No. 109).

132. NEW CONNECTICUT. Bos: Roberts Bros., 1887.
Ed. F.B. Sanborn. Also privately printed in 1881 (No. 121).

139. THE JOURNALS OF BRONSON ALCOTT. Bos: Little, Brown, 1938.
Ed. Odell Shepard.

Louisa May Alcott
1832–1888

142. FLOWER FABLES. Bos: Briggs, 1855.

*145. HOSPITAL SKETCHES. Bos: Redpath, 1863.

146. THE ROSE FAMILY. A FAIRY TALE. Bos: Redpath, 1864.

147. ON PICKET DUTY, AND OTHER TALES. Bos: Redpath, <1864>.

149. MOODS. Bos: Loring, 1865.
Revised edition published in 1882 (No. 199).

152. THE MYSTERIOUS KEY, AND WHAT IT OPENED. Bos: Elliott, Thomes & Talbot, <1867>.
Ten Cent Novelettes series of Standard American Authors, No. 50, ca.23 Dec. 1867.

153. MORNING-GLORIES, AND OTHER STORIES. Bos: Fuller, 1868.

*154. KITTY'S CLASS DAY. Bos: Loring, <1868>.

155. AUNT KIPP. Bos: Loring, <1868>.

156. PSYCHE'S ART. Bos: Loring, <1868>.

158. LITTLE WOMEN OR, MEG, JO, BETH AND AMY. Bos: Roberts Bros., 1868.

*159. LITTLE WOMEN OR MEG, JO, BETH AND AMY PART SECOND. Bos: Roberts Bros., 1869.

161. HOSPITAL SKETCHES AND CAMP AND FIRESIDE STORIES. Bos: Roberts Bros., 1869.

*163. AN OLD-FASHIONED GIRL. Bos: Roberts Bros., 1870.

164. WILL'S WONDER BOOK. Bos: Fuller, <1870>.
The Dirigo Series.

165. V.V.: OR, PLOTS AND COUNTERPLOTS. By A.M. Barnard. Bos: Thomes & Talbot, <1865, i.e. not before 1870>.
Ten Cent Novelettes series of Standard American Authors

166. LITTLE MEN: LIFE AT PLUMFIELD WITH JO'S BOYS. Lon: Low, Son, & Marston, 1871.

*167. LITTLE MEN: LIFE AT PLUMFIELD WITH JO'S BOYS. Bos: Roberts Bros., 1871.

168. AUNT JO'S SCRAP-BAG. MY BOYS. Bos: Roberts Bros., 1872.

LOUISA MAY ALCOTT (cont.)

171.   AUNT JO'S SCRAP-BAG. SHAWL-STRAPS. Bos: Roberts Bros., 1872.

173.   WORK: A STORY OF EXPERIENCE. Bos: Roberts Bros., 1873.
Published simultaneously (?) in the U.K. in 2v. & reprinted in 1875 with Vol. 2 entitled *Beginning Again* (No. 176).

174.   AUNT JO'S SCRAP-BAG. CUPID AND CHOW-CHOW, ETC. Bos: Roberts Bros., 1874.

*177.   EIGHT COUSINS; OR, THE AUNT-HILL. Bos: Roberts Bros., 1875.

180.   SILVER PITCHERS: AND INDEPENDENCE, A CENTENNIAL LOVE STORY. Bos: Roberts Bros., 1876.

*181.   ROSE IN BLOOM. Bos: Roberts Bros., 1876.
Sequel to *Eight Cousins.*

184.   A MODERN MEPHISTOPHELES. Bos: Roberts Bros., 1877.
Anon. *No Name Series.*

186.   AUNT JO'S SCRAP-BAG. MY GIRLS. Bos: Roberts Bros., 1878.

187.   UNDER THE LILACS. Lon: Low, Marston, et al, 1877–78.
11 parts.

188.   UNDER THE LILACS. Bos: Roberts Bros., 1878.

191.   AUNT JO'S SCRAP-BAG. JIMMY'S CRUISE IN THE PINAFORE. Bos: Roberts Bros., 1879.

195.   JACK AND JILL: A VILLAGE STORY. Bos: Roberts Bros., 1880.

202.   AUNT JO'S SCRAP-BAG. AN OLD-FASHIONED THANKSGIVING. Bos: Roberts Bros., 1882.

206.   SPINNING-WHEEL STORIES. Bos: Roberts Bros., 1884.

210.   LULU'S LIBRARY ... VOL. I. A CHRISTMAS DREAM. Bos: Roberts Bros., 1886.

*211.   JO'S BOYS, AND HOW THEY TURNED OUT. Bos: Roberts Bros., 1886.
Sequel to *Little Men.*

*212.   LULU'S LIBRARY ... VOL. II. THE FROST KING. Bos: Roberts Bros., 1887.

*217.   A GARLAND FOR GIRLS. Bos: Roberts Bros., 1888.

219.   A MODERN MEPHISTOPHELES AND A WHISPER IN THE DARK. Bos: Roberts Bros., 1889.

220.   LULU'S LIBRARY ... VOL. III. RECOLLECTIONS. Bos: Roberts Bros., 1889.

*221.   LOUISA MAY ALCOTT HER LIFE, LETTERS, AND JOURNALS. Bos: Roberts Bros., 1889.
Ed. Ednah D. Cheney.

224.   COMIC TRAGEDIES. Bos: Roberts Bros., 1893.
Written by "Jo" and "Meg" and acted by the "Little Women."

Thomas Bailey Aldrich
1836–1907

246.   THE BELLS: A COLLECTION OF CHIMES. By T.B.A. NY: Derby, 1855.

249.   DAISY'S NECKLACE: AND WHAT CAME OUT OF IT. NY: Derby & Jackson, 1857.

*251.   THE COURSE OF TRUE LOVE NEVER DID RUN SMOOTH. NY: Rudd & Carleton, 1858.

253.   THE BALLAD OF BABIE BELL AND OTHER POEMS. NY: Rudd & Carleton, 1859.

*256.   PAMPINEA AND OTHER POEMS. NY: Rudd & Carleton, 1861.

*257.   OUT OF HIS HEAD, A ROMANCE. NY: Carleton, 1862.

258.   POEMS. NY: Carleton, 1863.

262.   THE POEMS. Bos: Ticknor & Fields, 1865.
       Some of these poems reprinted in 1874 as *Cloth of Gold and Other Poems* (No. 280).

*269.   THE STORY OF A BAD BOY. Bos: Fields, Osgood, 1870.
       Reprinted in 1877 as *Tom Bailey's Adventures* (No. 293).

276.   MARJORIE DAW AND OTHER PEOPLE. Bos: Osgood, 1873.
       Extended edition published in 1885 as *Marjorie Daw and Other Stories* (No. 328).

278.   PRUDENCE PALFREY A NOVEL. Bos: Osgood, 1874.

289.   FLOWER AND THORN LATER POEMS. Bos: Osgood, 1877.

294.   A MIDNIGHT FANTASY, AND THE LITTLE VIOLINIST. Bos: Osgood, 1877.

295.   THE QUEEN OF SHEBA. Lon: Routledge & Sons, <n.d., 1877>.

296.   THE QUEEN OF SHEBA. Bos: Osgood, 1877.

307.   THE STILLWATER TRAGEDY. Bos: Houghton, Mifflin, 1880.

*318.   FROM PONKAPOG TO PESTH. Bos & NY: Houghton, Mifflin, 1883.

325.   MERCEDES, AND LATER LYRICS. Bos & NY: Houghton, Mifflin, 1884.
       Mercedes A Drama revised & published separately in 1894 (No. 369).

*329.   THE POEMS ... HOUSEHOLD EDITION. Bos & NY: Houghton, Mifflin, 1885.
       Reprinted with new material in 1890 (No. 390) & 1907 (No. 399).

*343.   THE SECOND SON A NOVEL. Bos & NY: Houghton, Mifflin, 1888.
       With Margaret Oliphant Wilson Oliphant.

350.   WYNDHAM TOWERS. Bos & NY: Houghton, Mifflin, 1890.

356.   THE SISTERS' TRAGEDY WITH OTHER POEMS, LYRICAL AND DRAMATIC. Bos & NY: Houghton, Mifflin, 1891.

*367.   AN OLD TOWN BY THE SEA. Bos & NY: Houghton, Mifflin, 1893.

*368.   TWO BITES AT A CHERRY WITH OTHER TALES. Bos & NY: Houghton, Mifflin, 1894.

*371.   UNGUARDED GATES AND OTHER POEMS. Bos & NY: Houghton, Mifflin, 1895.

THOMAS BAILEY ALDRICH (cont.)

*375.   JUDITH AND HOLOFERNES A POEM. Bos & NY: Houghton, Mifflin, 1896.

*379.   THE WRITINGS OF THOMAS BAILEY ALDRICH. Bos & NY: Houghton, Mifflin, 1897.
8v. Vols. 1–2, *The Poems* (No. 378), contain 7 new pieces.

*392.   A SEA TURN AND OTHER MATTERS. Bos & NY: Houghton, Mifflin, 1902.

*393.   PONKAPOG PAPERS. Bos & NY: Houghton, Mifflin, 1903.

*394.   JUDITH OF BETHULÎA A TRAGEDY. Bos: Houghton, Mifflin, 1904.

Elizabeth Akers Allen
(Florence Percy)
1832–1911

410.   FOREST BUDS, FROM THE WOODS OF MAINE. By Florence Percy. Bos: Brown, Bazin, 1856.

*412.   "ROCK ME TO SLEEP." 1860.
This noted poem was first printed in the *Saturday Evening Post*, 9 June 1860, & republished almost immediately as sheet music: the earliest has music by Ernest Leslie & was published by J.M. Russell of Boston. It was also frequently printed in readers, recitation books & as a broadside, leaflet or pamphlet. Collected in *Poems*, 1866, see next entry. For further details see BAL.

418.   POEMS. Bos: Ticknor & Fields, 1866.
Slightly revised edition published in 1867.

435.   THE TRIANGULAR SOCIETY LETTERS FROM THE LIFE OF A PORTLAND FAMILY. Portland: Hoyt, Fogg & Donham, 1886.
Anon.

437.   THE SILVER BRIDGE AND OTHER POEMS. Bos & NY: Houghton, Mifflin, 1886.

444.   THE HIGH-TOP SWEETING AND OTHER POEMS. NY: Scribner's Sons, 1891.

448.   THE SUNSET SONG AND OTHER VERSES. Bos: Lee & Shepard, 1902.

James Lane Allen
1849–1925

*451.   FLUTE AND VIOLIN AND OTHER KENTUCKY TALES AND ROMANCES. NY: Harper & Bros., 1891.

454.   THE BLUE-GRASS REGION OF KENTUCKY AND OTHER KENTUCKY ARTICLES. NY: Harper & Bros., 1892.

JAMES LANE ALLEN (cont.)

457. JOHN GRAY. A KENTUCKY TALE OF THE OLDEN TIME. Phila: Lippincott, 1893.
Originally published as the June 1892 issue of *Lippincott's Monthly Magazine* (No. 453).

*459. A KENTUCKY CARDINAL A STORY. NY: Harper & Bros., 1895.
For comment see next entry.

*460. AFTERMATH. NY: Harper & Bros., 1896.
Part Second of *A Kentucky Cardinal*. Both works revised & published together in 1v. in 1900 (No. 468).

461. SUMMER IN ARCADY A TALE OF NATURE. NY & Lon: Macmillan, 1896.

462. THE CHOIR INVISIBLE. NY & Lon: Macmillan, 1897.
Based on *John Gray*, 1893. Revised & corrected edition published in 1898 (No. 463).

*466. THE REIGN OF LAW A TALE OF THE KENTUCKY HEMP FIELDS. NY & Lon: Macmillan, 1900.
Published simultaneously in the U.K. as *The Increasing Purpose* (No. 467).

474. THE METTLE OF THE PASTURE. NY & Lon: Macmillan, 1903.

475. THE BRIDE OF THE MISTLETOE. NY: Macmillan, 1909.

477. THE DOCTOR'S CHRISTMAS EVE. NY: Macmillan, 1910.

478. THE HEROINE IN BRONZE OR A PORTRAIT OF A GIRL A PASTORAL OF THE CITY. NY: Macmillan, 1912.

480. THE LAST CHRISTMAS TREE AN IDYL OF IMMORTALITY. Portland: Mosher, 1914.

*481. THE SWORD OF YOUTH. NY: Century Co., 1915.

484. A CATHEDRAL SINGER. NY: Century Co., 1916.

486. THE KENTUCKY WARBLER. Garden City NY: Doubleday, Page, 1918.

487. THE EMBLEMS OF FIDELITY A COMEDY IN LETTERS. Garden City NY: Doubleday, Page, 1919.

491. THE ALABASTER BOX. NY & Lon: Harper & Bros., 1923.

492. THE LANDMARK. NY: Macmillan, 1925.

Washington Allston
1779–1843

493. THE SYLPHS OF THE SEASONS, WITH OTHER POEMS. Lon: Pople, 1813.

494. THE SYLPHS OF THE SEASONS, WITH OTHER POEMS. Bos: Cummings & Hilliard, 1813.

501. MONALDI: A TALE. Bos: Little & Brown, 1841.

508. LECTURES ON ART, AND POEMS. NY: Baker & Scribner, 1850.
Ed. Richard Henry Dana, Jr.

WASHINGTON ALLSTON (cont.)
509.   THE LIFE AND LETTERS OF WASHINGTON ALLSTON. NY: Scribner's Sons, 1892.
By Jared B. Flagg.

Jane Goodwin Austin
1831–1894

511.   FAIRY DREAMS; OR, WANDERINGS IN ELF-LAND. Bos: Tilton, <1859>.

512.   KINAH'S CURSE! OR, THE DOWNFALL OF CARNABY CEDARS. <Bos: Elliott, Thomes & Talbot, 1864>.
The Novelette, No. 101.

513.   THE TAILOR BOY. Bos: Tilton, 1865.
Anon.

514.   DORA DARLING: THE DAUGHTER OF THE REGIMENT. Bos: Tilton, 1865.
Anon.

515.   THE NOVICE: OR, MOTHER CHURCH THWARTED. Bos: Elliott, Thomes & Talbot, <1865>.
Ten Cent Novelettes, No. 22.

516.   THE OUTCAST: OR, THE MASTER OF FALCON'S EYRIE. Bos: <Elliott, Thomes & Talbot>, <1861, i.e. *ca.* 1865>.
The Novelette, No. 133.

517.   OUTPOST. Bos: Tilton, 1867.

519.   CIPHER: A ROMANCE. NY: Sheldon, 1869.

521.   THE SHADOW OF MOLOCH MOUNTAIN. NY: Sheldon, 1870.

522.   MOONFOLK. A TRUE ACCOUNT OF THE HOME OF THE FAIRY TALES. NY: Putnam's Sons, 1874.

*524.   MRS. BEAUCHAMP BROWN. Bos: Roberts Bros., 1880.
Anon. *No Name Series.*

525.   A NAMELESS NOBLEMAN. Bos: Osgood, 1881.
Anon. *Round-Robin Series.*

526.   THE DESMOND HUNDRED. Bos: Osgood, 1882.
Anon. *Round-Robin Series.*

527.   NANTUCKET SCRAPS BEING THE EXPERIENCES OF AN OFF-ISLANDER. Bos: Osgood, 1883.

535.   THE STORY OF A STORM.* A NOVEL. <NY: Lupton, 1886>.
The Leisure Hour Library, New Series, Vol. 1, No. 121, 16 Oct. 1886.

538.   STANDISH OF STANDISH A STORY OF THE PILGRIMS. Bos & NY: Houghton, Mifflin, 1889.

539.   DOLÓRES. A NOVEL. <NY: Lupton, 1890>.
The Leisure Hour Library, Vol. 3, No. 281, 1 April 1890.

540.   DR. LEBARON AND HIS DAUGHTERS A STORY OF THE OLD COLONY. Bos & NY: Houghton, Mifflin, 1890.

JANE G. AUSTIN (cont.)

542. BETTY ALDEN THE FIRST-BORN DAUGHTER OF THE PILGRIMS. Bos &
      NY: Houghton, Mifflin, 1891.

*543. QUEEN TEMPEST. NY: Ivers, <1892>.
      American Series, No. 271, 28 Nov. 1891.

*544. THE TWELVE GREAT DIAMONDS. A NOVEL. NY: Lupton, <1892>.
      The Idle Hour Series, No. 4, 5 March 1892.

545. IT NEVER DID RUN SMOOTH. A NOVEL. NY: Lupton, <1892>.
      The Idle Hour Series, No. 20, 30 April 1892.

*546. DAVID ALDEN'S DAUGHTER AND OTHER STORIES OF COLONIAL TIMES.
      Bos & NY: Houghton, Mifflin, 1892.

552. THE CEDAR SWAMP MYSTERY. <NY: Lupton, Lovell, 1901>.
      The Leisure Hour Library, No. 14.

Delia Salter Bacon
1811–1859

554. TALES OF THE PURITANS. THE REGICIDES. THE FAIR PILGRIM. CASTINE.
      New Haven: Maltby, 1831.
      Anon.

556. THE BRIDE OF FORT EDWARD, FOUNDED ON AN INCIDENT OF THE REVO-
      LUTION. NY: Colman, 1839.
      Anon.

558. THE PHILOSOPHY OF THE PLAYS OF SHAKSPERE UNFOLDED. Lon:
      Groombridge & Sons, 1857.
      With preface by Nathaniel Hawthorne.

559. THE PHILOSOPHY OF THE PLAYS OF SHAKSPERE UNFOLDED. Bos:
      Ticknor & Fields, 1857.
      With preface by Nathaniel Hawthorne

George William Bagby
1828–1883

560. MOZIS ADDUMS' NEW LETTERS. LETTUR WUN. Richmond: MacFarlane
      & Fergusson, Ptrs, 1860.
      Anon.

561. THE LETTERS OF MOZIS ADDUMS TO BILLY IVVINS. Richmond: West
      & Johnston, 1862.
      Anon. Revised edition published in 1878 as *Original Letters of Mozis Addums to Billy
      Ivvins* (No. 569).

563. JOHN M. DANIEL'S LATCH-KEY. Lynchburg VA: J.P. Bell, 1868.

GEORGE W. BAGBY (cont.)

566.   FOR VIRGINIANS ONLY. WHAT I DID WITH MY FIFTY MILLIONS. By Moses Adams. Phila: Lippincott, 1874.
"Edited from the posthumous MS. by Caesar Maurice, Esq., of the Richmond (VA.) Whig."

567.   MEEKINS'S TWINSES, A PERDUCKSHUN UV MOZIS ADDUMS. <Richmond: West & Johnston, 1877>.
Extended second edition also published in 1877 (No. 568).

570.   CANAL REMINISCENCES: RECOLLECTIONS OF TRAVEL IN THE OLD DAYS ON THE JAMES RIVER & KANAWHA CANAL. Richmond: West, Johnston, 1879.

571.   A WEEK IN HEPSIDAM. By Go. Wash. Meekins. Richmond: Gary, Ptr, 1879.

572.   1860–1880. JOHN BROWN AND WM. MAHONE. Richmond: C.F. Johnston, 1880.
Signed at end: *Edmund Ruffin's Shade.*

573.   YORKTOWN AND APPOMATTOX: A PLEA FOR THE UNION. Richmond: Ptd by Whittet & Shepperson, 1882.
Anon.

575.   SELECTIONS FROM THE MISCELLANEOUS WRITINGS. Richmond: Whittet & Shepperson, 1884–85.
2v. A selection, ed. Thomas Nelson Page, was published in 1910 as *The Old Virginia Gentleman and Other Sketches* (No. 576); see also next entry.

577.   THE OLD VIRGINIA GENTLEMAN AND OTHER SKETCHES. Richmond: Dietz PR, 1938.
Ed. Ellen M. Bagby. Extended edition published in 1943 (No. 578).

Joseph Glover Baldwin
1815–1864

580.   THE FLUSH TIMES OF ALABAMA AND MISSISSIPPI. A SERIES OF SKETCHES. NY & Lon: Appleton, 1853.

*581.   PARTY LEADERS; SKETCHES OF ... DISTINGUISHED AMERICAN STATESMEN. NY & Lon: Appleton, 1855.

George Bancroft
1800–1891

Note: Bancroft's *History of the United States* is listed here first, followed by his other literary works.

584.   A HISTORY OF THE UNITED STATES, FROM THE DISCOVERY OF THE AMERICAN CONTINENT TO THE PRESENT TIME. Bos: Bowen, 1834.
Vol. 1 of ten.

GEORGE BANCROFT (cont.)

*585.   HISTORY OF THE COLONIZATION OF THE UNITED STATES. Bos: Bowen, 1837.
Vol. 2 of ten.

586.   HISTORY OF THE COLONIZATION OF THE UNITED STATES. Bos: Little & Brown, 1840.
Vol. 3 of ten. Abridged 2v. edition of Vols. 1–3 published in 1841 (No. 595).

*587.   HISTORY OF THE UNITED STATES, FROM THE DISCOVERY OF THE AMERICAN CONTINENT. Bos: Little, Brown, 1852.
Vol. 4 of ten.

588.   HISTORY OF THE UNITED STATES, FROM THE DISCOVERY OF THE AMERICAN CONTINENT. Bos: Little, Brown, 1852.
Vol. 5 of ten.

589.   HISTORY OF THE UNITED STATES, FROM THE DISCOVERY OF THE AMERICAN CONTINENT. Bos: Little, Brown, 1854.
Vol. 6 of ten.

590.   HISTORY OF THE UNITED STATES, FROM THE DISCOVERY OF THE AMERICAN CONTINENT. Bos: Little, Brown, 1858.
Vol. 7 of ten.

591.   HISTORY OF THE UNITED STATES, FROM THE DISCOVERY OF THE AMERICAN CONTINENT. Bos: Little, Brown, 1860.
Vol. 8 of ten.

592.   HISTORY OF THE UNITED STATES, FROM THE DISCOVERY OF THE AMERICAN CONTINENT. Bos: Little, Brown, 1866.
Vol. 9 of ten.

593.   HISTORY OF THE UNITED STATES, FROM THE DISCOVERY OF THE AMERICAN CONTINENT. Bos: Little, Brown, 1874.
Vol. 10 of ten.

597.   HISTORY OF THE UNITED STATES, OF AMERICA, FROM THE DISCOVERY OF THE CONTINENT. Bos: Little, Brown, 1876.
6v. *Centenary Edition.* Revised.

598.   HISTORY OF THE UNITED STATES OF AMERICA, FROM THE DISCOVERY OF THE CONTINENT. NY: Appleton, 1883–85.
6v. "Author's last revision."

Other Works

600.   POEMS. Cambridge: Hilliard & Metcalf, 1823.

*644.   LITERARY AND HISTORICAL MISCELLANIES. NY: Harper & Bros., 1855.

680.   HISTORY OF THE FORMATION OF THE CONSTITUTION OF THE UNITED STATES OF AMERICA. NY: Appleton, 1882.
2v.

*684.   A PLEA FOR THE CONSTITUTION OF THE U.S. OF AMERICA WOUNDED IN THE HOUSE OF ITS GUARDIANS. NY: Harper & Bros., 1886.
Some copies issued as *Harper's Handy Series*, No. 53.

GEORGE BANCROFT (cont.)

686.   MARTIN VAN BUREN TO THE END OF HIS PUBLIC CAREER. NY: Harper & Bros., 1889.

687.   HISTORY OF THE BATTLE OF LAKE ERIE, AND MISCELLANEOUS PAPERS ... LIFE AND WRITINGS OF GEORGE BANCROFT. NY: Bonner's Sons, 1891.
By Oliver Dyer.

689.   THE LIFE AND LETTERS OF GEORGE BANCROFT. NY: Scribner's Sons, 1908.
2v. By M.A. DeWolfe Howe.

John Kendrick Bangs
1862–1922

694.   THE LORGNETTE 1886. NY: Coombes, <1886>.
Anon.

695.   ROGER CAMERDEN A STRANGE STORY. NY: Coombes, 1887.
Anon.

697.   NEW WAGGINGS OF OLD TALES. By Two Wags. Bos: Ticknor, 1888.
With Frank Dempster Sherman, see No. 17505 below.

*699.   KATHARINE A TRAVESTY. <NY: Gilliss Bros. & Turnuré,>, 1888.
Earlier (?) shorter version also published in 1888 (No. 698).

700.   MEPHISTOPHELES A PROFANATION. NY: Gilliss Bros. & Turnuré, 1889.

706.   TIDDLEDYWINK TALES. NY: Russell & Son, 1891.

708.   THE TIDDLEDYWINK'S POETRY BOOK. NY: Russell & Son, 1892.

710.   IN CAMP WITH A TIN SOLDIER. NY: Russell & Son, 1892.

*712.   COFFEE AND REPARTEE. NY: Harper & Bros., 1893.
Slightly revised & published in 1900 with *The Idiot*, 1895 (No. 742a).

713.   TOPPLETON'S CLIENT OR A SPIRIT IN EXILE. Lon: Osgood, McIlvaine, 1893.

714.   TOPPLETON'S CLIENT OR A SPIRIT IN EXILE. NY: Webster, 1893.

716.   HALF-HOURS WITH JIMMIEBOY. NY: Russell & Son, 1893.

719.   THREE WEEKS IN POLITICS. NY: Harper & Bros., 1894.

720.   THE WATER GHOST AND OTHERS. NY: Harper & Bros., 1894.

721.   THE IDIOT. NY: Harper & Bros., 1895.
For comment on a slightly revised edition see No. 712 above.

*722.   MR. BONAPARTE OF CORSICA. NY: Harper & Bros., 1895.

726.   A HOUSE-BOAT ON THE STYX. NY: Harper & Bros., 1896.

728.   THE BICYCLERS AND THREE OTHER FARCES. NY: Harper & Bros., 1896.

*729.   A REBELLIOUS HEROINE A STORY. NY: Harper & Bros., 1896.

730.   THE MANTEL-PIECE MINSTRELS, AND OTHER STORIES. NY: Russell & Son, 1896.

JOHN KENDRICK BANGS (cont.)

*731. THE PURSUIT OF THE HOUSE-BOAT. NY: Harper & Bros., 1897.

  732. A PROPHECY AND A PLEA … TWO POEMS. NY, 1897.
      Privately printed.

  735. PASTE JEWELS BEING SEVEN TALES OF DOMESTIC WOE. NY & Lon: Harper & Bros., 1897.

  737. GHOSTS I HAVE MET AND SOME OTHERS. NY & Lon: Harper & Bros., 1898.

  739. PEEPS AT PEOPLE. NY & Lon: Harper & Bros., 1899.
      "From the writings of Anne Warrington Witherup."

  741. THE DREAMERS A CLUB. NY & Lon: Harper & Bros., 1899.

  743. COBWEBS FROM A LIBRARY CORNER. NY & Lon: Harper & Bros., 1899.

*744. THE ENCHANTED TYPE-WRITER. NY & Lon: Harper & Bros., 1899.

*749. THE BOOMING OF ACRE HILL AND OTHER REMINISCENCES OF URBAN AND SUBURBAN LIFE. NY & Lon: Harper & Bros., 1900.

*750. THE IDIOT AT HOME. NY & Lon: Harper & Bros., 1900.

*752. OVER THE PLUM-PUDDING. NY & Lon: Harper & Bros., 1901.

*753. MR. MUNCHAUSEN. Bos: Noyes, Platt, 1901.

  755. UNCLE SAM TRUSTEE. NY: Riggs, 1902.

  756. OLYMPIAN NIGHTS. NY & Lon: Harper & Bros., 1902.

  757. BIKEY THE SKICYCLE & OTHER TALES OF JIMMIEBOY. NY: Riggs, 1902.

  758. MOLLIE AND THE UNWISEMAN. Phila: Coates, <1902>.

  759. EMBLEMLAND. NY: Russell, 1902.
      With Charles Raymond Macauley.

  763. THE INVENTIONS OF THE IDIOT. NY & Lon: Harper & Bros., 1904.

  766. THE WORSTED MAN A MUSICAL PLAY FOR AMATEURS. NY & Lon: Harper & Bros., 1905.

  767. MONSIEUR D'EN BROCHETTE. NY: Keppler & Schwarzmann, 1905.
      With Bert Leston Taylor & Arthur Hamilton Folwell.

  769. MRS. RAFFLES. NY & Lon: Harper & Bros., 1905.

  771. R. HOLMES & CO. NY & Lon: Harper & Bros., 1906.

  772. ANDIRON TALES. Phila: Winston, <1906>.

  775. ALICE IN BLUNDERLAND AN IRIDESCENT DREAM. NY: Doubleday, Page, 1907.

*777. POTTED FICTION. NY: Doubleday, Page, 1908.

  778. THE GENIAL IDIOT HIS VIEWS AND REVIEWS. NY & Lon: Harper & Bros., 1908.

  780. THE REAL THING AND THREE OTHER FARCES. NY & Lon: Harper & Bros., 1909.

  781. THE AUTOBIOGRAPHY OF METHUSELAH. NY: Dodge, 1909.

  783. SONGS OF CHEER. Bos: Sherman French, 1910.

JOHN KENDRICK BANGS (cont.)

785. MOLLIE AND THE UNWISEMAN ABROAD. Phila & Lon: Lippincott, 1910.

788. JACK AND THE CHECK BOOK. NY & Lon: Harper & Bros., 1911.

792. ECHOES OF CHEER. Bos: Sherman French, 1912.

793. A LITTLE BOOK OF CHRISTMAS. Bos: Little, Brown, 1912.

796. A LINE O' CHEER FOR EACH DAY O' THE YEAR. Bos: Little, Brown, 1913.

798. A CHAFING-DISH PARTY. NY & Lon: Harper & Bros., <1896, i.e. 1913>.

801. THE YOUNG FOLK'S MINSTRELS. NY & Lon: Harper & Bros., <1897, i.e. 1913>.

802. THE FOOTHILLS OF PARNASSUS. NY: Macmillan, 1914.

805. A QUEST FOR SONG. Bos: Little, Brown, 1915.

807. FROM PILLAR TO POST LEAVES FROM A LECTURER'S NOTE-BOOK. NY: Century Co., 1916.

809. HALF HOURS WITH THE IDIOT. Bos: Little, Brown, 1917.

*812. THE CHEERY WAY A BIT OF VERSE FOR EVERY DAY. NY & Lon: Harper & Bros., <1919>.

James Nelson Barker
1784–1858

823. THE INDIAN PRINCESS; OR, LA BELLE SAUVAGE. AN OPERATIC MELODRAME. Phila: Blake, 1808.
The songs were also published in 1808 in sheet music form (No. 822).

824. TEARS AND SMILES. A COMEDY. Phila: Blake, 1808.

828. MARMION; OR, THE BATTLE OF FLODDEN FIELD. A DRAMA. NY: D. Longworth, 1816.
Based on Sir Walter Scott's poem.

829. HOW TO TRY A LOVER. A COMEDY. NY: D. Longworth, 1817.
Anon.

836. THE TRAGEDY OF SUPERSTITION. Phila: Poole, <1826>.
"Carefully corrected … by M. Lopez, Prompter." At head of title: *Lopez and Wemyss' Edition. The Acting American Theatre*

Joel Barlow
1754–1812

Note: Barlow's many political writings are here omitted; for full listing see BAL. Some of these were collected & published in 1796 as *The Political Writings of Joel Barlow* (No. 894).

855. THE PROSPECT OF PEACE. A POETICAL COMPOSITION. New Haven: Ptd by T. & S. Green, 1788 <i.e. 1778>.
Delivered at Yale College, 23 July 1778.

JOEL BARLOW (cont.)

857.   A POEM, SPOKEN AT THE PUBLIC COMMENCEMENT AT YALE COLLEGE, IN NEW-HAVEN, SEPTEMBER 12, 1781. Hartford: Ptd by Hudson & Goodwin, <1781>.
Anon.

858.   AN ELEGY ON THE LATE HONORABLE TITUS HOSMER, ESQ. Hartford: Ptd by Hudson & Goodwin, <n.d., 1782>.

865.   THE VISION OF COLUMBUS; A POEM IN NINE BOOKS. Hartford: The Author, 1787.
Revised edition published in 1793 (No. 877). See also No. 906 below.

870.   THE CONSPIRACY OF KINGS; A POEM. Lon: J. Johnson, 1792.
Revised edition published in Paris in 1793 (Nos. 876 & 877).

884.   THE CONSPIRACY OF KINGS: A POEM. Newburyport: Robinson & Tucker, 1794.
Also (earlier?) published in the U.S. appended to *A Letter to the National Convention of France*, <n.d., 1793?> (No. 880).

890.   THE HASTY-PUDDING: A POEM, IN THREE CANTOS. <New Haven, 1796>.
15 pp. Evans No. 30022. For other 1796 editions see next 3 entries; no sequence established.

891.   THE HASTY-PUDDING: A POEM, IN THREE CANTOS. <New Haven, 1796>.
12 pp. Not in Evans.

892.   THE HASTY-PUDDING: A POEM, IN THREE CANTOS. NY: Fellows & Adam, 1796.
22 pp. Evans No. 30023.

893.   THE HASTY-PUDDING: A POEM, IN THREE CANTOS. NY: The Purchaser, <n.d., 1796>.
12 pp. Evans No. 30024.

*906.   THE COLUMBIAD A POEM. Phila: C. & A. Conrad, 1807.
Extensively revised & expanded version of *The Vision of Columbus*, 1787, see No. 865 above. Revised & corrected edition published in Paris in 1813 (No. 912) & in the U.S. in 1825 (No. 913).

915.   THE ANARCHIAD: A NEW ENGLAND POEM. New Haven: Pease, 1861.
With David Humphreys, John Trumbull & Dr. Lemuel Hopkins. Ed. Luther G. Riggs. See also No. 20552 below.

916.   LIFE AND LETTERS ... WITH EXTRACTS FROM HIS WORKS AND HITHERTO UNPUBLISHED POEMS. NY & Lon: Putnam's Sons, 1886.
By Charles Burr Todd.

Jeremy Belknap
1744–1798

918. AN ECLOGUE OCCASIONED BY THE DEATH OF THE REVEREND ALEXANDER CUMMING. Bos: J. Edwards, 1763.
Anon.

*922. THE HISTORY OF NEW-HAMPSHIRE. Phila: The Author, 1784.
Vol. 1 of three.

928. THE HISTORY OF NEW-HAMPSHIRE. Bos: The Author, 1791.
Vol. 2 of three.

*929. THE FORESTERS, AN AMERICAN TALE. Bos: Thomas & Andrews, 1792.
Anon. Revised edition published in 1796 (No. 938).

930. THE HISTORY OF NEW-HAMPSHIRE. Bos: The Author, 1792.
Vol. 3 of three.

931. A DISCOURSE, INTENDED TO COMMEMORATE THE DISCOVERY OF AMERICA BY CHRISTOPHER COLUMBUS ... TO WHICH ARE ADDED, FOUR DISSERTATIONS. Bos: Ptd by Belknap & Hall, 1792.
The discourse delivered at the request of the Massachusetts Historical Society, 23 Oct. 1792.

934. AMERICAN BIOGRAPHY. Bos: Ptd by Thomas & Andrews, 1794.
Vol. 1 of two.

935. DISSERTATIONS ON THE CHARACTER, DEATH & RESURRECTION OF JESUS CHRIST ... WITH REMARKS ON ... "THE AGE OF REASON." Bos: Ptd by Belknap, 1795.

942. AMERICAN BIOGRAPHY. Bos: Ptd by Thomas & Andrews, 1798.
Vol. 2 of two.

946. LIFE OF JEREMY BELKNAP, D.D. THE HISTORIAN OF NEW HAMPSHIRE. NY: Harper & Bros., 1847.
"With selections from his correspondence and other writings." Ed. Jane Belknap Marcou.

949. <THE BELKNAP PAPERS> COLLECTIONS OF THE MASSACHUSETTS HISTORICAL SOCIETY. Bos: The Society, 1877–91.
3v. *Historical Collections*, 5th Series, Vols. 2–3, & 6th Series, Vol.4. An extensive collection of Belknap papers & correspondence.

Edward Bellamy
1850–1898

Note: Bellamy's political writings on social theory are in general here omitted, but see Nos. 972 & 973 below.

952. SIX TO ONE; A NANTUCKET IDYL. NY: Putnam's Sons, 1878.
Anon.

EDWARD BELLAMY (cont.)

953. DR. HEIDENHOFF'S PROCESS. NY: Appleton, 1880.
Appletons' New Handy-Volume Series.

954. MISS LUDINGTON'S SISTER A ROMANCE OF IMMORTALITY. Bos: Osgood, 1884.

*956. LOOKING BACKWARD 2000–1887. Bos: Ticknor, 1888.
Published in 1889 with an additional "Postscript" (No. 958).

967. EQUALITY. NY: Appleton, 1897.
Many undated separate reprints of chapter 23 were published as *The Parable of the Water Tank* (No. 971).

968. THE BLINDMAN'S WORLD AND OTHER STORIES. Bos & NY: Houghton, Mifflin, 1898.

*970. THE DUKE OF STOCKBRIDGE A ROMANCE OF SHAYS' REBELLION. NY, Bos, &c: Silver, Burdett, 1900.

972. EDWARD BELLAMY SPEAKS AGAIN! ARTICLES PUBLIC ADDRESSES LETTERS. Kansas City MO: Peerage PR, 1937.

973. TALKS ON NATIONALISM. Chi: Peerage PR, <1938>.

Park Benjamin
1809–1864

976. A POEM ON THE MEDITATION OF NATURE. Hartford: Huntington, 1832.
Spoken before the Alumni of Washington College, 26 Sept. 1832.

977. THE HARBINGER; A MAY-GIFT. Bos: Carter, Hendee, 1833.
Anon. With Oliver Wendell Holmes & John O. Sargent; see No. 8723 below. Part 1 by Benjamin.

1008. POETRY: A SATIRE. NY: J. Winchester, 1842.
Pronounced before the Mercantile Library Association at its 22nd anniversary.

1016. INFATUATION: A POEM. Bos: Ticknor, 1844.
Spoken before the Mercantile Library Association of Boston, 9 Oct. 1844. "Published by the Association."

1046. POEMS OF PARK BENJAMIN. NY: Columbia U PR, 1948.
Ed. Merle M. Hoover.

Emerson Bennett
1822–1905

1047. THE BRIGAND. A POEM ... IN TWO CANTOS. NY: Xylographic PR, 1842.

1049. THE BANDITS OF THE OSAGE. A WESTERN ROMANCE. Cincinnati: Robinson & Jones, 1847.

1050. THE RENEGADE. A HISTORICAL ROMANCE OF BORDER LIFE. Cincinnati: Robinson & Jones, 1848.
Revised edition published in 1854 as *Ella Barnwell* (No. 1075).

EMERSON BENNETT (cont.)

1051. MIKE FINK: A LEGEND OF THE OHIO. Cincinnati: Robinson & Jones, 1848.
Revised edition published in 1852 (No. 1069).

1052. KATE CLARENDON: OR, NECROMANCY IN THE WILDERNESS. A TALE OF THE LITTLE MIAMI. Cincinnati & St. Louis: Stratton & Barnard, 1848.

1054. THE PRAIRIE FLOWER; OR, ADVENTURES IN THE FAR WEST. Cincinnati & St. Louis: Stratton & Barnard, 1849.
Revised editions published in 1850 (No. 1062) & 1881 (No. 1091).

1055. LENI-LEOTI; OR, ADVENTURES IN THE FAR WEST. Cincinnati & St. Louis: Stratton & Barnard, 1849.
Revised editions published in 1851 (No. 1063) & in 1881 with *The Prairie Flower* (No. 1091).

1056. OLIVER GOLDFINCH; OR, THE HYPOCRITE. Cincinnati: Stratton & Barnard, 1850.
Reprinted in 1853 as *The Forged Will* (No. 1073).

1057. THE FOREST ROSE; A TALE OF THE FRONTIER. Cincinnati: J.A. & U.P. James, 1850.
Revised edition published in 1852 (No. 1071).

1058. THE LEAGUE OF THE MIAMI. Louisville: C. Hagan, <1850>.

1059. THE TRAITOR; OR, THE FATE OF AMBITION. Cincinnati & St. Louis: Stratton & Barnard, 1850.

1060. THE TRAITOR; OR, THE FATE OF AMBITION ... PART II. Cincinnati: Stratton, 1850.

1064. THE UNKNOWN COUNTESS. Cincinnati: Stratton, 1851.

1065. THE FEMALE SPY; OR TREASON IN THE CAMP. A STORY OF THE REVOLUTION. Cincinnati: Stratton, <1851>.

*1066. THE PIONEER'S DAUGHTER. A TALE OF INDIAN CAPTIVITY. Phila: Peterson, <1851>.

1067. ROSALIE DU PONT; OR TREASON IN THE CAMP. Cincinnati: Stratton, <1851>.
Sequel to *The Female Spy*.

*1068. VIOLA; OR, ADVENTURES IN THE FAR SOUTH-WEST. Phila: Peterson, <1852>.
Companion to *The Prairie Flower.*

1070. WALDE-WARREN; A TALE OF CIRCUMSTANTIAL EVIDENCE. Phila: Peterson, <1852>.
Companion to *The Prairie Flower.*

*1072. CLARA MORELAND; OR, ADVENTURES IN THE FAR SOUTH-WEST. Phila: Peterson, <1853>.

1074. THE FAIR REBEL: A TALE OF COLONIAL TIMES. Cincinnati: Rulison, 1853.

EMERSON BENNETT (cont.)

*1076. THE BRIDE OF THE WILDERNESS. Phila: Peterson, <1854>.

1077. THE HEIRESS OF BELLEFONT. Phila: Peterson, <1855>.
Also reprints *Walde-Warren*, 1852, see No. 1070 above.

*1078. ELLEN NORBURY; OR, THE ADVENTURES OF AN ORPHAN. Phila: Peterson, <1855>.

1079. ALFRED MORLAND; OR, THE LEGACY. Cincinnati: <Rulison>, 1855.

*1080. THE BORDER ROVER. Phila: Peterson, <1857>.

1081. THE ARTIST'S BRIDE; OR, THE PAWNBROKER'S HEIR. NY: Garrett, Dick & Fitzgerald, <1856, i.e. 1857>.
Reprinted in 1874 as *Villeta Linden* (No. 1089).

1082. INTRIGUING FOR A PRINCESS. AN ADVENTURE WITH MEXICAN BANDITTI. Phila: Bradley, 1859.
Bradley's Railroad Library.

1083. WILD SCENES ON THE FRONTIERS; OR, HEROES OF THE WEST. Phila: Hamelin, 1859.
Reprinted in 1860 as *Forest and Prairie* (No. 1084).

1085. THE PHANTOM OF THE FOREST: A TALE OF THE DARK AND BLOODY GROUND. Phila: Potter, 1868.

1088. THE OUTLAW'S DAUGHTER; OR, ADVENTURES IN THE SOUTH. Phila: Claxton, Remsen & Haffelfinger, 1874.
Chapters 1–3 were published separately in 1871 (No. 1087) as an advertisement for the serial publication in *Saturday Night.*

1090. THE ORPHAN'S TRIALS; OR, ALONE IN A GREAT CITY. Phila: Peterson & Bros., <1874>.

Ambrose Gwinnett Bierce
1842–1914(?)

1096. THE FIEND'S DELIGHT. By Dod Grile. Lon: Hotten, <n.d., 1873>.

1097. THE FIEND'S DELIGHT. By Dod Grile. NY: Luyster, 1873.

*1099. NUGGETS AND DUST PANNED OUT IN CALIFORNIA. By Dod Grile. Lon: Chatto & Windus, <n.d., 1873>.
"Collected and loosely arranged by J. Milton Sloluck."

1100. COBWEBS FROM AN EMPTY SKULL. By Dod Grile. Lon & NY: Routledge & Sons, 1874.

1104. THE DANCE OF DEATH. By William Herman. <n.p., SF, 1877>.
With Thomas A. Harcourt. Revised edition published in 1877 (No. 1105).

1109. TALES OF SOLDIERS AND CIVILIANS. SF: Steele, 1891.

1111. BLACK BEETLES IN AMBER. SF & NY: Western Authors Pub. Co., 1892.

1112. THE MONK AND THE HANGMAN'S DAUGHTER. Chi: Schulte, 1892.
With Gustav Adolph Danzinger.

AMBROSE BIERCE (cont.)

1114. CAN SUCH THINGS BE? NY: Cassell, <1893>.

*1120. FANTASTIC FABLES. NY & Lon: Putnam's Sons, 1899.

*1122. SHAPES OF CLAY. SF: W.E. Wood, 1903.

*1124. THE CYNIC'S WORD BOOK. NY: Doubleday, Page, 1906.

1127. THE SHADOW ON THE DIAL AND OTHER ESSAYS. SF: Robertson, 1909.
Ed. S.O. Howes.

1128. WRITE IT RIGHT A LITTLE BLACKLIST OF LITERARY FAULTS. NY & Wash DC: Neale, 1909.

1129. THE COLLECTED WORKS. NY & Wash DC: Neale, 1909–12.
12v.

1137. THE LETTERS OF AMBROSE BIERCE. SF: Book Club of California, 1922.
Ed. Bertha Clark Pope.

Robert Montgomery Bird
1806–1854

1152. CALAVAR; OR, THE KNIGHT OF THE CONQUEST: A ROMANCE OF MEXICO. Phila: Carey, Lea, & Blanchard, 1834.
2v. Anon. Reprinted in 1839 as *Abdalla the Moor and the Spanish Knight* (No. 1163).

1154. THE INFIDEL; OR THE FALL OF MEXICO. A ROMANCE. Phila: Carey, Lea & Blanchard, 1835.
2v. Anon. Reprinted in 1840 as *The Infidel's Doom* (No. 1164).

1155. THE HAWKS OF HAWK-HOLLOW, A TRADITION OF PENNSYLVANIA. Phila: Carey, Lea, & Blanchard, 1835.
2v. Anon.

*1159. SHEPPARD LEE. WRITTEN BY HIMSELF. NY: Harper & Bros., 1836.
2v. Anon.

1160. NICK OF THE WOODS, OR THE JIBBENAINOSAY. A TALE OF KENTUCKY. Phila: Carey, Lea & Blanchard, 1837.
2v. Anon. Revised edition published in 1853 (No. 1172).

1161. PETER PILGRIM: OR A RAMBLER'S RECOLLECTIONS. Phila: Lea & Blanchard, 1838.
2v. Anon.

1162. THE ADVENTURES OF ROBIN DAY. Phila: Lea & Blanchard, 1839.
2v. Anon. Reprinted in 1840 as *Robin Day* (No. 1165).

1174. A BELATED REVENGE. FROM THE PAPERS OF IPSICO POE. Phila: Lippincott, <1889>.
With Frederic M. Bird. The Nov. 1889 issue of *Lippincott's Monthly Magazine* with title-page as above; not otherwise published in book form.

ROBERT MONTGOMERY BIRD (cont.)

1177. THE CITY LOOKING GLASS. A PHILADELPHIA COMEDY. NY: The Colophon, 1933.
Ed. Arthur Hobson Quinn.

1178. THE COWLED LOVER & OTHER PLAYS. Princeton: Princeton U PR, 1941.
Ed. Edward H. O'Neill. *America's Lost Plays*, Vol. 12.

George Henry Boker
1823–1890

1179. THE LESSON OF LIFE AND OTHER POEMS. Phila: G.S. Appleton, 1848.

1180. CALAYNOS: A TRAGEDY. Phila: Butler, 1848.

1185. ANNE BOLEYN: A TRAGEDY. Phila: Hart, 1850.

1189. THE PODESTA'S DAUGHTER AND OTHER MISCELLANEOUS POEMS. Phila: Hart, 1852.

1192. PLAYS AND POEMS. Bos: Ticknor & Fields, 1856.
2v.

1209. POEMS OF THE WAR. Bos: Ticknor & Fields, 1864.

1216. OUR HEROIC THEMES. A POEM. Bos: Ticknor & Fields, 1865.
Read before the Phi Beta Kappa Society of Harvard University, 20 July 1865.

1222. KÖNIGSMARK THE LEGEND OF THE HOUNDS AND OTHER POEMS. Phila: Lippincott, 1869.
Reprinted in 1929 as *The Legend of the Hounds* (No. 1235).

1228. THE BOOK OF THE DEAD. Phila & Lon: Lippincott, 1882.

1233. NYDIA A TRAGIC PLAY. Phila: U of Pennsylvania PR, 1929.
Ed. Edward Sculley Bradley.

1234. SONNETS A SEQUENCE ON PROFANE LOVE. Phila: U of Pennsylvania PR, 1929.
Ed. Edward Sculley Bradley.

1236. GLAUCUS & OTHER PLAYS. Princeton: Princeton U PR, 1940.
Ed. Sculley Bradley. *America's Lost Plays*, Vol. 3.

Hjalmar Hjorth Boyesen
1848–1895

1237. GUNNAR: A TALE OF NORSE LIFE. Bos: Osgood, 1874.

1238. A NORSEMAN'S PILGRIMAGE. NY: Sheldon, 1875.

1241. TALES FROM TWO HEMISPHERES. Bos: Osgood, 1877.

*1243. GOETHE AND SCHILLER: THEIR LIVES AND WORKS. NY: Scribner's Sons, 1879.

1244. FALCONBERG. NY: Scribner's Sons, 1879.

H. H. BOYESEN (cont.)

1245. ILKA ON THE HILL-TOP AND OTHER STORIES. NY: Scribner's Sons, 1881.
For dramatization of the title story see No. 1253 below.

1246. QUEEN TITANIA. NY: Scribner's Sons, 1881.

1250. IDYLS OF NORWAY AND OTHER POEMS. NY: Scribner's Sons, 1882.

1251. A DAUGHTER OF THE PHILISTINES. Bos: Roberts Bros., 1883.
Anon. *No Name Series.*

1253. ALPINE ROSES A COMEDY IN FOUR ACTS. <NY, n.d., 1884>.
"Privately printed for ... M.H. Mallory." Dramatization of "Ilka on the Hill-Top," see No. 1245 above.

*1259. THE STORY OF NORWAY. NY & Lon: Putnam's Sons, 1886.
The Story of the Nations series.

1261. THE MODERN VIKINGS STORIES OF LIFE AND SPORT IN THE NORSE-LAND. NY: Scribner's Sons, 1887.

1268. VAGABOND TALES. Bos: Lothrop, <1889>.

1269. THE LIGHT OF HER COUNTENANCE. NY: Appleton, 1889.
Cloth; and paper wrapper of *Appletons' Town and Country Library*, No. 34, 1 Aug. 1889. Originally published as the May 1888 issue of *Lippincott's Monthly Magazine* as *The Old Adam. A Novel* (No. 1266).

1273. AGAINST HEAVY ODDS A TALE OF NORSE HEROISM. NY: Scribner's Sons, 1890.

1275. THE MAMMON OF UNRIGHTEOUSNESS. NY: Lovell, <1891>.

1278. ESSAYS ON GERMAN LITERATURE. NY: Scribner's Sons, 1892.

*1279. BOYHOOD IN NORWAY STORIES OF BOY-LIFE IN THE LAND OF THE MID-NIGHT SUN. NY: Scribner's Sons, 1892.

1280. THE GOLDEN CALF A NOVEL. Meadville PA: Flood & Vincent, 1892.

1281. SOCIAL STRUGGLERS A NOVEL. NY: Scribner's Sons, 1893.

1285. A COMMENTARY ON THE WRITINGS OF HENRIK IBSEN. NY & Lon: Macmillan, 1894.

1286. LITERARY AND SOCIAL SILHOUETTES. NY: Harper & Bros., 1894.

1288. NORSELAND TALES. NY: Scribner's Sons, 1894.
The Norseland Series.

1289. ESSAYS ON SCANDINAVIAN LITERATURE. NY: Scribner's Sons, 1895.

Hugh Henry Brackenridge
1748–1816

1292. A POEM, ON THE RISING GLORY OF AMERICA. Phila: Aitken, 1772.
Anon. With Philip Freneau, see No. 6412 below. Delivered at the public commencement at Nassau-Hall, 25 Sept. 1771.

H. H. BRACKENRIDGE (cont.)

1293. A POEM ON DIVINE REVELATION. Phila: Aitken, 1774.
Anon. Delivered at the public commencement at Nassau-Hall, 28 Sept. 1774.

1294. THE BATTLE OF BUNKERS-HILL. A DRAMATIC PIECE, OF FIVE ACTS. By a Gentleman of Maryland. Phila: Bell, 1776.
Anon.

*1295. THE DEATH OF GENERAL MONTGOMERY, AT THE SIEGE OF QUEBEC. A TRAGEDY WITH AN ODE. Phila: Bell, 1777.
Anon.

1297. SIX POLITICAL DISCOURSES FOUNDED ON THE SCRIPTURE. Lancaster: Ptd by Bailey, <n.d., 1778>.

1298. AN EULOGIUM OF THE BRAVE MEN WHO HAVE FALLEN IN THE CONTEST WITH GREAT-BRITAIN. Phila: Ptd by F. Bailey, <1779>.
Delivered in the German Calvinist Church, Philadelphia, 5 July 1779.

*1300. MODERN CHIVALRY: CONTAINING THE ADVENTURES OF CAPTAIN JOHN FARRAGO, AND TEAGUE O'REGAN, HIS SERVANT. Phila: M'Culloch, 1792.
Vols. 1 & 2 of four; see also *Part 2* below. Vol. 2 misdated 1712. Revised editions published in 1804 (No. 1310), 1815 (No. 1322) & 1819 (No. 1323).

1301. MODERN CHIVALRY: CONTAINING THE ADVENTURES OF CAPTAIN JOHN FARRAGO, AND TEAGUE O'REGAN, HIS SERVANT. Pittsburgh: Scull, 1713 <i.e. 1793>.
Vol. 3 of four; see also *Part 2* below. Revised editions published in 1807 (No. 1316), 1815 (No. 1322) & 1819 (No. 1323).

1303. INCIDENTS OF THE INSURRECTION IN THE WESTERN PARTS OF PENNSYLVANIA, IN THE YEAR 1794. Phila: M'Culloch, 1795.
3v. in one.

1304. MODERN CHIVALRY: CONTAINING THE ADVENTURES OF CAPTAIN JOHN FARRAGO, AND TEAGUE O'REGAN, HIS SERVANT. Phila: M'Culloch, 1797.
Vol. 4 of four; see also *Part 2* below. Revised editions published in 1807 (no. 1316), 1815 (No. 1322) & 1819 (No. 1323).

1308. THE STANDARD OF LIBERTY, AN OCCASIONAL PAPER. By Democritus. <n.p., n.d.; Phila, 1802?>.

1309. MODERN CHIVALRY, CONTAINING THE ADVENTURES OF A CAPTAIN, &C. Carlisle: The Author, 1804.
Part 2, Vol. 1. Revised editions published in 1815 (No. 1322) & 1819 (No. 1323).

1312. MODERN CHIVALRY, CONTAINING THE ADVENTURES OF A CAPTAIN, &C. Carlisle: The Author, 1805.
Part 2, Vol. 2. Revised editions published in 1815 (No. 1322) & 1819 (No. 1323).

1313. GAZETTE PUBLICATIONS. Carlisle: Ptd by Alexander & Phillips, 1806.

1320. AN EPISTLE TO WALTER SCOTT. <Pittsburgh: Franklin Head Ptg-office, 1811(?)>.

John Gardiner Calkins Brainard
1796–1828

1325. LETTERS FOUND IN THE RUINS OF FORT BRADDOCK, INCLUDING AN
       INTERESTING AMERICAN TALE. NY: Wilder & Campbell, 1824.
       Anon. "Originally published in the Connecticut Mirror." Slightly abridged edi-
       tion published in 1827 as *Fort Braddock Letters* (No. 1328).

1327. OCCASIONAL PIECES OF POETRY. NY: Bliss & White, 1825.

1332. THE LITERARY REMAINS OF JOHN G.C. BRAINARD. Hartford: Goodsell,
       <1832>.
       By J.G. Whittier.

1333. THE POEMS ... A NEW AND AUTHENTIC COLLECTION, WITH AN ORIGI-
       NAL MEMOIR OF HIS LIFE. Hartford: Hopkins, 1842.

Charles Frederick Briggs
(Harry Franco)
1804–1877

1336. THE ADVENTURES OF HARRY FRANCO, A TALE OF THE GREAT PANIC.
       NY: Saunders, 1839.
       Anon.

1337. BANKRUPT STORIES. Edited by Harry Franco. NY: J. Allen, 1843.
       Issued in 5(?) parts.

1339. WORKING A PASSAGE: OR, LIFE IN A LINER. By B.C.F. NY: J. Allen,
       1844.

1343. THE TRIPPINGS OF TOM PEPPER; OR, THE RESULTS OF ROMANCING. AN
       AUTOBIOGRAPHY. By Harry Franco. NY: Burgess, Stringer, 1847.
       Mirror Library, New Series, No. 2.

1344. THE TRIPPINGS OF TOM PEPPER; OR THE RESULTS OF ROMANCING AN
       AUTOBIOGRAPHY. VOL. II. By Harry Franco. NY: Mirror Office, 1850.
       Mirror Library, New Series, No. 2.

1349. THE STORY OF THE TELEGRAPH, AND A HISTORY OF THE GREAT AT-
       LANTIC CABLE. NY: Rudd & Carleton, 1858.
       With Augustus Maverick.

Charles Timothy Brooks
1813–1883

Note: Brooks's many translations from the German are here reluctantly
omitted, but are listed in full in BAL.

1362. A POEM PRONOUNCED BEFORE THE PHI BETA KAPPA SOCIETY, AT
       CAMBRIDGE, AUGUST 28, 1845. Bos: Little & Brown, 1845.

CHARLES T. BROOKS (cont.)

1368. AQUIDNECK; A POEM. Providence: Burnett, 1848.
Pronounced on the 100th anniversary of the Redwood Library Company, Newport, RI, 24 Aug. 1847.

1373. THE CHILD'S ILLUSTRATED ALPHABET OF NATURAL HISTORY. Newport: Hammett, 1851.
Anon.

1382. SONGS OF FIELD AND FLOOD. Bos: Ptd by Wilson & Son, 1853.
Printed for the Ladies' Fair, Ocean Hall, Newport RI, August 1853.

1392. THE SIMPLICITY OF CHRIST'S TEACHINGS, SET FORTH IN SERMONS. Bos: Crosby, Nichols, 1859.

1436. ROMAN RHYMES: BEING WINTER WORK FOR A SUMMER FAIR. NEWPORT, R.I., AUGUST 27, 1869. By C.T.B. Cambridge: Ptd by Wilson & Son, 1869.

1477. WILLIAM ELLERY CHANNING: A CENTENNIAL MEMORY. Bos: Roberts Bros., 1880.

1493. POEMS, ORIGINAL AND TRANSLATED. Bos: Roberts Bros., 1885.
Ed. W.P. Andrews.

Maria Gowen Brooks
ca. 1794–1845

1494a. JUDITH, ESTHER, AND OTHER POEMS. By a Lover of the Fine Arts. Bos: Cummings & Hilliard, 1820.

1494b. ZOPHIEL, A POEM. Bos: Richardson & Lord, 1825.
Contains only Canto I of "Zóphiël" & 2 other pieces.

1494c. ZÓPHIËL; OR, THE BRIDE OF SEVEN. By Maria del Occidente. Bos: Carter & Hendee, 1833.
Complete text of "Zóphiël."

1494e. IDOMEN; OR THE VALE OF YUMURI. By Maria del Occidente. NY: Colman, 1843.

Charles Brockden Brown
1771–1810

1495. ALCUIN; A DIALOGUE. NY: Ptd by T. & J. Swords, 1798.
Anon.

1496. WIELAND; OR THE TRANSFORMATION. AN AMERICAN TALE. NY: Caritat, 1798.
Anon.

1497. ORMOND; OR THE SECRET WITNESS. NY: Caritat, 1799.
Anon.

CHARLES BROCKDEN BROWN (cont.)

1498. ARTHUR MERVYN; OR, MEMOIRS OF THE YEAR 1793. Phila: Maxwell, 1799.
Anon.

1499. EDGAR HUNTLY; OR, MEMOIRS OF A SLEEP-WALKER. Phila: Ptd by Maxwell, 1799.
Vols. 1–2 of three. Anon.

*1500. EDGAR HUNTLY; OR, MEMOIRS OF A SLEEP*WALKER. Phila: Ptd by Maxwell, 1799.
Vol. 3 of three. Anon.

1501. ARTHUR MERVYN; OR, MEMOIRS OF THE YEAR 1793. SECOND PART. NY: Hopkins, 1800.
Anon.

1502. CLARA HOWARD; IN A SERIES OF LETTERS. Phila: Dickins, 1801.
Anon. Reprinted in 1807 as *Philip Stanley* (No. 1510).

1503. JANE TALBOT, A NOVEL. Phila: J. Conrad, 1801.
Anon.

1515. THE LIFE OF CHARLES BROCKDEN BROWN. Phila: Parke, 1815.
2v. By William Dunlap, see No. 5017 below. "Together with selections ... from his original letters, and from his manuscripts before unpublished."

1516. THE NOVELS OF CHARLES BROCKDEN BROWN ... WITH A MEMOIR OF THE AUTHOR. Bos: Goodrich, 1827.
7v.

1517. THE RHAPSODIST AND OTHER UNCOLLECTED WRITINGS. NY: Scholars' Facsimiles & Reprints, 1943.
Ed. Harry R. Warfel

William Hill Brown
1766–1793

*1518. THE POWER OF SYMPATHY: OR, THE TRIUMPH OF NATURE. Bos: Thomas, 1789.
2v. Anon.

1520. THE BETTER SORT: OR, THE GIRL OF SPIRIT. AN OPERATICAL, COMICAL FARCE. Bos: Thomas, 1789.
Anon.

1523. IRA AND ISABELLA: OR THE NATURAL CHILDREN. A NOVEL. Bos: Belcher & Armstrong, 1807.

Charles Farrar Browne
(Artemus Ward)
1834–1867

Note: Artemus Ward's works were widely pirated in the U.K. The status of many of the U.K. editions and the attribution of some of the material contained therein to Browne has not been definitely established.

*1524. ARTEMUS WARD HIS BOOK. NY: Carleton, 1862.
>Published in the U.K. in 1865 by Hotten (No. 1526), whose "fourth edition" apparently contains 2 additional pieces, one of which is not by Browne.

*1527. ARTEMUS WARD; HIS TRAVELS. NY: Carleton, 1865.
>Also published in the U.K. in 1865 by Hotten (No. 1528) with 2 additional pieces.

*1529. ARTEMUS WARD AMONG THE FENIANS. Lon: Hotten, <n.d., 1866>.

 1532. ARTEMUS WARD IN LONDON, AND OTHER PAPERS. NY: Carleton, 1867.
>Published in the U.K. in 1870 by Hotten (No. 1535) with additional material.

*1533. ARTEMUS WARD'S LECTURE. (AS DELIVERED AT THE EGYPTIAN HALL, LONDON). Lon: Hotten, 1869.
>Ed. T.W. Robertson & E.P. Hingston. For U.S. edition see next entry.

 1534. ARTEMUS WARD'S PANORAMA. (AS EXHIBITED AT THE EGYPTIAN HALL, LONDON). NY: Carleton, 1869.
>Ed. T.W. Robertson & E.P. Hingston.

 1537. THE COMPLETE WORKS OF ARTEMUS WARD, (CHARLES FARRAR BROWNE). NY: G.W. Dillingham, 1898.
>"Revised edition." An earlier undated *Complete Works* published in the U.K. in 1870 by Hotten (No. 1536) contains 3 new pieces, possibly not by Browne.

 1538. LETTERS OF ARTEMUS WARD TO CHARLES E. WILSON 1858–1861. Cleveland: Rowfant Club, 1900.

Henry Howard Brownell
1820–1872

 1568. POEMS. NY: Appleton, 1847.

 1572. EPHEMERON. A POEM. NY: Appleton, 1855.

*1575. LYRICS OF A DAY: OR NEWSPAPER POETRY. Hartford: Case, Lockwood, 1863.
>Anon. Apparently printed for the author and not regularly published. Brownell's version of the "John Brown Song" is here collected; BAL also lists several ephemeral printings of this piece in 1863–64 (No. 1574).

 1576. LYRICS OF A DAY: OR NEWSPAPER POETRY. By a Volunteer in the U.S. Service. NY: Carleton, 1864.
>First published edition, with additional material; a further extended "second edition" also published in 1864 (No. 1577).

 1578. WAR-LYRICS AND OTHER POEMS. Bos: Ticknor & Fields, 1866.

H. H. BROWNELL (cont.)

1581. LINES OF BATTLE, AND OTHER POEMS. Bos & NY: Houghton Mifflin, 1912.
Ed. M.A. DeWolfe Howe.

William Cullen Bryant
1794–1878

Note: Anthologies edited by Bryant are here omitted. These include *Selections from the American Poets*, 1840 (No. 1617), *A Library of Poetry and Song*, 1871 (No. 1722) & *Picturesque America*, 1872–74 (No. 1732).

1582. THE EMBARGO, OR SKETCHES OF THE TIMES; A SATIRE. By a Youth of Thirteen. Bos: Ptd for the Purchasers, 1808.
Extended edition published in 1809 (No. 1583).

1587. POEMS. Cambridge: Ptd by Hilliard & Metcalf, 1821.
Ed. R.H. Dana Sr. & E.T. Channing. "Thanatopsis," here collected, was first published separately in 1874 (No. 1742).

1603. POEMS. NY: Bliss, 1832.
Later collections of Bryant's *Poems* containing new material published in 1834 (No. 1609), 1836 (No. 1612), 1839 (No. 1615), 1847 (No. 1633) & 1850 (No. 1643); see also Nos. 1656 & 1777 below.

*1621. THE FOUNTAIN AND OTHER POEMS. NY & Lon: Wiley & Putnam, 1842.

*1626. THE WHITE-FOOTED DEER AND OTHER POEMS. NY: Platt, 1844.
Some copies issued as *The Home Library. Poetical Series*, No. 1.

1642. LETTERS OF A TRAVELLER; OR, NOTES OF THINGS SEEN IN EUROPE AND AMERICA. NY: Putnam, 1850.
Reprinted in 1851 as *The Picturesque Souvenir. Letters of a Traveller* (No. 1645).

*1656. POEMS. NY & Lon: Appleton, 1855.
2v. "Collected and arranged by the author." Later 1v. editions, containing new material, published in 1858 (No. 1662a), 1871 (No. 1726) & 1876 (No. 1753).

*1665. LETTERS OF A TRAVELLER. SECOND SERIES. NY: Appleton, 1859.

*1683. THIRTY POEMS. NY & Lon: Appleton, 1864.

*1686. HYMNS. <n.p., n.d.; 1864>.
Slightly revised edition, also undated, published in 1869 (No. 1706).

*1707. LETTERS FROM THE EAST. NY: Putnam & Son, 1869.

*1714. THE ILIAD OF HOMER. Bos: Fields, Osgood, 1870.
2v. Translation.

1724. THE ODYSSEY OF HOMER. Bos: Osgood, 1871–72.
2v. Translation.

1735. ORATIONS AND ADDRESSES. NY: Putnam's Sons, 1873.

WILLIAM CULLEN BRYANT (cont.)

1776. A BIOGRAPHY OF WILLIAM CULLEN BRYANT, WITH EXTRACTS FROM HIS
PRIVATE CORRESPONDENCE. NY: Appleton, 1883.
2v. By Parke Godwin. *Life and Works,* Vols. 1–2.

1777. THE POETICAL WORKS OF WILLIAM CULLEN BRYANT. NY: Appleton,
1883.
2v. Ed. Parke Godwin. *Life and Works,* Vols. 3–4.

1781. PROSE WRITINGS OF WILLIAM CULLEN BRYANT. NY: Appleton, 1884.
2v. Ed. Parke Godwin. *Life and Works,* Vols. 5–6.

Henry Cuyler Bunner
1855–1896

1889. A WOMAN OF HONOR. Bos: Osgood, 1883.

*1891. AIRS FROM ARCADY AND ELSEWHERE. NY: Scribner's Sons, 1884.

1895. IN PARTNERSHIP STUDIES IN STORY-TELLING. NY: Scribner's Sons,
1884.
With Brander Matthews.

*1900. THE MIDGE. NY: Scribner's Sons, 1886.

*1907. THE STORY OF A NEW YORK HOUSE. NY: Scribner's Sons, 1887.
Two installments from the serialization in *Scribner's Magazine* were published as
an advertisement in 1886 (No. 1899).

*1913. "SHORT SIXES" STORIES TO BE READ WHILE THE CANDLE BURNS. NY:
Keppler & Schwarzmann, 1891.

*1914. ZADOC PINE AND OTHER STORIES. NY: Scribner's Sons, 1891.

*1919. THE RUNAWAY BROWNS A STORY OF SMALL STORIES. NY: Keppler &
Schwarzmann, 1892.

1921. ROWEN "SECOND CROP" SONGS. NY: Scribner's Sons, 1892.

*1924. "MADE IN FRANCE" FRENCH TALES RETOLD WITH A UNITED STATES
TWIST. NY: Keppler & Schwarzmann, 1893.

*1927. MORE "SHORT SIXES." NY: Keppler & Schwarzmann, 1894.

*1930. JERSEY STREET AND JERSEY LANE URBAN AND SUBURBAN SKETCHES.
NY: Scribner's Sons, 1896.

1931. THE SUBURBAN SAGE STRAY NOTES AND COMMENTS ON HIS SIMPLE
LIFE. NY: Keppler & Schwarzmann, 1896.

*1932. LOVE IN OLD CLOATHES AND OTHER STORIES. NY: Scribner's Sons,
1896.

1933. THE POEMS OF H.C. BUNNER. NY: Scribner's Sons, 1896.
Extended editions published in 1897 (No. 1938) & 1917 (No. 1951).

1936. THREE OPERETTAS. NY: Harper & Bros., 1897.
Music by Oscar Weil. "The Seven Old Ladies of Lavender Town," one of these
operettas, published separately in 1910 (No. 1946).

H. C. BUNNER (cont.)
   1953. THE LIFE AND LETTERS OF HENRY CUYLER BUNNER. Durham NC:
         Duke U PR, 1939.
         By Gerard E. Jensen.

Robert Jones Burdette
1844–1914

*1954. THE RISE AND FALL OF THE MUSTACHE AND OTHER "HAWK-EYETEMS."
       Burlington IA: Burlington Pub. Co., 1877.
       Extended edition published in 1878 (No. 1956).

 1958. HAWK-EYES. NY: Carleton, 1879.
       Reprinted in 1886 as *Innach Garden and Other Comic Sketches* (No. 1974) & in 1894
       as *Schooners that Pass in the Dark* (No. 2001).

 1963. WILLIAM PENN (1644–1718). NY: Holt, 1882.
       Lives of American Worthies.

 2003. THE MODERN TEMPLE AND TEMPLARS A SKETCH OF THE LIFE AND
       WORK OF RUSSELL H. CONWELL. NY, Bos, &c.: Silver, Burdett, 1894.

 2004. THE SONS OF ASAPH A SONG SERVICE OF YESTERDAY. <Phila: Times
       Ptg House, 1895>.

*2008. CHIMES FROM A JESTER'S BELLS STORIES AND SKETCHES … THE STORY
       OF ROLLO. Indianapolis & Kansas City: Bowen-Merrill, 1897.

 2011. SMILES YOKED WITH SIGHS. Indianapolis: Bowen-Merrill, <1900>.
       "Rime of the Ancient Miller," here collected, was issued in 1899 (?) as an adver-
       tisement for Galaxy Roller Mills (No. 2010).

 2020. THE SILVER TRUMPETS. Phila: Sunday School Times Co., <1912>.

 2021. OLD TIME AND YOUNG TOM. Indianapolis: Bobbs-Merrill, <1912>.
       "A Minute of Time," here slightly revised, was first printed separately for Burdette
       as a holiday token in 1902 (No. 2012).

 2022. A LITTLE PHILOSOPHY OF LIFE. <Pasadena CA, 1913>.
       "Designed and printed by Fred S. Lang Co., Los Angeles"

 2023. ALPHA AND OMEGA [A LITTLE CLUSTER OF EASTER BLOSSOMS]. <Pasa-
       dena CA: Clara Vista PR, 1914>.
       "Designed and printed by Fred S. Lang Co., Los Angeles"

 2025. THE DRUMS OF THE 47TH. Indianapolis: Bobbs-Merrill, <1914>.

 2028. ROBERT J. BURDETTE HIS MESSAGE. Phila, Chi, &c.: Winston, <1922>.
       Ed. Clara B. Burdette.

Frances Eliza Hodgson Burnett
1840–1924

*2033. THAT LASS O' LOWRIE'S. NY: Scribner, Armstrong, 1877.

*2035. "THEO." A LOVE STORY. Phila: Peterson & Bros., <1877>.
Revised edition published in 1879 (No. 2049).

*2036. SURLY TIM AND OTHER STORIES. NY: Scribner, Armstrong, 1877.

2037. DOLLY: A LOVE STORY. Phila: Porter & Coates, <1877>.
Revised edition published in 1884 as *Vagabondia* (No. 2062).

2038. PRETTY POLLY PEMBERTON. A LOVE STORY. Phila: Peterson & Bros.,
<1877>.
Revised edition published in 1878 (No. 2045).

*2039. KATHLEEN. A LOVE STORY. Phila: Peterson & Bros., <1878>.
Revised edition published also in 1878 as *Kathleen Mavourneen* (No.2043).

2040. OUR NEIGHBOUR OPPOSITE. Lon: Routledge & Sons, <n.d., 1878>.

2041. MISS CRESPIGNY. A LOVE STORY. Phila: Peterson & Bros., <1878>.
Revised edition published in 1879 (No. 2048).

2042. A QUIET LIFE; AND THE TIDE ON THE MOANING BAR. Phila: Peterson
& Bros., <1878>.
Published in U.K. as *The Tide on the Moaning Bar.*

2044. LINDSAY'S LUCK. NY: Scribner's Sons, <1878>.
The unrevised periodical text was published in 1879 by Peterson & Bros. (No.
2047).

2046. JARL'S DAUGHTER; AND OTHER STORIES. Phila: Peterson & Bros.,
<1879>.
Reprinted with 1 new story in 1883 (No. 2061).

2050. NATALIE AND OTHER STORIES. Lon: Warne, <n.d., 1879>.

2051. HAWORTH'S. NY: Scribner's Sons, 1879.

2053. LOUISIANA. NY: Scribner's Sons, 1880.

2054. A FAIR BARBARIAN. Lon: Warne, <n.d., 1881>.

*2055. A FAIR BARBARIAN. Bos: Osgood, 1881.

2056. ESMERALDA. A COMEDY-DRAMA. NY, 1881.
With William H. Gillette.

2058. THROUGH ONE ADMINISTRATION. Lon: Warne, 1883.
3v.

2059. THROUGH ONE ADMINISTRATION. Bos: Osgood, 1883.

*2064. LITTLE LORD FAUNTLEROY. NY: Scribner's Sons, 1886.
For dramatization see No. 2075 below.

2066. A WOMAN'S WILL OR MISS DEFARGE. Lon: Warne, <n.d., 1886>.
For U.S. edition see No. 2072 below.

FRANCES HODGSON BURNETT (cont.)

*2067. SARA CREWE OR WHAT HAPPENED AT MISS MINCHIN'S. NY: Scribner's Sons, 1888.
Revised edition published in 1905 as *The Little Princess* (No. 2101). For dramatization see No. 2114 below.

2069. SARA CREWE; OR WHAT HAPPENED AT MISS MINCHIN'S: AND EDITHA'S BURGLAR. Lon & NY: Warne, 1888.
For U.S. edition of "Editha's Burglar" see No. 2071 below.

2070. THE FORTUNES OF PHILIPPA FAIRFAX. Lon: Warne, <n.d., 1888>.

*2071. EDITHA'S BURGLAR A STORY FOR CHILDREN. Bos: Jordan, Marsh, 1888.

2072. MISS DEFARGE. Phila: Lippincott, 1888.
With *Brueton's Bayou*, by John Habberton. *Miss Defarge* originally published as the Dec. 1886 issue of *Lippincott's Monthly Magazine* (No. 2065); for U.K. edition as *A Woman's Will* see No. 2066 above.

*2073. THE PRETTY SISTER OF JOSÉ. NY: Scribner's Sons, 1889.

*2075. LITTLE LORD FAUNTLEROY A DRAMA. NY: French, <1889?>.
French's International Copyrighted Editions, No. 42. Dramatization presumably by Burnett, who also contributed to a French language dramatization published in 1895 (No. 2089).

2076. LITTLE SAINT ELIZABETH AND OTHER STORIES. Lon: Warne, 1889–90?
Not located. Title and imprint postulated.

2077. LITTLE SAINT ELIZABETH AND OTHER STORIES. NY: Scribner's Sons, 1890.

*2081. CHILDREN I HAVE KNOWN AND GIOVANNI AND THE OTHER. Lon: Osgood, McIlvaine, 1892.
For U.S. edition, containing 1 additional story, see next entry.

2082. GIOVANNI AND THE OTHER CHILDREN WHO HAVE MADE STORIES. NY: Scribner's Sons, 1892.

2083. THE DRURY LANE BOYS' CLUB. Wash DC: Press of "The Moon," 1892.

2084. THE ONE I KNEW THE BEST OF ALL A MEMORY OF THE MIND OF A CHILD. NY: Scribner's Sons, 1893.

2086. PICCINO AND OTHER CHILD STORIES. NY: Scribner's Sons, 1894.
Published in the U.K. in 1894 as *The Captain's Youngest* (No. 2087).

2088. TWO LITTLE PILGRIMS' PROGRESS A STORY OF THE CITY BEAUTIFUL. NY: Scribner's Sons, 1895.
Slightly revised edition published in 1897 (No. 2091).

*2090. A LADY OF QUALITY. NY: Scribner's Sons, 1896.

2092. HIS GRACE OF OSMONDE. NY: Scribner's Sons, 1897.

*2093. IN CONNECTION WITH THE DE WILLOUGHBY CLAIM. NY: Scribner's Sons, 1899.

FRANCES HODGSON BURNETT (cont.)

2096. THE MAKING OF A MARCHIONESS. NY: Stokes, <1901>.
For comment see next entry.

2097. THE METHODS OF LADY WALDERHURST. NY: Stokes, <1901>.
Reprinted with *The Making of a Marchioness* in 1909 as *Emily Fox-Seton* (No. 2111).

2100. IN THE CLOSED ROOM. NY: McClure, Phillips, 1904.

*2102. THE DAWN OF A TO-MORROW. NY: Scribner's Sons, 1906.

2103. QUEEN SILVER-BELL. NY: Century Co., 1906.
Published in the U.K. in 1907 as *The Troubles of Queen Silver-Bell* (No. 2105).

2104. RACKETTY-PACKETTY HOUSE. NY: Century Co., 1906.
For dramatization see No. 2133 below.

2106. THE COZY LION AS TOLD BY QUEEN CROSSPATCH. NY: Century Co., 1907.

*2107. THE SHUTTLE. NY: Stokes, <1907>.

2108. THE GOOD WOLF. NY: Moffat, Yard, 1908.

2109. THE SPRING CLEANING AS TOLD BY QUEEN CROSSPATCH. NY: Century Co., 1908.

2110. THE LAND OF THE BLUE FLOWER. NY: Moffat, Yard, 1909.

2112. BARTY CRUSOE AND HIS MAN SATURDAY. NY: Moffat, Yard, 1909.

*2114. THE LITTLE PRINCESS A PLAY FOR CHILDREN AND GROWN-UP CHILDREN. NY & Lon: French, 1911.
Dramatization of *Sara Crewe*, 1888. Burnett's outline of the play was published in 1903 (No. 2098).

*2115. THE SECRET GARDEN. NY: Stokes, <1911>.

2118. MY ROBIN. NY: Stokes, <1912>.

2119. T. TEMBAROM. NY: Century Co., 1913.

2122. THE LOST PRINCE. NY: Century Co., 1915.

2123. THE LITTLE HUNCHBACK ZIA. NY: Stokes, <1916>.

2124. THE WAY TO THE HOUSE OF SANTA CLAUS A CHRISTMAS STORY. NY & Lon: Harper & Bros., 1916.

*2125. THE WHITE PEOPLE. NY & Lon: Harper & Bros., <1917>.

2127. THE HEAD OF THE HOUSE OF COOMBE. NY: Stokes, <1922>.

2128. ROBIN. NY: Stokes, <1922>.

2130. IN THE GARDEN. Bos & NY: Medici Soc'y of America, 1925.

2133. RACKETTY-PACKETTY HOUSE A PLAY. NY: French, 1927.
First published in 1926 in *Another Treasury of Plays for Children*, ed. Montrose J. Moses (No. 2132); the leaves containing this work were extracted & issued separately (No. 2131), possibly for copyright purposes.

John Burroughs
1837–1921

Note: For a list of volumes of selected pieces from earlier works and information on collected sets of Burroughs's works see BAL (Nos. 2213–2223 & p. 446).

2134. NOTES ON WALT WHITMAN, AS POET AND PERSON. NY: American News Co., 1867.
These sheets reissued with additional material in 1871 as the "second edition" (No. 2136) by Redfield, New York.

2135. WAKE-ROBIN. NY: Hurd & Houghton, 1871.
Revised & extended "second edition" published in 1877 (No. 2139).

2138. WINTER SUNSHINE. NY: Hurd & Houghton, 1876.
Extended edition published in 1877 (No. 2141).

2140. BIRDS AND POETS WITH OTHER PAPERS. NY: Hurd & Houghton, 1877.

2142. LOCUSTS AND WILD HONEY. Bos: Houghton, Osgood, 1879.

2144. PEPACTON. Bos: Houghton, Mifflin, 1881.

*2146. FRESH FIELDS. Bos & NY: Houghton, Mifflin, 1885.

2147. SIGNS AND SEASONS. Bos & NY: Houghton, Mifflin, 1886.

2149. INDOOR STUDIES. Bos & NY: Houghton, Mifflin, 1889.

*2156. RIVERBY. Bos & NY: Houghton, Mifflin, 1894.

2162. WHITMAN A STUDY. Bos & NY: Houghton, Mifflin, 1896.

2166. THE LIGHT OF DAY RELIGIOUS DISCUSSIONS AND CRITICISMS. Bos & NY: Houghton, Mifflin, 1900.

*2167. SQUIRRELS AND OTHER FUR-BEARERS. Bos & NY: Houghton, Mifflin, 1900.

*2171. JOHN JAMES AUDUBON. Bos: Small, Maynard, 1902.

*2172. LITERARY VALUES AND OTHER PAPERS. Bos & NY: Houghton, Mifflin, 1902.

2173. FAR AND NEAR. Bos & NY: Houghton, Mifflin, 1904.

2176. WAYS OF NATURE. Bos & NY: Houghton, Mifflin, 1905.

2177. BIRD AND BOUGH. Bos & NY: Houghton, Mifflin, 1906.

2178. CAMPING WITH PRESIDENT ROOSEVELT. <Bos & NY>: Houghton, Mifflin, <1906>.
Extended edition published in 1907 as *Camping & Tramping with Roosevelt* (No. 2179).

2180. LEAF AND TENDRIL. Bos & NY: Houghton, Mifflin, 1908.

2185. TIME AND CHANGE. Bos & NY: Houghton Mifflin, 1912.

2186. THE SUMMIT OF THE YEARS. Bos & NY: Houghton Mifflin, 1913.

*2189. THE BREATH OF LIFE. Bos & NY: Houghton Mifflin, 1915.

2192. UNDER THE APPLE-TREES. Bos & NY: Houghton Mifflin, 1916.

JOHN BURROUGHS (cont.)
2199. FIELD AND STUDY. Bos & NY: Houghton Mifflin, 1919.
2200. ACCEPTING THE UNIVERSE. Bos & NY: Houghton Mifflin, 1920.
2201. UNDER THE MAPLES. Bos & NY: Houghton Mifflin, 1921.
2202. MY BOYHOOD. Garden City NY & Toronto: Doubleday, Page, 1922.
Conclusion by Julian Burroughs.
2203. THE LAST HARVEST. Bos & NY: Houghton Mifflin, 1922.
2207. JOHN BURROUGHS AND LUDELLA PECK. NY: Vinal, 1925.
2208. THE LIFE AND LETTERS OF JOHN BURROUGHS. Bos & NY: Houghton
Mifflin, 1925.
By Clara Barrus.
2212. THE HEART OF BURROUGHS'S JOURNALS. Bos & NY: Houghton
Mifflin, 1928.
Ed. Clara Barrus.

William Howard Allen Butler
1825–1902

2224. THE FUTURE; A POEM. NY: Craighead, Ptr, 1842.
Pronounced to the Philomathean Society, University of the City of New York, 27
Oct. 1842.

2226. BARNUM'S PARNASSUS; BEING CONFIDENTIAL DISCLOSURES OF THE
PRIZE COMMITTEE ON THE JENNY LIND SONG. NY: Appleton, 1850.
Anon.

*2228. NOTHING TO WEAR: AN EPISODE OF CITY LIFE. NY: Rudd & Carleton,
1857.
Anon. This popular satire was first published in *Harper's Weekly*, 7 Feb. 1857; BAL
lists several other early editions of unknown status, including one published as
Miss M'Flimsey: or Nothing to Wear.

2229. TWO MILLIONS. NY: Appleton, 1858.
2238. POEMS. Bos: Osgood, 1871.
2242. MRS. LIMBER'S RAFFLE; OR, A CHURCH FAIR AND ITS VICTIMS. A SHORT
STORY. NY: Appleton, 1876.
Anon.

2251. DOMESTICUS A TALE OF THE IMPERIAL CITY. NY: Scribner's Sons,
1886.
*2256. OBERAMMERGAU 1890. NY: Harper & Bros., 1891.
2258. THE ANIMAL BOOK A CHRISTMAS STORY. NY: Randolph, 1893.
2264. HOME POEMS AND RHYMES FOR THE NURSERY WITH "SEA SCRIBBLINGS"
AND "THE ANIMAL BOOK." NY: De Vinne PR, 1897.
"Printed for Private Circulation." "Sea Scribblings" was also privately printed in
1881 (No. 2250).

WILLIAM ALLEN BUTLER (cont.)

2265. NOTHING TO WEAR AND OTHER POEMS. NY: Harper & Bros., 1899.

*2269. A RETROSPECT OF FORTY YEARS 1825–1865. NY: Scribner's Sons, 1911.
Ed. Harriet Allen Butler.

Edwin Lassetter Bynner
1842–1893

2271. NIMPORT. Bos: Lockwood, Brooks, 1877.
Anon. *Wayside Series.*

2272. TRITONS. A NOVEL. Bos: Lockwood, Brooks, 1878.

2276. DAMEN'S GHOST. Bos: Osgood, 1881.
Anon. *Round-Robin Series.*

2277. AGNES SURRIAGE. Bos: Ticknor, 1887.
Issued in the U.K. in 1886 (No. 2276a); probably for copyright purposes only.

2278. PENELOPE'S SUITORS. Bos: Ticknor, 1887.

2279. AN UNCLOSETED SKELETON. Bos: Ticknor, <1888>.
With Lucretia Peabody Hale.

2280. THE BEGUM'S DAUGHTER. Bos: Little, Brown, 1890.

2281. THE CHASE OF THE METEOR AND OTHER STORIES. Bos: Little, Brown, 1891.

2283. ZACHARY PHIPS. Bos & NY: Houghton, Mifflin, 1892.

Brian Oswald Donn Byrne
1889–1928

2286. STORIES WITHOUT WOMEN (AND A FEW WITH WOMEN). NY: Hearst's Int'l Library Co., 1915.

2288. THE STRANGERS' BANQUET. NY & Lon: Harper & Bros., <1919>.

2289. THE FOOLISH MATRONS. NY & Lon: Harper & Bros., <1920>.

2291. MESSER MARCO POLO. NY: Century Co., 1921.

*2292. THE WIND BLOWETH. NY: Century Co., 1922.

2293. CHANGELING AND OTHER STORIES. NY & Lon: Century Co., <1923>.
Published in the U.K. in 1924 (No. 2295) with 1 new story.

2294. BLIND RAFTERY AND HIS WIFE, HILARIA. NY & Lon: Century Co., <1924>.

2296. O'MALLEY OF SHANGANAGH. NY & Lon: Century Co., <1925>.
Published in the U.K. in 1925 as *An Untitled Story* (No. 2297).

2300. HANGMAN'S HOUSE. Lon: Low, Marston, <n.d., 1926>.

*2301. HANGMAN'S HOUSE. NY & Lon: Century Co., <1926>.

2303. BROTHER SAUL. Lon: Low, Marston, <n.d., 1927>.

*2304. BROTHER SAUL. NY & Lon: Century Co., <1927>.

DONN BYRNE (cont.)

2305. CRUSADE. Lon: Low, Marston, <1928>.

*2306. CRUSADE. Bos: Little, Brown, 1928.

*2307. DESTINY BAY. Bos: Little, Brown, 1928.

2308. IRELAND THE ROCK WHENCE I WAS HEWN. Lon: Low, Marston, <n.d., 1929>.

2309. IRELAND THE ROCK WHENCE I WAS HEWN. Bos: Little, Brown, 1929.

*2310. FIELD OF HONOR. NY & Lon: Century Co., <1929>.
        Published in the U.K. in 1929 as *The Power of the Dog* (No. 2311).

2312. THE GOLDEN GOAT. Lon: Low, Marston, <n.d., 1930>.
        For U.S. edition see next entry.

2313. A PARTY OF BACCARAT. NY & Lon: Century Co., <1930>.

2315. RIVERS OF DAMASCUS AND OTHER STORIES. Lon: Low, Marston, <n.d., 1931>.

2316. RIVERS OF DAMASCUS AND OTHER STORIES. NY & Lon: Century Co., <1931>.

2317. SARGASSO SEA AND OTHER STORIES. Lon: Low, Marston, <n.d., 1932>.
        For U.S. edition see next entry.

2318. A WOMAN OF THE SHEE AND OTHER STORIES. NY & Lon: Century Co., <1932>.

2319. THE ISLAND OF YOUTH AND OTHER STORIES. Lon: Low, Marston, <n.d., 1932>.

2320. AN ALLEY OF FLASHING SPEARS AND OTHER STORIES. Lon: Low, Marston, <n.d., 1933>.

2321. THE ISLAND OF YOUTH AND OTHER STORIES. NY & Lon: Century Co., <n.d., 1933>.

2322. A DAUGHTER OF THE MEDICI AND OTHER STORIES. Lon: Low, Marston, <n.d., 1933>.

2323. THE HOUND OF IRELAND AND OTHER STORIES. Lon: Low, Marston, <n.d., 1934>.

2324. POEMS. Lon: Low, Marston, 1934.

2325. AN ALLEY OF FLASHING SPEARS AND OTHER STORIES. NY: Appleton-Century Co., 1934.

2327. THE HOUND OF IRELAND AND OTHER STORIES. NY: Appleton-Century Co., 1935.

2328. A DAUGHTER OF THE MEDICI AND OTHER STORIES. NY: Appleton-Century Co., 1935.

George Washington Cable
1844–1925

*2330. OLD CREOLE DAYS. NY: Scribner's Sons, 1879.

2331. THE GRANDISSIMES A STORY OF CREOLE LIFE. NY: Scribner's Sons, 1880.

2332. MADAME DELPHINE A NOVELETTE AND OTHER TALES. Lon: Warne, <1881>.

2333. MADAME DELPHINE. NY: Scribner's Sons, 1881.

2338. THE CREOLES OF LOUISIANA. NY: Scribner's Sons, 1884.

*2339. DR. SEVIER. Bos: Osgood, 1885.
A copyright printing was produced in 1883 (No. 2336).

2342. THE SILENT SOUTH TOGETHER WITH THE FREEDMAN'S CASE IN EQUITY AND THE CONVICT LEASE SYSTEM. NY: Scribner's Sons, 1885.
Extended edition published in 1889 (No. 2349).

2346. BONAVENTURE A PROSE PASTORAL OF ACADIAN LOUISIANA. NY: Scribner's Sons, 1888.
"Carancro" & "Grande Pointe," both here collected, were earlier published in the U.K. in 1887 with *Madame Delphine* (No. 2344).

2350. STRANGE TRUE STORIES OF LOUISIANA. NY: Scribner's Sons, 1889.

2353. THE NEGRO QUESTION. NY: Scribner's Sons, 1890.
Earlier versions of 2 of these papers, "The Negro Question" & "The Southern Struggle for Pure Government," were published separately in 1888 (No. 2348) & 1890 (No. 2352) respectively.

*2357. THE BUSY MAN'S BIBLE AND HOW TO STUDY AND TEACH IT. Meadville PA: Flood & Vincent, 1891.

2359. A MEMORY OF ROSWELL SMITH. <n.p., n.d.; NY, 1892>.
"Privately printed."

*2361. JOHN MARCH SOUTHERNER. NY: Scribner's Sons, 1894.

2365. STRONG HEARTS. NY: Scribner's Sons, 1899.

*2368. THE CAVALIER. NY: Scribner's Sons, 1901.

*2371. BYLOW HILL. NY: Scribner's Sons, 1902.

2376. KINCAID'S BATTERY. NY: Scribner's Sons, 1908.

2377. "POSSON JONE'" AND PÈRE RAPHAËL. NY: Scribner's Sons, 1909.
"Père Raphaël" was privately printed in 1901 (No. 2370); "Posson Jone'" is reprinted from *Old Creole Days*, 1879.

2381. GIDEON'S BAND A TALE OF THE MISSISSIPPI. NY: Scribner's Sons, 1914.

2382. THE AMATEUR GARDEN. NY: Scribner's Sons, 1914.

2384. THE FLOWER OF THE CHAPDELAINES. NY: Scribner's Sons, 1918.

2385. LOVERS OF LOUISIANA (TO-DAY). NY: Scribner's Sons, 1918.

2391. GEORGE W. CABLE HIS LIFE AND LETTERS. NY: Scribner's Sons, 1928.
By Lucy Leffingwell Cable Bikle.

George Henry Calvert
1803–1889

2394. A VOLUME FROM THE LIFE OF HERBERT BARCLAY. Baltimore: W. & J. Neal, 1833.
Anon.

2398. COUNT JULIAN; A TRAGEDY. Baltimore: Hickman, 1840.
Revised & privately printed for Calvert's use in 1879 as *Count Rudolf* (No. 2441).

2399. MISCELLANY OF VERSE AND PROSE. Baltimore: Hickman, 1840.

2400. CABIRO: A POEM ... CANTOS I. AND II. Baltimore: Hickman, 1840.
For Cantos 3 & 4 see No. 2419 below.

2402. SCENES AND THOUGHTS IN EUROPE. By an American. NY: Wiley & Putnam, 1846.
For comment see No. 2404 below.

2403. POEMS. Bos: Ticknor, 1847.

2404. SCENES AND THOUGHTS IN EUROPE ... SECOND SERIES. NY: Putnam, 1852.
Also issued with sheets of a later printing of the 1st series, 2v. in one; both series reprinted & published in 1860 2v. in one as *Travels in Europe* (No. 2413). Revised printings of both series published separately in 1863 (Nos. 2415 & 2416).

2409. INTRODUCTION TO SOCIAL SCIENCE A DISCOURSE IN THREE PARTS. NY: Redfield, 1856.

2410. COMEDIES. Bos: Phillips, Sampson, 1856.

2412. JOAN OF ARC: A POEM. IN FOUR BOOKS. <Cambridge>: Riverside PR, 1860.
Anon. Privately printed. First published edition, with corrected text, in 1883 (No. 2448).

2414. THE GENTLEMAN. Bos: Ticknor & Fields, 1863.

2417. ARNOLD AND ANDRÉ. AN HISTORICAL DRAMA. Bos: Little, Brown, 1864.
An early version collected in No. 2399 above; revised edition published in 1876 (No. 2434).

2419. CABIRO. A POEM ... CANTOS III. AND IV. Bos: Little, Brown, 1864.

2421. ANYTA AND OTHER POEMS. Bos: Dutton, 1866.

2422. FIRST YEARS IN EUROPE. Bos: Spencer, 1866.
These sheets reissued *ca.* 1883 by Lee & Shepard, Boston.

2424. ELLEN. A POEM FOR THE TIMES. NY: Carleton, 1867.
Anon. Extended edition published in 1869 (No. 2426).

2427. GOETHE: HIS LIFE AND WORKS. AN ESSAY. Bos: Lee & Shepard, 1872.

2428. MIRABEAU AN HISTORICAL DRAMA. Cambridge: Riverside PR, 1873.
Revised edition published in 1883 (No. 2447).

GEORGE H. CALVERT (cont.)

2430. THE MAID OF ORLEANS AN HISTORICAL TRAGEDY. NY: Putnam's Sons, 1874.
An earlier unrevised text was privately printed in 1873 (No. 2429).

2431. BRIEF ESSAYS AND BREVITIES. Bos: Lee & Shepard, 1874.

2432. ESSAYS AESTHETICAL. Bos: Lee & Shepard, 1875.

2435. A NATION'S BIRTH AND OTHER NATIONAL POEMS. Bos: Lee & Shepard, 1876.

2436. THE LIFE OF RUBENS. Bos: Lee & Shepard, 1876.

2437. CHARLOTTE VON STEIN: A MEMOIR. Bos: Lee & Shepard, 1877.

2439. WORDSWORTH. A BIOGRAPHIC AESTHETIC STUDY. Bos: Lee & Shepard, 1878.

2440. SHAKESPEARE A BIOGRAPHIC AESTHETIC STUDY. Bos: Lee & Shepard, 1879.

2442. COLERIDGE, SHELLEY, GOETHE. BIOGRAPHIC AESTHETIC STUDIES. Bos: Lee & Shepard, <1880>.

2444. LIFE, DEATH, AND OTHER POEMS. Bos: Lee & Shepard, <1882>.

2446. ANGELINE. A POEM. Bos: Lee & Shepard, <1883>.

2449. THREESCORE, AND OTHER POEMS. Bos: Lee & Shepard, <1883>.

2450. SIBYL A POEM. Bos: Lee & Shepard, <1883>.

2451. THE NAZARENE. A POEM. Bos: Lee & Shepard, <1883>.

2452. BRANGONAR A TRAGEDY. Bos: Lee & Shepard, <1883>.

2455. AUTOBIOGRAPHIC STUDY. Bos: Lee & Shepard, <n.d., 1885?>.
Apparently intended for private circulation only & never published.

William McKendree Carleton
1845–1912

2458. FAX. A CAMPAIGN POEM. Chi: Western News Co., 1868.

2460. POEMS. Chi: Lakeside Pub. & Ptg Co., 1871.

2464. FARM BALLADS. NY: Harper & Bros., 1873.
Revised & extended edition published in 1882 (No. 2485).

2468. FARM LEGENDS. NY: Harper & Bros., 1876.
Extended edition published in 1887 (No. 2498).

2469. YOUNG FOLKS' CENTENNIAL RHYMES. NY: Harper & Bros., 1876.

*2482. FARM FESTIVALS. NY: Harper & Bros., 1881.

2495. CITY BALLADS. NY: Harper & Bros., 1886.

2504. CITY LEGENDS. NY: Harper & Bros., 1890.

2511. CITY FESTIVALS. NY: Harper & Bros., 1892.

*2518. RHYMES OF OUR PLANET. NY: Harper & Bros., 1895.

2521. THE OLD INFANT AND SIMILAR STORIES. NY: Harper & Bros., 1896.

2535. SONGS OF TWO CENTURIES. NY & Lon: Harper & Bros., 1902.

WILL CARLETON (cont.)

2541. IN OLD SCHOOL DAYS. NY: Moffat, Yard, 1907.

2542. DRIFTED IN. NY: Moffat, Yard, 1908.

2543. A THOUSAND THOUGHTS FROM WILL CARLETON. NY, Lon, &c.: Every Where Pub. Co., <1908>.

2545. ARNOLD AND TALLEYRAND: A DRAMA. NY: Globe Literary Bureau, <1909>.

2546. THE BURGLAR-BRACELETS: A FARCE. NY: Globe Literary Bureau, <1909>.

2547. THE DUKE AND THE KING: A DRAMA. NY: Globe Literary Bureau, <1909>.

2548. LOWER THIRTEEN: A FARCE. NY: Globe Literary Bureau, <1909>.

2549. TAINTED MONEY: A DRAMA. NY: Globe Literary Bureau, <1909>.

2550. A THOUSAND MORE VERSES. NY: Every Where Pub. Co., <1912>.

William Bliss Carman
1861–1929

Note: Many of Carman's works appeared first in privately printed broadsides, leaflets & booklets, generally here omitted; for full details see BAL.

2606. LOW TIDE ON GRAND-PRÉ. By Bliss Carmen< *sic* >. Toronto: Copp, Clark, <n.d., 1889–90?>.
  Canadian Series of Booklets. Contains the title poem only.

2617. LOW TIDE ON GRAND PRÉ: A BOOK OF LYRICS. NY: Webster, 1893.
  Extended edition published in 1894 (No. 2620).

*2622. SONGS FROM VAGABONDIA. Bos: Copeland & Day, 1894.
  With Richard Hovey, see No. 9380 below.

*2623. A SEAMARK A THRENODY FOR ROBERT LOUIS STEVENSON. Bos: Copeland & Day, 1895.

2628. BEHIND THE ARRAS A BOOK OF THE UNSEEN. Bos & NY: Lamson, Wolffe, 1895.

*2634. MORE SONGS FROM VAGABONDIA. Bos: Copeland & Day, 1896.
  With Richard Hovey, see No. 9385 below.

2635. BALLADS OF LOST HAVEN A BOOK OF THE SEA. Bos, NY, &c.: Lamson, Wolffe, 1897.

2640. BY THE AURELIAN WALL AND OTHER ELEGIES. Bos, NY, &c.: Lamson, Wolffe, 1898.

2643. A WINTER HOLIDAY. Bos: Small, Maynard, 1899.

2646. LAST SONGS FROM VAGABONDIA. Bos: Small, Maynard, 1901.
  With Richard Hovey, see No. 9392.

BLISS CARMAN (cont.)

2649. BALLADS AND LYRICS. Lon: Bullen, 1902.
Another collection of similar material published with this title in Toronto in 1923 (No. 2742) & in the U.S. in 1924 (No. 2744).

2651. ODE ON THE CORONATION OF KING EDWARD. Bos: Page, 1902.

*2652. FROM THE BOOK OF MYTHS. Bos: Page, 1902.
Pipes of Pan, No. 1. Extended edition published in the U.K. in 1903 (No. 2655) & in the U.S. in 1904 (No. 2664).

*2656. FROM THE GREEN BOOK OF THE BARDS. Bos: Page, 1903.
Pipes of Pan, No. 2.

*2661. THE KINSHIP OF NATURE. Bos: Page, 1904.

2662. SONGS OF THE SEA CHILDREN. Bos: Page, 1904.
Pipes of Pan, No. 3.

*2663. SAPPHO ONE HUNDRED LYRICS. Bos: Page, 1904.

2665. THE FRIENDSHIP OF ART. Bos: Page, 1904.

2666. SONGS FROM A NORTHERN GARDEN. Bos: Page, 1904.
Pipes of Pan, No. 4. "Christmas Eve at S. Kavin's" & "The Word at St.Kavin's," both here collected, were printed separately in 1901 & 1903 respectively (Nos. 2648 & 2657).

2668. POEMS. NY: Scott-Thaw; Lon: Murray, 1904.
2v. The U.K. edition; for extended U.S. edition see No. 2673 below.

2669. FROM THE BOOK OF VALENTINES. Bos: Page, 1905.
Pipes of Pan, No. 5. An omnibus volume printed from the plates of Nos. 1–5 was published in 1906 as *Pipes of Pan* (No. 2674).

2671. THE POETRY OF LIFE. Bos: Page, 1905.

2673. POEMS. Bos: Page, 1905.
2v. Contains 1 poem not present in the U.K. edition.

2677. THE PRINCESS OF THE TOWER THE WISE MEN FROM THE EAST AND TO THE WINGED VICTORY. NY: Village PR, 1906.
"Privately printed."

2689. THE MAKING OF PERSONALITY. Bos: Page, 1908.

2692. THE ROUGH RIDER AND OTHER POEMS. NY: Kennerley, 1909.
"The Gate of Peace," here collected, was first printed separately in 1907 (No. 2687) & again in 1909 with added prologue & epilogue (No. 2691).

2703. ECHOES FROM VAGABONDIA. Bos: Small, Maynard, 1912.

2706. DAUGHTERS OF DAWN A LYRICAL PAGEANT. NY: Kennerley, 1913.
With Mary Perry King.

2712. EARTH DEITIES AND OTHER RHYTHMIC MASQUES. NY: Kennerley, 1914.
With Mary Perry King.

2717. APRIL AIRS A BOOK OF NEW ENGLAND LYRICS. Bos: Small, Maynard, 1916.

BLISS CARMAN (cont.)

2718. FOUR SONNETS. Bos: Small, Maynard, <1916>.

2731. LATER POEMS. Toronto: McClelland & Stewart, <1921>.

2735. LATER POEMS. Bos: Small, Maynard, <1922>.

2745. FAR HORIZONS. Bos: Small, Maynard, <1925>.

2747. TALKS ON POETRY AND LIFE BEING A SERIES OF FIVE LECTURES. Toronto: Ryerson PR, 1926.
Delivered before the University of Toronto, Dec. 1925. Ed. Blanche Hume.

2755. WILD GARDEN. NY: Dodd, Mead, 1929.

2759. SANCTUARY SUNSHINE HOUSE SONNETS. NY: Dodd, Mead, 1929.

2761. BLISS CARMAN'S POEMS. NY: Dodd, Mead, 1931.

Guy Wetmore Carryl
1873–1904

2777. FABLES FOR THE FRIVOLOUS. NY & Lon: Harper & Bros., 1898.

2780. MOTHER GOOSE FOR GROWN-UPS. NY & Lon: Harper & Bros., 1900.

2783. GRIMM TALES MADE GAY. Bos & NY: Houghton, Mifflin, <1902>.

2784. THE LIEUTENANT-GOVERNOR A NOVEL. Bos & NY: Houghton, Mifflin, 1903.

2785. ZUT AND OTHER PARISIANS. Bos & NY: Houghton, Mifflin, 1903.

2786. THE TRANSGRESSION OF ANDREW VANE A NOVEL. NY: Holt, 1904.

2787. FAR FROM THE MADDENING GIRLS. NY: McClure, Phillips, 1904.

2788. THE GARDEN OF YEARS AND OTHER POEMS. NY & Lon: Putnam's Sons, 1904.

William Alexander Caruthers
ca. 1800–1846

2790. THE KENTUCKIAN IN NEW-YORK. OR, THE ADVENTURES OF THREE SOUTHERNS. By a Virginian. NY: Harper & Bros., 1834.
2v.

2791. THE CAVALIERS OF VIRGINIA, OR THE RECLUSE OF JAMESTOWN. NY: Harper & Bros., 1834–35.
2v. Anon.

2795. THE KNIGHTS OF THE HORSE-SHOE; A TRADITIONARY TALE. Wetumpka AL: Yancey, 1845.
Anon.

Alice Cary
1820–1871

2798. POEMS OF ALICE AND PHOEBE CARY. Phila: Moss & Bro., 1850.

2804. CLOVERNOOK OR RECOLLECTIONS OF OUR NEIGHBORHOOD IN THE WEST. NY: Redfield, 1852.

2805. LYRA AND OTHER POEMS. NY: Redfield, 1852.

*2806. HAGAR, A STORY OF TO-DAY. NY: Redfield, 1852.

2808. CLOVERNOOK OR RECOLLECTIONS OF OUR NEIGHBORHOOD IN THE WEST SECOND SERIES. NY: Redfield, 1853.

2810. CLOVERNOOK CHILDREN. Bos: Ticknor & Fields, 1855.

2811. POEMS. Bos: Ticknor & Fields, 1855.

2812. MARRIED, NOT MATED; OR, HOW THEY LIVED AT WOODSIDE AND THROCKMORTON HALL. NY: Derby & Jackson, 1856.

2817. PICTURES OF COUNTRY LIFE. NY: Derby & Jackson, 1859.

2831. BALLADS, LYRICS, AND HYMNS. NY: Hurd & Houghton, 1866.

*2832. THE BISHOP'S SON A NOVEL. NY: Carleton, 1867.

2833. SNOW-BERRIES. A BOOK FOR YOUNG FOLKS. Bos: Ticknor & Fields, 1867.

2834. A LOVER'S DIARY. Bos: Ticknor & Fields, 1868.

2850. A MEMORIAL OF ALICE AND PHOEBE CARY, WITH SOME OF THEIR LATER POEMS. NY: Hurd & Houghton, 1873.
By Mary Clemmer Ames.

2852. THE LAST POEMS OF ALICE AND PHOEBE CARY. NY: Hurd & Houghton, 1873.
Ed. Mary Clemmer Ames.

2854. BALLADS FOR LITTLE FOLK. BY ALICE AND PHOEBE CARY. NY: Hurd & Houghton, 1874.
Ed. Mary Clemmer Ames.

2868. EARLY AND LATE POEMS OF ALICE AND PHOEBE CARY. Bos & NY: Houghton, Mifflin, 1887.

Phoebe Cary
1824–1871

2879. POEMS OF ALICE AND PHOEBE CARY. Phila: Moss & Bro., 1850.
For full entry see No. 2798 above.

2891. POEMS AND PARODIES. Bos: Ticknor, Reed, & Fields, 1854.

2907. POEMS OF FAITH, HOPE, AND LOVE. NY: Hurd & Houghton, 1868.

2914. A MEMORIAL OF ALICE AND PHOEBE CARY, WITH SOME OF THEIR LATER POEMS. NY: Hurd & Houghton, 1873.
By Mary Clemmer Ames. For full entry see No. 2850 above.

PHOEBE CARY (cont.)

2916. THE LAST POEMS OF ALICE AND PHOEBE CARY. NY: Hurd & Houghton, 1873.
Ed. Mary Clemmer Ames. For full entry see No. 2852 above.

2917. BALLADS FOR LITTLE FOLK. BY ALICE AND PHOEBE CARY. NY: Hurd & Houghton, 1874.
Ed. Mary Clemmer Ames. For full entry see No. 2854 above.

2927. EARLY AND LATE POEMS OF ALICE AND PHOEBE CARY. Bos & NY: Houghton, Mifflin, 1887.
For full entry see No. 2868 above.

Mary Hartwell Catherwood
1847–1902

*2934. A WOMAN IN ARMOR. By Mary Hartwell. NY: Carleton, 1875.

*2937. THE DOGBERRY BUNCH. Bos: Lothrop, <1879>.

2938. CRAQUE-O'-DOOM. A STORY. Phila: Lippincott, 1881.

2939. ROCKY FORK. Bos: Lothrop, <1882>.

2944. OLD CARAVAN DAYS. Bos: Lothrop, <1884>.

2951. THE SECRETS AT ROSELADIES. Bos: Lothrop, <1888>.

*2952. THE ROMANCE OF DOLLARD. NY: Century Co., <1889>.
For additional information see BAL (No. 15479).

2953. THE STORY OF TONTY. Chi: McClurg, 1890.

2955. THE LADY OF FORT ST. JOHN. Bos & NY: Houghton, Mifflin, 1891.

2959. OLD KASKASKIA. Bos & NY: Houghton, Mifflin, 1893.

2961. THE WHITE ISLANDER. NY: Century Co., 1893.

2963. THE CHASE OF SAINT-CASTIN AND OTHER STORIES. Bos & NY: Houghton, Mifflin, 1894.

2964. THE SPIRIT OF AN ILLINOIS TOWN AND THE LITTLE RENAULT TWO STORIES. Bos & NY: Houghton, Mifflin, 1897.

2966. THE DAYS OF JEANNE D'ARC. NY: Century Co., 1897.

*2967. BONY AND BAN THE STORY OF A PRINTING VENTURE. Bos: Lothrop, <1898>.

2969. HEROES OF THE MIDDLE WEST THE FRENCH. Bos: Ginn, 1898.

2970. THE QUEEN OF THE SWAMP AND OTHER PLAIN AMERICANS. Bos & NY: Houghton, Mifflin, 1899.

2971. MACKINAC AND LAKE STORIES. NY & Lon: Harper & Bros., 1899.

2972. SPANISH PEGGY A STORY OF YOUNG ILLINOIS. Chi & NY: Stone, 1899.

*2978. LAZARRE. Indianapolis: Bowen-Merrill, <1901>.
Two copyright printings were also produced in 1901 (Nos. 2976 & 2977).

Madison Julius Cawein
1865–1914

2986. BLOOMS OF THE BERRY. Louisville: Morton, 1887.

2987. THE TRIUMPH OF MUSIC AND OTHER LYRICS. <Louisville>: Morton, 1888.

2988. ACCOLON OF GAUL WITH OTHER POEMS. Louisville: Morton, 1889.

2989. LYRICS AND IDYLS. <Louisville>: Morton, 1890.

2991. DAYS AND DREAMS POEMS. NY & Lon: Putnam's Sons, 1891.

2992. MOODS AND MEMORIES POEMS. NY & Lon: Putnam's Sons, 1892.

2994. RED LEAVES AND ROSES POEMS. NY & Lon: Putnam's Sons, 1893.

2995. POEMS OF NATURE AND LOVE. NY & Lon: Putnam's Sons, 1893.
A selection with revisions & additions from Nos. 2988 & 2989 above.

2996. INTIMATIONS OF THE BEAUTIFUL AND POEMS. NY & Lon: Putnam's Sons, 1894.

*2998. VNDERTONES. Bos: Copeland & Day, 1896.

2999. THE GARDEN OF DREAMS. Louisville: Morton, 1896.

3000. SHAPES AND SHADOWS POEMS. NY: Russell, 1898.

3001. IDYLLIC MONOLOGUES ... OLD AND NEW WORLD VERSES. Louisville: Morton, <1898>.

3005. MYTH AND ROMANCE BEING A BOOK OF VERSES. NY & Lon: Putnam's Sons, 1899.

3007. WEEDS BY THE WALL VERSES. Louisville: Morton, 1901.

3008. ONE DAY & ANOTHER A LYRICAL ECLOGUE. Bos: Badger, 1901.
Revised & extended from No. 2991 above.

3010. KENTUCKY POEMS. Lon: Richards, 1902.
A selection with revisions from earlier books.

3011. A VOICE ON THE WIND AND OTHER POEMS. Louisville: Morton, 1902.

3012. KENTUCKY POEMS. NY: Dutton, 1902.
A selection with revisions from earlier books.

3014. THE VALE OF TEMPE POEMS. NY: Dutton, 1905.

3015. NATURE-NOTES AND IMPRESSIONS IN PROSE AND VERSE. NY: Dutton, 1906.

3016. AN ODE ... IN COMMEMORATION OF THE FOUNDING OF THE MASSA-CHUSETTS BAY COLONY. Louisville: Morton, 1908.
Read at the dedication of the monument erected at Gloucester, 15 Aug. 1907.

3017. THE POEMS OF MADISON CAWEIN. Indianapolis: Bobbs-Merrill, <1907, i.e.1908>.
5v. Contains revisions. A 1v. collection of *Poems* published in 1911 (No. 3025) contains 2 new poems.

3018. NEW POEMS. Lon: Richards, 1909.

MADISON CAWEIN (cont.)

3019. THE GIANT AND THE STAR LITTLE ANNALS IN RHYME. Bos: Small, Maynard, <1909>.

*3022. THE SHADOW GARDEN (A PHANTASY) AND OTHER PLAYS. NY & Lon: Putnam's Sons, 1910.

3030. THE POET, THE FOOL AND THE FAERIES. Bos: Small, Maynard, <1912>.

3034. THE REPUBLIC A LITTLE BOOK OF HOMESPUN VERSE. Cincinnati: Stewart & Kidd, <1913>.

3035. MINIONS OF THE MOON A LITTLE BOOK OF SONG AND STORY. Cincinnati: Stewart & Kidd, <1913>.

3043. THE POET AND NATURE ... THE MORNING ROAD. Louisville: Morton, <1914>.

*3048. THE CUP OF COMUS FACT AND FANCY. NY: Cameo PR, 1915.

3052. THE STORY OF A POET: MADISON CAWEIN HIS INTIMATE LIFE AS RE- VEALED BY HIS LETTERS AND OTHER HITHERTO UNPUBLISHED MATE- RIAL. Louisville: Morton, 1921.
By Otto A. Rothert. *Filson Club Publications,* No. 30.

William Ellery Channing
1818–1901

3057. POEMS. Bos: Little & Brown, 1843.

3061. POEMS ... SECOND SERIES. Bos: Munroe, 1847.

3062. CONVERSATIONS IN ROME: BETWEEN AN ARTIST, A CATHOLIC, AND A CRITIC. Bos: Crosby & Nichols, 1847.

3063. THE WOODMAN, AND OTHER POEMS. Bos: Munroe, 1849.

3065. NEAR HOME. A POEM. Bos: Munroe, 1858.
Anon.

3072. THE WANDERER. A COLLOQUIAL POEM. Bos: Osgood, 1871.

3074. THOREAU: THE POET-NATURALIST. Bos: Roberts Bros., 1873.
Extended edition published in 1902 (No. 3084).

3080. ELIOT. A POEM. Bos: Cupples, Upham, 1885.

3081. JOHN BROWN, AND THE HEROES OF HARPER'S FERRY. A POEM. Bos: Cupples, Upham, 1886.

3083. POEMS OF SIXTY-FIVE YEARS. Phila & Concord: J.H. Bentley, 1902.
Ed. F.B. Sanborn.

Lydia Maria Francis Child
1802–1880

Note: Most of Child's anti-slavery tracts are here omitted; for full details see BAL.

3087. HOBOMOK, A TALE OF EARLY TIMES. By an American. Bos: Cummings, Hilliard, 1824.

3088. EVENINGS IN NEW ENGLAND. By an American Lady. Bos: Cummings, Hilliard, 1824.

*3089. THE REBELS, OR BOSTON BEFORE THE REVOLUTION. Bos: Cummings, Hilliard, 1825.
Anon. Revised edition published in 1850 (No. 3167).

3091. EMILY PARKER, OR IMPULSE, NOT PRINCIPLE. Bos: Bowles & Dearborn, 1827.
Anon.

3097. BIOGRAPHICAL SKETCHES OF GREAT AND GOOD MEN. Bos: Putnam & Hunt, 1828.

*3100. THE FIRST SETTLERS OF NEW-ENGLAND: OR, CONQUEST OF THE PEQUODS, NARRAGANSETS AND POKANOKETS. By a Lady of Massachusetts. Bos: Munroe & Francis, <n.d., 1829>.

3101. THE FRUGAL HOUSEWIFE. Bos: Marsh & Capen, 1829.
Revised & extended "second edition" published in 1830 (No. 3104).

3108. THE LITTLE GIRL'S OWN BOOK. Bos: Carter, Hendee, & Babcock, 1831.
Extended edition published in 1834 (No. 3119) & reprinted, not before 1848, as *The Girls' Own Book* (No. 3117).

3109. THE MOTHER'S BOOK. Bos: Carter, Hendee, & Babcock, 1831.
Revised & extended "sixth edition" published in 1844 (No. 3148).

3110. THE CORONAL. A COLLECTION OF MISCELLANEOUS PIECES. Bos: Carter & Hendee, 1832.
Reprinted in the U.K., with additional material by Mary Howitt & Caroline Fry, in 1833 as *The Mother's Story Book; or, Western Coronal* (No. 3113).

3111. THE BIOGRAPHIES OF MADAME DE STAËL, AND MADAME ROLAND. Bos: Carter & Hendee, 1832.
Ladies' Family Library, Vol. 1. Revised edition published in 1847 as *Memoirs of Madame de Staël, and of Madame Roland* (No. 3159). *The Biography of Madame de Staël* published separately in 1836 (No. 3132).

3112. THE BIOGRAPHIES OF LADY RUSSELL, AND MADAME GUYON. Bos: Carter, Hendee, 1832.
Ladies' Family Library, Vol. 2. *The Biography of Lady Russell* published separately in 1836 (No. 3131).

LYDIA MARIA CHILD (cont.)

*3115. GOOD WIVES. Bos: Carter, Hendee, 1833.
  Ladies' Family Library, Vol. 3. Revised edition published in 1846 as *Biographies of Good Wives* (No. 3154); reprinted in 1858 as *Celebrated Women* (No. 3184) & in 1871 as *Married Women* (No. 3210).

3116. AN APPEAL IN FAVOR OF THAT CLASS OF AMERICANS CALLED AFRICANS. Bos: Allen & Ticknor, 1833.

3118. THE OASIS. Bos: Allen & Ticknor, 1834.
  Edited, with many contributions, by Child.

3121. THE HISTORY OF THE CONDITION OF WOMEN, IN VARIOUS AGES AND NATIONS ... VOL I. Bos: Allen, 1835.
  Ladies' Family Library, Vol. 4. "Comprising the women of Asia and Africa."

3122. THE HISTORY OF THE CONDITION OF WOMEN, IN VARIOUS AGES AND NATIONS ... VOL. II. Bos: Allen, 1835.
  Ladies' Family Library, Vol. 5. "Comprising the women of Europe, America, and South Sea Islands."

3130. PHILOTHEA. A ROMANCE. Bos: Otis, Broaders, 1836.
  Slightly revised edition published in 1845 (No. 3153).

3136. THE FAMILY NURSE; OR COMPANION OF THE FRUGAL HOUSEWIFE. Bos: Hendee, 1837.
  "Revised by a member of the Massachusetts Medical Society."

3144. LETTERS FROM NEW-YORK. NY: C.S. Francis, 1843.
  Extended "second edition" published in 1844 (No. 3147).

3149. FLOWERS FOR CHILDREN ... I. NY: C.S. Francis, 1844.
  "For children eight or nine years old." Reprinted in 1869 as *The Christ-Child, and Other Stories* (No. 3207).

3151. FLOWERS FOR CHILDREN ... II. NY: C.S. Francis, 1845.
  "For children from four to six years old." Reprinted in 1869 as *Good Little Mitty, and Other Stories* (No. 3208).

*3152. LETTERS FROM NEW YORK. SECOND SERIES. NY: C.S. Francis, 1845.

3155. FACT AND FICTION: A COLLECTION OF STORIES. NY: C.S. Francis, 1846.
  Reprinted in 1871 as *The Children of Mount Ida, and Other Stories* (No.3211). Another version of "The Youthful Emigrant," here collected, published in 1898 (No. 3224).

3157. FLOWERS FOR CHILDREN III. NY: C.S. Francis, 1847.
  "For children of eleven and twelve years of age." Reprinted in 1869 as *Making Something, and Other Stories* (No. 3209). The series reprinted in an omnibus volume in 1854 (No. 3178).

3170. SKETCHES FROM REAL LIFE. I. THE POWER OF KINDNESS. II. HOME AND POLITICS. Phila: Hazard & Mitchell, 1850.
  Reprinted in 1853 as *The Power of Kindness; and Other Stories* (No. 3175).

LYDIA MARIA CHILD (cont.)

3173. THE CHILDRENS' GEMS. THE BROTHER AND SISTER: AND OTHER STO-
RIES. Phila: New Church Book Store, <1852>.
Anon.

*3174. ISAAC T. HOPPER: A TRUE LIFE. Bos: Jewett, 1853.

*3180. THE PROGRESS OF RELIGIOUS IDEAS, THROUGH SUCCESSIVE AGES.
NY: C.S.Francis, 1855.
3v.

3182. A NEW FLOWER FOR CHILDREN. NY: C.S. Francis, 1856.
These stories reprinted in 1869 in 2v. as *The Adventures of Jamie and Jeannie, and
Other Stories* (No. 3205) & *The Boy's Heaven, and Other Stories* (No. 3206).

*3183. AUTUMNAL LEAVES: TALES AND SKETCHES IN PROSE AND RHYME. NY
& Bos: C.S.Francis, 1857.

*3187. CORRESPONDENCE BETWEEN LYDIA MARIA CHILD AND GOV. WISE AND
MRS. MASON, OF VIRGINIA. Bos: American Anti-Slavery Soc'y, 1860.
Also (later?) published in 1860 in New York by the American Anti-Slavery Society
(No. 3188) as *Anti-Slavery Tracts*, New Series, No. 1.

*3189. THE RIGHT WAY THE SAFE WAY, PROVED BY EMANCIPATION IN THE
BRITISH WEST INDIES, AND ELSEWHERE. NY, 1860.
Extended edition published in 1862 (No. 3195).

3192. INCIDENTS IN THE LIFE OF A SLAVE GIRL. WRITTEN BY HERSELF. Bos:
The Author, 1861.
By Harriet Brent Jacobs; edited by Child. Binder's title: *Linda*.

3198. LOOKING TOWARD SUNSET. FROM SOURCES OLD AND NEW, ORIGINAL
AND SELECTED. Bos: Ticknor & Fields, 1865.
Edited, with many contributions, by Child.

3199. THE FREEDMEN'S BOOK. Bos: Ticknor & Fields, 1865.
Edited, with many contributions, by Child.

3203. A ROMANCE OF THE REPUBLIC. Bos: Ticknor & Fields, 1867.

3204. AN APPEAL FOR THE INDIANS. NY: Tomlinson, <n.d., 1868>.

3218. IN BARTON WOODS. By Mrs. L.M. Childs< *sic* >. Bos: Lothrop, <n.d.,
ca.1881>.
By the subject of this list?

*3220. LETTERS OF LYDIA MARIA CHILD. Bos & NY: Houghton, Mifflin, 1883.

Thomas Holley Chivers
1809–1858

3225. THE PATH OF SORROW, OR, THE LAMENT OF YOUTH: A POEM. Franklin
TN: The Author, 1832.

3226. CONRAD AND EUDORA; OR, THE DEATH OF ALONZO. A TRAGEDY. Phila,
1834.

THOMAS HOLLEY CHIVERS (cont.)

3227. NACOOCHEE; OR, THE BEAUTIFUL STAR, WITH OTHER POEMS. NY: W.E. Dean, Ptr, 1837.

3228. THE LOST PLEIAD: AND OTHER POEMS. NY: Ptd by Jenkins, 1845.

3229. SEARCH AFTER TRUTH; OR, A NEW REVELATION OF THE PSYCHO-PHYSI-OLOGICAL NATURE OF MAN. NY: Ptd by Cobb & Yallalee, 1848.

3231. EONCHS OF RUBY. A GIFT OF LOVE. NY: Spalding & Shepard, 1851.
These sheets reissued in 1853 with new preliminaries as *Memoralia; or, Phials of Amber* (No. 3233).

*3232. VIRGINALIA; OR, SONGS OF MY SUMMER NIGHTS. Phila: Lippincott, Grambo, 1853.

3234. ATLANTA: OR THE TRUE BLESSED ISLAND OF POESY. Macon GA: Ptd at The Georgia Citizen Office, 1853.

3235. BIRTH-DAY SONG OF LIBERTY. A PAEAN OF GLORY FOR THE HEROES OF FREEDOM. Atlanta: Hanleiter, Ptrs, 1856.

3236. THE SONS OF USNA: A TRAGI-APOTHEOSIS. Phila: Sherman & Son, Ptrs, 1858.

3239. CHIVERS' LIFE OF POE. NY: Dutton, 1952.
Ed. Richard Beale Davis.

Kate O'Flaherty Chopin
1851–1904

3240. AT FAULT. A NOVEL. St. Louis: Nixon-Jones Ptg Co., 1890.

3244. BAYOU FOLK. Bos & NY: Houghton, Mifflin, 1894.

3245. A NIGHT IN ACADIE. Chi: Way & Williams, 1897.

3246. THE AWAKENING. Chi & NY: Stone, 1899.

*3248. KATE CHOPIN AND HER CREOLE STORIES. Phila: U of Pennsylvania PR, 1932.
By Daniel S. Rankin.

Willis Gaylord Clark
1808–1841

3260. THE SPIRIT OF LIFE: A POEM. Phila: Key & Biddle, 1833.
Pronounced before the Franklin Society of Brown University, 3 Sept. 1833.

3264. THE PAST AND PRESENT, A COMPARATIVE VIEW OF IDOLATRY AND RELIGION, AS AIDS TO LEARNING: A POEM. <Croydon PA>: Bristol College PR, 1834.
Pronounced before the Athenian Society of Bristol College, July 23, 1834. Clark's "Ode" for the Athenian Society's celebration, 4 July 1835, was also published as a broadside (No. 3266).

WILLIS GAYLORD CLARK (cont.)

3278.   AN ADDRESS ON THE CHARACTERS OF LAFAYETTE AND WASHINGTON.
Phila: Ptd by J. Crissy, 1840.
Pronounced before the Washington Society of Lafayette College, Easton PA,
4 July 1840.

*3282.   THE LITERARY REMAINS OF THE LATE WILLIS GAYLORD CLARK. NY:
Burgess, Stringer, 1844.
5 parts or 1v. Ed. Lewis Gaylord Clark.

3284.   THE POETICAL WRITINGS OF THE LATE WILLIS GAYLORD CLARK. NY:
Redfield, 1847.
"First complete edition."

3288.   THE LETTERS OF WILLIS GAYLORD CLARK AND LEWIS GAYLORD CLARK.
NY: New York Public Library, 1940.
Ed. Leslie W. Dunlap.

McDonald Clarke
1798–1842

3289.   THE EVE OF ETERNITY. NY: The Author, 1820.
At head of title: *To the old maids of Europe, Asia, Africa, and America.*

3291.   THE ELIXIR OF MOONSHINE; BEING A COLLECTION OF PROSE AND
POETRY. By the Mad Poet. Gotham: Ptd at the Sentimental
Epicure's Ordinary. A.M. 5822 <i.e. NY, 1822>.

*3292.   THE GOSSIP ... A SENTIMENTAL SATIRE; WITH OTHER POEMS ... NO.
ONE. NY: Ptd by Gray & Bunce, 1323 <i.e. 1823>.
Imprint dated 22 Oct. 1823 <"1323" in some copies>.

3293.   THE GOSSIP, NO. II ... AND OTHER POEMS. NY, 1824.
Imprint dated 24 April 1824.

3294.   SKETCHES. NY, 1826.
Imprint dated 18 June 1826.

3295.   SKETCHES. PART II. NY, 1826.
Imprint dated 1 Aug. 1826.

*3296.   AFARA, A POEM. NY, 1829.
Anon. Dated at end 18 April 1829.

3297.   AFARA. OR, THE BELLES OF BROADWAY. II. NY, 1829.
Anon. Dated at end 9 March 1829.

3298.   AFARA III. NY, 1829.
Anon. Dated at end 18 April 1829.

3299.   DEATH IN DISGUISE; A TEMPERANCE POEM. Bos: Mussey, 1833.

*3300.   POEMS. NY: Bell, 1836.
These sheets reissued in 1844 by Van Amringe & Bixby, New York.

3302.   A CROSS & CORONET! <NY>: Le Blanc, 1842.
Afara <2nd Series>, I.

McDONALD CLARKE (cont.)
3303. AFARA, II. IN WEEKLY NUMBERS. <NY: Le Blanc, 1842>.
3304. AFARA, III. IN WEEKLY NUMBERS. <NY>: Le Blanc, <n.d., 1842>.
3305. AFARA, IV. IN WEEKLY NUMBERS. <NY>: Le Blanc, <1842>.
3306. AFARA, V. IN WEEKLY NUMBERS. <NY: Le Blanc, 1842>.

Samuel Langhorne Clemens
(Mark Twain)
1835–1910

*3310. THE CELEBRATED JUMPING FROG OF CALAVERAS COUNTY, AND OTHER SKETCHES. NY: Webb, 1867.
Ed. John Paul <i.e. Charles Henry Webb>. U.K. editions with additional material published in 1870 (No. 3319) & 1872 (No. 3338).

*3316. THE INNOCENTS ABROAD, OR THE NEW PILGRIMS' PROGRESS. Hartford: American Pub. Co., 1869.
Slightly revised edition published in the U.K. in 1872 in 2v. as *The Innocents Abroad* (No. 3343) & *The New Pilgrims' Progress* (No. 3344).

*3326. MARK TWAIN'S (BURLESQUE) AUTOBIOGRAPHY AND FIRST ROMANCE. NY: Sheldon, <1871>.
Published in the U.K. in 1871 (No. 3329) with additional material; also published in an unauthorized & undated (1871?) Toronto edition (No. 3334) containing also selections from *Memoranda*, 1871, & other material.

3327. MARK TWAIN'S MEMORANDA. FROM THE GALAXY. Toronto: Canadian News Co., 1871.
Unauthorized. For another unauthorized Toronto edition (No. 3334) possibly published in 1871 see preceding entry.

*3335. "ROUGHING IT." Lon: Routledge & Sons, <n.d., 1872>.

*3336. THE INNOCENTS AT HOME. Lon: Routledge & Sons, <n.d., 1872>.
Also contains *Mark Twain's Burlesque Autobiography.*

3337. ROUGHING IT. Hartford: American Pub. Co., 1872.
Published in the U.K. in 2v., see preceding 2 entries.

*3340. A CURIOUS DREAM; AND OTHER SKETCHES. Lon: Routledge & Sons, <n.d., 1872>.

*3357. THE GILDED AGE A TALE OF TO-DAY. Hartford: American Pub. Co., 1873.
With Charles Dudley Warner, see No. 21117 below. Also a simultaneous (?) U.K. edition (No. 3359) with title-page dated 1874.

*3364. MARK TWAIN'S SKETCHES, NEW AND OLD. Hartford & Chi.: American Pub. Co., 1875.
Binder's title: *Sketches Old and New.* A pamphlet entitled *Mark Twain's Sketches*, No. 1, published in 1874 by the American News Co., New York (No. 3360) containing material not collected here; another collection of Twain's *Sketches* published in Toronto in 1879 (No. 3384) also contains new material.

S. L. CLEMENS (Mark Twain) (cont.)

3367. THE ADVENTURES OF TOM SAWYER. Lon: Chatto & Windus, 1876.

*3368. OLD TIMES ON THE MISSISSIPPI. Toronto: Belford Bros., 1876.
Unauthorized. Published in the U.K. in 1877 as *The Mississippi Pilot* (No. 3612).

*3369. THE ADVENTURES OF TOM SAWYER. Hartford, Chi, &c.: American Pub. Co., 1876.
A previously unpublished prologue was added to the Limited Editions Club edition of 1939 (No. 3562).

3373. A TRUE STORY, AND THE RECENT CARNIVAL OF CRIME. Bos: Osgood, 1877.

*3378. PUNCH, BROTHERS, PUNCH! AND OTHER SKETCHES. NY: Slote, Woodman, <1878>.
Published in the U.K. in 1878 as *An Idle Excursion and Other Papers* (No. 3615). An unauthorized Toronto edition of some of this material published as *An Idle Excursion* (No. 3377) may have preceded the U.S. edition by a few days. Twain's version of "Punch, Brothers, Punch!" was also included in numerous other publications in 1876–77 (No. 3366A–F).

*3386. A TRAMP ABROAD. Hartford: American Pub. Co., 1880.

3396. THE PRINCE AND THE PAUPER. A TALE FOR YOUNG PEOPLE OF ALL AGES. Lon: Chatto & Windus, 1881.
Also a simultaneous authorized Canadian edition (No. 3397).

3402. THE PRINCE AND THE PAUPER A TALE FOR YOUNG PEOPLE OF ALL AGES. Bos: Osgood, 1882.

*3403. THE STOLEN WHITE ELEPHANT. Lon: Chatto & Windus, 1882.

3404. THE STOLEN WHITE ELEPHANT ETC. Bos: Osgood, 1882.
"A Curious Experience," here collected, was also published separately in an undated & unauthorized Canadian edition probably in late 1881 (No. 3395).

3407. DATE 1601. CONVERSATION, AS IT WAS BY THE SOCIAL FIRESIDE, IN THE TIME OF THE TUDORS. <West Point NY: Ye Academie Presse, 1882>.
First authorized edition. An unauthorized edition was possibly printed in 1880 (No. 3388).

3410. LIFE ON THE MISSISSIPPI. Lon: Chatto & Windus, 1883.

*3411. LIFE ON THE MISSISSIPPI. Bos: Osgood, 1883.
A "Suppressed Chapter" was first printed separately *ca.* 1913 (No. 3519) & included with other suppressed passages in the Limited Editions Club edition of 1944 (No. 3571).

*3414. THE ADVENTURES OF HUCKLEBERRY FINN (TOM SAWYER'S COMRADE). Lon: Chatto & Windus, 1884.

*3415. ADVENTURES OF HUCKLEBERRY FINN (TOM SAWYER'S COMRADE). NY: Webster, 1885.

*3429. A CONNECTICUT YANKEE IN KING ARTHUR'S COURT. NY: Webster, 1889.

3434. THE AMERICAN CLAIMANT. NY: Webster, 1892.

S. L. CLEMENS (Mark Twain) (cont.)

3435. MERRY TALES. NY: Webster, 1892.

3436. THE £1,000,000 BANK-NOTE AND OTHER NEW STORIES. NY: Webster, 1893.

3440. TOM SAWYER ABROAD BY HUCK FINN. NY: Webster, 1894.

3441. PUDD'NHEAD WILSON A TALE. Lon: Chatto & Windus, 1894.

*3442. THE TRAGEDY OF PUDD'NHEAD WILSON AND THE COMEDY OF THOSE EXTRAORDINARY TWINS. Hartford: American Pub. Co., 1894.

*3446. PERSONAL RECOLLECTIONS OF JOAN OF ARC. By the Sieur Louis de Conte. NY: Harper & Bros., 1896.
"Freely translated out of the ancient French ... by Jean François Alden <i.e. Clemens>."

3447. TOM SAWYER ABROAD TOM SAWYER, DETECTIVE AND OTHER STORIES. NY: Harper & Bros., 1896.

3448. TOM SAWYER, DETECTIVE AS TOLD BY HUCK FINN AND OTHER TALES. Lon: Chatto & Windus, 1897.

3449. HOW TO TELL A STORY AND OTHER ESSAYS. NY: Harper & Bros., 1897.
Extended edition published in 1900 (No. 3458) as *The Writings*, Vol. 22, see No. 3456 below.

*3451. FOLLOWING THE EQUATOR A JOURNEY AROUND THE WORLD. Hartford: American Pub. Co., 1897.
Published simultaneously (?) in the U.K. in 1897 as *More Tramps Abroad* (No. 3453). A "Suppressed Chapter" was privately printed in 1928 (No.3546) but later destroyed.

3456. THE WRITINGS OF MARK TWAIN. Hartford: American Pub. Co., 1899–1907.
25v. *Autograph edition.*

*3459. THE MAN THAT CORRUPTED HADLEYBURG AND OTHER STORIES AND ESSAYS. NY & Lon: Harper & Bros., 1900.
The U.K. edition with additional material also published in 1900 (No. 3460).

*3465. ENGLISH AS SHE IS TAUGHT. Bos: Mutual Book Co., <1900>.
Earlier published in the U.K. as a commentary in Caroline B. Le Row's *English as She Is Taught*, 1887 (No. 3420).

*3471. A DOUBLE BARRELLED DETECTIVE STORY. NY & Lon: Harper & Bros., 1902.
Tauchnitz edition with additional material also published in 1902 (No.3472).

3480. EXTRACTS FROM ADAM'S DIARY. NY & Lon: Harper & Bros., 1904.
"Translated from the original MS." An earlier version was published in *The Niagara Book*, 1893 (No. 3437), & collected in No. 3448 above.

3483. A DOG'S TALE. NY & Lon: Harper & Bros., 1904.
First U.S. edition. Earlier periodical text published in the U.K. by the National Anti-Vivisection Soc'y in 1903–04 (No. 3479).

S. L. CLEMENS (Mark Twain) (cont.)

*3485. KING LEOPOLD'S SOLILOQUY A DEFENSE OF HIS CONGO RULE. Bos: P.R.Warren, 1905.

*3489. EVE'S DIARY. Lon & NY: Harper & Bros., 1906.
First U.S. edition. "Translated from the original MS." First published in *Their Husband's Wives*, 1906 (No. 3488).

*3492. THE $30,000 BEQUEST AND OTHER STORIES. NY & Lon: Harper & Bros., 1906.

*3497. CHRISTIAN SCIENCE WITH NOTES CONTAINING CORRECTIONS TO DATE. NY & Lon: Harper & Bros., 1907.
Some copies issued as *The Writings*, Vol. 25, see No. 3456 above.

 3500. A HORSE'S TALE. NY & Lon: Harper & Bros., 1907.

*3509. IS SHAKESPEARE DEAD? FROM MY AUTOBIOGRAPHY. NY & Lon: Harper & Bros., 1909.

*3511. EXTRACT FROM CAPTAIN STORMFIELD'S VISIT TO HEAVEN. NY & Lon: Harper & Bros., 1909.
Extended edition published in 1952 as *Report from Paradise* (No. 3581).

 3513. MARK TWAIN'S SPEECHES. NY & Lon: Harper & Bros., 1910.
Ed. F.A. Nast. For an extended edition see No. 3535 below.

 3520. THE MYSTERIOUS STRANGER A ROMANCE. NY & Lon: Harper & Bros., <1916>.

*3524. WHAT IS MAN? AND OTHER ESSAYS. NY & Lon: Harper & Bros., 1917.
The title essay was privately printed in 1906 (No. 3490).

*3525. MARK TWAIN'S LETTERS. NY & Lon: Harper & Bros., <1917>.
2v. Ed. Albert Bigelow Paine.

 3527. THE CURIOUS REPUBLIC OF GONDOUR AND OTHER WHIMSICAL SKETCHES. NY: Boni & Liveright, 1919.

 3534. THE MYSTERIOUS STRANGER AND OTHER STORIES. NY & Lon: Harper & Bros., 1922.

 3535. MARK TWAIN'S SPEECHES. NY & Lon: Harper & Bros., <1923>.

 3536. EUROPE AND ELSEWHERE. NY & Lon: Harper & Bros., <1923>.

*3537. MARK TWAIN'S AUTOBIOGRAPHY. NY & Lon: Harper & Bros., 1924.
2v. A partial copyright printing was produced in 1906–07 as *Chapters from My Autobiography* (No. 3491).

*3539. SKETCHES OF THE SIXTIES. SF: Howell, 1926.
With Bret Harte, see No. 7410 below. "Now collected for the first time from The Californian 1864–67." Extended edition published in 1927 (No. 3541).

 3544. THE ADVENTURES OF THOMAS JEFFERSON SNODGRASS. Chi: Covici, 1928.
Ed. Charles Honce.

 3554. MARK TWAIN THE LETTER WRITER. Bos: Meador, 1932.
Ed. Cyril Clemens.

S. L. CLEMENS (Mark Twain) (cont.)
*3556.   MARK TWAIN'S NOTEBOOK. NY & Lon: Harper & Bros., 1935.
Ed. Albert Bigelow Paine.

3558.   LETTERS FROM THE SANDWICH ISLANDS WRITTEN FOR THE SACRA-
MENTO UNION. SF: Grabhorn PR, 1937.
An extended collection of this material was published in 1939 as *Letters from Honolulu* (No. 3561) & a complete collection in 1947 as *Mark Twain and Hawaii* (No. 3576).

3559.   THE WASHOE GIANT IN SAN FRANCISCO BEING HERETOFORE UNCOL-
LECTED SKETCHES. SF: Fields, 1938.
Ed. Franklin Walker.

3563.   MARK TWAIN'S TRAVELS WITH MR. BROWN. NY: Knopf, 1940.
Ed. Franklin Walker & G. Ezra Dane. "Heretofore uncollected sketches written for the San Francisco Alta California in 1866 & 1867."

*3564.   MARK TWAIN IN ERUPTION HITHERTO UNPUBLISHED PAGES ABOUT
MEN AND EVENTS. NY & Lon: Harper & Bros., <1940>.
Ed. Bernard DeVoto.

3573.   MARK TWAIN, BUSINESS MAN. Bos: Little, Brown, 1946.
Ed. Samuel Charles Webster.

3575.   THE LETTERS OF QUINTUS CURTIUS SNODGRASS. Dallas: Southern
Methodist U PR, 1946.
Ed. Ernest E. Leisy.

3578.   MARK TWAIN TO MRS. FAIRBANKS. San Marino CA: Huntington Library, 1949.
Ed. Dixon Wecter.

*3579.   THE LOVE LETTERS OF MARK TWAIN. NY: Harper & Bros., 1949.
Ed. Dixon Wecter.

John Esten Cooke
1830–1886

3709.   LEATHER STOCKING AND SILK; OR, HUNTER JOHN MYERS AND HIS
TIMES. NY: Harper & Bros., 1854.
Anon. Reprinted in 1896 as *Leather and Silk* (No. 3766).

*3710.   THE YOUTH OF JEFFERSON OR A CHRONICLE OF COLLEGE SCRAPES AT
WILLIAMSBURG IN VIRGINIA, A.D. 1764. NY: Redfield, 1854.
Anon.

3711.   THE VIRGINIA COMEDIANS: OR, OLD DAYS IN THE OLD DOMINION. NY
& Lon: Appleton, 1854.
2v. Anon. "Edited from the mss. of C. Effingham, Esq." Reprinted in 1892 in 2v. as *Beatrice Hallam* (No. 3760) & *Captain Ralph* (No. 3761).

3712.   ELLIE: OR, THE HUMAN COMEDY. Richmond: A. Morris, 1855.

JOHN ESTEN COOKE (cont.)

3714. THE LAST OF THE FORESTERS: OR, HUMORS ON THE BORDER. NY: Derby & Jackson, 1856.

3716. HENRY ST. JOHN, GENTLEMAN, OF "FLOWER OF HUNDREDS," IN THE COUNTY OF PRINCE GEORGE, VIRGINIA. NY: Harper & Bros., 1859.
Reprinted in 1883 as *Bonnybel Vane* (No. 3751) & in 1892 as *Miss Bonnybel* (No. 3762).

3718. THE LIFE OF STONEWALL JACKSON. By a Virginian. Richmond: Ayres & Wade, 1863.
Reprinted in New York also in 1863. Revised edition published in 1866 as *Stonewall Jackson: A Military Biography* (No. 3722).

3721. SURRY OF EAGLE'S-NEST; OR, THE MEMOIRS OF A STAFF-OFFICER SERVING IN VIRGINIA. NY: Bunce & Huntington, 1866.
"Edited, from the mss. of Colonel Surry."

*3725. WEARING OF THE GRAY; BEING PERSONAL PORTRAITS, SCENES AND ADVENTURES OF THE WAR. NY: Treat, 1867.
Reprinted in 1871 as *Personal Portraits, Scenes and Adventures of the War* (No. 3734).

*3726. FAIRFAX: OR, THE MASTER OF GREENWAY COURT. NY: Carleton, 1868.
Reprinted in 1888 as *Lord Fairfax* (No. 3757).

3727. MOHUN. OR, THE LAST DAYS OF LEE AND HIS PALADINS. NY: Huntington, 1869.
"From the mss. of Colonel Surry, of Eagle's Nest."

*3728. HILT TO HILT; OR, DAYS AND NIGHTS ON THE BANKS OF THE SHENANDOAH IN THE AUTUMN OF 1864. NY: Carleton, 1869.
"From the mss. of Colonel Surry of Eagle's Nest."

*3730. HAMMER AND RAPIER. NY: Carleton, 1870.

3731. THE HEIR OF GAYMOUNT: A NOVEL. NY: Van Evrie, Horton, <1870>.

3732. OUT OF THE FOAM. A NOVEL. NY: Carleton, 1871.
Reprinted in 1891 as *Westbrooke Hall* (No. 3759).

3733. A LIFE OF GEN. ROBERT E. LEE. NY: Appleton, 1871.
Reprinted in 1889 as *Our Leader and Defender* (No. 3758) & in 1893 as *Robert E. Lee* (No. 3763).

3736. DOCTOR VANDYKE. A NOVEL. NY: Appleton, 1872.

3738. HER MAJESTY THE QUEEN. A NOVEL. Phila: Lippincott, 1873.

3739. PRETTY MRS. GASTON, AND OTHER STORIES. NY: Judd, <1874>.

*3740. JUSTIN HARLEY: A ROMANCE OF OLD VIRGINIA. Phila: Claxton, Remsen & Haffelfinger, 1875.

3741. CANOLLES: THE FORTUNES OF A PARTISAN OF '81. Detroit: E.B. Smith, 1877.

3742. PROFESSOR PRESSENSEE MATERIALIST AND INVENTOR. NY: Harper & Bros., 1878.
Harper's Half-Hour Series.

JOHN ESTEN COOKE (cont.)

3743. STORIES OF THE OLD DOMINION FROM THE SETTLEMENT TO THE END OF THE REVOLUTION. NY: Harper & Bros., 1879.

3744. MR. GRANTLEY'S IDEA. NY: Harper & Bros., 1879.
Harper's Half-Hour Series.

3746. THE VIRGINIA BOHEMIANS A NOVEL. NY: Harper & Bros., 1880.
Harper's Library of American Fiction.

3749. FANCHETTE BY ONE OF HER ADMIRERS. Bos: Osgood, 1883.
Anon. *Round-Robin Series.*

3750. VIRGINIA A HISTORY OF THE PEOPLE. Bos & NY: Houghton, Mifflin, 1883.
American Commonwealths series.

3752. MY LADY POKAHONTAS A TRUE RELATION OF VIRGINIA. Bos & NY: Houghton, Mifflin, 1885.
"Writ by Anas Todkill, Puritan and Pilgrim."

3753. THE MAURICE MYSTERY. NY: Appleton, 1885.
Reprinted in 1893 as *Col. Ross of Piedmont* (No. 3764).

3768. STONEWALL JACKSON AND THE OLD STONEWALL BRIGADE. Charlottesville: U of Virginia PR, <1954>.
Ed. Richard Barksdale Harwell.

Rose Terry Cooke
1827–1892

3770. POEMS. By Rose Terry. Bos: Ticknor & Fields, 1861.

3781. HAPPY DODD; OR, "SHE HATH DONE WHAT SHE COULD." Bos: Hoyt, <1878>.

*3784. SOMEBODY'S NEIGHBORS. Bos: Osgood, 1881.

*3795. A LAY PREACHER. Bos: Congregational Sunday-School & Pub. Soc'y, <1884>.

3801. ROOT-BOUND AND OTHER SKETCHES. Bos: Congregational Sunday-School & Pub. Soc'y, 1885.
"The Deacon's Week," here collected, was also published separately in several editions in 1884–85 (Nos. 3797, 3798, 3799).

3804. THE SPHINX'S CHILDREN AND OTHER PEOPLE'S. Bos: Ticknor, 1886.

3805. NO. NY: Phillips & Hunt, 1886.

3809. POEMS. NY: Gottsberger, 1888.
These sheets reissued *ca.* 1895 with title-page of George Gottsberger Peck, New York.

3810. THE OLD GARDEN. Bos: Prang, 1888.

3812. STEADFAST THE STORY OF A SAINT AND A SINNER. Bos: Ticknor, 1889.

3818. HUCKLEBERRIES GATHERED FROM NEW ENGLAND HILLS. Bos & NY: Houghton, Mifflin, 1891.

ROSE TERRY COOKE (cont.)
3822.   LITTLE FOXES. Phila: Altemus, <1904>.
        Illustrated Holly-Tree Series, No. 8.

James Fenimore Cooper
1789–1851

Note: During the 1830s & 1840s many of Cooper's works were published
in Paris by Baudry or Galignani: although precise dates of publication
are not known, these most probably derive from & follow the U.K.
editions (see No. 3835). For the posthumous collection of Cooper's
Works, edited by his daughter Susan Fenimore Cooper, see BAL (Nos.
3980–3994).

3825.   PRECAUTION, A NOVEL. NY: Goodrich, 1820.
        2v. Anon. Revised editions published in 1839 (Nos. 3889 & 3890).

*3826. THE SPY; A TALE OF THE NEUTRAL GROUND. NY: Wiley & Halsted,
        1821.
        2v. Anon. Revised editions published in 1822 (Nos. 3827 & 3828), 1831 (No.
        3932) & 1849 (No. 3848).

*3829. THE PIONEERS, OR THE SOURCES OF THE SUSQUEHANNA. NY: Wiley,
        1823.
        2v. Anon. Revised editions published in 1832 (No. 3855) & 1851 (No. 3938).

3830.   TALES FOR FIFTEEN; OR IMAGINATION AND HEART. By Jane Morgan.
        NY: Wiley, 1823.

3831.   THE PILOT; A TALE OF THE SEA. NY: Wiley, 1823.
        2v. Anon. Revised edition published in 1849 (No. 3933). Reprinted in 1874 in an
        omnibus volume entitled *Sea Tales* (No. 3954).

3832.   LIONEL LINCOLN; OR, THE LEAGUER OF BOSTON. NY: Wiley, 1825–
        24.
        2v. Anon. Vol. 2 dated 1824. Revised edition published in 1832 (No. 3859).

*3833. THE LAST OF THE MOHICANS; A NARRATIVE OF 1757. Phila: Carey &
        Lea, 1826.
        2v. Anon. Revised editions published in 1831 (No. 3849) & 1850 (No. 3937).

3834.   THE PRAIRIE, A TALE. Lon: Colburn, 1827.
        3v. Anon. Also published in Paris in 1827 (No. 3835).

*3836. THE PRAIRIE; A TALE. Phila: Carey, Lea & Carey, 1827.
        2v. Anon. Revised editions published in 1832 (No. 3856) & 1851 (No. 3940).

3837.   THE RED ROVER, A TALE. Paris: Bossange, 1827.
        3v. Anon. Also published in the U.K. in 1827 (No. 3838).

3839.   THE RED ROVER, A TALE. Phila: Carey, Lea & Carey, 1828–27.
        2v. Anon. Revised editions published in 1834 (No. 3865) & 1850 (No. 3934).
        Reprinted in 1874 in an omnibus volume entitled *Sea Tales* (No. 3954).

JAMES FENIMORE COOPER (cont.)

3841. NOTIONS OF THE AMERICANS: PICKED UP BY A TRAVELLING BACHELOR. Lon: Colburn, 1828.
2v. Anon. Reprinted in 1836 as *America and the Americans* (No. 3869).

3842. NOTIONS OF THE AMERICANS: PICKED UP BY A TRAVELLING BACHELOR. Phila: Carey, Lea & Carey, 1828.
2v. Anon. Reprinted in 1856 as *The Travelling Bachelor* (No. 3950).

3843. THE BORDERERS: A TALE. Lon: Colburn & Bentley, 1829.
3v. Anon. For U.S. edition see next entry. Revised edition published in 1833 (No. 3862) & reprinted in 1854 as *The Heathcotes* (No. 3947). *Note:* Though first printed in Florence as *The Wept of Wish Ton-Wish*, the Italian edition was apparently published after the U.K. but before the U.S. edition.

3844. THE WEPT OF WISH TON-WISH: A TALE. Phila: Carey, Lea & Carey, 1829.
2v. Anon. For comment see preceding entry.

3845. THE WATER WITCH OR THE SKIMMER OF THE SEAS. A TALE. Dresden: Walther, 1830.
3v. Anon. Also published in the U.K. in 1830 (No. 3846).

3847. THE WATER-WITCH, OR THE SKIMMER OF THE SEAS. A TALE. Phila: Carey & Lea, 1831.
Anon. Revised editions published in 1834 (No. 3863) & 1851 (No. 3943). Reprinted in 1874 in an omnibus volume entitled *Sea Tales* (No. 3954).

*3850. THE BRAVO. A VENETIAN STORY. Lon: Colburn & Bentley, 1831.
3v. Anon.

*3852. THE BRAVO: A TALE. Phila: Carey & Lea, 1831.
2v. Anon. Revised edition published in 1834 (No. 3864).

3857. THE HEIDENMAUER; OR THE BENEDICTINES. Lon: Colburn & Bentley, 1832.
3v. Anon.

*3858. THE HEIDENMAUER; OR, THE BENEDICTINES. A LEGEND OF THE RHINE. Phila: Carey & Lea, 1832.
2v. Anon.

3860. THE HEADSMAN; OR, THE ABBAYE DES VIGNERONS. A TALE. Lon: Bentley, 1833.
3v. Anon.

3861. THE HEADSMAN; OR, THE ABBAYE DES VIGNERONS. A TALE. Phila: Carey, Lea & Blanchard, 1833.
2v. Anon.

3866. A LETTER TO HIS COUNTRYMEN. NY: Wiley, 1834.

3867. THE MONIKINS. A TALE. Lon: Bentley, 1835.
3v. Anon.

3868. THE MONIKINS. Phila: Carey, Lea, & Blanchard, 1835.
2v. Anon.

JAMES FENIMORE COOPER (cont.)

3871. SKETCHES OF SWITZERLAND. By an American. Phila: Carey, Lea & Blanchard, 1836.
2v. Published in the U.K. in 1836 as *Excursions in Switzerland* (No. 3872).

3873. A RESIDENCE IN FRANCE; WITH AN EXCURSION UP THE RHINE, AND A SECOND VISIT TO SWITZERLAND. Lon: Bentley, 1836.
2v. For U.S. edition see next entry.

3874. SKETCHES OF SWITZERLAND ... PART SECOND. By an American. Phila: Carey, Lea & Blanchard, 1836.
2v.

3875. RECOLLECTIONS OF EUROPE. Lon: Bentley, 1837.
2v. For U.S. edition see next entry.

3876. GLEANINGS IN EUROPE <FRANCE>. By an American. Phila: Carey, Lea & Blanchard, 1837.
2v.

3877. ENGLAND. WITH SKETCHES OF SOCIETY IN THE METROPOLIS. Lon: Bentley, 1837.
3v. For U.S. edition see next entry.

3878. GLEANINGS IN EUROPE. ENGLAND. By an American. Phila: Carey, Lea, & Blanchard, 1837.
2v.

*3879. EXCURSIONS IN ITALY. Lon: Bentley, 1838.
2v. For U.S. edition see No. 3882 below.

3880. THE AMERICAN DEMOCRAT, OR HINTS ON THE SOCIAL AND CIVIC RELATIONS OF THE UNITED STATES OF AMERICA. Cooperstown: H. & E. Phinney, 1838.

3881. HOMEWARD BOUND: OR, THE CHASE. A TALE OF THE SEA. Lon: Bentley, 1838.
3v.

3882. GLEANINGS IN EUROPE. ITALY. By an American. Phila: Carey, Lea, & Blanchard, 1838.
2v.

3883. HOMEWARD BOUND: OR, THE CHASE. A TALE OF THE SEA. Phila: Carey, Lea & Blanchard, 1838.
2v. Anon. Revised "new edition" also published in 1838 (No. 3887).

*3884. HOME AS FOUND. Phila: Lea & Blanchard, 1838.
2v. Anon. Published in the U.K. in 1838 as *Eve Effingham; or, Home as Found* (No. 3885).

3886. THE CHRONICLES OF COOPERSTOWN. Cooperstown: H. & E. Phinney, 1838.
Anon.

JAMES FENIMORE COOPER (cont.)

3888.   THE HISTORY OF THE NAVY OF THE UNITED STATES OF AMERICA. Phila: Lea & Blanchard, 1839.
2v. Revised & extended editions published in 1840 (No. 3894), 1846 (No. 3923), 1853 (No. 3946) & 1854 (No. 3948); abridged edition in 1841 (No. 3896).

3891.   THE PATHFINDER; OR, THE INLAND SEA. Lon: Bentley, 1840.
3v. Anon.

*3892. THE PATHFINDER: OR, THE INLAND SEA. Phila: Lea & Blanchard, 1840.
2v. Anon. Revised edition published in 1851 (No. 3939).

3893.   MERCEDES OF CASTILE: OR, THE VOYAGE TO CATHAY. Phila: Lea & Blanchard, 1840.
2v. Anon. These sheets reissued in 1842.

3895.   THE DEERSLAYER: OR, THE FIRST WAR-PATH. A TALE. Phila: Lea & Blanchard, 1841.
2v. Anon. Revised edition published in 1850 (No. 3936).

3898.   THE TWO ADMIRALS. A TALE OF THE SEA. Lon: Bentley, 1842.
3v.

3899.   THE TWO ADMIRALS. A TALE. Phila: Lea & Blanchard, 1842.
2v. Anon. Revised edition published in 1851 (No. 3942). Reprinted in 1874 in an omnibus volume entitled *Sea Tales* (No. 3954).

3900.   THE JACK O'LANTERN; (LE FEU-FOLLET;) OR, THE PRIVATEER. Lon: Bentley, 1842.
3v. For U.S. edition see next entry.

3901.   THE WING-AND-WING, OR LE FEU-FOLLET; A TALE. Phila: Lea & Blanchard, 1842.
2v. Anon. Revised edition published in 1851 (No. 3941). Reprinted in 1874 in an omnibus volume entitled *Sea Tales* (No. 3954).

3902.   LE MOUCHOIR; AN AUTOBIOGRAPHICAL ROMANCE. NY: Wilson, <1843>.
Brother Jonathan, Extra Sheet, No. 22, 22 Mar. 1843. Published in the U.K. in 1843 as *The French Governess* (No. 3903).

3904.   THE BATTLE OF LAKE ERIE: OR ANSWERS TO MESSRS. BURGES, DUER, AND MACKENZIE. Cooperstown: H. & E. Phinney, 1843.

3905.   WYANDOTTÉ; OR, THE HUTTED KNOLL. Lon: Bentley, 1843.
3v.

3906.   WYANDOTTÉ, OR THE HUTTED KNOLL. A TALE. Phila: Lea & Blanchard, 1843.
2v. Anon.

3907.   NED MYERS; OR, A LIFE BEFORE THE MAST. Lon: Bentley, 1843.
2v.

JAMES FENIMORE COOPER (cont.)

3908. NED MYERS; OR, A LIFE BEFORE THE MAST. Phila: Lea & Blanchard, 1843.

3909. AFLOAT AND ASHORE; OR, THE ADVENTURES OF MILES WALLINGFORD. Lon: Bentley, 1844.
3v. Anon.

*3910. AFLOAT AND ASHORE; OR THE ADVENTURES OF MILES WALLINGFORD. Phila: The Author, 1844.
Vols. 1–2 of four. Anon.

3911. LUCY HARDINGE: A SECOND SERIES OF AFLOAT & ASHORE. Lon: Bentley, 1844.
3v. Anon. Reprinted in 1854 as *Miles Wallingford* (No. 3949). For U.S. edition see next entry.

*3912. AFLOAT AND ASHORE; OR THE ADVENTURES OF MILES WALLINGFORD. Phila: The Author, 1844.
Vols. 3–4 of four. Anon.

3914. SATANSTOE; OR, THE FAMILY OF LITTLEPAGE. A TALE OF THE COLONY. Lon: Bentley, 1845.
3v.

3915. SATANSTOE; OR, THE LITTLEPAGE MANUSCRIPTS. A TALE OF THE COLONY. NY: Burgess, Stringer, 1845.
2v. Anon.

3916. THE CHAINBEARER; OR, THE LITTLEPAGE MANUSCRIPTS. Lon: Bentley, 1845.
3v. Anon.

3917. THE CHAINBEARER; OR, THE LITTLEPAGE MANUSCRIPTS. NY: Burgess, Stringer, 1845.
2v. Anon.

3920. LIVES OF DISTINGUISHED AMERICAN NAVAL OFFICERS. Phila: Carey & Hart, 1846.
2v.

3921. RAVENSNEST; OR, THE REDSKINS. Lon: Bentley, 1846.
3v. Anon. For U.S. edition see next entry.

3922. THE REDSKINS; OR, INDIAN AND INJIN. BEING THE CONCLUSION OF THE LITTLEPAGE MANUSCRIPTS. NY: Burgess & Stringer, 1846.
2v. Anon.

3924. MARK'S REEF; OR, THE CRATER. A TALE OF THE PACIFIC. Lon: Bentley, 1847.
3v. Anon. For U.S. edition see next entry.

*3925. THE CRATER; OR, VULCAN'S PEAK. A TALE OF THE PACIFIC. NY: Burgess, Stringer, 1847.
2v. Anon.

JAMES FENIMORE COOPER (cont.)

3926. CAPTAIN SPIKE; OR, THE ISLETS OF THE GULF. Lon: Bentley, 1848.
3v. For U.S. edition see next entry.

3927. JACK TIER; OR, THE FLORIDA REEF. NY: Burgess, Stringer, 1848.
2v. Anon.

3928. THE BEE-HUNTER; OR, THE OAK OPENINGS. Lon: Bentley, 1848.
3v. Anon. For U.S. edition see next entry.

3929. THE OAK OPENINGS; OR, THE BEE-HUNTER. NY: Burgess, Stringer, 1848.
2v. Anon.

3930. THE SEA LIONS; OR, THE LOST SEALERS. Lon: Bentley, 1849.
3v. Anon.

3931. THE SEA LIONS; OR, THE LOST SEALERS. NY: Stringer & Townsend, 1849.
2v. Anon.

*3935. THE WAYS OF THE HOUR; A TALE. NY: Putnam, 1850.
Anon.

*3955. CORRESPONDENCE OF JAMES FENIMORE-COOPER. New Haven: Yale U PR, 1922.
2v. Ed. Cooper's grandson James Fenimore Cooper.

Susan Augusta Fenimore Cooper
1813–1894

3959. ELINOR WYLLYS. A TALE. Lon: Bentley, 1845.
3v. Anon. Ed. J. Fenimore Cooper.

3960. ELINOR WYLLYS; OR, THE YOUNG FOLK OF LONGBRIDGE. A TALE. By Amabel Penfeather. Phila: Carey & Hart, 1846.
2v. Ed. J. Fenimore Cooper.

*3961. RURAL HOURS. By a Lady. NY: Putnam, 1850.
Revised editions published in 1868 (No. 3970) & 1887 (No. 3976).

3967. MOUNT VERNON: A LETTER TO THE CHILDREN OF AMERICA. NY: Appleton, 1859.
Anon.

Frederic Swartwout Cozzens
1818–1869

3995. PRISMATICS. By Richard Haywarde. NY & Lon: Appleton, 1853.

*3998. THE SPARROWGRASS PAPERS: OR, LIVING IN THE COUNTRY. NY: Derby & Jackson, 1856.

*4001. ACADIA; OR, A MONTH WITH THE BLUE NOSES. NY: Derby & Jackson, 1859.

FREDERIC S. COZZENS (cont.)

1008. THE SAYINGS OF DR. BUSH-WHACKER, AND OTHER LEARNED MEN. NY:
Simpson, 1867.
Extended edition published in 1871 (No. 4011) & reprinted in 1880 as *Sayings,*
Wise and Otherwise (No. 4013).

4014. THE SOUND OF A VOICE; OR THE SONG OF THE DÉBARDEUR. Phila:
Lippincott, <1891>.
The March 1891 issue of *Lippincott's Monthly Magazine* with title-page as above;
this work published only in this form.

Christopher Pearse Cranch
1813–1892

4017. A POEM DELIVERED IN THE FIRST CONGREGATIONAL CHURCH IN THE
TOWN OF QUINCY, MAY 25, 1840. Bos: Munroe, 1840.
For the 200th anniversary of the incorporation of Quincy.

4022. POEMS. Phila: Carey & Hart, 1844.

4029. THE LAST OF THE HUGGERMUGGERS. A GIANT STORY. Bos: Phillips,
Sampson, 1856.
Reprinted in 1860 in an omnibus volume entitled *Giant Hunting* (No. 4033).

4031. KOBBOLTOZO: A SEQUEL TO THE LAST OF THE HUGGERMUGGERS. Bos:
Phillips, Sampson, 1857.
Reprinted in 1860 in an omnibus volume entitled *Giant Hunting* (No. 4033).

4039. THE AENEID OF VIRGIL. Bos: Osgood, 1872.
Translation.

4042. SATAN: A LIBRETTO. Bos: Roberts Bros., 1874.

4047. THE BIRD AND THE BELL, WITH OTHER POEMS. Bos: Osgood, 1875.

4059. ARIEL AND CALIBAN WITH OTHER POEMS. Bos & NY: Houghton,
Mifflin, 1887.

4065. THE LIFE AND LETTERS OF CHRISTOPHER PEARSE CRANCH. Bos & NY:
Houghton Mifflin, 1917.
By Leonora Cranch Scott.

Stephen Crane
1871–1900

4068. MAGGIE A GIRL OF THE STREETS (A STORY OF NEW YORK). By Johnston
Smith. <n.p., n.d.; NY, 1893>.
Printed for the author. For revised edition see No. 4075 below.

*4070. THE BLACK RIDERS AND OTHER LINES. Bos: Copeland & Day, 1895.
Privately reprinted in 1905 (No. 4098).

*4071. THE RED BADGE OF COURAGE AN EPISODE OF THE AMERICAN CIVIL
WAR. NY: Appleton, 1895.
Extended editions published in 1900 (No. 4088) & 1951 (No. 4114).

STEPHEN CRANE (cont.)

4073. GEORGE'S MOTHER. NY & Lon: Arnold, 1896.

*4075. MAGGIE A GIRL OF THE STREETS. NY: Appleton, 1896.
Revised.

*4076. THE LITTLE REGIMENT AND OTHER EPISODES OF THE AMERICAN CIVIL
WAR. NY: Appleton, 1896.

4078. THE THIRD VIOLET. NY: Appleton, 1897.

4079. THE OPEN BOAT AND OTHER TALES OF ADVENTURE. NY: Doubleday
& McClure, 1898.
Contains only 8 stories.

*4080. THE OPEN BOAT AND OTHER STORIES. Lon: Heinemann, 1898.
Contains 17 stories.

4083. WAR IS KIND. NY: Stokes, 1899.

4084. ACTIVE SERVICE A NOVEL. NY: Stokes, <1899>.

4085. THE MONSTER AND OTHER STORIES. NY & Lon: Harper & Bros.,
1899.
For U.K. edition see No. 4095 below.

4089. WHILOMVILLE STORIES. NY & Lon: Harper & Bros., 1900.

4090. WOUNDS IN THE RAIN A COLLECTION OF STORIES. Lon: Methuen,
1900.

4091. WOUNDS IN THE RAIN WAR STORIES. NY: Stokes, <1900>.

4094. GREAT BATTLES OF THE WORLD. Phila: Lippincott, 1901.

4095. THE MONSTER AND OTHER STORIES. Lon & NY: Harper & Bros.,
1901.
Contains 4 stories not in the U.S. edition.

4096. LAST WORDS. Lon: Digby, Long, 1902.

4097. THE O'RUDDY A ROMANCE. NY: Stokes, <1903>.
With Robert Barr.

*4100. MEN, WOMEN AND BOATS. NY: Boni & Liveright, <1921>.
Ed. Vincent Starrett.

4101. THE WORK OF STEPHEN CRANE. NY: Knopf, <1925–26>.
12v. Ed. Wilson Follett.

4103. THE COLLECTED POEMS. NY & Lon: Knopf, 1930.
Ed. Wilson Follett.

4107. A BATTLE IN GREECE. Mount Vernon NY: Peter Pauper PR, 1936.

4112. THE SULLIVAN COUNTY SKETCHES. <Syracuse>: Syracuse U PR,
<1949>.
Ed. Melvin Schoberlin.

4116. STEPHEN CRANE'S LOVE LETTERS TO NELLIE CROUSE WITH SIX OTHER
LETTERS. <Syracuse>: Syracuse U PR, 1954.
Ed. Edwin H. Cady & Lester G. Wells.

Adelaide Crapsey
1878–1914

4120. VERSE. Rochester: The Manas PR, 1915.
Extended editions published in 1922 (No. 4124) & 1934 (No. 4126) by Knopf, New York.

4122. A STUDY IN ENGLISH METRICS. NY: Knopf, 1918.

Francis Marion Crawford
1854–1909

4129. MR. ISAACS A TALE OF MODERN INDIA. Lon: Macmillan, 1882.

4130. MR. ISAACS A TALE OF MODERN INDIA. NY: Macmillan, 1882.

4131. DOCTOR CLAUDIUS A TRUE STORY. Lon: Macmillan, 1883.

4132. DOCTOR CLAUDIUS A TRUE STORY. NY: Macmillan, 1883.

4133. TO LEEWARD. Lon: Chapman & Hall, 1884.
2v.

4134. TO LEEWARD. Bos & NY: Houghton, Mifflin, 1884.
Revised edition published in 1893 (No. 4176).

*4135. A ROMAN SINGER. Bos & NY: Houghton, Mifflin, 1884.
Slightly revised edition published in 1893 (No. 4174).

*4137. AN AMERICAN POLITICIAN A NOVEL. Bos & NY: Houghton, Mifflin, 1885.
These sheets reissued in 1893 with cancel title-page of Macmillan, New York & London. Published simultaneously (?) in the U.K. with title-page dated 1884 (No. 4136).

4138. ZOROASTER. Lon: Macmillan, 1885.
2v.

*4139. ZOROASTER. Lon & NY: Macmillan, 1885.
1v. First U.S. edition.

4142. A TALE OF A LONELY PARISH. Lon: Macmillan, 1886.
2v.

4143. A TALE OF A LONELY PARISH. Lon & NY: Macmillan, 1886.
1v. First U.S. edition.

4146. SARACINESCA. Edinburgh & Lon: Blackwood & Sons, 1887.
3v.

4147. SARACINESCA. NY: Macmillan, 1887.

4148. MARZIO'S CRUCIFIX. Lon & NY: Macmillan, 1887.
2v.

4149. PAUL PATOFF. Lon & NY: Macmillan, 1887.
3v.

4150. MARZIO'S CRUCIFIX. Lon & NY: Macmillan, 1887.
1v. First U.S. edition.

F. MARION CRAWFORD (cont.)

4151. PAUL PATOFF. Bos & NY: Houghton, Mifflin, 1887.
Revised edition published in 1893 (No. 4177).

4153. WITH THE IMMORTALS. Lon & NY: Macmillan, 1888.
2v.

4154. WITH THE IMMORTALS. Lon & NY: Macmillan, 1888.
1v. First U.S. edition.

4155. GREIFENSTEIN. Lon & NY: Macmillan, 1889.
3v.

4156. GREIFENSTEIN. Lon & NY: Macmillan, 1889.
1v. First U.S. edition.

4157. SANT' ILARIO. Lon & NY: Macmillan, 1889.
3v.

4158. SANT' ILARIO. Lon & NY: Macmillan, 1889.
1v. First U.S. edition.

4163. A CIGARETTE-MAKER'S ROMANCE. Lon & NY: Macmillan, 1890.
2v.

4164. A CIGARETTE-MAKER'S ROMANCE. Lon & NY: Macmillan, 1890.
1v. First U.S. edition.

4165. KHALED A TALE OF ARABIA. Lon & NY: Macmillan, 1891.
2v.

4166. KHALED A TALE OF ARABIA. Lon & NY: Macmillan, 1891.
1v. First U.S. edition.

4167. THE WITCH OF PRAGUE. Lon & NY: Macmillan, 1891.
3v.

4168. THE WITCH OF PRAGUE A FANTASTIC TALE. Lon & NY: Macmillan, 1891.
1v. First U.S. edition.

4169. THE THREE FATES. Lon & NY: Macmillan, 1892.
3v.

4170. THE THREE FATES. Lon & NY: Macmillan, 1892.
1v. First U.S. edition.

4172. DON ORSINO. NY & Lon: Macmillan, 1892.
Published simultaneously (?) in the U.K. in 3v.

4173. THE CHILDREN OF THE KING A TALE OF SOUTHERN ITALY. NY & Lon: Macmillan, 1893.
Published simultaneously in the U.K. in 2v.

*4175. THE NOVEL WHAT IT IS. NY & Lon: Macmillan, 1893.

4178. PIETRO GHISLERI. NY & Lon: Macmillan, 1893.
Published simultaneously in the U.K. in 3v. A copyright printing produced in 1892 as *Laura Arden* (No. 4171).

F. MARION CRAWFORD (cont.)

4179. MARION DARCHE A STORY WITHOUT COMMENT. NY & Lon: Macmillan, 1893.
Published simultaneously in the U.K. in 2v.

4180. KATHARINE LAUDERDALE. NY & Lon: Macmillan, 1894.
2v. Published simultaneously in the U.K. in 3v.

4181. THE UPPER BERTH. Lon: Unwin, 1894.

*4184. THE UPPER BERTH. NY & Lon: Putnam's Sons, 1894.
The Autonym Library, No. 1.

4186. LOVE IN IDLENESS A BAR HARBOUR TALE. Lon & NY: Macmillan, 1894.

4187. LOVE IN IDLENESS A TALE OF BAR HARBOUR. NY & Lon: Macmillan, 1894.
Published simultaneously in the U.K. A copyright printing was also produced in 1894 (No. 4182).

4188. THE RALSTONS. NY & Lon: Macmillan, 1895.
2v. A copyright printing was probably produced in 1894, *not located*.

*4191. CONSTANTINOPLE. NY: Scribner's Sons, 1895.

4192. CASA BRACCIO. NY & Lon: Macmillan, 1895.
2v. Published simultaneously in the U.K. A copyright printing was produced in 1894 (No. 4185).

4193. ADAM JOHNSTONE'S SON. Lon: Macmillan, 1896.

4194. ADAM JOHNSTONE'S SON. NY: Macmillan, 1896.
A copyright printing was produced in 1895 (No. 4190).

4198. TAQUISARA. NY: Macmillan, 1896.
2v. These sheets issued simultaneously (?) in the U.K. (No. 4197). A copyright printing was produced in 1895 (No. 4189).

4199. A ROSE OF YESTERDAY. Lon: Macmillan, 1897.

4200. A ROSE OF YESTERDAY. NY: Macmillan, 1897.

4202. CORLEONE A TALE OF SICILY. NY: Macmillan, 1897.
2v. These sheets issued simultaneously (?) in the U.K. (No. 4201). A copyright printing was produced in 1896 (No. 4195).

*4203. AVE ROMA IMMORTALIS STUDIES FROM THE CHRONICLES OF ROME. NY: Macmillan, 1898.
2v. Revised edition published in 1902 (No. 4214).

4204. VIA CRUCIS A ROMANCE OF THE SECOND CRUSADE. NY: Macmillan, 1899.

*4206. THE RULERS OF THE SOUTH SICILY, CALBARIA, MALTA. NY: Macmillan, 1900.
2v. Reprinted in 1905 as *Southern Italy and Sicily and the Rulers of the South* (No. 4222).

F. MARION CRAWFORD (cont.)

4207. IN THE PALACE OF THE KING A LOVE STORY OF OLD MADRID. NY: Macmillan, 1900.
Published simultaneously in the U.K.

4209. MARIETTA A MAID OF VENICE. NY: Macmillan, 1901.
Published simultaneously (?) in the U.K.

4210. FRANCESCA DA RIMINI A PLAY IN FOUR ACTS. NY: Macmillan, 1902.
Copyright printing. "12 copies only ... printed April, 1902." A French translation by Marcel Schwob published in 1902 (No. 4211) contains a new preface by Crawford.

4212. CECILIA A STORY OF MODERN ROME. Lon: Macmillan, 1902.

4213. CECILIA A STORY OF MODERN ROME. NY: Macmillan, 1902.

4216. MAN OVERBOARD! NY: Macmillan, 1903.
A copyright printing also produced in 1903 (No. 4215).

4217. THE HEART OF ROME A TALE OF THE 'LOST WATER.' Lon: Macmillan, 1903.

4218. THE HEART OF ROME A TALE OF THE "LOST WATER." NY: Macmillan, 1903.

4220. WHOSOEVER SHALL OFFEND. Lon: Macmillan, 1904.

4221. WHOSOEVER SHALL OFFEND. NY: Macmillan, 1904.

4223. SOPRANO A PORTRAIT. Lon: Macmillan, 1905.
For U.S. edition see next entry.

4224. FAIR MARGARET A PORTRAIT. NY: Macmillan, 1905.

4225. SALVE VENETIA GLEANINGS FROM VENETIAN HISTORY. NY: Macmillan, 1905.
2v. Published simultaneously in the U.K. as *Gleanings from Venetian History* (No. 4226). Reprinted in 1909 as *Venice The Place and the People* (No. 4240).

4227. A LADY OF ROME. NY: Macmillan, 1906.
Published simultaneously in the U.K.

4230. ARETHUSA. Lon: Macmillan, 1907.

*4231. ARETHUSA. NY: Macmillan, 1907.
A copyright printing was also produced in 1907 (No. 4229).

4232. THE LITTLE CITY OF HOPE A CHRISTMAS STORY. Lon: Macmillan, 1907.

4233. THE LITTLE CITY OF HOPE. A CHRISTMAS STORY. NY: Macmillan, 1907.

4234. THE PRIMADONNA. Lon: Macmillan, 1908.
Sequel to *Soprano*, 1905.

4235. THE PRIMADONNA. NY: Macmillan, 1908.
Sequel to *Fair Margaret*, 1905.

4237. THE DIVA'S RUBY. Lon: Macmillan, 1908.
Sequel to *The Primadonna*, 1908.

F. MARION CRAWFORD (cont.)

4238. THE DIVA'S RUBY. NY: Macmillan, 1908.
Sequel to *The Primadonna*, 1908.

4241. THE WHITE SISTER. Lon: Macmillan, 1909.

4242. THE WHITE SISTER. NY: Macmillan, 1909.
For a dramatization see No. 4251 below.

4245. STRADELLA AN OLD ITALIAN LOVE TALE. Lon: Macmillan, 1909.
A copyright printing was produced in 1908 (No. 4236).

4246. STRADELLA. NY: Macmillan, 1909.
A copyright printing was also produced in 1909 (No. 4239).

4247. THE UNDESIRABLE GOVERNESS. NY: Macmillan, 1910.
A copyright printing was produced in 1909 (No. 4244).

4248. UNCANNY TALES. Lon: Unwin, 1911.
For U.S. edition see next entry.

4249. WANDERING GHOSTS. NY: Macmillan, 1911.

4251. THE WHITE SISTER ROMANTIC DRAMA IN THREE ACTS. <n.p.>: Dramatists Play Service, 1937.
With Walter Hackett.

Maria Susanna Cummins
1827–1866

4252. THE LAMPLIGHTER. Bos: Jewett, 1854.
Anon.

*4253. MABEL VAUGHAN. Bos: Jewett, 1857.
Anon.

4254. EL FUREIDÎS. Bos: Ticknor & Fields, 1860.
Anon.

4255. HAUNTED HEARTS. Bos: Tilton, 1864.
Anon.

George William Curtis
1824–1892

4259. NILE NOTES OF A HOWADJI. NY: Harper & Bros., 1851.
Anon.

4260. THE WANDERER IN SYRIA. Lon: Bentley, 1852.
For U.S. edition see next entry.

4261. THE HOWADJI IN SYRIA. NY: Harper & Bros., 1852.

4262. LOTOS-EATING: A SUMMER BOOK. Lon: Bentley, 1852.

4263. LOTUS-EATING: A SUMMER BOOK. NY: Harper & Bros., 1852.

*4267. THE POTIPHAR PAPERS. NY: Putnam, 1853.
Anon.

GEORGE W. CURTIS (cont.)

4269. NEW AND UNIFORM EDITION OF CURTIS'S WORKS. NY: Dix, Edwards,
       1856.
       5v. Revised.

4270. PRUE AND I. NY: Dix, Edwards, 1856.
       Some copies issued as Curtis's *Works*, Vol. 5, see preceding entry.

4280. TRUMPS. A NOVEL. NY: Harper & Bros., 1861.

4390. WASHINGTON IRVING A SKETCH. NY: Grolier Club, 1891.

*4391. FROM THE EASY CHAIR. NY: Harper & Bros., 1892.

4394. JAMES RUSSELL LOWELL AN ADDRESS. NY: Harper & Bros., 1892.

4398. OTHER ESSAYS FROM THE EASY CHAIR. NY: Harper & Bros., 1893.
       Reprinted in 1894 as *From the Easy Chair ... Second Series* (No. 4403).

*4399. ORATIONS AND ADDRESSES. NY: Harper & Bros., 1894.
       3v. Ed. Charles Eliot Norton. Many of these addresses were first published sepa-
       rately, for details see BAL.

4400. FROM THE EASY CHAIR ... THIRD SERIES. NY: Harper & Bros., 1894.

4405. LITERARY AND SOCIAL ESSAYS. NY: Harper & Bros., 1895.

4409. ARS RECTE VIVENDI BEING ESSAYS CONTRIBUTED TO "THE EASY CHAIR."
       NY & Lon: Harper & Bros., 1898.

4410. EARLY LETTERS OF GEORGE WM. CURTIS TO JOHN S. DWIGHT. NY &
       Lon: Harper & Bros., 1898.
       Ed. George Willis Cooke.

Richard Henry Dana, Sr.
1787–1879

4414. AN ORATION. Cambridge: Ptd by Hilliard & Metcalf, 1814.
       Delivered before the Washington Benevolent Society, Cambridge, 4 July 1814.

4415. THE IDLE MAN. <NO. I.> NY: Wiley & Halsted, 1821.
       Edited, with contributions, by Dana.

4416. THE IDLE MAN. NO. II. NY: Wiley & Halsted, 1821.
       Edited, with contributions, by Dana.

4418. THE IDLE MAN. NO. III. NY: Wiley & Halsted, 1821.
       Edited, with a substantial contribution, by Dana.

4419. THE IDLE MAN. NO. IV. NY: Wiley & Halsted, 1822.
       Edited, with a contribution, by Dana.

4420. THE IDLE MAN. VOL I. <NO. V.> NY: Wiley & Halsted, 1821–22.
       Edited, with a substantial contribution, by Dana.

4421. THE IDLE MAN. NO. I.—VOL. II. NY: Wiley & Halsted, 1822.
       Edited, with a substantial contribution, by Dana.

4422. POEMS. Bos: Bowles & Dearborn, 1827.

RICHARD HENRY DANA, SR. (cont.)

4424.   A POEM DELIVERED BEFORE THE PORTER RHETORICAL SOCIETY,
        ANDOVER THEOLOGICAL SEMINARY, SEPTEMBER 22, 1829. Bos: Perkins
        & Marvin, 1829.

*4426. POEMS AND PROSE WRITINGS. Bos: Russell, Odiorne, 1833.
        A collection of Dana's poems, all reprints, was published in the U.K. in 1844 as
        The Buccaneer, and Other Poems (No. 4428).

*4430. POEMS AND PROSE WRITINGS. NY: Baker & Scribner, 1850.
        2v.

Richard Henry Dana, Jr.
1815–1882

*4434. TWO YEARS BEFORE THE MAST. A PERSONAL NARRATIVE OF LIFE AT SEA.
        NY: Harper & Bros., 1840.
        Anon. *Family Library*, No. 106. Revised edition published in 1869 (No. 4471).

4435.   THE SEAMAN'S FRIEND; CONTAINING A TREATISE ON PRACTICAL SEA-
        MANSHIP. Bos: Little & Brown, <1841>.
        Published in the U.K. "with alterations and notes for the English market" in 1841
        as *The Seaman's Manual* (No. 4436).

4447.   TO CUBA AND BACK. A VACATION VOYAGE. Bos: Ticknor & Fields,
        1859.

4487.   SPEECHES IN STIRRING TIMES AND LETTERS TO A SON. Bos & NY:
        Houghton Mifflin, 1910.
        Ed. Richard H. Dana, 3rd.

4489.   AN AUTOBIOGRAPHICAL SKETCH (1815–1842). Hamden CT: Shoe
        String PR, 1953.
        Ed. Robert F. Metzdorf.

Charles Augustus Davis
1795–1867

Note: Davis was one of several imitators to use Seba Smith's pseudonym
Major Jack Downing: his work appeared with Downing material by Smith
and others in several publications in 1833–34, for details see BAL. Davis
used the pseudonym *Peter Scriber* for 3 political tracts on protection and
currency published in 1844, 1849 & 1857 (Nos. 4505, 4506, 4507).

4494.   LETTERS OF J. DOWNING, MAJOR ... TO HIS OLD FRIEND, MR. DWIGHT,
        OF THE NEW-YORK DAILY ADVERTISER. NY: Harper & Bros., 1834.
        Originally with only 29 letters. Later printings, also dated 1834 (Nos. 4495–4501),
        contain additional letters up to 45, with the final letter dated 1 Feb. 1835.

Richard Harding Davis
1864–1916

4508. THE ADVENTURES OF MY FRESHMAN. <Bethlehem PA: Moravian Print; n.d., 1884>.

*4510. GALLEGHER AND OTHER STORIES. NY: Scribner's Sons, 1891.

4511. STORIES FOR BOYS. NY: Scribner's Sons, 1891.

*4512. VAN BIBBER AND OTHERS. NY: Harper & Bros., 1892.

4513. THE WEST FROM A CAR-WINDOW. NY: Harper & Bros., 1892.

*4515. THE RULERS OF THE MEDITERRANEAN. NY: Harper & Bros., 1894.

*4516. OUR ENGLISH COUSINS. NY: Harper & Bros., 1894.

4517. THE EXILES AND OTHER STORIES. NY: Harper & Bros., 1894.

*4518. THE PRINCESS ALINE. NY: Harper & Bros., 1895.

4519. ABOUT PARIS. NY: Harper & Bros., 1895.

4521. THREE GRINGOS IN VENEZUELA AND CENTRAL AMERICA. NY: Harper & Bros., 1896.

4522. CINDERELLA AND OTHER STORIES. NY: Scribner's Sons, 1896.

4523. DR. JAMESON'S RAIDERS *vs.* THE JOHANNESBURG REFORMERS. NY: Russell, 1897.

4524. CUBA IN WAR TIME. NY: Russell, 1897.

4525. SOLDIERS OF FORTUNE. NY: Scribner's Sons, 1897.

4526. A YEAR FROM A REPORTER'S NOTE-BOOK. NY & Lon: Harper & Bros., 1898.
Published in the U.K. in 1898 as *A Year from a Correspondent's Note-Book* (No. 4527).

*4528. THE KING'S JACKAL. NY: Scribner's Sons, 1898.

*4529. THE CUBAN AND PORTO RICAN CAMPAIGNS. NY: Scribner's Sons, 1898.

4530. THE LION AND THE UNICORN. NY: Scribner's Sons, 1899.

*4533. WITH BOTH ARMIES IN SOUTH AFRICA. NY: Scribner's Sons, 1900.

4537. IN THE FOG. NY: Russell, 1901.

*4538. RANSON'S FOLLY. NY: Scribner's Sons, 1902.

4539. CAPTAIN MACKLIN HIS MEMOIRS. NY: Scribner's Sons, 1902.

4543. "MISS CIVILIZATION" A COMEDY IN ONE ACT. NY: Scribner's Sons, 1905.

*4544. FARCES THE DICTATOR THE GALLOPER "MISS CIVILIZATION." NY: Scribner's Sons, 1906.

4545. REAL SOLDIERS OF FORTUNE. NY: Scribner's Sons, 1906.

4546. THE SCARLET CAR. NY: Scribner's Sons, 1907.

4547. THE CONGO AND COASTS OF AFRICA. NY: Scribner's Sons, 1907.

*4548. VERA THE MEDIUM. NY: Scribner's Sons, 1908.

4549. THE WHITE MICE. NY: Scribner's Sons, 1909.

RICHARD HARDING DAVIS (cont.)

  4552. ONCE UPON A TIME. NY: Scribner's Sons, 1910.

  4553. NOTES OF A WAR CORRESPONDENT. NY: Scribner's Sons, 1910.

  4554. THE CONSUL. NY: Scribner's Sons, 1911.

  4555. THE MAN WHO COULD NOT LOSE. NY: Scribner's Sons, 1911.
          The title story was also published separately in 1911 (No. 4556).

  4557. THE RED CROSS GIRL. NY: Scribner's Sons, 1912.

  4560. THE LOST ROAD. NY: Scribner's Sons, 1913.

 *4562. PEACE MANOEUVRES A PLAY. NY: French, 1914.

 *4563. THE ZONE POLICE A PLAY. NY: French, 1914.

  4564. THE BOY SCOUT. NY: Scribner's Sons, 1914.

  4565. WITH THE ALLIES. NY: Scribner's Sons, 1914.

  4570. "SOMEWHERE IN FRANCE." NY: Scribner's Sons, 1915.

  4573. WITH THE FRENCH IN FRANCE AND SALONIKA. NY: Scribner's Sons,
          1916.

 *4574. THE NOVELS AND STORIES OF RICHARD HARDING DAVIS. NY:
          Scribner's Sons, 1916.
          12v. *Crossroads Edition.*

  4579. ADVENTURES AND LETTERS OF RICHARD HARDING DAVIS. NY:
          Scribner's Sons, 1917.
          Ed. Charles Belmont Davis.

Rufus Dawes
1803–1859

  4587. STROKES AND STRICTURES. By Samuel Smythe. Bos: Office of the
          New England Galaxy, 1830.

  4588. THE VALLEY OF THE NASHAWAY: AND OTHER POEMS. Bos: Carter
          & Hendee, 1830.

  4590. ATHENIA OF DAMASCUS. A TRAGEDY. NY: Colman, 1839.
          These sheets reissued not before 1840 by Giffing, New York, in a nonce collec-
          tion entitled *American Dramatic Library* (No. 4594).

  4591. GERALDINE, ATHENIA OF DAMASCUS, AND MISCELLANEOUS POEMS.
          NY: Colman, 1839.
          Library of American Poets.

  4592. NIX'S MATE: AN HISTORICAL ROMANCE OF AMERICA. NY: Colman,
          1839.
          2v. Anon.

John William De Forest
1826–1906

*4599. HISTORY OF THE INDIANS OF CONNECTICUT. Hartford: Hamersley, 1851.

4600. ORIENTAL ACQUAINTANCE: OR, LETTERS FROM SYRIA. NY: Dix, Edwards, 1856.

4602. EUROPEAN ACQUAINTANCE: BEING SKETCHES OF PEOPLE IN EUROPE. NY: Harper & Bros., 1858.

4603. SEACLIFF OR THE MYSTERY OF THE WESTERVELTS. Bos: Phillips, Sampson, 1859.

4605. MISS RAVENEL'S CONVERSION FROM SECESSION TO LOYALTY. NY: Harper & Bros., 1867.
Revised edition published in 1939 (No. 4630).

4606. OVERLAND. A NOVEL. NY: Sheldon, <1871>.

*4607. KATE BEAUMONT. Bos: Osgood, 1872.

4609. THE WETHEREL AFFAIR. NY: Sheldon, 1873.

4611. HONEST JOHN VANE. A STORY. New Haven: Richmond & Patten, 1875.

4612. PLAYING THE MISCHIEF. A NOVEL. NY: Harper & Bros., 1875.
Harper's Library of Select Novels, No. 442.

4614. JUSTINE'S LOVERS A NOVEL. NY: Harper & Bros., 1878.
Anon. *Harper's Library of American Fiction*, No. 2.

4616. IRENE THE MISSIONARY. Bos: Roberts Bros., 1879.
Anon.

4619. THE BLOODY CHASM. A NOVEL. NY: Appleton, 1881.
Reprinted in 1882 as *The Oddest of Courtships* (No. 4620).

4625. A LOVER'S REVOLT. NY, Lon, &c: Longmans, Green, 1898.

4626. THE DE FORESTS OF AVESNES (AND OF NEW NETHERLAND). New Haven: Tuttle, Morehouse & Taylor, 1900.

4627. THE DOWNING LEGENDS STORIES IN RHYME. New Haven: Tuttle, Morehouse & Taylor, 1901.

4628. POEMS MEDLEY AND PALESTINA. New Haven: Tuttle, Morehouse & Taylor, 1902.

4631. A VOLUNTEER'S ADVENTURES A UNION CAPTAIN'S RECORD OF THE CIVIL WAR. New Haven: Yale U PR, 1946.
Ed. James H. Croushore.

4632. A UNION OFFICER IN THE RECONSTRUCTION. New Haven: Yale U PR, 1948.
Ed. James H. Croushore & David Morris Potter.

Joseph Dennie
1768–1812

4633. THE LAY PREACHER; OR SHORT SERMONS, FOR IDLE READERS. Walpole
NH: Carlisle, 1796.
Anon. Only 2 of these sermons are reprinted in the 1817 collection with this title.

4636. THE SPIRIT OF THE FARMERS' MUSEUM, AND LAY PREACHER'S GAZETTE.
Walpole NH: Thomas & Thomas, 1801.
Edited, with contributions, by Dennie.

4642. THE LAY PREACHER. Phila: H. Hall, 1817.
Ed. John E. Hall. An additional piece was published separately in 1818 as *The
Relicks of Dennie* (No. 4643). Other fugitive pieces by Dennie were collected in J.E.
Hall's *The Philadelphia Souvenir*, 1826 (No. 4644), & Joseph T. Buckingham's *Speci-
mens of Newspaper Literature*, 1850 (No. 4645).

George Horatio Derby
1823–1861

*4650. PHOENIXIANA: OR, SKETCHES AND BURLESQUES. By John Phoenix.
NY: Appleton, 1856.
Ed. John Judson Ames. Extended editions published in 1897 (No. 4652) & 1937
(BAL II, p. 445).

*4651. THE SQUIBOB PAPERS. NY: Carleton, 1865.
Ed. Mary Angeline Coons Derby & Charles H. Poole.

Emily Elizabeth Dickinson
1830–1886

*4654. A MASQUE OF POETS. Bos: Roberts Bros., 1878.
Anon. *No Name Series*. Contains Dickinson's "Success," p. 174. For full entry see
No. 11423 below & BAL (No. 118).

4655. POEMS. Bos: Roberts Bros., 1890.
Ed. Mabel Loomis Todd & T.W. Higginson. The "fourth edition" published in
1891 (No. 4658) has minor corrections.

4656. POEMS ... SECOND SERIES. Bos: Roberts Bros., 1891.
Ed. T.W. Higginson & Mabel Loomis Todd.

*4660. LETTERS OF EMILY DICKINSON. Bos: Roberts Bros., 1894.
2v. Ed. Mabel Loomis Todd. Extended edition published in 1931 (No. 4685).

4661. POEMS ... THIRD SERIES. Bos: Roberts Bros., 1896.
Ed. Mabel Loomis Todd.

4669. THE SINGLE HOUND POEMS OF A LIFETIME. Bos: Little, Brown, 1914.

EMILY DICKINSON (cont.)

4673. THE LIFE AND LETTERS OF EMILY DICKINSON. Bos & NY: Houghton Mifflin, 1924.

By Martha Dickinson Bianchi. Reprinted, with additions & revisions, in 1924 (twice), 1925 (once) & 1929 (twice).

*4683. FURTHER POEMS OF EMILY DICKINSON. Bos: Little, Brown, 1929.

Ed. Martha Dickinson Bianchi & Alfred Leete Hampson.

4688. UNPUBLISHED POEMS OF EMILY DICKINSON. Bos: Little, Brown, 1935.

Ed. Martha Dickinson Bianchi & Alfred Leete Hampson. Limited edition; the trade edition published in 1936 (No. 4689).

4695. BOLTS OF MELODY NEW POEMS OF EMILY DICKINSON. NY & Lon: Harper & Bros., 1945.

Ed. Mabel Loomis Todd & Millicent Todd Bingham.

4699. EMILY DICKINSON'S LETTERS TO DR. AND MRS. JOSIAH GILBERT HOLLAND. Cambridge: Harvard U PR, 1951.

Ed. Theodora Van Wagenen Ward.

4701. THE POEMS OF EMILY DICKINSON. Cambridge: Harvard U PR, 1955.

3v. Ed. Thomas H. Johnson. The definitive edition; earlier collected editions, containing 2 new poems & 1 new poem respectively, are *The Complete Poems,* 1924 (No. 4674), & *The Poems ... Centenary Edition,* 1930 (No. 4684).

Mary Abigail Dodge
(Gail Hamilton)
1833–1896

Note: All works listed here, with the sole exception of No. 4718, were published under Dodge's pseudonym *Gail Hamilton.*

4702. COUNTRY LIVING AND COUNTRY THINKING. Bos: Ticknor & Fields, 1862.

4705. GALA-DAYS. Bos: Ticknor & Fields, 1863.

4708. STUMBLING-BLOCKS. Bos: Ticknor & Fields, 1864.

*4710. A NEW ATMOSPHERE. Bos: Ticknor & Fields, 1865.

4711. SKIRMISHES AND SKETCHES. Bos: Ticknor & Fields, 1865.

4713. SUMMER REST. Bos: Ticknor & Fields, 1866.

4714. RED-LETTER DAYS IN APPLETHORPE. Bos: Ticknor & Fields, 1866.

4715. WOOL-GATHERING. Bos: Ticknor & Fields, 1867.

*4717. WOMAN'S WRONGS: A COUNTER-IRRITANT. Bos: Ticknor & Fields, 1868.

4718. MEMORIAL. MRS. HANNAH STANWOOD DODGE. Cambridge: Riverside PR, 1869.

Privately printed according to a statement signed *Mary Abby Dodge* on the title-page verso.

MARY A. DODGE (Gail Hamilton) (cont.)

4720. A BATTLE OF THE BOOKS, RECORDED BY AN UNKNOWN WRITER, FOR THE USE OF AUTHORS AND PUBLISHERS. Cambridge: Riverside PR, 1870.
"Edited and published by Gail Hamilton."

4723. WOMAN'S WORTH AND WORTHLESSNESS. THE COMPLEMENT TO "A NEW ATMOSPHERE." NY: Harper & Bros., 1872.

4724. LITTLE FOLK LIFE. NY: Harper & Bros., 1872.

4725. CHILD WORLD. Bos: Shepard & Gill, 1873.

4726. CHILD WORLD ... PART SECOND. Bos: Shepard & Gill, 1873.

4727. TWELVE MILES FROM A LEMON. NY: Harper & Bros., 1874.

4728. NURSERY NOONINGS. NY: Harper & Bros., 1875.

4731. SERMONS TO THE CLERGY. Bos: Gill, 1876.

4732. FIRST LOVE IS BEST. A SENTIMENTAL SKETCH. Bos: Estes & Lauriat, 1877.

4733. WHAT THINK YE OF CHRIST THE TESTIMONY OF THE ENGLISH BIBLE. Bos: Estes & Lauriat, 1877.

*4735. OUR COMMON SCHOOL SYSTEM. Bos: Estes & Lauriat, <1880>.

4736. DIVINE GUIDANCE. MEMORIAL OF ALLEN W. DODGE. NY: Appleton, 1881.

4743. A WASHINGTON BIBLE-CLASS. NY: Appleton, 1891.

4744. ENGLISH KINGS IN A NUTSHELL AN AID TO THE MEMORY. NY, Cincinnati, &c: American Book Co., 1893.

*4746. BIOGRAPHY OF JAMES G. BLAINE. Norwich CT: H. Bill, 1895.

*4748. X RAYS. <n.p.; Hamilton MA, 1896>.
Extended edition, ed. H. Augusta Dodge, also published in 1896 (No. 4749).

4750. GAIL HAMILTON'S LIFE IN LETTERS. Bos: Lee & Shepard, 1901.
2v. Ed. H. Augusta Dodge.

4751. CHIPS, FRAGMENTS AND VESTIGES. Bos: Lee & Shepard, 1902.
Ed. H. Augusta Dodge.

Mary Elizabeth Mapes Dodge
1831–1905

4752. THE IRVINGTON STORIES. By M.E. Dodge. NY: O'Kane, 1865.
A "fourth edition," with 1 substitution, published in 1867 (No. 4754); revised & extended edition in 1898 (No. 4790).

4753. HANS BRINKER; OR, THE SILVER SKATES. By M.E. Dodge. NY: O'Kane, 1866.
Slightly revised edition published in 1875 (No. 4766).

MARY MAPES DODGE (cont.)

4755. A FEW FRIENDS AND HOW THEY AMUSED THEMSELVES. By M.E. Dodge. Phila: Lippincott, 1869.

*4764. RHYMES AND JINGLES. NY: Scribner, Armstrong, 1875.
Extended editions published in 1881 (No. 4774) & 1904 (No. 4801).

4769. THEOPHILUS AND OTHERS. NY: Scribner, Armstrong, 1876.

4773. ALONG THE WAY. NY: Scribner's Sons, 1879.
For an extended edition see No. 4800 below.

4776. DONALD AND DOROTHY. Bos: Roberts Bros., 1883.
Published simultaneously (?) in the U.K. as *The Adventures of Donald and Dorothy* (No. 4775A).

4786. THE LAND OF PLUCK STORIES AND SKETCHES FOR YOUNG FOLK. NY: Century Co., 1894.

4787. WHEN LIFE IS YOUNG A COLLECTION OF VERSE FOR BOYS AND GIRLS. NY: Century Co., 1894.

4800. POEMS AND VERSES. NY: Century Co., 1904.

Ignatius Loyola Donnelly
1831–1901

4807. THE MOURNER'S VISION. A POEM. Phila, 1850.

4812. ATLANTIS: THE ANTEDILUVIAN WORLD. NY: Harper & Bros., 1882.

*4813. RAGNAROK: THE AGE OF FIRE AND GRAVEL. NY: Appleton, 1883.

4814. THE GREAT CRYPTOGRAM: FRANCIS BACON'S CIPHER IN THE SO-CALLED SHAKESPEARE PLAYS. Lon: Low, Marston, et al, 1888.
2v.

4815. THE GREAT CRYPTOGRAM: FRANCIS BACON'S CIPHER IN THE SO-CALLED SHAKESPEARE-PLAYS. Chi, NY, &c.: Peale, 1888.

4816. CAESAR'S COLUMN. A STORY OF THE TWENTIETH CENTURY. By Edmund Boisgilbert, M.D. Chi: Schulte, <1890>.

*4817. DOCTOR HUGUET A NOVEL. Chi: Schulte, <1891>.

4818. THE GOLDEN BOTTLE OR THE STORY OF EPHRAIM BENEZET OF KANSAS. NY & St.Paul: Merrill, 1892.
Merrill's Library, No. 1, Sept. 1892.

4819. THE AMERICAN PEOPLE'S MONEY. Chi: Laird & Lee, 1895.
Cloth; and paper wrapper of *The Pastime Series*, No. 141, June 1895.

4821. THE CIPHER IN THE PLAYS, AND ON THE TOMBSTONE. Minneapolis: Verulam Pub. Co., 1899.

Joseph Rodman Drake
1795–1820

4822. POEMS. By Croaker, Croaker & Co. and Croaker, Jun. NY: Pub'd for the Reader, 1819.
With Fitz-Greene Halleck, see No. 6958 below. The "first complete edition" of this material published in 1860 as *The Croakers* (Nos. 4835 & 6991) contains 7 additional poems by Drake.

4825. THE CULPRIT FAY AND OTHER POEMS. NY: Dearborn, 1835.

4842. THE LIFE AND WORKS OF JOSEPH RODMAN DRAKE ... A MEMOIR AND COMPLETE TEXT OF HIS POEMS & PROSE. Bos: The Author, 1935.
Ed. Frank Lester Pleadwell.

Augustine Joseph Hickey Duganne
1823–1884

4844. THE TWO CLERKS, OR THE ORPHAN'S GRATITUDE. Bos: Brainard, 1843.

*4845. MASSACHUSETTS AND OTHER POEMS. Bos: Ticknor, 1843.

4846. SECRET GUILT, OR THE COUNTERFEITERS. AN AMERICAN TALE. Bos: Brainard, 1844.

4847. THE KNIGHTS OF THE SEAL: OR, THE MYSTERIES OF THE THREE CITIES. Phila: Colon & Adriance, 1845.
Anon. Reprinted *ca.* 1854 as *The Mysteries of Three Cities!* (No. 4876).

4852. THE DAGUERREOTYPE MINIATURE; OR, LIFE IN THE EMPIRE CITY. Phila: Zieber, 1846.
Anon. Reprinted ca. 1865 as *Rose Warrington; or, the Daguerreotype Miniature* (No. 4903).

4856. EUSTACE BARCOURT: OR THE ILLEGITIMATE. Phila: Zieber, 1848.
Anon.

4859. EMILY HARPER, OR THE COQUETTE'S DESTINY. Worcester: Drew, <n.d., 1848?>.

4861. THE GOSPEL OF LABOR: A POEM. Bos: The Association, 1849.
Delivered before the Mechanic Apprentices' Library Assn, 22 Feb. 1849.

4865. THE BRAVO'S DAUGHTER; OR, THE TORY OF CAROLINA. NY: E. Winchester, 1850.

*4867. PARNASSUS IN PILLORY. A SATIRE. By Motley Manners, Esq. NY: Adriance, Sherman, 1851.

4869. ART'S TRUE MISSION IN AMERICA. NY: G.S. Appleton, 1853.

4870. THE MISSION OF INTELLECT; A POEM. NY: Larkin, Stearns, 1853.
Delivered at Metropolitan Hall, New York, 20 Dec. 1852.

A. J. H. DUGANNE (cont.)

*4871. A SOUND LITERATURE THE SAFEGUARD OF OUR NATIONAL INSTITU-
TIONS. NY: <Union Book Assn, 1853>.

4874. BIANCA; OR, THE STAR OF THE VALLEY. NY: French, <n.d., 1854?>.

4877. THE PRINCE CORSAIR: OR, THE THREE BROTHERS OF GUZAN. NY:
French, <n.d., 1854?>.
With material by others, pp. <75>–100.

4878. THE POETICAL WORKS OF AUGUSTINE DUGANNE. Phila: Parry &
McMillan, 1855.
These sheets reissued 1865 as the *Autograph Edition* (No. 4900).

4880. THE TENANT-HOUSE; OR, EMBERS FROM POVERTY'S HEARTHSTONE.
NY: De Witt, <1857>.
Anon.

4882. THE WAR IN EUROPE: BEING A RETROSPECT OF WARS AND TREATIES.
NY: De Witt, 1859.

4884. A HISTORY OF GOVERNMENTS. NY: De Witt, <1860>.
Revised edition published in 1882 as *Governments of the World* (No. 4913).

*4885. MASSASOIT'S DAUGHTER; OR, THE FRENCH CAPTIVES. NY & Lon:
Beadle, <1861>.

4886. THE PEON PRINCE; OR THE YANKEE KNIGHT ERRANT. NY & Lon:
Beadle, <1861>.
Beadle's Dime Novel, No. 25, 15 June 1861.

4887. PUTNAM POMFRET'S WARD OR A VERMONTER'S ADVENTURES IN
MEXICO. NY & Lon: Beadle, <1861>.
Anon. *Beadle's Dime Novel*, No. 30, 19 Oct. 1861.

4891. THE KING'S MAN: A TALE OF SOUTH CAROLINA. NY & Lon: Beadle,
<1862>.
Beadle's Dime Novel, No. 42, 6 Aug. 1862.

4894. THE RING OF DESTINY; OR, THE ASTROLOGER'S PLOT. Bos: Gleason,
1863.
Not located.

4898. UTTERANCES. NY: De Witt, 1865.

4899. CAMPS AND PRISONS. TWENTY MONTHS IN THE DEPARTMENT OF
THE GULF. NY, 1865.
"Subscriber's edition."

4904. THE FIGHTING QUAKERS, A TRUE STORY OF THE WAR FOR OUR
UNION. NY: Robens, 1866.
"With letters from the brothers to their mother: and a funeral sermon by Rev.
O.B. Frothingham." Reprinted in 1869 as *The Quaker Soldiers* (No. 4908).

*4910. WOMAN'S VOWS AND MASON'S OATHS. A PLAY. NY: De Witt, 1874.
De Witt's Acting Plays, No. 161

A. J. H. DUGANNE (cont.)
    4912. CORN-BREAD. POEM. NY: 1880.
        Read at the Academy of Music, New York, on the 13th celebration of Decoration
        Day.

    4914. INJURESOUL; A SATIRE FOR SCIENCE. NY: American Book-Print Co.,
        1884.

Paul Laurence (Lawrence) Dunbar
1872–1906

Note: Copyright printings & sheet music editions of Dunbar's lyrics
written for the musical stage are here omitted.

    4916. OAK AND IVY. Dayton OH: United Brethren Pub. House, 1893.
    4917. MAJORS AND MINORS: POEMS. <Toledo OH, 1895>.
    4918. LYRICS OF LOWLY LIFE. NY: Dodd, Mead, 1896.
    4921. FOLKS FROM DIXIE. NY: Dodd, Mead, 1898.
    4923. THE UNCALLED A NOVEL. NY: Dodd, Mead, 1898.
        Originally published as the May 1898 issue of *Lippincott's Monthly Magazine* (No.
        4922).

    4925. LYRICS OF THE HEARTHSIDE. NY: Dodd, Mead, 1899.
    4930. THE STRENGTH OF GIDEON AND OTHER STORIES. NY: Dodd, Mead,
        1900.

    4932. THE LOVE OF LANDRY. NY: Dodd, Mead, 1900.
    4936. THE FANATICS. NY: Dodd, Mead, 1901.
    4939. THE SPORT OF THE GODS. NY: Dodd, Mead, 1902.
    4945. LYRICS OF LOVE AND LAUGHTER. NY: Dodd, Mead, 1903.
        Contains 11 poems here first collected.

    *4946. IN OLD PLANTATION DAYS. NY: Dodd, Mead, 1903.
    4950. THE HEART OF HAPPY HOLLOW. NY: Dodd, Mead, 1904.
    4954. LYRICS OF SUNSHINE AND SHADOW. NY: Dodd, Mead, 1905.
    4961. THE COMPLETE POEMS. NY: Dodd, Mead, 1913.
        Contains only 3 new poems. Other collections of Dunbar's verse published by
        Dodd, Mead are reprints or print only a single new piece: *Poems of Cabin and Field,*
        1899 (No. 4927), *Candle-Lightin' Time,* 1901 (No. 4937), *When Malindy Sings,* 1903
        (No. 4948), *Li'l' Gal,* 1904 (No. 4951), *Howdy Honey Howdy,* 1905 (No. 4955),
        Joggin' Erlong, 1906 (No. 4956), *Chris'mus Is A'Comin' & Other Poems,* 1907 (No.
        4957) & *Speakin' o' Christmas and Other Christmas ... Poems,* 1914 (No. 4962).

William Dunlap
1766–1839

4974. THE FATHER; OR, AMERICAN SHANDY-ISM. A COMEDY. NY: Ptd by Hodge, Allen & Campbell, 1789.

Anon. For comment on a revised edition see No. 4999 below.

4975. DARBY'S RETURN. A COMIC SKETCH. NY: Ptd by Hodge, Allen, & Campbell, 1789.

4977. THE ARCHERS, OR MOUNTAINEERS OF SWITZERLAND: AN OPERA ... TO WHICH IS SUBJOINED A BRIEF HISTORICAL ACCOUNT OF SWITZERLAND. NY: Ptd by T. & J. Swords, 1796.

4978. TELL THE TRUTH AND SHAME THE DEVIL: A COMEDY. NY: Ptd by T. & J. Swords, 1797.

Adaptation of *Jérôme Pointu* by A.L.B. Robineau.

4980. ANDRE; A TRAGEDY ... TO WHICH ARE ADDED, AUTHENTIC DOCUMENTS RESPECTING MAJOR ANDRE. NY: Ptd by T. & J. Swords, 1798.

4982. THE WILD-GOOSE CHACE: A PLAY. NY: Dunlap, 1800.

Adaptation of *Der Wildfang* by Augustus von Kotzebue.

4983. THE VIRGIN OF THE SUN: A PLAY. NY: Dunlap, 1800.

Adaptation of *Die Sonnenjungfrau* by Augustus von Kotzebue.

4984. PIZARRO IN PERU; OR, THE DEATH OF ROLLA. A PLAY. NY: Dunlap, 1800.

Adaptation of *Die Spanier in Peru* by Augustus von Kotzebue, based in large part on Sheridan's adaptation.

4988. ABAELLINO, THE GREAT BANDIT. NY: D. Longworth, 1802.

Translation of the dramatic version of *Aballino der Grosse Bandit* by Johann Heinrich Daniel Zschokke. Another edition published with imprint Bos: Ptd by Russell & Cutler, 1802; this edition misattributes the original to Schiller.

4990. THE GLORY OF COLUMBIA; HER YEOMANRY. A PLAY. NY: D. Longworth, 1803.

Anon. Contains only the "songs, duets, and chorusses."

*4993. RIBBEMONT, OR THE FEUDAL BARON, A TRAGEDY. NY: D. Longworth, 1803.

4994. THE VOICE OF NATURE, A DRAMA. NY: D. Longworth, 1803.

Adaptation of *Le Jugement de Salomon* by L.C. Caigniez.

4996. THE WIFE OF TWO HUSBANDS. A DRAMA. NY: D. Longworth, 1804.

Adaptation of *La Femme à Deux Maris* by Guilbert de Pixeré court.

4999. THE DRAMATIC WORKS OF WILLIAM DUNLAP. Phila: Ptd by T. & G. Palmer, 1806–16.

Only 3 of a projected 10v. were published. Sheets of the 4 plays in Vol. 1 were also issued separately by D. Longworth in 1807: *Darby's Return* (No. 5000) is a reprint; *The Father of an Only Child* (No. 5001) is a revision of *The Father,* 1789; *Fountainville Abbey* (No. 5002) & *Leicester* (No. 5003) are here first published in book form.

WILLIAM DUNLAP (cont.)

*5004. THE MAN OF FORTITUDE; OR, THE KNIGHT'S ADVENTURE. A DRAMA. NY: D.Longworth, 1807.
An adaptation by John Hodgkinson, whose name appears alone on the title-page, of Dunlap's *The Knight's Adventure.*

5005. FRATERNAL DISCORD: A DRAMA. NY: D. Longworth, 1809.
Adaptation of *Die Versöhnung* by Augustus von Kotzebue.

5006. THE ITALIAN FATHER: A COMEDY. NY: D. Longworth, 1810.
Based on *The Honest Whore* by Thomas Dekker.

5008. YANKEE CHRONOLOGY; OR, HUZZA FOR THE CONSTITUTION! A MUSICAL INTERLUDE ... TO WHICH ARE ADDED ... PATRIOTIC SONGS. NY: D. Longworth, 1812.

5010. MEMOIRS OF THE LIFE OF GEORGE FREDERICK COOKE, ESQUIRE. NY: D. Longworth, 1813.
2v.

5012. LOVERS VOWS; A PLAY. NY: D. Longworth, 1814.
Adaptation of *Das Kind der Liebe* by Augustus von Kotzebue.

5013. THE GOOD NEIGHBOR; AN INTERLUDE. NY: D. Longworth, 1814.
"Altered from a scene of <August Wilhelm> Iffland's."

*5014. PETER THE GREAT; OR, THE RUSSIAN MOTHER: A PLAY. NY: D. Longworth, 1814.
Adaptation of *Die Strelizen* by J.M. Babo.

5016. A NARRATIVE OF THE EVENTS WHICH FOLLOWED BONAPARTE'S CAMPAIGN IN RUSSIA TO THE PERIOD OF HIS DETHRONEMENT. Hartford: Sheldon, 1814.
Also published as an appendix in Sir Robert Ker Porter's *A Narrative of the Campaign in Russia, during the Year 1812* (Hartford: Andrus, Starr, 1814).

5017. THE LIFE OF CHARLES BROCKDEN BROWN. Phila: Parke, 1815.
2v. For full entry see No. 1515 above. Reprinted in the U.K. in 1822 as *Memoirs of Charles Brockden Brown* (No. 5020).

5018. THE GLORY OF COLUMBIA HER YEOMANRY! A PLAY. NY: D. Longworth, 1817.

5023. A TRIP TO NIAGARA; OR, TRAVELLERS IN AMERICA. A FARCE. NY: Clayton, 1830.

5025. A HISTORY OF THE AMERICAN THEATRE. NY: Harper, 1832.

5026. HISTORY OF THE RISE AND PROGRESS OF THE ARTS OF DESIGN IN THE UNITED STATES. NY: Scott, Ptrs, 1834.
2v.

5028. THIRTY YEARS AGO; OR THE MEMOIRS OF A WATER DRINKER. NY: Bancroft & Holley, 1836.
2v. Anon. The "second edition" published in 1837 as *Memoirs of a Water Drinker* (No. 5030).

WILLIAM DUNLAP (cont.)

5029.   A HISTORY OF NEW YORK, FOR SCHOOLS. NY: Collins, Keese, 1837.
2v. or 2v. in one.

5031.   HISTORY OF THE NEW NETHERLANDS, PROVINCE OF NEW YORK, AND
STATE OF NEW YORK. NY: The Author, 1839–40.
2v.

5032.   DIARY OF WILLIAM DUNLAP (1766–1839). NY: New York Historical
Soc'y, 1930.
3v.

5033.   FALSE SHAME AND THIRTY YEARS TWO PLAYS. Princeton: Princeton
U PR, 1940.
Ed. Oral Sumner Coad. *America's Lost Plays* series.

Timothy Dwight
1752–1817

Note: Dwight's separately printed sermons & addresses are here generally omitted; for full details see BAL.

5034.   A DISSERTATION ON THE HISTORY, ELOQUENCE, AND POETRY OF
THE BIBLE. New Haven: Ptd by T. & S. Green, 1772.
Delivered at the Public Commencement, New-Haven.

5037.   AMERICA: OR, A POEM ON THE SETTLEMENT OF THE BRITISH
COLONIES. By a Gentleman Educated at Yale-College. New Ha-
ven: Ptd by T. & S. Green, <n.d. 1780?>.
"Addressed to the Friends of Freedom, and Their Country."

5040.   THE CONQUEST OF CANÄAN; A POEM, IN ELEVEN BOOKS. Hartford:
Babcock, 1785.

*5041.   THE TRIUMPH OF INFIDELITY: A POEM. <n.p.> Ptd in the World, 1788.
Anon.

5048.   GREENFIELD HILL: A POEM, IN SEVEN PARTS. NY: Ptd by Childs &
Swaine, 1794.

5071.   REMARKS ON THE REVIEW OF INCHIQUIN'S LETTERS, PUBLISHED IN
THE QUARTERLY REVIEW. By an Inhabitant of New-England. Bos:
Armstrong, 1815.

5074.   THEOLOGY; EXPLAINED AND DEFENDED, IN A SERIES OF SERMONS. New
Haven: Dwight, 1818–19.
5v.

5075.   TRAVELS; IN NEW-ENGLAND AND NEW-YORK. New Haven: Dwight,
1821–22.
4v.

5081.   SERMONS. Edinburgh: Waugh & Innes, 1828.
2v.

5082.   SERMONS. New Haven: Howe, 1828.
2v.

Edward Eggleston
1837–1902

Note: Omitted from this list are Eggleston's sunday school manuals and history school texts.

5093. MR. BLAKE'S WALKING-STICK: A CHRISTMAS STORY FOR BOYS AND GIRLS. Chi: Adams, Blackmer, & Lyon, 1870.

5095. THE BOOK OF QUEER STORIES, AND STORIES TOLD ON A CELLAR DOOR. Chi: Adams, Blackmer, & Lyon, 1871.

*5096. THE HOOSIER SCHOOL-MASTER. A NOVEL. NY: Judd, <1871>.
Revised edition published in 1892 (No. 5150).

5098. THE END OF THE WORLD: A LOVE STORY. Lon: Routledge & Sons, 1872.

*5099. THE END OF THE WORLD. A LOVE STORY. NY: Judd, <1872>.

5103. THE MYSTERY OF METROPOLISVILLE. NY: Judd, <1873>.

5105. THE CIRCUIT RIDER: A TALE OF THE HEROIC AGE. Lon: Routledge & Sons, 1874.

*5106. THE CIRCUIT RIDER: A TALE OF THE HEROIC AGE. NY: Ford, 1874.

5107. THE SCHOOLMASTER'S STORIES, FOR BOYS AND GIRLS. Bos: Shepard, 1874.
Reprint of Nos. 5095 & 5093 above with 6 additional stories. Revised & extended edition published in 1884 as *Queer Stories for Boys and Girls* (No. 5128).

5113. ROXY. NY: Scribner's Sons, 1878.

5114. TECUMSEH AND THE SHAWNEE PROPHET. NY: Dodd, Mead, 1878.
With Lillie Eggleston Seelye. *Famous American Indians* series. Published in the U.K. in 1880 as *The Shawnee Prophet* (No. 5118).

*5116. POCAHONTAS. NY: Dodd, Mead, <1879>.
With Lillie Eggleston Seelye. *Famous American Indians* series. Published in the U.K. in 1881 as *The Indian Princess* (No. 5119B)

5117. BRANT AND RED JACKET. NY: Dodd, Mead, 1879.
With Lillie Eggleston Seelye. *Famous American Indians* series. Published in the U.K. in 1881 as *The Rival Warriors* (No. 5119A).

5119. MONTEZUMA AND THE CONQUEST OF MEXICO. NY: Dodd, Mead, 1880.
With Lillie Eggleston Seelye. *Famous American Indians* series. Published in the U.K. in 1881 as *The Mexican Prince* (No. 5119C).

5121. THE HOOSIER SCHOOL-BOY. Lon: Warne, <1882>.
The Columbia Library.

*5126. THE HOOSIER SCHOOL-BOY. NY: Scribner's Sons, 1883.
Edition arranged for school use published in 1890 (No. 5143).

5133. THE GRAYSONS A STORY OF ILLINOIS. NY: Century Co., <1887, i.e. 1888>.

EDWARD EGGLESTON (cont.)

*5147. THE FAITH DOCTOR A STORY OF NEW YORK. NY: Appleton, 1891.

 5152. DUFFELS. NY: Appleton, 1893.
        "Sister Tabea," here collected, reprinted separately for Mrs. Eggleston in 1896
        (No. 5160).

 5161. THE BEGINNERS OF A NATION A HISTORY OF THE SOURCE AND RISE
        OF THE EARLIEST ENGLISH SETTLEMENTS IN AMERICA. NY: Appleton,
        1896.

 5168. THE TRANSIT OF CIVILIZATION FROM ENGLAND TO AMERICA IN THE
        SEVENTEENTH CENTURY. NY: Appleton, 1901.

Ralph Waldo Emerson
1803–1882

*5181. NATURE. Bos: Munroe, 1836.
        Anon.

 5183. AN ORATION, DELIVERED BEFORE THE PHI BETA KAPPA SOCIETY, AT
        CAMBRIDGE, AUGUST 31, 1837. Bos: Munroe, 1837.
        Otherwise "The American Scholar." Published in the U.K. in 1844 as *Man Think-
        ing* (No. 5341).

 5184. AN ADDRESS DELIVERED BEFORE THE SENIOR CLASS IN DIVINITY
        COLLEGE, CAMBRIDGE … 15 JULY, 1838. Bos: Munroe, 1838.

 5189. ESSAYS. Bos: Munroe, 1841.
        Revised & extended edition published in 1847 (No. 5213).

*5196. NATURE; AN ESSAY. AND LECTURES ON THE TIMES. Lon: H.G. Clarke,
        1844.

 5197. ORATIONS, LECTURES, AND ADDRESSES. Lon: H.G. Clarke, 1844.
        "The Young American," here first printed, was also published separately in the
        U.K. in 1844 (No. 5343).

 5198. ESSAYS: SECOND SERIES. Bos: Munroe, 1844.
        The "second edition" published in 1850 (No. 5220) contains 1 additional poem.

 5210. POEMS. Lon: Chapman, Bros., 1847.

 5211. POEMS. Bos: Munroe, 1847.
        Emerson's *Selected Poems* published in 1876 (No. 5274) contains 7 new pieces.

 5218. NATURE; ADDRESSES, AND LECTURES. Bos & Cambridge: Munroe,
        1849.

*5219. REPRESENTATIVE MEN: SEVEN LECTURES. Bos: Phillips, Sampson,
        1850.

 5226. ENGLISH TRAITS. Bos: Phillips, Sampson, 1856.

*5231. THE CONDUCT OF LIFE. Bos: Ticknor & Fields, 1860.

 5250. MAY-DAY AND OTHER PIECES. Bos: Ticknor & Fields, 1867.

*5260. SOCIETY AND SOLITUDE. TWELVE CHAPTERS. Bos: Fields, Osgood,
        1870.

RALPH WALDO EMERSON (cont.)

5272. LETTERS AND SOCIAL AIMS. Bos: Osgood, 1876.

*5289. THE CORRESPONDENCE OF THOMAS CARLYLE AND RALPH WALDO EMERSON 1834–1872. Bos: Osgood, 1883.
2v. Ed. Charles Eliot Norton. Published simultaneously (?) in the U.K. See also No. 5299 below.

5290. THE WORKS OF RALPH WALDO EMERSON. Lon: Bell & Sons, 1883.
3v. Vol. 3 contains 8 pieces collected for the first time.

*5291. MISCELLANIES. Bos & NY: Houghton, Mifflin, 1884.
Riverside Edition of Emerson's Complete Works, Vol. 11 (No. 5414). Extended edition published in 1904 as the "Centenary Edition" of Emerson's *Complete Works*, Vol. 11 (Nos. 5315 & 5463).

*5292. POEMS ... NEW AND REVISED EDITION. Bos & NY: Houghton, Mifflin, 1884.
Riverside Edition of Emerson's Complete Works, Vol. 9 (No. 5414).Extended edition published in 1904 as the "Centenary Edition" of Emerson's *Complete Works*, Vol. 9 (Nos. 5314 & 5463).

*5293. LECTURES AND BIOGRAPHICAL SKETCHES. Bos & NY: Houghton, Mifflin, 1884.
Ed. J.E. Cabot. *Little Classic* edition. Published simultaneously as *Riverside Edition of Emerson's Complete Works*, Vol. 10 (Nos. 5294 & 5414).

5299. THE CORRESPONDENCE OF THOMAS CARLYLE AND RALPH WALDO EMERSON 1834–1872 SUPPLEMENTARY LETTERS. Bos: Ticknor, 1886.
Later included in an extended edition of No. 5289 above.

*5302. NATURAL HISTORY OF INTELLECT AND OTHER PAPERS. Bos & NY: Houghton, Mifflin, 1893.
Ed. J.E. Cabot. *Little Classic* edition. Published simultaneously as *Riverside Edition of Emerson's Complete Works*, Vol. 12. (Nos. 5303 & 5414). Extended edition published in 1904 as the "Centenary Edition" of Emerson's *Complete Works*, Vol. 12 (Nos. 5316 & 5463).

5304. TWO UNPUBLISHED ESSAYS THE CHARACTER OF SOCRATES THE PRESENT STATE OF ETHICAL PHILOSOPHY. Bos & NY: Lamson Wolffe, 1896.

5306. A CORRESPONDENCE BETWEEN JOHN STERLING AND RALPH WALDO EMERSON. Bos & NY: Houghton, Mifflin, 1897.

5307. LETTERS FROM RALPH WALDO EMERSON TO A FRIEND 1838–1853. Bos & NY: Houghton, Mifflin, 1899.
Ed. Charles Eliot Norton.

5312. CORRESPONDENCE BETWEEN RALPH WALDO EMERSON AND HERMAN GRIMM. Bos & NY: Houghton, Mifflin, 1903.
Ed. Frederick William Holls.

*5318. JOURNALS ... 1820–1824. Bos & NY: Houghton Mifflin, 1909.
Vol. 1 of ten. Ed. Edward Waldo Emerson & Waldo Emerson Forbes. Uniform with the 12v. "Centenary Edition" of Emerson's *Complete Works*, 1903–04 (No. 5463).

RALPH WALDO EMERSON (cont.)

*5319.   JOURNALS ... 1824–1832. Bos & NY: Houghton Mifflin, 1909.
Vol. 2 of ten. For comment see No. 5318 above.

*5320.   JOURNALS ... 1833–1835. Bos & NY: Houghton Mifflin, 1910.
Vol. 3 of ten. For comment see No. 5318 above.

*5321.   JOURNALS ... 1836–1838. Bos & NY: Houghton Mifflin, 1910.
Vol. 4 of ten. For comment see No. 5318 above.

 5322.   RECORDS OF A LIFELONG FRIENDSHIP 1807 1882 RALPH WALDO
EMERSON AND WILLIAM HENRY FURNESS. Bos & NY: Houghton
Mifflin, 1910.
Ed. Horace Howard Furness.

*5323.   JOURNALS ... 1838–1841. Bos & NY: Houghton Mifflin, 1911.
Vol. 5 of ten. For comment see No. 5318 above.

*5324.   JOURNALS ... 1841–1844. Bos & NY: Houghton Mifflin, 1911.
Vol. 6 of ten. For comment see No. 5318 above.

 5325.   UNCOLLECTED WRITINGS ESSAYS, ADDRESSES, POEMS, REVIEWS AND
LETTERS. NY: Lamb, <1912>.

*5326.   JOURNALS ... 1845–1848. Bos & NY: Houghton Mifflin, 1912.
Vol. 7 of ten. For comment see No. 5318 above.

*5327.   JOURNALS ... 1849–1855. Bos & NY: Houghton Mifflin, 1912.
Vol. 8 of ten. For comment see No. 5318 above.

*5328.   JOURNALS ... 1856–1863. Bos & NY: Houghton Mifflin, 1913.
Vol. 9 of ten. For comment see No. 5318 above.

*5329.   JOURNALS ... 1864–1876. Bos & NY: Houghton Mifflin, 1914.
Vol. 10 of ten. For comment see No. 5318 above.

 5330.   UNCOLLECTED LECTURES ... REPORTS OF LECTURES ON AMERICAN
LIFE AND NATURAL RELIGION. NY: Rudge, 1932.
Ed. Clarence Gohdes.

 5331.   EMERSON-CLOUGH LETTERS. Cleveland: The Rowfant Club, 1934.
Ed. Howard F. Lowry & Ralph Leslie Rusk.

 5333.   YOUNG EMERSON SPEAKS UNPUBLISHED DISCOURSES ON MANY
SUBJECTS. Bos: Houghton Mifflin, 1938.
Ed. Arthur Cushman McGiffert, Jr.

 5334.   THE LETTERS OF RALPH WALDO EMERSON. NY: Columbia U PR, 1939.
6v. Ed. Ralph L. Rusk.

Thomas Dunn English
1819–1902

 5504.   ZEPHANIAH DOOLITTLE: A POEM. Phila: Ptd by C. Alexander, 1838.
"From the Manuscripts of Montmorency Sneerlip Snags, Esq."

 5514.   1844; OR, THE POWER OF THE "S.F." A TALE. NY: Burgess, Stringer,
1847.
Mirror Library—New Series.

THOMAS DUNN ENGLISH (cont.)

5515. WALTER WOOLFE; OR, THE DOOM OF THE DRINKER. NY: W.B. Smith, 1847.

5517. THE FRENCH REVOLUTION OF 1848: ITS CAUSES, ACTORS, EVENTS AND INFLUENCES. Phila: Zieber, 1848.
With G.G. Foster.

*5518. THE MORMONS; OR, LIFE AT SALT LAKE CITY. A DRAMA. NY: French, <1858>.
French's Standard Drama, No. 205.

5523. AMBROSE FECIT; OR, THE PEER AND THE PRINTER. A NOVEL. NY: Hilton, 1867.

5525. ZARA; OR, THE GIRL OF THE PERIOD. A NOVEL. NY: Hilton & Syme, <n.d., 1869>.

5535. GASOLOGY A SATIRE. By John Donkey. Phila: Donkey, 1878.

5540. AMERICAN BALLADS. NY: Harper & Bros., 1880.
Harper's Half-Hour Series.

5547. THE BOY'S BOOK OF BATTLE-LYRICS A COLLECTION OF VERSES ILLUSTRATING ... THE HISTORY OF THE UNITED STATES OF AMERICA. NY: Harper & Bros. 1885.

5549. JACOB SCHUYLER'S MILLIONS. A NOVEL. NY: Appleton, 1886.
Anon.

5572. THE SELECT POEMS ... (EXCLUSIVE OF THE "BATTLE LYRICS"). Newark NJ, 1894.
"Published by private subscription." Ed. Alice English.

5574. FAIRY STORIES AND WONDER TALES. NY: Stokes, <1897>.
Ed. Florence English Noll.

5577. THE LITTLE GIANT THE BIG DWARF AND TWO OTHER WONDER-TALES. Chi: McClurg, 1904.

Sumner Lincoln Fairfield
1803–1844

5578. THE BATTLE OF BORODINO; WITH OTHER POEMS. Savannah: The Author, 1821.

5580. THE SIEGE OF CONSTANTINOPLE. A POEM. Charleston: W. Riley, 1822.

5581. POEMS. NY: Bliss & White, 1823.

5582. LAYS OF MELPOMENE. Portland: Ptd by Todd & Smith, 1824.
Also issued with *The Sisters of St Clara,* see next entry.

5583. THE SISTERS OF ST CLARA. A PORTUGUESE TALE. Portland: Ptd by Todd & Smith, 1825.
Issued bound with *Lays of Melpomene,* 1824. Also issued separately?

5584. MINA, A DRAMATIC SKETCH: WITH OTHER POEMS. Baltimore: J. Robinson, 1825.

S. L. FAIRFIELD (cont.)

5585. THE PASSAGE OF THE SEA; A POEM. WITH OTHER PIECES. NY: Ptd by Folsom & Allen, 1826.

5587. THE CITIES OF THE PLAIN. A SCRIPTURE POEM. Bos: Greene, 1827.

5589. THE CITIES OF THE PLAIN, WITH OTHER POEMS ... THIRD EDITION. Phila: Simpson, 1828.
Actually the second edition of the title poem in book form.

5590. THE HEIR OF THE WORLD, AND LESSER POEMS. Phila: Maxwell, 1829.

5592. ABADDON, THE SPIRIT OF DESTRUCTION; AND OTHER POEMS. NY: Sleight & Robinson, 1830.

5593. THE LAST NIGHT OF POMPEII; A POEM: AND LAYS AND LEGENDS. NY: Elliott & Palmer, 1832.

5594. THE POEMS AND PROSE WRITINGS. Phila: The Proprietor, 1841.
These sheets reissued in 1842 as *The Poetical Works* (No. 5595).

Edgar Fawcett
1847–1904

5598. SHORT POEMS FOR SHORT PEOPLE. NY: Felt, 1872.

5599. PURPLE AND FINE LINEN. A NOVEL. NY: Carleton, 1873.

5602. ELLEN STORY A NOVEL. NY: Hale & Son, 1876.

5610. FANTASY AND PASSION. Bos: Roberts Bros., 1878.

5617. A HOPELESS CASE. Bos: Houghton, Mifflin, 1880.

*5619. A GENTLEMAN OF LEISURE A NOVEL. Bos: Houghton, Mifflin, 1881.

*5622. AN AMBITIOUS WOMAN A NOVEL. Bos & NY: Houghton, Mifflin, 1884.

5623. TINKLING CYMBALS A NOVEL. Bos: Osgood, 1884.

5624. SONG AND STORY LATER POEMS. Bos: Osgood, 1884.

5625. RUTHERFORD. NY & Lon: Funk & Wagnalls, 1884.
Standard Library, No. 121, 11 Aug. 1884.

5626. THE ADVENTURES OF A WIDOW A NOVEL. Bos: Osgood, 1884.

5627. THE BUNTLING BALL A GRAECO-AMERICAN PLAY. NY & Lon: Funk & Wagnalls, 1884.

5628. SOCIAL SILHOUETTES (BEING THE IMPRESSIONS OF MR. MARK MAN-HATTAN). Bos: Ticknor, 1885.

5629. THE NEW KING ARTHUR AN OPERA WITHOUT MUSIC. NY & Lon: Funk & Wagnalls, 1885.
Anon.

5631. ROMANCE AND REVERY POEMS. Bos: Ticknor, 1886.

5633. THE HOUSE AT HIGH BRIDGE A NOVEL. Bos: Ticknor, 1887.

5635. THE CONFESSIONS OF CLAUD A ROMANCE. Bos: Ticknor, 1887.

5637. A MAN'S WILL. A NOVEL. NY & Lon: Funk & Wagnalls, 1888.

EDGAR FAWCETT (cont.)

5638. OLIVIA DELAPLAINE A NOVEL. Bos: Ticknor, 1888.

5639. DOUGLAS DUANE. Phila: Lippincott, 1888.
With "Sinfire" by Julian Hawthorne. Originally published as the April 1887 issue
of *Lippincott's Monthly Magazine* (No. 5634).

5640. DIVIDED LIVES A NOVEL. Chi, NY, &c.: Belford, Clarke, <1888>.
Cloth; and paper wrapper of *The Household Library*, No. 1, Vol. 4, 15 Nov. 1888.

5641. MIRIAM BALESTIER A NOVEL. Chi, NY, &c.: Belford, Clarke, <1888>.
Cloth; and paper wrapper of *The Household Library*, Vol. 4, No. 10, 15 Nov. 1888.

5642. A DEMORALIZING MARRIAGE. Phila: Lippincott, 1889.
Cloth; and paper wrapper of *American Novels* series.

5644. AGNOSTICISM AND OTHER ESSAYS. NY, Chi, &c.: Belford, Clarke,
<1889>.

5645. SOLARION. A ROMANCE. Phila: Lippincott, <1889>.
The Sept. 1889 issue of *Lippincott's Monthly Magazine* with title-page as above; not
otherwise published in book form.

*5648. THE EVIL THAT MEN DO A NOVEL. NY: Belford, <1889>.
Cloth; and paper wrapper of *Belford American Novel Series*, No. 7, 7 Dec. 1889.

5650. A DAUGHTER OF SILENCE A NOVEL. NY: Belford, <1890>.
Cloth; and paper wrapper of *Belford American Novel Series*, No. 25, 14 April 1890.

*5653. FABIAN DIMITRY A NOVEL. Chi & NY: Rand, McNally, 1890.
Cloth; and paper wrappers of *The Rialto Series*, Vol. 1, No. 25, May 1890, & *The
Globe Library*, Vol. 1, No. 123, 27 Jan. 1890.

5654. HOW A HUSBAND FORGAVE A NOVEL. NY: Belford, <1890>.
Cloth; and paper wrapper of *Belford American Novel Series*, Vol. 2, No. 10, 4 Aug.
1890.

*5656. A NEW YORK FAMILY A NOVEL. NY: Cassell, <1891>.

5658. SONGS OF DOUBT AND DREAM (POEMS). NY, Toronto, &c.: Funk &
Wagnalls, 1891.

5659. A ROMANCE OF TWO BROTHERS. NY: Minerva Pub. Co., 1891.
Romantic Series, No. 7, Dec. 1891.

5660. WOMEN MUST WEEP A NOVEL. Chi: Laird & Lee, <1891>.
The Library of Choice Fiction, No. 38, Jan. 1892. These sheets reissued in 1895 as *A
Story of Three Girls* (No. 5673).

5661. AN HEIR TO MILLIONS. Chi: Schulte, <1892>.
The Ariel Library, No. 19, July 1892. Also issued in cloth?

5662. THE ADOPTED DAUGHTER. Chi & NY: Neely, <1892>.
Neely's Library of Choice Literature, Vol. 1, No. 1, Sept. 1892.

5663. AMERICAN PUSH. Chi: Schulte, <1892; i.e. 1893>.
Cloth; and paper wrapper of *The Ariel Library*, No. 24, Dec. 1892.

*5665. LOADED DICE A NOVEL. NY: Tait, Sons, <1891, i.e. 1893>.

5666. THE NEW NERO A REALISTIC ROMANCE. NY: Collier, 1893.
Once a Week Library, Vol. 10, No. 22, 6 May 1893.

EDGAR FAWCETT (cont.)

5667.   A MARTYR OF DESTINY. NY: Collier, 1894.
        Once a Week Semi-Monthly Library, Vol. 11, No. 22, 5 May 1894. Also (simultaneously?)
        published as *Outrageous Fortune* with the imprint of the Concord Press, C.T.
        Dillingham & Co., agents (No. 5668); both printed from the same plates.

5669.   HER FAIR FAME A NOVEL. NY: Merrill & Baker, 1894.

5671.   A MILD BARBARIAN A NOVEL. NY: Appleton, 1894.
        Cloth; and paper wrapper of *Appletons' Town and Country Library*, No. 153, 15 Oct.
        1894.

5674.   THE GHOST OF GUY THYRLE. <NY>: Collier, 1895.
        Once a Week Library, Vol. 12, No. 19, 21 March 1895.

5675.   LIFE'S FITFUL FEVER BEING THE MEMOIRS OF CLEMENCE DISOSWAY
        TORRINGTON ... PART ONE. <NY>: Collier, 1896.
        The Fortnightly Library, Vol. 15, No. 13, 24 Dec. 1896.

5676.   LIFE'S FITFUL FEVER BEING THE MEMOIRS OF CLEMENCE DISOSWAY
        TORRINGTON ... PART TWO. <NY>: Collier, 1896.
        The Fortnightly Library, Vol. 15, No. 14, 7 Jan. 1897.

5677.   A ROMANCE OF OLD NEW YORK. Phila & Lon: Lippincott, 1897.

5678.   TWO DAUGHTERS OF ONE RACE. Phila: Lippincott, <1897>.
        The Aug. 1897 issue of *Lippincott's Monthly Magazine* with title-page as above; not
        otherwise published in book form.

5679.   NEW YORK. A NOVEL. NY & Lon: Neely, <1898>.
        Cloth; and paper wrapper of *Neely's Continental Library*, No. 17.

*5681. THE VULGARIANS. NY & Lon: Smart Set Pub. Co., 1903.

5682.   VOICES AND VISIONS LATER VERSES. Lon: Nash, 1903.
        Blooms and Brambles, an earlier collection of verse, reprints save for a prefatory
        poem, was published in the U.K. in 1889 (No. 5646).

Theodore Sedgwick Fay
1807–1898

5687.   DREAMS AND REVERIES OF A QUIET MAN CONSISTING OF THE LITTLE
        GENIUS, AND OTHER ESSAYS. NY: J. & J. Harper, 1832.
        2v.

5692.   NORMAN LESLIE. A TALE OF THE PRESENT TIMES. NY: Harper & Bros.,
        1835.
        2v. Anon. Revised edition published in 1869 (No. 5718).

5696.   SYDNEY CLIFTON; OR, VICISSITUDES IN BOTH HEMISPHERES. NY:
        Harper & Bros., 1839.
        2v. Anon.

5697.   THE COUNTESS. Lon: Bentley, 1840.
        3v. For U.S. edition see next entry.

T. S. FAY (cont.)

5698. THE COUNTESS IDA. A TALE OF BERLIN. NY: Harper & Bros., 1840.
2v. Anon.

5700. THE DOUBLE DUEL; OR, HOBOKEN. Lon: Bentley, 1843.
3v. Reprinted in 1844 as *The Brothers* (No. 5703) with an additional sketch of unknown authorship. For U.S. edition see next entry.

5701. HOBOKEN: A ROMANCE OF NEW-YORK. NY: Harper & Bros., 1843.
2v.

5702. ROBERT RUEFUL; OR, A LESSON TO VALETUDINARIANS. Phila: Godey, 1844.
Godey's Library of Elegant Literature, Lady's Book Extra, No. 2.

*5706. ULRIC; OR, THE VOICES. NY: Appleton, 1851.

*5722. THE THREE GERMANYS GLIMPSES INTO THEIR HISTORY. NY: The Author, <1889>.
2v.

Eugene Field
1850–1895

5725. TRIBUNE PRIMER. <Denver: Tribune Pub. Co.; n.d., 1881>.
Tribune Series, No. 2. Editions with additional material published in 1882 as *The Model Primer* (No. 5726), in 1900 as *Eugene Field's First Book* (No. 5785) & in 1901 as *The Complete Tribune Primer* (No. 5788); some additional *Clippings* were privately printed in 1909 (No. 5797). See also No. 5789 below.

5733. CULTURE'S GARLAND BEING MEMORANDA OF THE GRADUAL RISE OF LITERATURE, ART, MUSIC AND SOCIETY IN CHICAGO. Bos: Ticknor, 1887.
Cloth; and paper wrapper of *Ticknor's Paper Series*, No. 16, 20 Aug. 1887.

*5742. A LITTLE BOOK OF PROFITABLE TALES. NY: Scribner's Sons, 1890.
First edition privately printed for subscribers in 1889 (No. 5738). "The Symbol and the Saint," here collected, was printed separately in facsimile of Field's manuscript in 1886 (No. 5731).

5743. A LITTLE BOOK OF WESTERN VERSE. NY: Scribner's Sons, 1890.
First edition privately printed for subscribers in 1889 (No. 5739). "Dutch Lullaby" (otherwise "Wynken, Blynken, and Nod") & "Little Boy Blue" are both here collected; BAL notes several earlier printings of the latter poem in 1888–89 (Nos. 5735 & 5737).

*5744. ECHOES FROM THE SABINE FARM BEING CERTAIN HORATIAN LYRICS. New Rochelle: F. Wilson, 1891.
Translation, with Roswell M. Field. Revised edition published in 1893 (No. 5754). First trade edition published in 1895 (No. 5812).

*5750. WITH TRUMPET AND DRUM. NY: Scribner's Sons, 1892.
Limited edition; first trade edition also published in 1892 (No. 5808A).

EUGENE FIELD (cont.)

*5751. SECOND BOOK OF VERSE. Chi: M.E. Stone, 1892.
Limited edition; first trade edition published in 1893 (No. 5810A).

*5757. THE HOLY-CROSS AND OTHER TALES. Cambridge & Chi: Stone & Kimball, 1893.
Extended edition published in 1896 as *The Writings*, Vol. 5 (Nos. 5773 & 5815).

*5761. LOVE-SONGS OF CHILDHOOD. NY: Scribner's Sons, 1894.

*5769. LITTLE WILLIE. <n.p., 1895?>.
Dated at end of text: *October 19, 1895*. One of many unauthorized editions; for comment and another, possibly earlier, edition see BAL (No. 5768). First known authorized publication is in Slason Thompson's *Life of Eugene Field*, 1927, pp. 159–60.

*5771. THE LOVE AFFAIRS OF A BIBLIOMANIAC. NY: Scribner's Sons, 1896.

*5772. THE HOUSE AN EPISODE IN THE LIVES OF REUBEN BAKER, ASTRONO-MER, AND OF HIS WIFE ALICE. NY: Scribner's Sons, 1896.

 5774. SONGS AND OTHER VERSE. NY: Scribner's Sons, 1896.
The Writings in Prose and Verse, Vol. 9 (No. 5815). Also published separately later in 1896 (No. 5819).

 5775. SECOND BOOK OF TALES. NY: Scribner's Sons, 1896.
The Writings in Prose and Verse, Vol. 10 (No. 5815). Also published separately later in 1896 (No. 5818).

*5779. FLORENCE BARDSLEY'S STORY THE LIFE AND DEATH OF A REMARKABLE WOMAN. Chi: Way, 1897.

 5782. HOW ONE FRIAR MET THE DEVIL AND TWO PURSUED HIM. Chi: F.M. Morris, <1900>.
Also privately printed at the Cadmus Press of NY in 1900 as *The Temptation of the Friar Gonsol* (No. 5783); no sequence established.

 5784. SHARPS AND FLATS. NY: Scribner's Sons, 1900.
2v. "Collated by Slason Thompson."

*5789. A LITTLE BOOK OF TRIBUNE VERSE A NUMBER OF HITHERTO UNCOL-LECTED POEMS, GRAVE AND GAY. Denver: Tandy, Wheeler, 1901.
Ed. Joseph G. Brown.

*5790. THE STARS: A SLUMBER STORY. NY: New Amsterdam Book Co., 1901.

*5795. HOOSIER LYRICS. Chi: Donohue, <1905>.
Ed. Charles Walter Brown. Contains 31 new poems. *The Clink of the Ice and Other Poems Worth Reading* (No. 5794) & *John Smith U.S.A.* (No. 5796), also published by Donohue in 1905, contain poems reprinted from Field's earlier books, some under revised titles, with some additional poems first collected; *The Clink of the Ice* was first published in 1902–03 (No. 5792) by Ogilvie, Chicago.

 5798. THE POEMS OF EUGENE FIELD COMPLETE EDITION. NY: Scribner's Sons, 1910.

 5803. SOME LOVE LETTERS OF EUGENE FIELD. Buffalo NY, 1927.
"Privately printed."

James Thomas Fields
1817–1881

5903. ANNIVERSARY POEM, DELIVERED BEFORE THE MERCANTILE LIBRARY ASSOCIATION OF BOSTON, SEPTEMBER 13, 1838. Bos: Ticknor, 1838.
Published together with *An Address* by Edward Everett. Revised & collected in *Poems*, 1849, as "Commerce"; see next entry.

5926. POEMS. Bos: Ticknor, 1849.

5937. POEMS. Cambridge: Ptd by Metcalf, <n.d., 1854>.

5941. A FEW VERSES FOR A FEW FRIENDS. <Cambridge: Riverside PR; n.d., 1858>.
Anon.

5956. YESTERDAYS WITH AUTHORS. Bos: Osgood, 1872.
The chapters on Hawthorne & Dickens were revised & published separately in 1876 (Nos. 5965 & 5967).

5966. OLD ACQUAINTANCE. BARRY CORNWALL AND SOME OF HIS FRIENDS. Bos: Osgood, 1876.

5969. UNDERBRUSH. Bos: Osgood, 1877.
Extended edition published in 1881 (No. 5984). "A Conversational Pitcher," here collected, was also published separately in 1877 (No. 5970).

5976. VERSES FOR A FEW FRIENDS. Cambridge: University PR, <1879>.
"Privately printed."

*5983. BALLADS AND OTHER VERSES. Bos: Houghton, Mifflin, 1881.

5987. JAMES T. FIELDS BIOGRAPHICAL NOTES AND PERSONAL SKETCHES. Bos: Houghton, Mifflin, 1881.

John Fiske
1842–1901

*5993. TOBACCO AND ALCOHOL. NY: Leypoldt & Holt, 1869.

5997. MYTHS AND MYTH-MAKERS: OLD TALES AND SUPERSTITIONS INTERPRETED BY COMPARATIVE MYTHOLOGY. Bos: Osgood, 1873.

*5999. OUTLINES OF COSMIC PHILOSOPHY, BASED ON THE DOCTRINE OF EVOLUTION. Bos: Osgood, 1875.
2v.

6000. THE UNSEEN WORLD, AND OTHER ESSAYS. Bos: Osgood, 1876.

6002. DARWINISM AND OTHER ESSAYS. Lon & NY: Macmillan, 1879.
For first U.S. edition, revised & extended, see No. 6017.

6011. EXCURSIONS OF AN EVOLUTIONIST. Bos & NY: Houghton, Mifflin, 1884.

6013. THE DESTINY OF MAN VIEWED IN THE LIGHT OF HIS ORIGIN. Bos & NY: Houghton, Mifflin, 1884.
These sheets issued in the U.K. as *Man's Destiny Viewed in the Light of his Origin* (No. 6014).

JOHN FISKE (cont.)

*6016. AMERICAN POLITICAL IDEAS VIEWED FROM THE STANDPOINT OF UNI-
VERSAL HISTORY. NY: Harper & Bros., 1885.
"Three lectures delivered at the Royal Institution of Great Britain in May 1880."
Reprinted, with an additional address, in 1911 (No. 6073).

6017. DARWINISM, AND OTHER ESSAYS. Bos & NY: Houghton, Mifflin, 1885.

6018. THE IDEA OF GOD AS AFFECTED BY MODERN KNOWLEDGE. Bos & NY:
Houghton, Mifflin, 1886.

*6021. THE CRITICAL PERIOD OF AMERICAN HISTORY 1783–1789. Bos & NY:
Houghton, Mifflin, 1888.
Revised edition published in 1898 (No. 6048).

*6023. THE BEGINNINGS OF NEW ENGLAND. Bos & NY: Houghton, Mifflin,
1889.
Revised edition published in 1898 (No. 6050).

*6024. THE WAR OF INDEPENDENCE. Bos & NY: Houghton, Mifflin, 1889.
Riverside Library for Young People.

*6026. CIVIL GOVERNMENT IN THE UNITED STATES CONSIDERED WITH SOME
REFERENCE TO ITS ORIGINS. Bos & NY: Houghton, Mifflin, 1890.

6028. THE AMERICAN REVOLUTION. Bos & NY: Houghton, Mifflin, 1891.
2v. Revised edition published in 1896 (No. 6042).

*6031. THE DISCOVERY OF AMERICA WITH SOME ACCOUNT OF ANCIENT
AMERICA AND THE SPANISH CONQUEST. Bos & NY: Houghton,
Mifflin, 1892.
2v. or 2v. in four.

6037. EDWARD LIVINGSTON YOUMANS INTERPRETER OF SCIENCE FOR THE
PEOPLE. NY: Appleton, 1894.

6039. A HISTORY OF THE UNITED STATES FOR SCHOOLS. Bos, NY, &c.:
Houghton, Mifflin, 1894.
Later printings were revised & extended. The *First Five Chapters of a History of the
United States* published in April 1894 as *Riverside Literature Series*, No. 62, extra
(No. 6038).

6047. OLD VIRGINIA AND HER NEIGHBOURS. Bos & NY: Houghton,
Mifflin, 1897.
2v.

*6052. THROUGH NATURE TO GOD. Bos & NY: Houghton, Mifflin, 1899.

*6053. THE DUTCH AND QUAKER COLONIES IN AMERICA. Bos & NY:
Houghton, Mifflin, 1899.
2v.

6054. A CENTURY OF SCIENCE AND OTHER ESSAYS. Bos & NY: Houghton,
Mifflin, 1899.

*6055. THE MISSISSIPPI VALLEY IN THE CIVIL WAR. Bos & NY: Houghton,
Mifflin, 1900.

JOHN FISKE (cont.)

*6059. LIFE EVERLASTING. Bos & NY: Houghton, Mifflin, 1901.

 6062. COLONIZATION OF THE NEW WORLD. Phila & NY: Lea Bros., <1902>.
Ed. John Henry Wright. *History of the Two Americas*, Vol. 1 (also *A History of All Nations*, Vol. 21).

 6063. INDEPENDENCE OF THE NEW WORLD. Phila & NY: Lea Bros., <1902>.
Ed. John Henry Wright. *History of the Two Americas*, Vol. 2 (also *A History of All Nations*, Vol. 22).

 6064. MODERN DEVELOPMENT OF THE NEW WORLD. Phila & NY: Lea Bros., <1902>.
Ed. John Henry Wright. *History of the Two Americas*, Vol. 3 (also *A History of All Nations*, Vol. 23).

*6065. NEW FRANCE AND NEW ENGLAND. Bos & NY: Houghton, Mifflin, 1902.
Some copies issued in the *Collected Writings*, see No. 6067 below.

 6066. ESSAYS HISTORICAL AND LITERARY. NY: Macmillan, 1902.
2v.

*6067. COLLECTED WRITINGS. Bos & NY: Houghton, Mifflin, 1902.
24v.

 6072. UNPUBLISHED ORATIONS. Bos: The Bibliophile Soc'y, 1909.

 6074. THE LIFE AND LETTERS OF JOHN FISKE. Bos & NY: Houghton Mifflin, 1917.
2v. By John Spencer Clark.

 6077. THE PERSONAL LETTERS OF JOHN FISKE. Cedar Rapids IA: Torch PR, 1939.
"A small edition privately printed for members of the Bibliophile Society."

 6078. THE LETTERS OF JOHN FISKE. NY: Macmillan, 1940.
Ed. Ethel F. Fisk.

William Clyde Fitch
1865–1909

 6082. THE KNIGHTING OF THE TWINS, AND TEN OTHER TALES. Bos: Roberts Bros., <1891>.

 6083. PAMELA'S PRODIGY A LIVELY COMEDY. NY: G.M. Allen, 1893.

 6085. SOME CORRESPONDENCE AND SIX CONVERSATIONS. NY: Stone & Kimball, 1896.

 6086. THE SMART SET CORRESPONDENCE & CONVERSATIONS. Chi & NY: Stone, 1897.

 6087. NATHAN HALE A PLAY. NY: Russell, 1899.

 6088. BARBARA FRIETCHIE, THE FREDERICK GIRL. A PLAY. NY: Life Pub. Co., 1900.

CLYDE FITCH (cont.)

6089. CAPTAIN JINKS OF THE HORSE MARINES A FANTASTIC COMEDY. NY: Doubleday, Page, 1902.

6090. THE GIRL WITH THE GREEN EYES A PLAY. NY: Macmillan, 1905.

6091. THE CLIMBERS A PLAY. NY: Macmillan, 1906.

6092. THE STUBBORNNESS OF GERALDINE A PLAY. NY: Macmillan, 1906.

6093. HER OWN WAY A PLAY. NY: Macmillan, 1907.

6094. THE TRUTH A PLAY. NY: Macmillan, 1907.

6095. THE COWBOY AND THE LADY. NY: Kauser, <1908>.
Possibly prepared for copyright purposes only. Later published by French, New York.

6096. THE FRISKY MRS. JOHNSON. NY: Kauser, <1908>.
Possibly prepared for copyright purposes only.

6097. THE MOTH AND THE FLAME. NY: Kauser, <1908>.
Possibly prepared for copyright purposes only.

*6098. BEAU BRUMMEL A PLAY. NY: Lane, 1908.
"Written for Richard Mansfield."

6099. A WAVE OF LIFE A NOVEL. NY: Kennerley, <1891, i.e. 1909>.
Originally published as the Feb. 1891 issue of *Lippincott's Monthly Magazine* (No. 6081).

6103. PLAYS. Bos: Little, Brown, 1915.
4v. *Memorial Edition.* Ed. Montrose J. Moses & Virginia Gerson. Sheets of 3 of these plays were issued separately (Nos. 6100, 6101 & 6102), possibly for copyright purposes only. Similarly, "Her Great Match," first published in *Representative American Plays*, ed. Arthur Hobson Quinn, 1917 (No. 6105), was also issued separately for copyright purposes (No. 6104).

6106. CLYDE FITCH AND HIS LETTERS. Bos: Little, Brown, 1924.
By Montrose J. Moses & Virginia Gerson.

Timothy Flint
1780–1840

6113. RECOLLECTIONS OF THE LAST TEN YEARS, PASSED IN OCCASIONAL RESIDENCES AND JOURNEYINGS IN THE VALLEY OF THE MISSISSIPPI. Bos: Cummings, Hilliard, 1826.
"In a series of letters to the Rev. James Flint."

6114. FRANCIS BERRIAN, OR THE MEXICAN PATRIOT. Bos: Cummings, Hilliard, 1826.
2v. Anon.

6115. THE LIFE AND ADVENTURES OF ARTHUR CLENNING. Phila: Towar & Hogan, 1828.
2v. Anon.

TIMOTHY FLINT (cont.)

6117. A CONDENSED GEOGRAPHY AND HISTORY OF THE WESTERN STATES, OR THE MISSISSIPPI VALLEY. Cincinnati: E.H. Flint, 1828.
2v. Vol. 2 issued with imprint of W.M. Farnsworth, Ptr. For extended edition see No. 6125 below.

6118. GEORGE MASON, THE YOUNG BACKWOODSMAN. Bos: Hilliard, Gray, et al, 1829.
Anon. Abridged & published in the U.K. in 1833 as *Don't Give up the Ship* (No. 6133).

*6120. THE LOST CHILD. Bos: Carter & Hendee; Putnam & Hunt, 1830.
Reprinted in 1847 as *Little Henry* (No. 6138).

6121. THE SHOSHONEE VALLEY; A ROMANCE. Cincinnati: E.H. Flint, 1830.
2v. Anon.

6122. THE PERSONAL NARRATIVE OF JAMES O. PATTIE, OF KENTUCKY. Cincinnati: J.H. Wood, 1831.
These sheets reissued in 1833 with imprint of E.H. Flint, Cincinnati. Abridged & published in 1847 as *The Hunters of Kentucky* (No. 6137).

6125. THE HISTORY AND GEOGRAPHY OF THE MISSISSIPPI VALLEY ... SECOND EDITION. Cincinnati: Flint & Lincoln, 1832.
2v. Vol. 2 has title *The United States and the Other Divisions of the American Continent.*

6127. LECTURES UPON NATURAL HISTORY, GEOLOGY, CHEMISTRY, THE APPLICATION OF STEAM, AND INTERESTING DISCOVERIES IN THE ARTS. Bos: Lilly, Wait, et al, 1833.

6128. INDIAN WARS OF THE WEST. Cincinnati: E.H. Flint, 1833.

*6130. BIOGRAPHICAL MEMOIR OF DANIEL BOONE, THE FIRST SETTLER OF KENTUCKY. Cincinnati: N. & G. Guilford, 1833.
Reprinted in 1847 as *The First White Man of the West* (No. 6136) & in 1868 as *The Life and Adventures of Daniel Boone* (No. 6139).

6135. JOURNAL OF THE REV. TIMOTHY FLINT, FROM THE RED RIVER, TO THE OUACHITTA OR WASHITA, IN LOUISIANA, IN 1835. <n.p., n.d.; Phila, 1836?>.
"From Waldie's Select Circulating Library."

Paul Leicester Ford
1865–1902

Note: Ford's privately printed historical & genealogical studies are here omitted, as are his editions & collections of the writings of historical figures.

6206. THE HONORABLE PETER STIRLING AND WHAT PEOPLE THOUGHT OF HIM. NY: Holt, 1894.

6210. THE TRUE GEORGE WASHINGTON. Phila: Lippincott, 1896.
Reprinted in 1926 as *George Washington* (No. 6239).

PAUL LEICESTER FORD (cont.)

*6213. THE GREAT K. & A. ROBBERY. NY: Dodd Mead, 1897.
Originally published as the Aug. 1896 issue of *Lippincott's Monthly Magazine* (No. 6209).

 6215. THE STORY OF AN UNTOLD LOVE. Bos & NY: Houghton, Mifflin, 1897.

 6220. TATTLE-TALES OF CUPID. NY: Dodd, Mead, 1898.
Two versions of "The Best Laid Plans," here collected, were printed privately in 1889 (Nos. 6174 & 6175).

 6221. WASHINGTON AND THE THEATRE. NY: The Dunlap Soc'y, 1899.
Publications of the Dunlap Society, New Series, No. 8.

 6223. THE MANY-SIDED FRANKLIN. NY: Century Co., 1899.

*6224. JANICE MEREDITH A STORY OF THE AMERICAN REVOLUTION. NY: Dodd, Mead, 1899.
A partial printing was also produced in 1899 for copyright purposes (No. 6222).

 6226. WANTED A MATCH MAKER. NY: Dodd Mead, 1900.

 6229. A HOUSE PARTY AN ACCOUNT OF THE STORIES TOLD AT A GATHERING OF FAMOUS AMERICAN AUTHORS. Bos: Small, Maynard, 1901.
Edited by Ford, who with 11 others contributed a chapter. A copyright printing of Ford's chapter, "A Family Tradition," was also produced in 1901 (No. 6227).

*6232. WANTED—A CHAPERON. NY: Dodd Mead, 1902.

 6233. A CHECKED LOVE AFFAIR AND "THE CORTELYOU FEUD." NY: Dodd Mead, 1903.

 6235. LOVE FINDS THE WAY. NY: Dodd Mead, 1904.

Hannah Webster Foster
1759–1840

 6241. THE COQUETTE; OR, THE HISTORY OF ELIZA WHARTON; A NOVEL. By a Lady of Massachusetts. Bos: Larkin, 1797.

 6242. THE BOARDING SCHOOL; OR, LESSONS OF A PRECEPTRESS TO HER PUPILS. By a Lady of Massachusetts. Bos: Thomas & Andrews, 1798.

John William Fox, Jr.
1862–1919

*6243. A CUMBERLAND VENDETTA AND OTHER STORIES. NY: Harper & Bros., 1896.

 6244. "HELL FER SARTAIN" AND OTHER STORIES. NY: Harper & Bros., 1897.

 6245. THE KENTUCKIANS A NOVEL. NY & Lon: Harper & Bros., 1898.

 6246. A MOUNTAIN EUROPA. NY & Lon: Harper & Bros., 1899.

 6248. CRITTENDEN A KENTUCKY STORY OF LOVE AND WAR. NY: Scribner's Sons, 1900.

JOHN WILLIAM FOX, JR. (CONT.)
6249. BLUE-GRASS AND RHODODENDRON OUT-DOORS IN OLD KENTUCKY. NY: Scribner's Sons, 1901.
*6250. THE LITTLE SHEPHERD OF KINGDOM COME. NY: Scribner's Sons, 1903.
*6252. CHRISTMAS EVE ON LONESOME AND OTHER STORIES. NY: Scribner's Sons, 1904.
6254. FOLLOWING THE SUN-FLAG A VAIN PURSUIT THROUGH MANCHURIA. NY: Scribner's Sons, 1905.
6255. A KNIGHT OF THE CUMBERLAND. NY: Scribner's Sons, 1906.
*6256. THE TRAIL OF THE LONESOME PINE. NY: Scribner's Sons, 1908.
*6259. THE HEART OF THE HILLS. NY: Scribner's Sons, 1913.
6262. IN HAPPY VALLEY. NY: Scribner's Sons, 1917.
6263. ERSKINE DALE PIONEER. NY: Scribner's Sons, 1920.

Harold Frederic
1856–1898

*6266. SETH'S BROTHER'S WIFE A STUDY OF LIFE IN THE GREATER NEW YORK. NY: Scribner's Sons, 1887.
6267. THE LAWTON GIRL. Lon: Chatto & Windus, 1890.
*6268. THE LAWTON GIRL. NY: Scribner's Sons, 1890.
6269. IN THE VALLEY. NY: Scribner's Sons, 1890.
6270. THE YOUNG EMPEROR WILLIAM II OF GERMANY. Lon: Unwin, 1891.
Revised "second edition" published in 1892 (No. 6272).
6271. THE YOUNG EMPEROR WILLIAM II OF GERMANY. NY: Putnam's Sons, 1891.
Revised "second edition" published in 1892 (No. 6277).
6273. THE NEW EXODUS A STUDY OF ISRAEL IN RUSSIA. Lon: Heinemann, 1892.
*6274. THE RETURN OF THE O'MAHONY A NOVEL. NY: Bonner's Sons, 1892.
Issued in both *The Ledger Library*, No. 71, 15 Oct. 1892, & *The Choice Series*, No. 71, 15 Oct. 1892.
6276. THE NEW EXODUS A STUDY OF ISRAEL IN RUSSIA. NY: Putnam's Sons, 1892.
6278. THE COPPERHEAD. NY: Scribner's Sons, 1893.
Contains the title-story only.
6280. THE COPPERHEAD AND OTHER STORIES OF THE NORTH DURING THE AMERICAN WAR. Lon: Heinemann, 1894.
*6281. MARSENA AND OTHER STORIES OF THE WARTIME. NY: Scribner's Sons, 1894.
6282. THE DAMNATION OF THERON WARE. Chi: Stone & Kimball, 1896.
Also published in the U.K. in 1896 as *Illumination* (No. 6283).

HAROLD FREDERIC (cont.)

6284.   MRS ALBERT GRUNDY OBSERVATIONS IN PHILISTIA. Lon: Lane;
        NY: Merriam, 1896.
        169pp.

*6285. MRS ALBERT GRUNDY OBSERVATIONS IN PHILISTIA. Lon: Lane;
        NY: Merriam, 1896.
        263pp. First U.S. edition.

6286.   MARCH HARES. By George Forth. Lon: Lane, 1896.
        Lane's Library, No. 1.

6290.   MARCH HARES. NY: Appleton, 1896.
        A copyright printing, under the pseudonym George Forth, was also produced in
        1896 (No. 6287).

6292.   THE DESERTER AND OTHER STORIES A BOOK OF TWO WARS. Bos:
        Lothrop, <1898>.

6293.   GLORIA MUNDI A NOVEL. Chi & NY: Stone, 1898.
        Published simultaneously (?) in the U.K. Abridged reprint published in the U.K.
        in 1913 as *Pomps and Vanities* (No. 6295).

6294.   THE MARKET-PLACE. NY: Stokes, <1899>.

Mary Eleanor Wilkins Freeman
1852–1930

6302.   DECORATIVE PLAQUES. Bos: Lothrop, <1883>.

6303.   GOODY TWO-SHOES AND OTHER FAMOUS NURSERY TALES. Bos:
        Lothrop, <1883>.
        With Clara Doty Bates.

6305.   THE COW WITH GOLDEN HORNS AND OTHER STORIES. Bos: Lothrop,
        <1884, i.e. *ca.* 1886>.

6313.   THE ADVENTURES OF ANN STORIES OF COLONIAL TIMES. Bos:
        Lothrop, <1886>.

6317.   A HUMBLE ROMANCE AND OTHER STORIES. NY & Lon: Harper &
        Bros., 1887.

6325.   A NEW ENGLAND NUN AND OTHER STORIES. NY: Harper & Bros.,
        1891.

6327.   THE POT OF GOLD AND OTHER STORIES. Bos: Lothrop, <1892>.

6329.   YOUNG LUCRETIA AND OTHER STORIES. NY: Harper & Bros., 1892.

6332.   JANE FIELD A NOVEL. Lon: Osgood, McIlvaine 1892.

6333.   JANE FIELD A NOVEL. NY: Harper & Bros., 1893.

6334.   GILES COREY, YEOMAN A PLAY. NY: Harper & Bros., 1893.

*6337. PEMBROKE A NOVEL. NY: Harper & Bros., 1894.

*6340. COMFORT PEASE AND HER GOLD RING. NY, Chi, &c.: Revell, 1895.
        The Renaissance Booklets series.

MARY E. WILKINS FREEMAN (cont.)
*6344.   MADELON A NOVEL. NY: Harper & Bros., 1896.
 6346.   ONCE UPON A TIME AND OTHER CHILD-VERSES. Bos: Lothrop, <1897>.
 6347.   JEROME, A POOR MAN A NOVEL. NY & Lon: Harper & Bros., 1897.
 6350.   SILENCE AND OTHER STORIES. NY & Lon: Harper & Bros., 1898.
*6351.   THE PEOPLE OF OUR NEIGHBORHOOD. Phila: Curtis, <1898>.
         Ladies' Home Journal Library of Fiction.
*6353.   THE JAMESONS. NY: Doubleday & McClure, 1899.
*6361.   THE LOVE OF PARSON LORD AND OTHER STORIES. NY & Lon: Harper
         & Bros., 1900.
*6362.   THE HEART'S HIGHWAY A ROMANCE OF VIRGINIA IN THE SEVEN-
         TEENTH CENTURY. NY: Doubleday, Page, 1900.
*6365.   UNDERSTUDIES. NY & Lon: Harper & Bros., 1901.
*6366.   THE PORTION OF LABOR. NY & Lon: Harper & Bros., 1901.
 6370.   SIX TREES. NY & Lon: Harper & Bros., 1903.
 6371.   THE WIND IN THE ROSE-BUSH AND OTHER STORIES OF THE SUPER-
         NATURAL. NY: Doubleday, Page, 1903.
*6372.   THE GIVERS. NY & Lon: Harper & Bros., 1904.
 6377.   THE DEBTOR A NOVEL. NY & Lon: Harper & Bros., 1905.
*6380.   "DOC." GORDON. NY & Lon: The Authors & Newspapers Assn, 1906.
*6383.   BY THE LIGHT OF THE SOUL A NOVEL. NY & Lon: Harper & Bros.,
         1907.
 6386.   THE FAIR LAVINIA AND OTHERS. NY & Lon: Harper & Bros., 1907.
 6388.   THE SHOULDERS OF ATLAS A NOVEL. NY & Lon: Harper & Bros.,
         1908.
 6391.   THE WINNING LADY AND OTHERS. NY & Lon: Harper & Bros., 1909.
 6392.   THE GREEN DOOR. NY: Moffat, Yard, 1910.
 6395.   THE BUTTERFLY HOUSE. NY: Dodd, Mead, 1912.
 6396.   THE YATES PRIDE A ROMANCE. NY & Lon: Harper & Bros., 1912.
 6397.   THE COPY-CAT & OTHER STORIES. NY & Lon: Harper & Bros., 1914.
 6400.   AN ALABASTER BOX. NY & Lon: Appleton, 1917.
         With Florence Morse Kingsley.
 6403.   EDGEWATER PEOPLE. NY & Lon: Harper & Bros., <1918>.
 6406.   THE BEST STORIES OF MARY E. WILKINS. NY & Lon: Harper & Bros.,
         1927.
         Ed. Henry Wysham Lanier. Reprint save for "The Gospel According to Joan."

Philip Morin Freneau
1752–1832

6412. A POEM, ON THE RISING GLORY OF AMERICA. Phila, 1772.
Anon. With H.H. Brackenridge, see No. 1292 above.

6413. THE AMERICAN VILLAGE, A POEM TO WHICH ARE ADDED, SEVERAL OTHER ORIGINAL PIECES IN VERSE. NY: Ptd by Inslee & Car, 1772.

*6415. AMERICAN LIBERTY, A POEM. NY: Ptd by J. Anderson, 1775.
Anon.

*6417. A VOYAGE TO BOSTON. A POEM. NY: Ptd by J. Anderson, <n.d., 1775>.
Anon.

6418. GENERAL GAGE'S CONFESSION. <n.p., NY: H. Gaine>, 1775.
Anon.

6422. THE BRITISH PRISON-SHIP. A POEM, IN FOUR CANTOES. Phila: Ptd by F. Bailey, 1781.
Anon.

6435. THE POEMS OF PHILIP FRENEAU WRITTEN CHIEFLY DURING THE LATE WAR. Phila: Ptd by F. Bailey, 1786.
Reprinted in the U.K. in 1861 (No. 6455).

6437. A JOURNEY FROM PHILADELPHIA TO NEW-YORK, BY WAY OF BURLINGTON AND SOUTH-AMBOY. By Robert Slender, Stocking Weaver. Phila: Ptd by F. Bailey, 1787.
Revised edition published in 1809 as *A Laughable Poem* (No. 6453).

*6440. THE MISCELLANEOUS WORKS OF MR. PHILIP FRENEAU CONTAINING HIS ESSAYS, AND ADDITIONAL POEMS. Phila: Ptd by F. Bailey, 1788.

6443. THE VILLAGE MERCHANT: A POEM. TO WHICH IS ADDED THE COUNTRY PRINTER. Phila: Ptd by Hoff & Derrick, 1794.
Anon.

6445. POEMS WRITTEN BETWEEN THE YEARS 1768 & 1794. Monmouth NJ: The Author, 1795.
"A new edition, revised and corrected."

*6450. LETTERS ON VARIOUS INTERESTING AND IMPORTANT SUBJECTS; MANY OF WHICH HAVE APPEARED IN THE AURORA. By Robert Slender. Phila: The Author, 1799.
"Corrected and much enlarged."

*6452. POEMS WRITTEN AND PUBLISHED DURING THE AMERICAN REVOLUTIONARY WAR. Phila: L.R. Bailey, 1809.
2v. "The third edition."

6454. A COLLECTION OF POEMS, ON AMERICAN AFFAIRS, AND A VARIETY OF OTHER SUBJECTS, CHIEFLY MORAL AND POLITICAL. NY: D. Longworth, 1815.
2v. "Written between the year 1797 and the present time."

PHILIP FRENEAU (cont.)
  6457. SOME ACCOUNT OF THE CAPTURE OF THE SHIP "AURORA." NY: Mansfield & Wessels, <1899>.
        Ed. Jay Milles.

  6458. THE POEMS OF PHILIP FRENEAU. Princeton: U Library, 1902–07.
        3v. Ed. Fred Lewis Pattee for the Princeton Historical Association.

  6460. THE LAST POEMS OF PHILIP FRENEAU. New Brunswick: Rutgers U PR, 1945.
        Ed. Lewis Leary.

  6461. THE PROSE OF PHILIP FRENEAU. New Brunswick: Scarecrow PR, 1955.
        Ed. Philip M. Marsh.

Henry Blake Fuller
1857–1929

  6462. THE CHEVALIER OF PENSIERI-VANI TOGETHER WITH FREQUENT REFERENCES TO THE PROREGE OF ARCOPIA. By Stanton Page. Bos: Cupples, <1890>.
        Revised edition published in 1892 (No. 6463).

  6464. THE CHATELAINE OF LA TRINITÉ. NY: Century Co., 1892.
 *6465. THE CLIFF-DWELLERS A NOVEL. NY: Harper & Bros., 1893.
 *6466. WITH THE PROCESSION A NOVEL. NY: Harper & Bros., 1895.
  6467. THE PUPPET-BOOTH TWELVE PLAYS. NY: Century Co., 1896.
  6468. FROM THE OTHER SIDE STORIES OF TRANSATLANTIC TRAVEL. Bos & NY: Houghton, Mifflin, 1898.
  6469. THE NEW FLAG SATIRES. <n.p., Chi?, 1899>.
  6470. THE LAST REFUGE A SICILIAN ROMANCE. Bos & NY: Houghton, Mifflin, 1900.
  6471. UNDER THE SKYLIGHTS. NY: Appleton, 1901.
  6473. WALDO TRENCH AND OTHERS STORIES OF AMERICANS IN ITALY. NY: Scribner's Sons, 1908.
  6475. LINES LONG AND SHORT BIOGRAPHICAL SKETCHES IN VARIOUS RHYTHMS. Bos & NY: Houghton Mifflin, 1917.
  6476. ON THE STAIRS. Bos & NY: Houghton Mifflin, 1918.
  6478. BERTRAM COPE'S YEAR A NOVEL. Chi: Seymour, 1919.
 *6484. GARDENS OF THIS WORLD. NY: Knopf, 1929.
  6485. NOT ON THE SCREEN. NY & Lon: Knopf, 1930.

Sarah Margaret Fuller
(Marchesa d'Ossoli)
1810–1850

6490. CONVERSATIONS WITH GOETHE IN THE LAST YEARS OF HIS LIFE. Bos: Hilliard, Gray, 1839.
From the German of Eckermann. *Specimens of Foreign Standard Literature*, ed. George Ripley, Vol. 4.

6491. GÜNDERODE. Bos: Peabody, 1842.
From the German of Bettina Brentano von Arnim & Karoline von Günderode.

6492. SUMMER ON THE LAKES, IN 1843. Bos: Little & Brown, 1844.

6493. WOMAN IN THE NINETEENTH CENTURY. NY: Greeley & McElrath, 1845.
For extended edition see No. 6503.

*6496. PAPERS ON LITERATURE AND ART. NY: Wiley & Putnam, 1846.
2v. *Library of American Books*, Nos. 19–20. Reprinted in 1852 as *Literature and Art* (No. 6502) & with 1 additional piece in 1860 as *Art, Literature, and the Drama* as part of Fuller's *Collected Works*, see No. 6506 below.

*6500. MEMOIRS OF MARGARET FULLER OSSOLI. Bos: Phillips, Sampson, 1852.
2v. Ed. Ralph Waldo Emerson, James Freeman Clarke & W.H. Channing. Also published simultaneously (?) in the U.K. (No. 6501).

6503. WOMAN IN THE NINETEENTH CENTURY, AND KINDRED PAPERS RELATING TO THE SPHERE, CONDITION AND DUTIES, OF WOMAN. Bos: Jewett, 1855.
Ed. Arthur B. Fuller. Extended editions published as part of Fuller's *Collected Works* in 1860, see No. 6506 below, & 1869 (No. 6507).

*6504. AT HOME AND ABROAD, OR THINGS AND THOUGHTS IN AMERICA AND EUROPE. Bos: Crosby, Nichols, 1856.
Ed. Arthur B. Fuller.

6505. LIFE WITHOUT AND LIFE WITHIN; OR, REVIEWS, NARRATIVES, ESSAYS, AND POEMS. Bos: Brown, Taggard & Chase, 1860.
Ed. Arthur B. Fuller. Part of *Collected Works*, see next entry.

6506. COLLECTED WORKS. Bos: Brown, Taggard & Chase, 1860.
6v. Ed. Arthur B. Fuller. The volumes, several of which collect new pieces, are not identified as part of a set although issued as such. The set reprinted with 1 additional piece in 1869 (No. 6507).

6511. LOVE-LETTERS OF MARGARET FULLER 1845–1846. NY: Appleton, 1903.

William Davis Gallagher
1808–1894

6513. ERATO, NUMBER I. Cincinnati: Drake, 1835.

6514. ERATO, NUMBER II. Cincinnati: Flash, 1835.
For comment on reissue see next entry.

6515. ERATO, NUMBER III. Cincinnati: Flash, 1837.
Sheets of Nos. 2 & 3 reissued in 1837 as *Poems* (No. 6516).

6517. SELECTIONS FROM THE POETICAL LITERATURE OF THE WEST. Cincinnati: U.P. James, 1841.
Edited, with contributions, by Gallagher.

6523. FACTS AND CONDITIONS OF PROGRESS IN THE NORTH-WEST. Cincinnati: Derby, 1850.
Annual discourse before the Historical and Philosophical Society of Ohio, 8 April 1850.

6529. MIAMI WOODS A GOLDEN WEDDING AND OTHER POEMS. Cincinnati: Clarke, 1881.

Richard Watson Gilder
1844–1909

6536. THE NEW DAY A POEM IN SONGS AND SONNETS. NY: Scribner, Armstrong, 1876.
Reprinted with 1 additional sonnet in 1880 (No.6540).

6538. THE POET AND HIS MASTER AND OTHER POEMS. NY: Scribner's Sons, 1878.

6543. LYRICS AND OTHER POEMS. NY: Scribner's Sons, 1885.
Extended "second edition" published in 1887 (No. 6550). Further extended edition published in 1894 (No. 6570) & a slightly revised "fourth edition" in 1900 (No. 6589), both as *Five Books of Song*.

6549. THE CELESTIAL PASSION. NY: Century Co., <1887>.

*6559. TWO WORLDS AND OTHER POEMS. NY: Century Co., 1891.

6565. THE GREAT REMEMBRANCE AND OTHER POEMS. NY: Century Co., 1893.

6588. IN PALESTINE AND OTHER POEMS. NY: Century Co., <1898>.

6593. POEMS AND INSCRIPTIONS. NY: Century Co., 1901.
"Inscriptions for the Pan-American Exposition at Buffalo 1901," here collected, also printed separately in 1901 (?) (No. 6591).

6605. "IN THE HEIGHTS." NY: Century Co., 1905.

6611. A BOOK OF MUSIC. NY: Century Co., 1906.
Contains 9 new poems.

6615. THE FIRE DIVINE. NY: Century Co., 1907.

RICHARD WATSON GILDER (cont.)

*6621. THE POEMS OF RICHARD WATSON GILDER. Bos & NY: Houghton
Mifflin, 1908.

 6624. LINCOLN THE LEADER AND LINCOLN'S GENIUS FOR EXPRESSION.
Bos & NY: Houghton Mifflin, 1909.

 6631. GROVER CLEVELAND: A RECORD OF FRIENDSHIP. NY: Century Co.,
1910.

*6636. LETTERS OF RICHARD WATSON GILDER. Bos & NY: Houghton Mifflin,
1916.
Ed. Rosamond Gilder.

Rufus Wilmot Griswold
1815–1857

Note: In addition to the major anthologies listed here, Griswold was
responsible for compiling & editing numerous other collections; for
full details see BAL.

*6643. GEMS FROM AMERICAN FEMALE POETS, WITH BRIEF BIOGRAPHICAL
NOTICES. Phila: Hooker, 1842.

*6644. THE POETS AND POETRY OF AMERICA WITH AN HISTORICAL INTRO-
DUCTION. Phila: Carey & Hart, 1842.
Frequently reprinted, often with alterations or revisions, 1842–73.

*6676. THE PROSE WRITERS OF AMERICA. Phila: Carey & Hart, 1847.
For full publication information see BAL (No. 3158). Revised editions published
in 1847 & 1851.

 6677. WASHINGTON AND THE GENERALS OF THE AMERICAN REVOLUTION.
Phila: Carey & Hart, 1847.
2v. Anon. With W.G. Simms and others. Corrected edition published in 1848
(No. 6679).

*6681. THE FEMALE POETS OF AMERICA. Phila: Carey & Hart, 1849.
In large part extracted from No. 6644 above. Slightly revised "second edition"
also published in 1849; revised & extended by R.H. Stoddard in 1874 (No. 19113).

 6701. THE REPUBLICAN COURT OR AMERICAN SOCIETY IN THE DAYS OF
WASHINGTON. NY & Lon: Appleton, 1855.
Revised & extended editions published in 1856 (No. 6705) & 1859 (No. 6709).

 6707. WASHINGTON. A BIOGRAPHY. NY: Virtue, Emmins, 1856–60.
3v. in 45 parts. Begun by Griswold, who completed only the first 200 pp., but
written in large part by Benson J. Lossing.

 6712. PASSAGES FROM THE CORRESPONDENCE AND OTHER PAPERS OF
RUFUS W. GRISWOLD. Cambridge: W.M. Griswold, 1898.
Ed. William M. Griswold.

Louise Imogen Guiney
1861–1920

6715. SONGS AT THE START. Bos: Cupples, Upham, 1884.
Sheets reissued in 1895 by Houghton, Mifflin, Boston.

6716. GOOSE-QUILL PAPERS. Bos: Roberts Bros., 1885.

6719. THE WHITE SAIL AND OTHER POEMS. Bos: Ticknor, <1887>.

6721. BROWNIES AND BOGLES. Bos: Lothrop, <1888>.

*6726. "MONSIEUR HENRI" A FOOT-NOTE TO FRENCH HISTORY. NY: Harper & Bros., 1892.

6727. A ROADSIDE HARP A BOOK OF VERSES. Bos & NY: Houghton Mifflin, 1893.

6728. A LITTLE ENGLISH GALLERY. NY: Harper & Bros., 1894.

*6729. THREE HEROINES OF NEW ENGLAND ROMANCE. Bos: Little Brown, 1894.
With Harriet Prescott Spofford & Alice Brown, see No. 18512 below.

6733. NINE SONNETS WRITTEN AT OXFORD. <Cambridge>, 1895.

*6737. LOVERS' SAINT RUTH'S AND THREE OTHER TALES. Bos: Copeland & Day, 1895.

6741. JAMES CLARENCE MANGAN HIS SELECTED POEMS. Bos: Lamson Wolffe, 1897.
Edited by Guiney, who contributed the "Study" of Mangan, pp. 3–112.

6742. PATRINS TO WHICH IS ADDED AN INQUIRENDO INTO THE WIT ... OF ... KING CHARLES THE SECOND. Bos: Copeland & Day, 1897.

6744. "ENGLAND AND YESTERDAY" A BOOK OF SHORT POEMS. Lon: Richards, 1898.

*6749. THE MARTYRS' IDYL AND SHORTER POEMS. Bos & NY: Houghton, Mifflin, 1899.

6754. ROBERT EMMET A SURVEY OF HIS REBELLION AND OF HIS ROMANCE. Lon: Nutt, 1904.

6760. BLESSED EDMUND CAMPION. Lon: MacDonald & Evans, 1908.

6761. BLESSED EDMUND CAMPION. NY, Cincinnati, &c.: Benziger Bros., 1908.

6762. HAPPY ENDING ... COLLECTED LYRICS. Bos & NY: Houghton Mifflin, 1909.
Revised & extended edition published in 1927 (No. 6770).

6769. LETTERS. NY & Lon: Harper & Bros., 1926.
2v. Ed. Grace Guiney.

Sarah Josepha Buell Hale
1788–1879

6774.   THE GENIUS OF OBLIVION; AND OTHER ORIGINAL POEMS. By a Lady of New-Hampshire. Concord <NH>: J.B. Moore, 1823.

6776.   NORTHWOOD; A TALE OF NEW ENGLAND. Bos: Bowles & Dearborn, 1827.
2v. Revised (?) & published in 1852 as *Northwood; or, Life North and South* (No. 6879).

6784.   SKETCHES OF AMERICAN CHARACTER. Bos: Putnam & Hunt, 1829.

6788.   CONVERSATIONS ON THE BURMAN MISSION. By a Lady of New Hampshire. Bos: Mass. Sabbath School Union, 1830.

6789.   POEMS FOR OUR CHILDREN ... PART FIRST. Bos: Marsh, Capen, & Lyon, 1830.
All issued. "Mary's Lamb" (otherwise "Mary Had a Little Lamb") here collected.

*6792.   FLORA'S INTERPRETER: OR, THE AMERICAN BOOK OF FLOWERS AND SENTIMENTS. Bos: Marsh, Capen & Lyon, 1832.
Edited by Hale. Frequently reprinted, often with alterations & revisions, 1832–60. Adapted & published in the U.K. in 1836 as *The Book of Flowers* (No. 6807).

6796.   THE SCHOOL SONG BOOK. Bos: Allen & Ticknor, 1834.
Reprinted in 1841 as *My Little Song Book* (No. 6833).

6802.   TRAITS OF AMERICAN LIFE. Phila: Carey & Hart, 1835.

6812.   THE LADIES' WREATH; A SELECTION FROM THE FEMALE POETIC WRITERS OF ENGLAND AND AMERICA. Bos: Marsh, Capen & Lyon, 1837.
Edited, with notes & contributions, by Hale. The "second edition" published in 1839 (No. 6823) contains 2 additional poems by Hale.

6849.   KEEPING HOUSE AND HOUSE KEEPING. A STORY OF DOMESTIC LIFE. NY: Harper & Bros., 1845.

6851.   ALICE RAY: A ROMANCE IN RHYME. Phila, 1845.

6852.   "BOARDING OUT." A TALE OF DOMESTIC LIFE. NY: Harper & Bros., 1846.
Anon.

6860.   THREE HOURS; OR, THE VIGIL OF LOVE: AND OTHER POEMS. Phila: Carey & Hart, 1848.

6861.   HARRY GUY, THE WIDOW'S SON. A STORY OF THE SEA. Bos: Mussey, 1848.

6880.   WOMAN'S RECORD; OR, SKETCHES OF ALL DISTINGUISHED WOMEN FROM "THE BEGINNING" TILL A.D. 1850. NY: Harper & Bros., 1853.
Revised editions published in 1855 (No. 6886) & 1870 (No. 6900); reprinted in 1876 as *Biography of Distinguished Women* (No. 6903).

6882.   LIBERIA; OR, MR. PEYTON'S EXPERIMENTS. NY: Harper & Bros., 1853.

*6897.   MANNERS; OR, HAPPY HOMES AND GOOD SOCIETY ALL THE YEAR ROUND. Bos: Tilton, 1868.

SARAH J. HALE (cont.)
6901. LOVE; OR WOMAN'S DESTINY… WITH OTHER POEMS. Phila: Ashmead, 1870.

Baynard Rush Hall
1798–1863

6908. THE NEW PURCHASE: OR, SEVEN AND A HALF YEARS IN THE FAR WEST. By Robert Carlton, Esq. NY: Appleton, 1843.
2v. Revised "second edition" published in 1855 (No. 6913).

6909. SOMETHING FOR EVERYBODY: GLEANED IN THE OLD PURCHASE, FROM FIELDS OFTEN REAPED. By Robert Carlton, Esq. NY: Appleton, 1846.

6910. TEACHING, A SCIENCE: THE TEACHER AN ARTIST. NY: Baker & Scribner, 1848.

6912. FRANK FREEMAN'S BARBER SHOP; A TALE. NY: Scribner, 1852.

James Hall
1793–1868

6919. LETTERS FROM THE WEST; CONTAINING SKETCHES OF SCENERY, MANNERS, AND CUSTOMS. Lon: Colburn, 1828.

6920. THE WESTERN SOUVENIR, A CHRISTMAS AND NEW YEAR'S GIFT FOR 1829. Cincinnati: N. & G. Guilford, <n.d.; 1828>.
Edited & largely written by Hall.

6927. LEGENDS OF THE WEST. Phila: H. Hall, 1832.
Revised edition published in 1853 (No. 6954).

6928. THE SOLDIER'S BRIDE AND OTHER TALES. Phila: Key & Biddle, 1833.

6929. THE HARPE'S HEAD; A LEGEND OF KENTUCKY. Phila: Key & Biddle, 1833.
Published in the U.K. in 1834 as *Kentucky. A Tale* (No. 6936).

*6934. HISTORY OF THE INDIAN TRIBES OF NORTH AMERICA. Phila, 1836–44.
3v. in 20 parts. With Thomas L. M'Kenney. Published by 4 successive publishers: Biddle; Greenough; Bowen; Rice & Clark.

6935. SKETCHES OF HISTORY, LIFE, AND MANNERS IN THE WEST … VOLUME I. Cincinnati: Hubbard & Edmands, 1834.
All published; extended edition in 2v. published in 1835 (No. 6939).

6938. TALES OF THE BORDER. Phila: H. Hall, 1835.

6940. A MEMOIR OF THE PUBLIC SERVICES OF WILLIAM HENRY HARRISON, OF OHIO. Phila: Key & Biddle, 1836.

JAMES HALL (cont.)
*6941. STATISTICS OF THE WEST, AT THE CLOSE OF THE YEAR 1836. Cincinnati: J.A. James, 1836.
Extended editions published in 1838 as *Notes on the Western States* (No. 6943) & in 1848 as both *The West: Its Commerce and Navigation* (No. 6951) & *The West: Its Soil, Surface, and Productions* (No. 6952).

*6949. THE WILDERNESS AND THE WAR PATH. NY: Wiley & Putnam, 1846.
Library of American Books, No. 15.

6955. THE ROMANCE OF WESTERN HISTORY: OR, SKETCHES OF HISTORY, LIFE, AND MANNERS, IN THE WEST. Cincinnati: Applegate, 1857.

Fitz-Greene Halleck
1790–1867

6958. POEMS. By Croaker, Croaker & Co. and Croaker, Jun. NY: Published for the Reader, 1819.
With Joseph Rodman Drake, see No. 4822 above. The "first complete edition" of this material published in 1860 as *The Croakers* (No. 6991) contains 11 additional poems by Halleck, 2 written in collaboration with Drake.

*6960. FANNY. NY: Wiley, 1819.
Anon. Extended "second edition" published in 1821 (No. 6962); privately printed with added notes in 1866 (No. 6998).

6965. ALNWICK CASTLE, WITH OTHER POEMS. NY: G. & C. Carvill, 1827.
Anon. Extended editions published in 1836 (No. 6971) & 1845 (No. 6975).

6972. FANNY, WITH OTHER POEMS. NY: Harper & Bros., 1839.
Anon. "Lines to the Recorder," here collected, was privately printed with added notes in 1866 (No. 6999).

6979. THE POETICAL WORKS. NY: Appleton, 1847.
Extended editions published in 1852 (No. 6982) & 1858 (Nos. 6987 & 6988).

6996. YOUNG AMERICA: A POEM. NY: Appleton, 1865.

*7000. THE POETICAL WRITINGS OF FITZ-GREENE HALLECK. NY: Appleton, 1869.
"With extracts from … Joseph Rodman Drake." Ed. James Grant Wilson. For full entry see BAL (No. 4840).

*7001. THE LIFE AND LETTERS. NY: Appleton, 1869.
By James Grant Wilson.

Charles Graham Halpine
(Private Miles O'Reilly)
1829–1868

7007. LYRICS. By the Letter H. NY: Derby, 1854.

*7010. THE LIFE AND ADVENTURES, SONGS, SERVICES, AND SPEECHES OF PRIVATE MILES O'REILLY. NY: Carleton, 1864.

7021. BAKED MEATS OF THE FUNERAL. A COLLECTION OF ESSAYS, POEMS, SPEECHES, HISTORIES, AND BANQUETS. By Private Miles O'Reilly. NY: Carleton, 1866.

7027. THE POETICAL WORKS. NY: Harper & Bros., 1869.
Ed. Robert B. Roosevelt.

Arthur Sherburne Hardy
1847–1930

7033. FRANCESCA OF RIMINI. A POEM. By A.S.H. Phila: Lippincott, 1878.

*7036. BUT YET A WOMAN A NOVEL. Bos & NY: Houghton, Mifflin, 1883.

7038. THE WIND OF DESTINY. Bos & NY: Houghton, Mifflin, 1886.

7043. PASSE ROSE. Bos & NY: Houghton, Mifflin, 1889.

7045. LIFE AND LETTERS OF JOSEPH HARDY NEESIMA. Bos & NY: Houghton, Mifflin, 1891.

7048. SONGS OF TWO. NY: Scribner's Sons, 1900.

7049. HIS DAUGHTER FIRST. Bos & NY: Houghton, Mifflin, 1903.

7050. AURÉLIE. NY & Lon: Harper & Bros., 1912.

7051. DIANE AND HER FRIENDS. Bos & NY: Houghton Mifflin, 1914.

7052. HELEN. Bos & NY: Houghton Mifflin, 1916.

7054. NO. 13 RUE DU BON DIABLE. Bos & NY: Houghton Mifflin, 1917.

7056. PETER. Bos & NY: Houghton Mifflin, 1920.

7058. THINGS REMEMBERED. Bos & NY: Houghton Mifflin, 1923.

7060. A MAY AND NOVEMBER CORRESPONDENCE. Bos & NY: Houghton Mifflin, 1928.
Correspondence with Dorothy Hardy Richardson.

Henry Harland
(Sidney Luska)
1861–1905

*7061. AS IT WAS WRITTEN A JEWISH MUSICIAN'S STORY. By Sidney Luska. NY: Cassell, <1885>.

7062. MRS PEIXADA. By Sidney Luska. NY: Cassell, <1886>.

*7064. THE YOKE OF THE THORAH. By Sidney Luska. NY: Cassell, <1887>.

HENRY HARLAND (cont.)

7066. MY UNCLE FLORIMOND. Bos: Lothrop, <1888>.

7067. A LATIN-QUARTER COURTSHIP AND OTHER STORIES. NY: Cassell, <1889>.

The title story was originally published as the Aug. 1887 issue of *Lippincott's Monthly Magazine* (No. 7065) as *A Land of Love*.

7068. GRANDISON MATHER OR AN ACCOUNT OF THE FORTUNES OF MR. AND MRS. THOMAS GARDINER. NY: Cassell, <1889>.

7069. TWO WOMEN OR ONE? FROM THE MSS. OF DR. LEONARD BENARY. Lon, Paris, &c.: Cassell, 1890.

7070. TWO VOICES. NY: Cassell, <1890>.

7071. TWO WOMEN OR ONE? FROM THE MSS. OF DR. LEONARD BENARY. NY: Cassell, <1890>.

7074. MEA CULPA A WOMAN'S LAST WORD. Lon: Heinemann, 1891.
3v.

7076. MEA CULPA A WOMAN'S LAST WORD. NY: Lovell, <1891>.

7078. MADEMOISELLE MISS AND OTHER STORIES. Lon: Heinemann, 1893.

7079. MADEMOISELLE MISS TO WHICH IS ADDED: THE FUNERAL MARCH OF A MARIONETTE <& 3 other titles>. NY: Lovell, Coryell, <1893>.

7081. GREY ROSES. Lon: Lane, 1895.

7082. GRAY ROSES. Bos: Roberts Bros., 1895.

*7083. COMEDIES & ERRORS. Lon & NY: Lane, 1898.

*7084. THE CARDINAL'S SNUFF-BOX. Lon & NY: Lane, 1900.
These sheets issued simultaneously (?) in the U.S. & the U.K.

7085. THE LADY PARAMOUNT. Lon & NY: Lane, 1902.
Published simultaneously (?) in the U.S. & the U.K.

*7089. MY FRIEND PROSPERO A NOVEL. NY: McClure, Phillips, 1904.

7091. THE ROYAL END A ROMANCE. Lon: Hutchinson, 1909.
Completed by Mrs. Harland.

7092. THE ROYAL END A ROMANCE. NY: Dodd, Mead, 1909.
Completed by Mrs. Harland.

George Washington Harris
1814–1869

*7095. SUT LOVINGOOD. YARNS SPUN BY A "NAT'RAL BORN DURN'D FOOL. NY: Dick & Fitzgerald, <1867>.
Three of these pieces are here revised & collected from S.P. Avery's popular compilation *The Harp of a Thousand Strings*, 1858 (No. 7094).

7096. SUT LOVINGOOD TRAVELS WITH OLD ABE LINCOLN. Chi: Black Cat PR, 1937.

Joel Chandler Harris
1848–1908

*7100. UNCLE REMUS HIS SONGS AND HIS SAYINGS THE FOLK-LORE OF THE OLD PLANTATION. NY: Appleton, 1881.
Revised edition published in 1895 (No. 7131). This material published in the U.K. in 1881 & 1884 as *Uncle Remus and his Legends of the Old Plantation* (Nos. 7101 & 7113) & in 1881 as *Uncle Remus or Mr. Fox, Mr. Rabbit, and Mr. Terrapin* (No. 7102).

7109. NIGHTS WITH UNCLE REMUS MYTHS AND LEGENDS OF THE OLD PLANTATION. Bos: Osgood, 1883.
Also a simultaneous (?) U.K. edition dated 1884 (No. 7110); a copyright printing was produced in 1883 (No. 7108).

7112. MINGO AND OTHER SKETCHES IN BLACK AND WHITE. Bos: Osgood, 1884.

7114. FREE JOE AND OTHER GEORGIAN SKETCHES. NY: Scribner's Sons, 1887.

7117. DADDY JAKE THE RUNAWAY AND SHORT STORIES TOLD AFTER DARK. NY: Century Co., <1889>.

*7122. BALAAM AND HIS MASTER AND OTHER SKETCHES AND STORIES. Bos & NY: Houghton, Mifflin, 1891.

7123. A PLANTATION PRINTER THE ADVENTURES OF A GEORGIA BOY DURING THE WAR. Lon: Osgood, McIlvaine, 1892.
For U.S. edition see next entry.

7124. ON THE PLANTATION A STORY OF A GEORGIA BOY'S ADVENTURES DURING THE WAR. NY: Appleton, 1892.
Contains 1 chapter not in the U.K. edition.

7125. UNCLE REMUS AND HIS FRIENDS OLD PLANTATION STORIES, SONGS, AND BALLADS. Bos & NY: Houghton, Mifflin, 1892.

7129. LITTLE MR. THIMBLEFINGER AND HIS QUEER COUNTRY. Bos & NY: Houghton, Mifflin, 1894.

*7132. MR. RABBIT AT HOME. Bos & NY: Houghton, Mifflin, 1895.
Sequel to *Little Mr. Thimblefinger.*

*7135. THE STORY OF AARON (SO NAMED) THE SON OF BEN ALI. Bos & NY: Houghton, Mifflin, 1896.

7136. STORIES OF GEORGIA. NY, Cincinnati, &c.: American Book Co., 1896.
Reprinted in 1896 as *Stories from American History Georgia* (No. 7137). Revised edition published *ca.* 1910.

*7138. SISTER JANE HER FRIENDS AND ACQUAINTANCES. Bos & NY: Houghton, Mifflin, 1896.
"Transcribed from the papers of the late William Wornum."

JOEL CHANDLER HARRIS (cont.)

*7140. AARON IN THE WILDWOODS. Bos & NY: Houghton, Mifflin, 1897.

7141. TALES OF THE HOME FOLKS IN PEACE AND WAR. Bos & NY: Houghton, Mifflin, 1898.

7142. PLANTATION PAGEANTS. Bos & NY: Houghton, Mifflin, 1899.

7143. THE CHRONICLES OF AUNT MINERVY ANN. NY: Scribner's Sons, 1899.

7145. ON THE WING OF OCCASIONS. NY: Doubleday, Page, 1900.
Reprinted in 1909 as *The Kidnapping of President Lincoln and Other War Detective Stories* (No. 7163).

7148. THE MAKING OF A STATESMAN AND OTHER STORIES. NY: McClure, Phillips, 1902.

*7149. GABRIEL TOLLIVER A STORY OF RECONSTRUCTION. NY: McClure, Phillips, 1902.

7152. WALLY WANDEROON AND HIS STORY-TELLING MACHINE. NY: McClure, Phillips, 1903.

7153. A LITTLE UNION SCOUT. NY: McClure, Phillips, 1904.

7154. THE TAR-BABY AND OTHER RHYMES OF UNCLE REMUS. NY: Appleton, 1904.

7156. TOLD BY UNCLE REMUS NEW STORIES OF THE OLD PLANTATION. NY: McClure, Phillips, 1905.

7160. UNCLE REMUS AND BRER RABBIT. NY: Stokes, 1907.

7161. THE BISHOP AND THE BOOGERMAN. NY: Doubleday, Page, 1909.

7162. THE SHADOW BETWEEN HIS SHOULDER-BLADES. Bos: Small, Maynard, <1909>.

7165. UNCLE REMUS AND THE LITTLE BOY. Bos: Small, Maynard, <1910>.

7168. UNCLE REMUS RETURNS. Bos & NY: Houghton Mifflin, 1918.

7169. THE LIFE AND LETTERS OF JOEL CHANDLER HARRIS. Bos & NY: Houghton Mifflin, 1918.
By Julia Collier Harris.

7170. THE WITCH WOLF AN UNCLE REMUS STORY. Cambridge: Bacon & Brown, 1921.

7172. JOEL CHANDLER HARRIS EDITOR AND ESSAYIST MISCELLANEOUS LITERARY, POLITICAL, AND SOCIAL WRITINGS. Chapel Hill: U of North Carolina PR, 1931.
Ed. Julia Collier Harris.

7174. QUA: A ROMANCE OF THE REVOLUTION. Atlanta: Emory U Library, 1946.
Ed. Thomas H. English. *Emory University Publications Sources & Reprints,* Series 3, No. 2.

7175. SEVEN TALES OF UNCLE REMUS. Atlanta: Emory U Library, 1948.
Ed. Thomas H. English. *Emory University Publications Sources & Reprints,* Series 5, No. 2.

JOEL CHANDLER HARRIS (cont.)
7177. THE COMPLETE TALES OF UNCLE REMUS. Bos: Houghton Mifflin, 1955.
Ed. Richard Chase.

Constance Cary Harrison
(Mrs. Burton Harrison)
1843–1920

Note: Harrison's dramatic adaptations & translations are here omitted. These include *Short Comedies for Amateur Players*, <1889> (No. 7186), *A Russia Honeymoon*, 1890 (No. 7187) & *Alice in Wonderland*, 1890 (No. 7190).

7178. GOLDEN-ROD AN IDYL OF MOUNT DESERT. NY: Harper & Bros., 1880.
Anon. *Harper's Half-Hour Series*, No. 130.

*7179. WOMAN'S HANDIWORK IN MODERN HOMES. <NY>: Scribner's Sons, 1881.
Revised & published in 1894 as part of *The Woman's Book* (No. 7204).

7180. THE STORY OF HELEN TROY. NY: Harper & Bros., 1881.
Anon.

7181. THE OLD-FASHIONED FAIRY BOOK. NY: Scribner's Sons, 1884.

7182. BRIC-A-BRAC STORIES. NY: Scribner's Sons, 1885.
Published in the U.K. in 1885 as *Folk and Fairy Tales* (No. 7183).

7184. BAR HARBOR DAYS. NY: Harper & Bros., 1887.

7188. THE ANGLOMANIACS. NY: Cassell, <1890>.
Anon.

*7189. FLOWER DE HUNDRED THE STORY OF A VIRGINIA PLANTATION. NY: Cassell, <1890>.

7192. A DAUGHTER OF THE SOUTH AND SHORTER STORIES. NY: Cassell, <1892>.

7193. AN EDELWEISS OF THE SIERRAS, GOLDEN-ROD AND OTHER TALES. NY: Harper & Bros., 1892.

7195. BELHAVEN TALES CROW'S NEST UNA AND KING DAVID. NY: Century Co., 1892.

*7202. SWEET BELLS OUT OF TUNE. NY: Century Co., 1893.

*7205. A BACHELOR MAID. NY: Century Co., 1894.

7207. AN ERRANT WOOING. NY: Century Co., 1895.

7208. A VIRGINIA COUSIN & BAR HARBOR TALES. Bos & NY: Lamson Wolffe, 1895.

*7210. THE MERRY MAID OF ARCADY, HIS LORDSHIP AND OTHER STORIES. Bos, Lon, &c.: Lamson, Wolffe, 1897.

7211. A SON OF THE OLD DOMINION. Bos, NY, &c.: Lamson, Wolffe, 1897.

7212. GOOD AMERICANS. NY: Century Co., 1898.

7213. THE WELL-BRED GIRL IN SOCIETY. Phila: Curtis, <1898>.
Ladies' Home Journal Girl's Library.

CONSTANCE CARY HARRISON (cont.)

7214. A TRIPLE ENTANGLEMENT. Lon: Unwin, 1898.

7215. A TRIPLE ENTANGLEMENT. Phila: Lippincott, 1899.

7216. THE CARCELLINI EMERALD WITH OTHER TALES. Chi & NY: Stone, 1899.

7217. THE CIRCLE OF A CENTURY. NY: Century Co., 1899.

7218. A PRINCESS OF THE HILLS AN ITALIAN ROMANCE. Bos: Lothrop, <1901>.

7221. THE UNWELCOME MRS. HATCH. NY: Appleton, 1903.
       Novelization of an unpublished drama, of which a presumed copyright printing was produced in 1901 (No. 7220).

7222. SYLVIA'S HUSBAND. NY: Appleton, 1904.

7223. THE CARLYLES A STORY OF THE FALL OF THE CONFEDERACY. NY: Appleton, 1905.

7224. LATTER-DAY SWEETHEARTS. Lon: Unwin, 1906.

*7227. LATTER-DAY SWEETHEARTS. NY & Lon: The Authors & Newspapers Assn, 1907.
       A copyright printing was produced in 1906 (No. 7225).

7228. THE COUNT AND THE CONGRESSMAN. NY: Cupples & Leon, <1908>.

7231. TRANSPLANTED DAUGHTERS. Lon: Unwin, 1909.

7232. RECOLLECTIONS GRAVE AND GAY. NY: Scribner's Sons, 1911.

Bret Harte
(Francis Brett Harte)
1836–1902

Note: Harte's poems & sketches were collected & published in the U.K. in the 1870s in various combinations & with various titles. A completely satisfactory publication sequence of these editions has not been established, and most have been here omitted although some almost certainly print first edition material. Similarly, many of the Tauchnitz editions of Harte's works contain some first edition material but are here omitted. For comment on U.S. publication of some of this material see No. 7314 below; for further details see BAL.

7240. CONDENSED NOVELS. AND OTHER PAPERS. NY: Carleton, 1867.
       Extended edition published in 1871 (No. 7255).

7242. THE LOST GALLEON AND OTHER TALES. SF: Towne & Bacon, Ptrs, 1867.

*7246. THE LUCK OF ROARING CAMP, AND OTHER SKETCHES. Bos: Fields, Osgood, 1870.
       Extended edition also published in 1870 (No. 7247).

BRET HARTE (cont.)

*7248. THE HEATHEN CHINEE. 1870.
This popular poem first appeared in the *Overland Monthly*, Sept. 1870, as "Plain Language from Truthful James" & was first published separately in Nov. 1870 by the Western News Co., Chicago, as "The Heathen Chinee" on 9 lithographed cards in an envelope. Collected in *Poems*, 1871, & reprinted separately in book form in 1871 (No. 7425). BAL lists numerous other early separate printings as sheet music, pamphlets & broadsides.

*7253. POEMS. Bos: Fields, Osgood, 1871.

7256. EAST AND WEST POEMS. Bos: Osgood, 1871.

7266. MRS. SKAGGS'S HUSBANDS, AND OTHER SKETCHES. Bos: Osgood, 1873.

7270. AN EPISODE OF FIDDLETOWN AND OTHER SKETCHES. Lon: Routledge & Sons, <n.d., 1873>.

*7271. MLISS. AN IDYL OF RED MOUNTAIN. A STORY OF CALIFORNIA IN 1863. NY: De Witt, <n.d., 1873>.
Unauthorized piracy.

*7278. ECHOES OF THE FOOT-HILLS. Bos: Osgood, 1875.

*7280. TALES OF THE ARGONAUTS, AND OTHER SKETCHES. Bos: Osgood, 1875.

7283. GABRIEL CONROY. A NOVEL. Lon: Warne, <1876>.
3v. Also (partially?) printed in 30 parts in 1875 (No. 7281), possibly for copyright purposes.

*7285. GABRIEL CONROY. Hartford CT: American Pub. Co., 1876.
"Issued by Subscription Only."

7286. TWO MEN OF SANDY BAR. A DRAMA. Bos: Osgood, 1876.
A copyright printing was also produced in 1876 (No. 7284).

7288. THANKFUL BLOSSOM A ROMANCE OF THE JERSEYS 1779. Bos: Osgood, 1877.
Also (earlier?) published in Toronto (No. 7287). The U.K. edition published in 1877 (No. 7289) has a brief additional conclusion.

7292. THE STORY OF A MINE. Lon: Routledge & Sons, <n.d., 1877>.

7295. THE STORY OF A MINE. Bos: Osgood, 1878.

*7296. THE MAN ON THE BEACH. Lon: Routledge & Sons, <n.d., 1878>.

*7297. "JINNY." Lon: Routledge & Sons, <n.d., 1878>.

7300. DRIFT FROM TWO SHORES. Bos: Houghton, Osgood, 1878.

7306. AN HEIRESS OF RED DOG AND OTHER TALES. Lon: Chatto & Windus, 1879.

*7308. THE TWINS OF TABLE MOUNTAIN. Lon: Chatto & Windus, 1879.

7309. THE TWINS OF TABLE MOUNTAIN, AND OTHER STORIES. Bos: Houghton, Osgood, 1879.

BRET HARTE (cont.)

7314. THE COMPLETE WORKS. Lon: Chatto & Windus, 1880–1900.
10v. "Collected and revised by the author." The 5v. "Riverside Edition" of Harte's *Works* published in Boston in 1882 (No. 7319) contains only reprinted material, but is the first collected appearance in the U.S. of many pieces first published abroad. See also No. 7384 below.

7320. FLIP AND OTHER STORIES. Lon: Chatto & Windus, 1882.

*7321. FLIP AND FOUND AT BLAZING STAR. Bos & NY: Houghton, Mifflin, 1882.

7324. IN THE CARQUINEZ WOODS. Lon: Longmans, Green, 1883.

7326. ON THE FRONTIER. Lon: Longmans, Green, 1884.

7327. ON THE FRONTIER. Bos & NY: Houghton, Mifflin, 1884.

*7328. IN THE CARQUINEZ WOODS. Bos & NY: Houghton, Mifflin, 1884.

*7330. BY SHORE AND SEDGE. Bos & NY: Houghton, Mifflin, 1885.

7331. MARUJA. Lon: Chatto & Windus, 1885.

*7333. MARUJA. Bos & NY: Houghton, Mifflin, 1885.

7335. SNOW-BOUND AT EAGLE'S. Bos & NY: Houghton, Mifflin, 1886.
A partial U.K. copyright printing was produced in 1885 (No. 7334).

7337. THE QUEEN OF THE PIRATE ISLE. Lon: Chatto & Windus, <n.d., 1886>.

7338. THE QUEEN OF THE PIRATE ISLE. Bos & NY: Houghton, Mifflin, 1887.

*7339. A MILLIONAIRE OF ROUGH-AND-READY AND DEVIL'S FORD. Bos & NY: Houghton, Mifflin, 1887.

*7340. THE CRUSADE OF THE EXCELSIOR. Bos & NY: Houghton, Mifflin, 1887.

*7342. A PHYLLIS OF THE SIERRAS AND A DRIFT FROM REDWOOD CAMP. Bos & NY: Houghton, Mifflin, 1888.

7344. THE ARGONAUTS OF NORTH LIBERTY. Bos & NY: Houghton, Mifflin, 1888.

7345. CRESSY. Lon & NY: Macmillan, 1889.
2v.

7346. CRESSY. Bos & NY: Houghton, Mifflin, 1889.

7348. THE HERITAGE OF DEDLOW MARSH AND OTHER TALES. Bos & NY: Houghton, Mifflin, 1889.

7349. A WAIF OF THE PLAINS. Lon: Chatto & Windus, 1890.

*7350. A WAIF OF THE PLAINS. Bos & NY: Houghton, Mifflin, 1890.

7353. A WARD OF THE GOLDEN GATE. Lon: Chatto & Windus, 1890.

7355. A WARD OF THE GOLDEN GATE. Bos & NY: Houghton, Mifflin, 1890.

7356. A SAPPHO OF GREEN SPRINGS AND OTHER TALES. Lon: Chatto & Windus, 1891.

BRET HARTE (cont.)

*7357. A SAPPHO OF GREEN SPRINGS AND OTHER STORIES. Bos & NY: Houghton, Mifflin, 1891.
The title story was originally published as the May 1890 issue of *Lippincott's Monthly Magazine* (No. 7352).

7359. A FIRST FAMILY OF TASAJARA. Lon & NY: Macmillan, 1891.
2v.

7360. COLONEL STARBOTTLE'S CLIENT AND SOME OTHER PEOPLE. Lon: Chatto & Windus, 1892.

*7361. A FIRST FAMILY OF TASAJARA. Bos & NY: Houghton, Mifflin, 1892.

7362. COLONEL STARBOTTLE'S CLIENT AND SOME OTHER PEOPLE. Bos & NY: Houghton, Mifflin, 1892.

*7365. SUSY A STORY OF THE PLAINS. Bos & NY: Houghton, Mifflin, 1893.

7366. SALLY DOWS ETC. Lon: Chatto & Windus, 1893.

*7367. SALLY DOWS AND OTHER STORIES. Bos & NY: Houghton, Mifflin, 1893.

*7368. A PROTÉGÉE OF JACK HAMLIN'S AND OTHER STORIES. Bos & NY: Houghton, Mifflin, 1894.
The U.K. edition published in 1894 contains 1 additional story (No. 7369).

7372. THE BELL-RINGER OF ANGEL'S AND OTHER STORIES. Bos & NY: Houghton, Mifflin, 1894.
Also a simultaneous (?) U.K. edition with slightly different contents (No. 7373).

7375. CLARENCE. Lon: Chatto & Windus, 1895.

7376. CLARENCE. Bos & NY: Houghton, Mifflin, 1895.

7377. IN A HOLLOW OF THE HILLS. Lon: Chapman & Hall, 1895.

7378. IN A HOLLOW OF THE HILLS. Bos & NY: Houghton, Mifflin, 1895.

7381. BARKER'S LUCK AND OTHER STORIES. Bos & NY: Houghton, Mifflin, 1896.

7382. THE POETICAL WORKS. Bos & NY: Houghton, Mifflin, <1896>.
Household Edition. Another edition with title *Poems and Two Men of Sandy Bar* (No. 7383) published simultaneously as *Writings*, Vol. 12, see next entry. A slightly extended edition published not before 1902 (No. 7401).

*7384. WRITINGS. Bos & NY: Houghton, Mifflin, 1896–1914.
20v. See also No. 7314 above.

7385. THREE PARTNERS OR THE BIG STRIKE ON HEAVY TREE HILL. Bos & NY: Houghton, Mifflin, 1897.

7387. TALES OF TRAIL AND TOWN. Bos & NY: Houghton, Mifflin, 1898.

7388. SOME LATER VERSES. Lon: Chatto & Windus, 1898.
Contains 6 new poems. These sheets reissued not before 1905 by The Times Book Club, London.

7389. STORIES IN LIGHT AND SHADOW. Lon: Pearson, 1898.

7390. STORIES IN LIGHT AND SHADOW. Bos & NY: Houghton, Mifflin, 1898.

BRET HARTE (cont.)

7392. MR. JACK HAMLIN'S MEDIATION AND OTHER STORIES. Bos & NY: Houghton, Mifflin, 1899.

7394. FROM SAND HILL TO PINE. Bos & NY: Houghton, Mifflin, 1900.

*7396. UNDER THE REDWOODS. Bos & NY: Houghton, Mifflin, 1901.

7397. ON THE OLD TRAIL. Lon: Pearson, 1902.
For simultaneous (?) U.S. edition see next entry.

*7398. OPENINGS IN THE OLD TRAIL. Bos & NY: Houghton, Mifflin, 1902.

7399. CONDENSED NOVELS SECOND SERIES NEW BURLESQUES. Bos & NY: Houghton, Mifflin, 1902.

7400. SUE: A PLAY. Lon: Greening, 1902.
With T. Edgar Pemberton.

7403. TRENT'S TRUST AND OTHER STORIES. Lon: Nash, 1903.

7404. TRENT'S TRUST AND OTHER STORIES. Bos & NY: Houghton, Mifflin, 1903.

*7407. THE LECTURES OF BRET HARTE. Brooklyn: Kozlay, 1909.

*7408. STORIES AND POEMS AND OTHER UNCOLLECTED WRITINGS. Bos & NY: Houghton Mifflin, 1914.
Ed. Charles Meeker Kozlay. Also issued as Harte's *Writings*, Vol. 20, see No. 7384 above.

7409. THE LETTERS OF BRET HARTE. Bos & NY: Houghton Mifflin, 1926.
Ed. Geoffrey Bret Harte.

7410. SKETCHES OF THE SIXTIES. SF: Howell, 1926.
With Mark Twain, see No. 3539 above. "Now collected for the first time from The Californian 1864–67." Extended edition published in 1927 (Nos. 7411 & 3541).

7415. SAN FRANCISCO IN 1866. SF: Book Club of California, 1951.
"Letters to the Springfield Republican." Ed. George R. Stewart & Edwin S. Fussell.

Nathaniel Hawthorne
1804–1864

7570. FANSHAWE, A TALE. Bos: Marsh & Capen, 1828.
Anon.

7581. TWICE-TOLD TALES. Bos: American Stationers Co., 1837.
For an extended edition see No. 7594 below.

7590. GRANDFATHER'S CHAIR: A HISTORY FOR YOUTH. Bos: Peabody, 1841.
Revised & extended edition published in 1842 (No. 7593) & later reissued, see No. 7595 below.

7591. FAMOUS OLD PEOPLE: BEING THE SECOND EPOCH OF GRANDFATHER'S CHAIR. Bos: Peabody, 1841.
For comment see No. 7595 below.

NATHANIEL HAWTHORNE (cont.)

*7592. LIBERTY TREE: WITH THE LAST WORDS OF GRANDFATHER'S CHAIR. Bos: Peabody, 1841.
These sheets reissued in 1851 both separately & with other works, see No. 7595 below.

7594. TWICE-TOLD TALES. Bos: Munroe, 1842.
2v.

7595. BIOGRAPHICAL STORIES FOR CHILDREN. Bos: Tappan & Dennet, 1842.
These sheets later reissued with reprints of Nos. 7590, 7591 & 7592 above in 2v. with binder's title *Hawthorne's Historical Tales for Youth* (No. 7652); the 4 works reprinted in 1v. in 1851 as *True Stories from History and Biography* (No. 7655).

*7596. THE CELESTIAL RAIL-ROAD. Bos: Wilder, 1843.

*7597. JOURNAL OF AN AFRICAN CRUISER ... BY AN OFFICER OF THE U.S. NAVY. NY & Lon: Wiley & Putnam, 1845.
By Horatio Bridge; edited by Hawthorne. *Library of American Books*, No. 1. These sheets also issued in the U.K. in 1845 & reissued in 1848 with imprint of Wiley, New York.

*7598. MOSSES FROM AN OLD MANSE. NY: Wiley & Putnam, 1846.
2v. *Library of American Books*, Nos. 17–18. Revised edition published in 1854 (No. 7615) with 3 additonal stories.

7600. THE SCARLET LETTER, A ROMANCE. Bos: Ticknor, Reed, & Fields, 1850.
Corrected "second edition" also published in 1850 (No. 7601).

7604. THE HOUSE OF THE SEVEN GABLES, A ROMANCE. Bos: Ticknor, Reed, & Fields, 1851.

7606. A WONDER-BOOK FOR GIRLS AND BOYS. Bos: Ticknor, Reed, & Fields, 1852.

7607. THE SNOW-IMAGE, AND OTHER TWICE-TOLD TALES. Bos: Ticknor, Reed, & Fields, 1852.
Also a simultaneous (?) U.K. edition dated 1851 (No. 7605).

7610. THE BLITHEDALE ROMANCE. Lon: Chapman & Hall, 1852.
2v.

7611. THE BLITHEDALE ROMANCE. Bos: Ticknor, Reed, & Fields, 1852.

7612. LIFE OF FRANKLIN PIERCE. Bos: Ticknor, Reed, & Fields, 1852.

7613. TANGLEWOOD TALES, FOR GIRLS AND BOYS: BEING A SECOND WONDER-BOOK. Lon: Chapman & Hall, 1853.

*7614. TANGLEWOOD TALES, FOR GIRLS AND BOYS: BEING A SECOND WONDER-BOOK. Bos: Ticknor, Reed, & Fields, 1853.

7620. TRANSFORMATION: OR, THE ROMANCE OF MONTE BENI. Lon: Smith, Elder, 1860.
3v. For simultaneous (?) U.S. edition see next entry. The "second edition," also published in 1860, has an added "Postscript" (No. 7622).

NATHANIEL HAWTHORNE (cont.)

*7621. THE MARBLE FAUN: OR, THE ROMANCE OF MONTE BENI. Bos: Ticknor & Fields, 1860.
2v. Reprinted in 1860 with an added "Conclusion" (No. 7624).

*7626. OUR OLD HOME: A SERIES OF ENGLISH SKETCHES. Bos: Ticknor & Fields, 1863.

7627. PANSIE: A FRAGMENT. Lon: Hotten, <n.d., 1864>.
"The last literary effort of Nathaniel Hawthorne."

*7632. PASSAGES FROM THE AMERICAN NOTE-BOOKS OF NATHANIEL HAWTHORNE. Bos: Ticknor & Fields, 1868.
2v. Ed. Sophia Hawthorne. Reprinted in the U.K. in 1869 as *Passages from the Note-Books of the Late Nathaniel Hawthorne* (No. 7633) with some additional material which was collected in the U.S. in *Passages from the English Note-Books,* see next entry. Critical edition published in 1932.

7634. PASSAGES FROM THE ENGLISH NOTE-BOOKS OF NATHANIEL HAWTHORNE. Bos: Fields, Osgood, 1870.
2v. Ed. Sophia Hawthorne. Critical edition published in 1941.

7635. PASSAGES FROM THE FRENCH AND ITALIAN NOTE-BOOKS OF NATHANIEL HAWTHORNE. Lon: Strahan, 1871.
2v. Ed. Una Hawthorne.

7636. PASSAGES FROM THE FRENCH AND ITALIAN NOTE-BOOKS OF NATHANIEL HAWTHORNE. Bos: Osgood, 1872.
2v. Ed. Una Hawthorne.

*7637. SEPTIMIUS: A ROMANCE. Lon: King, 1872.
Ed. Una Hawthorne & Robert Browning.

7638. SEPTIMIUS FELTON; OR THE ELIXIR OF LIFE. Bos: Osgood, 1872.
Ed. Una Hawthorne & Robert Browning.

7640. THE DOLLIVER ROMANCE AND OTHER PIECES. Bos: Osgood, 1876.
Ed. Sophia Hawthorne.

7641. FANSHAWE AND OTHER PIECES. Bos: Osgood, 1876.

*7642. DOCTOR GRIMSHAWE'S SECRET A ROMANCE. Bos: Osgood, 1883.
Ed. Julian Hawthorne.

7645. THE COMPLETE WRITINGS. Bos & NY: Houghton, Mifflin, 1900.
22v. *Autograph edition.* An earlier "Riverside Edition" of Hawthorne's *Writings* in 12v. published in 1883 (No. 7643).

7647. LOVE LETTERS OF NATHANIEL HAWTHORNE. Chi: Soc'y of the Dofobs, 1907.
2v. "Privately printed."

7648. LETTERS OF HAWTHORNE TO WILLIAM D. TICKNOR. Newark: Carteret Book Club, 1910.
2v.

NATHANIEL HAWTHORNE (cont.)

7650.   THE HEART OF HAWTHORNE'S JOURNALS. Bos & NY: Houghton Mifflin, 1929.
Ed. Newton Arvin.

7651.   HAWTHORNE AS EDITOR. University LA: Louisiana State U PR, 1941.
Ed. Arlin Turner. *Louisiana State University Studies,* No. 42. "Selections from his writings in the American Magazine of Useful and Entertaining Knowledge."

John Milton Hay
1838–1905

*7739.   JIM BLUDSO OF THE PRAIRIE BELLE, AND LITTLE BREECHES. Bos: Osgood, 1871.
These sheets reissued *ca.* 1876. These poems appeared first in *The New-York <Weekly> Tribune,* 30 Nov. 1870, & *The New-York Semi-Weekly Tribune,* 6 Jan. 1871, respectively. They were also published in a variety of other forms in 1871, for details see BAL (Nos. 7734, 7737, 7741 & 7815).

7740.   PIKE COUNTY BALLADS AND OTHER PIECES. Bos: Osgood, 1871.

*7742.   CASTILIAN DAYS. Bos: Osgood, 1871.
Revised edition published in 1890 (No. 7770); further revised & abridged edition in 1903 (No. 7793).

*7762.   THE BREAD-WINNERS A SOCIAL STUDY. NY: Harper & Bros., 1884.
Anon. Also a simultaneous (?) U.K. edition with title-page dated 1883. The *Century Magazine* text of chaps. 1–11 was also published separately in 1883 (No. 7760).

*7769.   POEMS. Bos & NY: Houghton, Mifflin, 1890.

7772.   ABRAHAM LINCOLN A HISTORY. NY: Century Co., 1890.
10v. With John G. Nicolay. Lincoln's *Complete Works* in 2v., ed. Nicolay & Hay, published in 1894 (No. 7774).

7802.   ADDRESSES. NY: Century Co., 1906.
"Omar Khayyam" (otherwise "In Praise of Omar"), here collected, was first published in a variety of forms in 1898 (No. 7781); other addresses here collected were also first published separately.

7803.   LETTERS OF JOHN HAY AND EXTRACTS FROM DIARY. Wash DC, 1908.
3v. "Printed but not published." Ed. Henry Adams.

7805.   A POET IN EXILE EARLY LETTERS OF JOHN HAY. Bos & NY: Houghton Mifflin, 1910.
Ed. Caroline Ticknor.

*7806.   THE LIFE AND LETTERS OF JOHN HAY. Bos & NY: Houghton Mifflin, 1915.
2v. By William Roscoe Thayer.

7808.   THE COMPLETE POETICAL WORKS. Bos & NY: Houghton Mifflin, 1916.

JOHN HAY (cont.)
7811. A COLLEGE FRIENDSHIP A SERIES OF LETTERS FROM JOHN HAY TO HANNAH ANGELL. Bos, 1938.
"Privately printed."

7813. LINCOLN AND THE CIVIL WAR IN THE DIARIES AND LETTERS OF JOHN HAY. NY: Dodd, Mead, 1939.
Ed. Tyler Dennett.

Paul Hamilton Hayne
1830–1886

7850. POEMS. Bos: Ticknor & Fields, 1855.

7851. SONNETS, AND OTHER POEMS. Charleston: Harper & Calvo, 1857.

7853. AVOLIO; A LEGEND OF THE ISLAND OF COS. WITH POEMS, LYRICAL, MISCELLANEOUS, AND DRAMATIC. Bos: Ticknor & Fields, 1860.

7857. M.M.S. OF VOLUME FIRST OF THE WORK ENTITLED "POLITICS OF SOUTH CAROLINA,—F.W. PICKENS' SPEECHES, REPORTS, &C." <n.p., n.d.; *ca.* 1865>.
Incomplete & presumably never formally published.

7865. LEGENDS AND LYRICS. Phila: Lippincott, 1872.

7868. THE MOUNTAIN OF THE LOVERS; WITH POEMS OF NATURE AND TRADITION. NY: Hale & Son, 1875.

7871. LIVES OF ROBERT YOUNG HAYNE AND HUGH SWINTON LEGARÉ. Charleston: Walker, Evans & Cogswell, 1878.

7889. POEMS ... COMPLETE EDITION. Bos: Lothrop, 1882.
"W. Gilmore Simms," here collected, was first published separately in 1877 (No. 7870).

7907. A COLLECTION OF HAYNE LETTERS. Austin: U of Texas PR, 1944.
Ed. Daniel Morley McKeithan.

7908. THE CORRESPONDENCE OF BAYARD TAYLOR AND PAUL HAMILTON HAYNE. Baton Rouge: Louisiana State U PR, 1945.
Ed. Charles Duffy.

Lafcadio Hearn
1850–1904

Note: Hearn's translations from the French are here omitted, as are the posthumous editions of Hearn's literary criticism edited from lecture notes kept by his students.

7912. STRAY LEAVES FROM STRANGE LITERATURE. Bos: Osgood, 1884.

7916. SOME CHINESE GHOSTS. Bos: Roberts Bros., 1887.

7918. CHITA: A MEMORY OF LAST ISLAND. NY: Harper & Bros., 1889.

7920. TWO YEARS IN THE FRENCH WEST INDIES. NY: Harper & Bros., 1890.

LAFCADIO HEARN (cont.)

7921. YOUMA THE STORY OF A WEST-INDIAN SLAVE. NY: Harper & Bros., 1890.

*7926. GLIMPSES OF UNFAMILIAR JAPAN. Bos & NY: Houghton, Mifflin, 1894.
2v.

*7927. "OUT OF THE EAST" REVERIES AND STUDIES IN NEW JAPAN. Bos & NY: Houghton, Mifflin, 1895.

7928. KOKORO HINTS AND ECHOES OF JAPANESE INNER LIFE. Bos & NY: Houghton, Mifflin, 1896.
Extended Japanese edition published in 1921 (No. 7968).

7929. GLEANINGS IN BUDDHA-FIELDS STUDIES OF HAND AND SOUL IN THE FAR EAST. Bos & NY: Houghton, Mifflin, 1897.

7931. EXOTICS AND RETROSPECTIVES. Bos: Little, Brown, 1898.

7934. IN GHOSTLY JAPAN. Bos: Little, Brown, 1899.

7935. SHADOWINGS. Bos: Little, Brown, 1900.

*7936. A JAPANESE MISCELLANY. Bos: Little, Brown, 1901.

*7938. KOTTŌ BEING JAPANESE CURIOS, WITH SUNDRY COBWEBS. NY: Macmillan, 1902.

*7940. KWAIDAN: STORIES AND STUDIES OF STRANGE THINGS. Bos & NY: Houghton, Mifflin, 1904.

7941. JAPAN AN ATTEMPT AT INTERPRETATION. NY: Macmillan, 1904.
The 4th printing, also published in 1904, has an added appendix (No. 7942).

7943. THE ROMANCE OF THE MILKY WAY AND OTHER STUDIES & STORIES. Bos & NY: Houghton Mifflin, 1905.

*7944. THE LIFE AND LETTERS OF LAFCADIO HEARN. Bos & NY: Houghton, Mifflin, 1906.
2v. By Elizabeth Bisland.

7945. LETTERS FROM THE RAVEN BEING THE CORRESPONDENCE OF LAFCADIO HEARN WITH HENRY WATKIN. NY: Brentano's, 1907.
Ed. Milton Bronner.

*7950. THE JAPANESE LETTERS OF LAFCADIO HEARN. Bos & NY: Houghton Mifflin, 1910.
Ed. Elizabeth Bisland.

7953. LEAVES FROM THE DIARY OF AN IMPRESSIONIST EARLY WRITINGS BY LAFCADIO HEARN. Bos & NY: Houghton Mifflin, 1911.

7954. EDITORIALS FROM THE KOBE CHRONICLE. <n.p., n.d.; NY, 1913>.
Ed. Merle Johnson.

7955. FANTASTICS AND OTHER FANCIES. Bos & NY: Houghton Mifflin, 1914.
Ed. Charles Woodward Hutson.

7956. JAPANESE LYRICS. Bos & NY: Houghton Mifflin, 1915.
Translation.

LAFCADIO HEARN (cont.)

7960.   JAPANESE FAIRY TALES. NY: Boni & Liveright, 1918.
Translation by Hearn & others. Hearn's translations were previously published separately in Tokyo in 1897 (No. 7930), 1899 (No. 7932), 1902 (No. 7937) & 1903 (No. 7939).

7961.   KARMA. NY: Boni & Liveright, 1918.
Ed. Albert Mordell.

7976.   LEAVES FROM THE DIARY OF AN IMPRESSIONIST CREOLE SKETCHES AND SOME CHINESE GHOSTS. Bos & NY: Houghton Mifflin, 1922.
The Writings, Vol. 1, see next entry.

7977.   THE WRITINGS OF LAFCADIO HEARN. Bos & NY: Houghton Mifflin, 1922.
16v. *Large-Paper Edition.* Reprinted in 1923 as the "Koizumi Edition" (No. 7981).

7979.   ESSAYS IN EUROPEAN AND ORIENTAL LITERATURE. NY: Dodd, Mead, 1923.
Ed. Albert Mordell.

7982.   CREOLE SKETCHES. Bos & NY: Houghton Mifflin, 1924.
Ed. Charles Woodward Hutson.

7984.   AN AMERICAN MISCELLANY ... ARTICLES AND STORIES. NY: Dodd, Mead, 1924.
2v. Ed. Albert Mordell. These sheets issued in the U.K. edition as *Miscellanies* (No. 7985).

7990.   OCCIDENTAL GLEANINGS ... SKETCHES AND ESSAYS. NY: Dodd, Mead, 1925.
2v. Ed. Albert Mordell.

7992.   SOME NEW LETTERS AND WRITINGS OF LAFCADIO HEARN. Tokyo: Kenkyusha, 1925.
Ed. Sanki Ichikawa.

*7994.   EDITORIALS. Bos & NY: Houghton Mifflin, 1926.
Ed. Charles Woodward Hutson.

8011.   ESSAYS ON AMERICAN LITERATURE. Tokyo: Hokuseido PR, 1929.
Ed. Sanki Ichikawa.

8039.   BARBAROUS BARBERS AND OTHER STORIES. <Tokyo>: Hokuseido PR, <1939>.
Ed. Ichiro Nishizaki.

8040.   BUYING CHRISTMAS TOYS AND OTHER ESSAYS. <Tokyo>: Hokuseido PR, <1939>.
Ed. Ichiro Nishizaki.

8041.   LITERARY ESSAYS. <Tokyo>: Hokuseido PR, <1939>.
Ed. Ichiro Nishizaki.

8042.   THE NEW RADIANCE AND OTHER SCIENTIFIC SKETCHES. <Tokyo>: Hokuseido PR, <1939>.
Ed. Ichiro Nishizaki.

LAFCADIO HEARN (cont.)
    8043. ORIENTAL ARTICLES. <Tokyo>: Hokuseido PR, <1939>.
        Ed. Ichiro Nishizaki.

Henry William Herbert
(Frank Forester)
1807–1858

*8057. THE BROTHERS. A TALE OF THE FRONDE. NY: Harper & Bros., 1835.
        2v. Anon. Published in the U.K. in 1844 (No. 8077) with additional stories.

  8061. CROMWELL. AN HISTORICAL NOVEL. NY: Harper & Bros., 1838.
        2v. Anon. Revised edition published in 1856 as *Oliver Cromwell* (No.8152). The
        U.K. edition published in 1840 as *Oliver Cromwell* (No. 8062) was revised by Horace
        Smith.

8071A. MARMADUKE WYVIL; OR, THE MAID'S REVENGE. Lon: Colburn, 1843.
        3v.

  8072. MARMADUKE WYVIL; OR, THE MAID'S REVENGE. NY: Winchester,
        <1843>.
        Reprinted *ca.* 1856 as *Old Noll; or, the Days of the Ironsides* (No. 8156). Revised
        "fourteenth edition" published in 1853 (No. 8137).

  8073. THE VILLAGE INN; OR THE ADVENTURE OF BELLECHASSAIGNE. NY:
        Winchester, 1843.

  8075. RINGWOOD THE ROVER, A TALE OF FLORIDA. Phila: Graham, 1843.
        For comment see next entry.

  8078. GUARICA, THE CHARIB BRIDE. A LEGEND OF HISPANIOLA. Phila:
        Rockafellar, 1844.
        Reprinted with No. 8075 in 1847 as *Tales of the Spanish Seas* (No. 8102).

  8079. THE LORD OF THE MANOR; OR ROSE CASTLETON'S TEMPTATION.
        Phila: Rockafellar, 1844.

  8084. RUTH WHALLEY; OR, THE FAIR PURITAN. A ROMANCE OF THE BAY
        PROVINCE. Bos: H.L. Williams, 1845.
        For comment see No. 8087 below.

  8085. THE WARWICK WOODLANDS, OR THINGS AS THEY WERE THERE, TEN
        YEARS AGO. Phila: Zieber, 1845.
        Revised edition published in 1851 (No. 8124). See also Nos. 8114 & 8132 below.

  8086. THE INNOCENT WITCH, A CONTINUATION OF RUTH WHALLEY. Bos:
        H.L. Williams, 1845.
        For comment see next entry.

  8087. THE REVOLT OF BOSTON. A CONTINUATION OF RUTH WHALLEY. Bos:
        H.L. Williams, 1845.
        Reprinted with Nos. 8084 & 8086 in 1875 as *The Fair Puritan. An Historical Ro-
        mance of the Days of Witchcraft* (No. 8175).

H. W. HERBERT (Frank Forester) (cont.)
*8091. MY SHOOTING BOX. Phila: Carey & Hart, 1846.
For comment see Nos. 8114 & 8132 below.

8092. THE ROMAN TRAITOR; A TRUE TALE OF THE REPUBLIC. Lon: Colburn, 1846.
3v.

8099. THE ROMAN TRAITOR: A TRUE TALE OF THE REPUBLIC. NY: W. Taylor, 1846.
2v.

*8100. THE MILLER OF MARTIGNÈ. A ROMANCE. NY: Richards, <1847>.

8101. INGLEBOROUGH HALL, AND LORD OF THE MANOR. NY: Burgess, Stringer, 1847.

8106. ISABEL GRAHAM, OR, CHARITY'S REWARD. NY: Williams, Bros., 1848.

8107. PIERRE, THE PARTISAN; A TALE OF THE MEXICAN MARCHES. NY: Williams Bros., 1848.
Reprinted in 1870 as *The Silent Rifleman* (No. 8171).

8108. FIELD SPORTS IN THE UNITED STATES, AND THE BRITISH PROVINCES OF AMERICA. By Frank Forester. Lon: Bentley, 1848.
2v.

*8112. FRANK FORESTER'S FIELD SPORTS OF THE UNITED STATES, AND BRITISH PROVINCES, OF NORTH AMERICA. NY: Stringer & Townsend, 1849.
2v. Frequently reprinted; the 1852 "fourth edition" is revised (No. 8129).

8114. THE DEERSTALKERS; OR, CIRCUMSTANTIAL EVIDENCE: A TALE OF THE SOUTH-WESTERN COUNTIES. By Frank Forester. Phila: Carey & Hart, 1849.
Published first in the U.K. together with Nos. 8085 & 8091 in 3v. in 1849 as *Frank Forester and His Friends* (No. 8113). See also No. 8132 below.

8115. DERMOT O'BRIEN: OR THE TAKING OF TREDAGH. A TALE OF 1649. NY: Stringer& Townsend, 1849.

8117. FRANK FORESTER'S FISH AND FISHING OF THE UNITED STATES AND BRITISH PROVINCES OF NORTH AMERICA. NY: Stringer & Townsend, 1850 <i.e. 1849>.
Also a simultaneous (?) U.K. edition (No. 8118) with title-page dated 1849. Revised "third edition" published in 1851 (No. 8125); a further revised edition in 1859 (No. 8166). See also next entry.

8119. SUPPLEMENT TO FRANK FORESTER'S FISH AND FISHING OF THE UNITED STATESAND BRITISH PROVINCES OF NORTH AMERICA. NY: Stringer & Townsend, 1850.
These sheets were apparently also issued bound with sheets of No. 8117 above (No. 8120).

*8127. THE CAPTAINS OF THE OLD WORLD; AS COMPARED WITH THE GREAT MODERN STRATEGISTS. NY: Scribner, 1851.

H. W. HERBERT (Frank Forester) (cont.)

8130. THE CAVALIERS OF ENGLAND, OR THE TIMES OF THE REVOLUTIONS OF 1642 AND 1688. NY: Redfield, 1852.

8131. THE KNIGHTS OF ENGLAND, FRANCE, AND SCOTLAND. NY: Redfield, 1852.

8132. THE QUORNDON HOUNDS; OR, A VIRGINIAN AT MELTON MOWBRAY. Phila: Getz, Buck, 1852.
Reprinted together with Nos. 8085, 8091, 8114 in 2v. in 1857 as *Frank Forester's Sporting Scenes and Characters* (No. 8157).

8135. THE CHEVALIERS OF FRANCE FROM THE CRUSADERS TO THE MARECHALS OF LOUIS XIV. NY: Redfield, 1853.

*8138. AMERICAN GAME IN ITS SEASONS. NY: Scribner, 1853.

8141. PERSONS AND PICTURES FROM THE HISTORIES OF FRANCE AND ENGLAND FROM THE NORMAN CONQUEST TO THE FALL OF THE STUARTS. NY: Riker, Thorne, 1854.

8142. THE CAPTAINS OF THE ROMAN REPUBLIC, AS COMPARED WITH THE GREAT MODERN STRATEGISTS. NY: Scribner, 1854.

*8146. MEMOIRS OF HENRY THE EIGHTH OF ENGLAND. NY & Auburn: Miller, Orton & Mulligan, 1855.

8147. WAGER OF BATTLE; A TALE OF SAXON SLAVERY IN SHERWOOD FOREST. NY: Mason Bros., 1855.

8153. THE COMPLETE MANUAL FOR YOUNG SPORTSMEN. By Frank Forester. NY: Stringer & Townsend, 1856.

8159. FRANK FORESTER'S HORSE AND HORSEMANSHIP OF THE UNITED STATES AND BRITISH PROVINCES OF NORTH AMERICA. NY: Stringer & Townsend, 1857.
2v.

8162. FISHING WITH HOOK AND LINE; A MANUAL FOR AMATEUR ANGLERS. By Frank Forrester<sic>. NY: Brother Jonathan Office, <1858>.
Reprinted *ca.* 1870 as *Frank Forrester's<sic> Fishermens' Guide* (No. 8173).

*8163. TRICKS AND TRAPS OF HORSE DEALERS. By Frank Forester. NY: Dinsmore, 1858.

8165. HINTS TO HORSE-KEEPERS, A COMPLETE MANUAL FOR HORSEMEN. NY: A.O. Moore, 1859.

8176. FRANK FORESTER'S FUGITIVE SPORTING SKETCHES. Westfield WI, 1879.
Ed. Will Wildwood <i.e. Frederick Eugene Pond>.

8178. LIFE AND WRITINGS OF FRANK FORESTER. NY: Judd, 1882.
2v. Ed. David W. Judd.

8179. POEMS OF "FRANK FORESTER." NY: Wiley & Sons, 1888.
Ed. Morgan Herbert <i.e. Margaret Morgan Herbert Mather>.

Thomas Wentworth Storrow Higginson
1823–1911

Note: Higginson's separately published addresses, lectures & sermons are here omitted, as are offprints from periodicals and his U.S. & English school histories.

8197.   THE BIRTHDAY IN FAIRY-LAND: A STORY FOR CHILDREN. Bos: Crosby & Nichols, 1850.

*8218.   WOMAN AND HER WISHES; AN ESSAY. Bos: Wallcut, 1853.
"Inscribed to the Massachusetts Constitutional Convention."

8249.   OUT-DOOR PAPERS. Bos: Ticknor & Fields, 1863.

8253.   HARVARD MEMORIAL BIOGRAPHIES. Cambridge: Sever & Francis, 1866.
2v. Edited by Higginson, who contributed numerous sketches. Revised edition published in 1867 (No. 8255).

8264.   MALBONE: AN OLDPORT ROMANCE. Bos: Fields, Osgood, 1869.

8271.   ARMY LIFE IN A BLACK REGIMENT. Bos: Fields, Osgood, 1870.
Extended edition published in 1900 as *The Writings,* Vol. 2, see No. 8440 below.

8277.   ATLANTIC ESSAYS. Bos: Osgood, 1871.

8282.   OLDPORT DAYS. Bos: Osgood, 1873.

8312.   SHORT STUDIES OF AMERICAN AUTHORS. Bos: Lee & Shepard, 1880.
Extended edition published in 1888 (No. 8356).

8327.   COMMON SENSE ABOUT WOMEN. Bos: Lee & Shepard, 1882.
Reprinted in 1900 as *The Writings,* Vol. 4, with title *Women and the Alphabet,* see No. 8440 below.

8338.   MARGARET FULLER OSSOLI. Bos & NY: Houghton, Mifflin, 1884.
American Men of Letters series.

8346.   THE MONARCH OF DREAMS. Bos: Lee & Shepard, 1887.

8349.   HINTS ON WRITING AND SPEECH-MAKING. Bos: Lee & Shepard, 1887.
Handbook Series.

8354.   WOMEN AND MEN. NY: Harper & Bros., 1888.

8362.   TRAVELLERS AND OUTLAWS EPISODES IN AMERICAN HISTORY. Bos: Lee & Shepard, 1889.

8363.   THE AFTERNOON LANDSCAPE POEMS AND TRANSLATIONS. NY & Lon: Longmans, Green, 1889.

8381.   LIFE OF FRANCIS HIGGINSON FIRST MINISTER IN THE MASSACHUSETTS BAY COLONY. NY: Dodd, Mead, <1891>.
Makers of America series.

8390.   THE NEW WORLD AND THE NEW BOOK AN ADDRESS ... WITH KINDRED ESSAYS. Bos: Lee & Shepard, 1892.

*8392.   CONCERNING ALL OF US. NY: Harper & Bros., 1892.

8398.   SUCH AS THEY ARE POEMS. Bos: Roberts Bros., 1893.
With Mary Thacher Higginson.

THOMAS WENTWORTH HIGGINSON (cont.)

8417. BOOK AND HEART ESSAYS ON LITERATURE AND LIFE. NY: Harper & Bros., 1897.

*8422. CHEERFUL YESTERDAYS. Bos & NY: Houghton, Mifflin, 1898.

8425. TALES OF THE ENCHANTED ISLANDS OF THE ATLANTIC. NY: Macmillan, 1898.

8429. OLD CAMBRIDGE. NY: Macmillan, 1899.

8433. CONTEMPORARIES. Bos & NY: Houghton, Mifflin, 1899.

*8440. THE WRITINGS OF THOMAS WENTWORTH HIGGINSON. Bos & NY: Houghton, Mifflin, 1900.
7v.

8444. AMERICAN ORATORS AND ORATORY. Cleveland: Imperial PR, March 1901.
"A report of lectures delivered ... at Western Reserve University."

*8448. HENRY WADSWORTH LONGFELLOW. Bos & NY: Houghton, Mifflin, 1902.
American Men of Letters series.

8449. JOHN GREENLEAF WHITTIER. NY: Macmillan, 1902.
English Men of Letters series.

8460. A READER'S HISTORY OF AMERICAN LITERATURE. Bos, NY, &c.: Houghton, Mifflin, <1903>.
With Henry Walcott Boynton.

8472. PART OF A MAN'S LIFE. Bos & NY: Houghton, Mifflin, 1905.

8481. LIFE AND TIMES OF STEPHEN HIGGINSON. Bos & NY: Houghton, Mifflin, 1907.

8488. THINGS WORTH WHILE. NY: Huebsch, 1908.
The Art of Life Series.

8495. CARLYLE'S LAUGH AND OTHER SURPRISES. Bos & NY: Houghton Mifflin, 1909.

8501. DESCENDANTS OF THE REVEREND FRANCIS HIGGINSON. <n.p.>, 1910.
"Privately printed."

8508. LETTERS AND JOURNALS OF THOMAS WENTWORTH HIGGINSON 1846–1906. Bos & NY: Houghton Mifflin, 1921.
Ed. Mary Thacher Higginson.

James Abraham Hillhouse
1789–1841

8510. PERCY'S MASQUE: A DRAMA. Lon: J. Miller, 1819.
Anon.

8511. PERCY'S MASQUE, A DRAMA. NY: Ptd by Van Winkle, 1820.
Anon. "From the London edition, with alterations."

JAMES A. HILLHOUSE (cont.)

8512. THE JUDGMENT, A VISION. NY: Eastburn, 1821.
Anon.

*8513. HADAD, A DRAMATIC POEM. NY: Bliss & White, 1825.

*8518. SACHEM'S-WOOD: A SHORT POEM, WITH NOTES. New Haven: B. & W. Noyes, 1838.
Anon.

8519. DRAMAS, DISCOURSES, AND OTHER PIECES. Bos: Little & Brown, 1839.
2v.

Charles Fenno Hoffman
1806–1884

8521. A WINTER IN THE WEST. By a New-Yorker. NY: Harper & Bros., 1835.
2v. Revised "second edition" also published in 1835 (No. 8522).

8525. WILD SCENES IN THE FOREST AND PRAIRIE. Lon: Bentley, 1839.
2v. For U.S. edition see No. 8535 below.

8526. GREYSLAER: A ROMANCE OF THE MOHAWK. Lon: Bentley, 1840.
3v.

8527. GREYSLAER: A ROMANCE OF THE MOHAWK. NY: Harper & Bros., 1840.
2v. Anon. Revised editions published in 1841 (No. 8529) & 1849 (No. 8569).

8535. THE VIGIL OF FAITH, AND OTHER POEMS. NY: Colman, 1842.
Published in the U.K. in 1844 with additional material (No. 8544); the U.S. "fourth edition" published in 1845 (No. 8556) & "fifth edition" published in 1846 as *Songs and Other Poems* (No. 8559) both contain new material. Earlier collections of Hoffman's verse were published in "extra numbers" of the *Quadruple Boston Notion* dated 10 June 1841 (No. 8530) & 15 July 1841 (No. 8531).

8538. WILD SCENES IN THE FOREST AND PRAIRIE, WITH SKETCHES OF AMERICAN LIFE. NY: Colyer, 1843.
2v.

8546. THE ECHO: OR, BORROWED NOTES FOR HOME CIRCULATION. Phila: Lindsay & Blakiston, 1844.

8564. LOVE'S CALENDAR, LAYS OF THE HUDSON, AND OTHER POEMS. NY: Appleton, 1847.

8565. THE PIONEERS OF NEW-YORK. AN ANNIVERSARY DISCOURSE. NY: Stanford & Swords, 1848.
Delivered before the St. Nicholas Society of Manhattan, 6 Dec. 1847.

8575. THE POEMS OF CHARLES FENNO HOFFMAN. Phila: Porter & Coates, 1873.
Ed. Edward Fenno Hoffman.

Josiah Gilbert Holland
(Timothy Titcomb)
1819–1881

8578. HISTORY OF WESTERN MASSACHUSETTS. THE COUNTIES OF HAMPDEN, HAMPSHIRE, FRANKLIN, AND BERKSHIRE. Springfield: Bowles, 1855. 2v.

8581. THE BAY-PATH; A TALE OF NEW ENGLAND COLONIAL LIFE. NY: Putnam, 1857.

8582. TITCOMB'S LETTERS TO YOUNG PEOPLE, SINGLE AND MARRIED. By Timothy Titcomb, Esq. NY: Scribner, 1858.
Revised "fiftieth edition" published in 1881 (No. 8637).

8583. BITTER-SWEET A POEM. NY: Scribner, 1859.
Revised (?) edition published in 1881 (No. 8635). See also No. 8611 below.

8585. GOLD-FOIL, HAMMERED FROM POPULAR PROVERBS. By Timothy Titcomb. NY: Scribner, 1859.
Revised edition published in 1881 (No. 8636).

8586. MISS GILBERT'S CAREER: AN AMERICAN STORY. NY: Scribner, 1860.
An unauthorized, altered edition published in the U.K. in 1867 as *The Heroes of Crampton* (No. 8603).

8589. LESSONS IN LIFE. A SERIES OF FAMILIAR ESSAYS. By Timothy Titcomb. NY: Scribner, 1861.
Revised edition published in 1881 (No. 8639).

8592. LETTERS TO THE JONESES. By Timothy Titcomb. NY: Scribner, 1863.
Revised edition published in 1881 as *Concerning the Jones Family* (No. 8641).

8600. THE LIFE OF ABRAHAM LINCOLN. Springfield: G. Bill, 1866.

8601. PLAIN TALKS ON FAMILIAR SUBJECTS. A SERIES OF POPULAR LECTURES. NY: Scribner, 1866.
Revised & extended edition published in 1881 (No. 8640).

8605. KATHRINA: HER LIFE AND MINE, IN A POEM. NY: Scribner, 1867.
Revised (?) edition published in 1881 (No. 8638). See also next entry.

*8611. THE MARBLE PROPHECY, AND OTHER POEMS. NY: Scribner, Armstrong, 1872.
Reprinted in 1873 with Nos. 8583 & 8605 above in an omnibus volume as *Garnered Sheaves* (No. 8612).

8614. ARTHUR BONNICASTLE, AN AMERICAN NOVEL. Lon: Routledge & Sons, <n.d., 1873>.

*8615. ARTHUR BONNICASTLE, AN AMERICAN NOVEL. NY: Scribner, Armstrong, 1873.

8616. ILLUSTRATED LIBRARY OF FAVORITE SONG. NY: Scribner, Armstrong, <1873>.
Edited, with contributions, by Holland. "Sold by subscription only." For full entry see BAL (No. 2853).

J. G. HOLLAND (cont.)

8617. THE MISTRESS OF THE MANSE. Lon: Low, Marston, et al, 1874.

*8618. THE MISTRESS OF THE MANSE. NY: Scribner, Armstrong, 1874.
       Revised editions published in 1877 (No. 8625) & 1881 (No. 8642).

8620. SEVENOAKS A STORY OF TO-DAY. NY: Scribner, Armstrong, 1875.
       Published in the U.K. in 1880 as *Paul Benedict* (No. 8632).

8623. EVERY-DAY TOPICS A BOOK OF BRIEFS. NY: Scribner, Armstrong, 1876.

*8624. NICHOLAS MINTURN. A STUDY IN A STORY. NY: Scribner, Armstrong,
       1877.

8628. THE COMPLETE POETICAL WRITINGS OF J G HOLLAND. NY: Scribner's
       Sons, 1879.

8645. EVERY-DAY TOPICS A BOOK OF BRIEFS ... SECOND SERIES. NY: Scribner's
       Sons, 1882.

Mary Jane Hawes Holmes
1825–1907

Note: Many of Holmes's early works were republished after *ca.* 1895 in
cheap editions, many of which appear under new titles and are truncated, rearranged or otherwise revised. These altered reprints are not
noted here unless there is clear evidence that Holmes herself made the
revisions.

*8649. TEMPEST AND SUNSHINE; OR, LIFE IN KENTUCKY. NY: Appleton, 1854.

*8650. THE ENGLISH ORPHANS; OR, A HOME IN THE NEW WORLD. NY & Lon:
       Appleton, 1855.

8651. THE HOMESTEAD ON THE HILLSIDE, AND OTHER TALES. NY &
       Auburn: Miller, Orton & Mulligan, 1856.

8652. 'LENA RIVERS. NY & Auburn: Miller, Orton & Mulligan, 1856.

8653. MEADOW BROOK. NY: Miller, Orton, 1857.

8654. DORA DEANE, OR THE EAST INDIA UNCLE; AND MAGGIE MILLER, OR
       OLD HAGAR'S SECRET. NY: Saxton, 1859.

8655. COUSIN MAUDE AND ROSAMOND. NY: Saxton, Barker, 1860.

*8656. MARIAN GREY; OR, THE HEIRESS OF REDSTONE HALL. NY: Carleton,
       1863.
       Revised edition published in 1899 (No. 8687).

8657. DARKNESS AND DAYLIGHT. A NOVEL. NY: Carleton, 1864.

*8658. HUGH WORTHINGTON. OF <sic> A NOVEL. NY: Carleton, 1865.

8659. THE CAMERON PRIDE; OR, PURIFIED BY SUFFERING. A NOVEL. NY:
       Carleton, 1867.

8660. ROSE MATHER: A TALE OF THE WAR. NY: Carleton, 1868.

8661. THE CHRISTMAS FONT. A STORY FOR YOUNG FOLKS. NY: Carleton,
       1868.

MARY J. HOLMES (cont.)

8662. ETHELYN'S MISTAKE; OR, THE HOME IN THE WEST. A NOVEL. NY: Carleton, 1869.

8663. MILLBANK; OR, ROGER IRVING'S WARD. A NOVEL. NY: Carleton, 1871.

8664. EDNA BROWNING; OR THE LEIGHTON HOMESTEAD. A NOVEL. NY: Carleton, 1872.

8665. WEST LAWN AND THE RECTOR OF ST. MARK'S. NY: Carleton, 1874.

8666. EDITH LYLE. A NOVEL. NY: Carleton, 1876.

*8667. MILDRED. A NOVEL. NY: Carleton, 1877.

*8668. DAISY THORNTON AND JESSIE GRAHAM. NY: Carleton, 1878.

*8669. FORREST HOUSE. A NOVEL. NY: Carleton, 1879.

*8670. CHATEAU D'OR. NORAH AND KITTY CRAIG. NY: Carleton, 1880.

8671. RED-BIRD. A BROWN COTTAGE STORY. NY: Carleton, 1880.
Reprinted in 1892 as *Red-Bird's Christmas Story* (No. 8680).

*8672. MADELINE. A NOVEL. NY: Carleton, 1881.

8673. QUEENIE HETHERTON. A NOVEL. NY: Carleton, 1883.

8674. CHRISTMAS STORIES. NY: Carleton, 1885.

8675. BESSIE'S FORTUNE. A NOVEL. NY: Carleton, 1886.

*8676. GRETCHEN. A NOVEL. NY: G.W. Dillingham, 1887.

8678. MARGUERITE. A NOVEL. NY: G.W. Dillingham, 1891.

*8683. DOCTOR HATHERN'S DAUGHTERS. A STORY OF VIRGINIA. NY: G.W. Dillingham, 1895.

*8684. MRS. HALLAM'S COMPANION. AND THE SPRING FARM, AND OTHER TALES. NY: G.W. Dillingham, 1896.
The title story was originally published as the Dec. 1894 issue of *Lippincott's Monthly Magazine* (No. 8681).

*8686. PAUL RALSTON. A NOVEL. NY: G.W. Dillingham, 1897.

8688. THE TRACY DIAMONDS. NY: G.W. Dillingham, 1899.

*8693. THE CROMPTONS. NY: G.W. Dillingham, <1902>.

*8694. THE MERIVALE BANKS. NY: G.W. Dillingham, <1903>.

8696. RENA'S EXPERIMENT. NY: G.W. Dillingham, <1904>.

8700. THE ABANDONED FARM AND CONNIE'S MISTAKE. NY: G.W. Dillingham, <1905>.

8701. LUCY HARDING A ROMANCE OF RUSSIA. NY: American News Co., <1905>.

Oliver Wendell Holmes
1809–1894

Note: Holmes's many addresses, orations and lectures are here omitted save for 2 early medical lectures, Nos. 8736 & 8738, and No. 8876; for collections of some of this material see Nos. 8803 & 8975. Similarly, separate printings of his occasional verse are also omitted save for 2 early pieces, Nos. 8745 & 8757.

8716. ILLUSTRATIONS OF THE ATHENÆUM GALLERY OF PAINTINGS. Bos: F.S. Hill, 1830.
Anon. Contains 9 poems by Holmes.

8723. THE HARBINGER; A MAY-GIFT. Bos: Carter, Hendee, 1833.
Anon. With Park Benjamin & John O. Sargent; see No. 977 above. Part 2 by Holmes.

8729. POEMS. Bos: Otis, Broaders, 1836.

8736. HOMŒOPATHY, AND ITS KINDRED DELUSIONS; TWO LECTURES. Bos: Ticknor, 1842.
Delivered before the Boston Society for the Diffusion of Useful Knowledge.

8738. THE CONTAGIOUSNESS OF PUERPERAL FEVER. <n.p., n.d.; Boston 1843? 1844?>.
Read before the Boston Society for Medical Improvement. "Published at the request of The Society." Reprinted with a new introduction in 1855 as *Puerperal Fever* (No. 8768).

8743. POEMS. Lon: Rich & Sons, 1846.
The edition prepared for publication in the U.S. by Ticknor, Boston.

8745. URANIA: A RHYMED LESSON. Bos: Ticknor, 1846.
Pronounced before the Mercantile Library Association, 14 Oct. 1846.

8750. POEMS ... NEW AND ENLARGED EDITION. Bos: Ticknor, 1849.
An extended edition was also published in 1849 with imprint of Ticknor, Reed & Fields (No. 8753). Other collections with a few new pieces are the "first English edition" of *The Poetical Works*, 1852 (No. 8762), the blue & gold edition of *The Poems*, 1862 (No. 8817) & *Humorous Poems*, 1865 (No. 8847). See also Nos. 8919, 9033 & 9059 below.

*8757. ASTRÆA: THE BALANCE OF ILLUSIONS. A POEM. Bos: Ticknor, Reed, & Fields, 1850.
Delivered before the Phi Beta Kappa Society of Yale College, 14 Aug. 1850.

8766. SONGS OF THE CLASS OF MDCCCXXIX. Bos: Prentiss & Sawyer, Ptrs, 1854.
Contains 3 poems by Holmes. Later editions published in 1859 (No. 8785), 1868 (No. 8863) & 1881 (No. 9150) contain additional Holmes material.

OLIVER WENDELL HOLMES (cont.)

*8781. THE AUTOCRAT OF THE BREAKFAST-TABLE. Bos: Phillips, Sampson, 1858.
Anon. These sheets also issued in the U.K. (No. 8781A). Revised edition published in 1883 (No. 8970). Another 1883 edition published in the U.K. (No. 8979) with 1 additional piece.

*8791. THE PROFESSOR AT THE BREAKFAST-TABLE; WITH THE STORY OF IRIS. Bos: Ticknor & Fields, 1860.
Revised edition published in 1883 (No. 8972).

*8801. ELSIE VENNER: A ROMANCE OF DESTINY. Bos: Ticknor & Fields, 1861.
2v.

 8803. CURRENTS AND COUNTER-CURRENTS IN MEDICAL SCIENCE. WITH OTHER ADDRESSES AND ESSAYS. Bos: Ticknor & Fields, 1861.

*8813. SONGS IN MANY KEYS. Bos: Ticknor & Fields, 1862.

 8829. SOUNDINGS FROM THE ATLANTIC. Bos: Ticknor & Fields, 1864.

 8856. THE GUARDIAN ANGEL. Lon: Low, Son, & Marston, 1867.
2v.

 8857. THE GUARDIAN ANGEL. Bos: Ticknor & Fields, 1867.

*8876. MECHANISM IN THOUGHT AND MORALS. AN ADDRESS. Bos: Osgood, 1871.
Delivered before the Phi Beta Kappa Society, Harvard University, 29 June 1870. Also a simultaneous (?) U.K. edition.

*8881. THE POET AT THE BREAKFAST-TABLE. Bos: Osgood, 1872.
Anon.

*8895. SONGS OF MANY SEASONS. 1862–1874. Bos: Osgood, 1875.

 8919. THE POETICAL WORKS. Bos: Osgood, 1877.
Household Edition. Other collections with a few new pieces are *The Poetical Works,* 1881 (No. 8954) & *Illustrated Poems,* 1885 (No. 8985). See also Nos. 9033 & 9059 below.

 8928. JOHN LOTHROP MOTLEY. A MEMOIR. Lon: Trübner, 1878.

 8931. THE SCHOOL-BOY. Bos: Houghton, Osgood, 1879.
Also privately printed for the author's use in 1878 (No. 8925).

*8933. JOHN LOTHROP MOTLEY. A MEMOIR. Bos: Houghton, Osgood, 1879.
Slightly revised reprint also published in 1879 (No. 8934).

 8949. THE IRON GATE, AND OTHER POEMS. Bos: Houghton, Mifflin, 1880.

 8975. MEDICAL ESSAYS 1842–1882. Bos & NY: Houghton, Mifflin, 1883.

*8978. PAGES FROM AN OLD VOLUME OF LIFE A COLLECTION OF ESSAYS 1857–1881. Bos & NY: Houghton, Mifflin, 1883.

 8986. RALPH WALDO EMERSON. Bos & NY: Houghton, Mifflin, 1885.
American Men of Letters series.

*8989. A MORTAL ANTIPATHY FIRST OPENING OF THE NEW PORTFOLIO. Bos & NY: Houghton, Mifflin, 1885.
A partial copyright printing was also produced in 1885 (No. 8988).

OLIVER WENDELL HOLMES (cont.)

9005.   OUR HUNDRED DAYS IN EUROPE. Lon: Low, Marston, et al, 1887.

9006.   OUR HUNDRED DAYS IN EUROPE. Bos & NY: Houghton, Mifflin, 1887.

*9012. BEFORE THE CURFEW AND OTHER POEMS, CHIEFLY OCCASIONAL. Bos & NY: Houghton, Mifflin, 1888.

*9027. OVER THE TEACUPS. Bos & NY: Houghton, Mifflin, 1891 <i.e. 1890>.

*9033. THE WRITINGS OF OLIVER WENDELL HOLMES. Bos & NY: Houghton, Mifflin, 1891–92.
        14v. Contains new prefaces in Vols. 1–9 & 4 new poems in Vol. 13, *The Poetical Works*, Vol. 3.

9059.   THE COMPLETE POETICAL WORKS OF OLIVER WENDELL HOLMES. Bos & NY: Houghton, Mifflin, <1895>.
        Cambridge Edition. Several poems here collected are also included in an extended edition of the "Household Edition" published not before 1894 (No. 9054).

*9060. LIFE AND LETTERS OF OLIVER WENDELL HOLMES. Bos & NY: Houghton, Mifflin, 1896.
        2v. By John T. Morse, Jr.

9076.   THE AUTOCRAT'S MISCELLANIES. NY: Twayne, <1959>.
        Ed. Albert Mordell.

William Howe Cuyler Hosmer
1814–1877

9286.   THE PIONEERS OF WESTERN NEW-YORK: A POEM. Geneva NY: Ptd by I. Merrell, 1838.
        Pronounced before the Literary Societies of Geneva College, 1 Aug. 1838.

9289.   THE PROSPECTS OF THE AGE. A POEM. Burlington: Goodrich, 1841.
        Delivered before the Literary Societies of the University of Vermont, Burlington, 3 Aug. 1841.

9292.   THEMES OF SONG: A POEM. Rochester: Ptd by W. Alling, 1842.
        Read before the Amphictyon Association of the Genesee Wesleyan Seminary, 30 Sept. 1842.

9293.   YONNONDIO, OR WARRIOR OF THE GENESEE: A TALE OF THE SEVEN-TEENTH CENTURY. NY: Wiley & Putnam, 1844.

9297.   THE MONTHS. Bos: Ticknor, 1847.

9300.   THE POETICAL WORKS OF WILLIAM H.C. HOSMER. NY: Redfield, 1854.
        2v.

9311.   LATER LAYS AND LYRICS. Rochester: Dewey, 1873.

Emerson Hough
1857–1923

9314. THE SINGING MOUSE STORIES. NY: Forest & Stream Pub. Co., 1895.
Revised & extended edition published in 1910 (No. 9334).

9315. THE STORY OF THE COWBOY. NY: Appleton, 1897.
Reprinted in 1908 as *The Cowboy* (No. 9329).

*9316. THE GIRL AT THE HALFWAY HOUSE A STORY OF THE PLAINS. NY: Appleton, 1900.

*9318. THE MISSISSIPPI BUBBLE ... A NOVEL. Indianapolis: Bowen-Merrill, <1902>.

9319. THE WAY TO THE WEST AND THE LIVES OF THREE EARLY AMERICANS BOONE—CROCKETT—CARSON. Indianapolis: Bobbs-Merrill, <1903>.

9322. THE LAW OF THE LAND ... A NOVEL. Indianapolis: Bobbs-Merrill, <1904>.

9323. HEART'S DESIRE. NY: Macmillan, 1905.

*9325. THE KING OF GEE-WHIZ. Indianapolis: Bobbs-Merrill, <1906>.
Lyrics by Wilbur D. Nesbit.

9326. THE STORY OF THE OUTLAW A STUDY OF THE WESTERN DESPERADO. NY: Outing Pub. Co., 1907.

9327. THE WAY OF A MAN. NY: Outing Pub. Co., 1907.

9328. THE YOUNG ALASKANS. NY & Lon: Harper & Bros., 1908.

*9330. 54–40 OR FIGHT. Indianapolis: Bobbs-Merrill, <1909>.

9331. THE SOWING A "YANKEE'S" VIEW OF ENGLAND'S DUTY TO HERSELF AND TO CANADA. Chi, Lon, &c.: Vanderhoof-Gunn, 1909.

*9333. THE PURCHASE PRICE OR THE CAUSE OF COMPROMISE. Indianapolis: Bobbs-Merrill, <1910>.

9335. THE YOUNG ALASKANS ON THE TRAIL. NY & Lon: Harper & Bros., 1911.

*9336. JOHN RAWN PROMINENT CITIZEN. Indianapolis: Bobbs-Merrill, <1912>.

9339. THE LADY AND THE PIRATE. Indianapolis: Bobbs-Merrill, <1913>.

9340. THE YOUNG ALASKANS IN THE ROCKIES. NY & Lon: Harper & Bros., 1913.

9341. GETTING A WRONG START A TRUTHFUL AUTOBIOGRAPHY. NY: Macmillan, 1915.
Anon.

9342. OUT OF DOORS. NY & Lon: Appleton, 1915.

9343. LET US GO AFIELD. NY & Lon: Appleton, 1916.

9344. THE MAGNIFICENT ADVENTURE. NY & Lon: Appleton, 1916.

9347. THE MAN NEXT DOOR. NY & Lon: Appleton, 1917.

9348. THE BROKEN GATE. NY & Lon: Appleton, 1917.

EMERSON HOUGH (cont.)

9349. THE WAY OUT A STORY OF THE CUMBERLANDS TO-DAY. NY & Lon: Appleton, 1918.

9350. THE PASSING OF THE FRONTIER A CHRONICLE OF THE OLD WEST. New Haven: Yale U PR, 1918.
The Chronicles of America series, Abraham Lincoln Edition, Vol. 26. Reprinted in 1924 as part 2 of The Last Frontier (No. 9364).

9351. YOUNG ALASKANS IN THE FAR NORTH. NY & Lon: Harper & Bros., <1918>.

9353. THE SAGEBRUSHER A STORY OF THE WEST. NY & Lon: Appleton, 1919.

9354. THE WEB. Chi: Reilly & Lee, <1919>.
"The authorized history of the American Protective League."

9357. MAW'S VACATION   THE STORY OF A HUMAN BEING IN THE YELLOWSTONE. St. Paul: Haynes, 1921.

9359. THE COVERED WAGON. NY & Lon: Appleton, 1922.

9360. THE YOUNG ALASKANS ON THE MISSOURI. NY & Lon: Harper & Bros., <1922>.

9362. NORTH OF 36. NY & Lon: Appleton, 1923.

9363. MOTHER OF GOLD. NY & Lon: Appleton, 1924.

9365. THE SHIP OF SOULS. NY & Lon: Appleton, 1925.

Richard Hovey
1864–1900

9367. POEMS. Wash DC: N.B. Smith, Ptr, 1880.

9369. HANOVER BY GASLIGHT OR WAYS THAT ARE DARK BEING AN EXPOSÉ OF THE SOPHOMORIC CAREER OF '85. <n.p., n.d.; Hanover NH, 1883?>.
"Imprinted for the Class of '85."

9371. THE LAUREL; AN ODE. TO MARY DAY LANIER. Wash DC: The Author, 1889.

9372. HARMONICS. <n.p., n.d.; probably Wash DC, ca. 1890>.

9375. LAUNCELOT AND GUENEVERE A POEM IN DRAMAS. NY: United States Book Co., <1891>.
Revised editions of portions of the text published separately in 1895 as The Marriage of Guenevere (No. 9382) & in 1898 as The Quest of Merlin (No. 9386).

9376. SEAWARD AN ELEGY ON THE DEATH OF THOMAS WILLIAM PARSONS. Bos: Lothrop, 1893.

*9380. SONGS FROM VAGABONDIA. Bos: Copeland & Day, 1894.
With Bliss Carman, see No. 2622 above.

*9385. MORE SONGS FROM VAGABONDIA. Bos: Copeland & Day, 1896.
With Bliss Carman, see No. 2634 above.

9387. THE BIRTH OF GALAHAD. Bos: Small Maynard, 1898.

9389. ALONG THE TRAIL A BOOK OF LYRICS. Bos: Small, Maynard, 1898.

*9391. TALIESIN A MASQUE. Bos: Small Maynard, 1900.

9392. LAST SONGS FROM VAGABONDIA. Bos: Small, Maynard, 1901.
With Bliss Carman, see No. 2646 above.

9395. THE HOLY GRAAL AND OTHER FRAGMENTS. NY: Duffield, 1907.
Ed. Mrs. Richard Hovey.

9397. TO THE END OF THE TRAIL. NY: Duffield, 1908.
Ed. Mrs. Richard Hovey.

9401. DARTMOUTH LYRICS. Bos: Small, Maynard, <1924>.
Ed. Edwin Osgood Grover.

Julia Ward Howe
1819–1910

9409. PASSION-FLOWERS. Bos: Ticknor, Reed, & Fields, 1854.
Anon.

9411. WORDS FOR THE HOUR. Bos: Ticknor & Fields, 1857.
Anon.

*9412. THE WORLD'S OWN. Bos: Ticknor & Fields, 1857.
Another version was also published in 1857 by Baker & Godwin, New York, with title *Leonore; or, The World's Own* & issued as *Stuart's Repertory of Original American Plays,* No. 1. Sequence not established.

9414. A TRIP TO CUBA. Bos: Ticknor & Fields, 1860.

*9416. BATTLE HYMN OF THE REPUBLIC. 1862.
First printed in *The Atlantic Monthly,* Feb. 1862. Published separately as sheet music by Oliver Ditson, Boston, March 1862. BAL lists other significant appearances from 1862–63. Collected in *Later Lyrics,* 1866.

9427. LATER LYRICS. Bos: Tilton, 1866.

9429. FROM THE OAK TO THE OLIVE. A PLAIN RECORD OF A PLEASANT JOURNEY. Bos: Lee & Shepard, 1868.

9448. MEMOIR OF DR. SAMUEL GRIDLEY HOWE ... WITH OTHER MEMORIAL TRIBUTES. Bos: Howe Memorial Committee, 1876

9458. MODERN SOCIETY. Bos: Roberts Bros., 1881.

9462. MARGARET FULLER (MARCHESA OSSOLI). Bos: Roberts Bros., 1883.
Famous Women series.

9492. IS POLITE SOCIETY POLITE? AND OTHER ESSAYS. Bos & NY: Lamson, Wolffe, 1895.
These sheets reissued in 1899 by Houghton, Mifflin.

9496. FROM SUNSET RIDGE POEMS OLD AND NEW. Bos & NY: Houghton, Mifflin, 1898.

9501. REMINISCENCES 1819–1899. Bos & NY: Houghton, Mifflin, 1899.

*9519. ORIGINAL POEMS AND OTHER VERSE SET TO MUSIC AS SONGS. <Bos>: Boston Music Co., 1908.

JULIA WARD HOWE (cont.)

9526. AT SUNSET. Bos & NY: Houghton Mifflin, 1910.
Ed. Laura E. Richards.

9529. JULIA WARD HOWE AND THE WOMAN SUFFRAGE MOVEMENT A
SELECTION FROM HER SPEECHES AND ESSAYS. Bos: Estes, <1913>.

9530. JULIA WARD HOWE 1819–1910. Bos & NY: Houghton Mifflin, 1915.
2v. By Laura E. Richards & Maud Howe Elliott, assisted by Florence Howe Hall.

9531. THE WALK WITH GOD … EXTRACTS FROM MRS HOWE'S PRIVATE
JOURNALS. NY: Dutton, <1919>.
Ed. Laura E. Richards.

William Dean Howells
1837–1920

9537. POEMS OF TWO FRIENDS. Columbus: Follett, Foster, 1860.
With John J. Piatt, see No. 15983 below.

*9538. LIVES AND SPEECHES OF ABRAHAM LINCOLN AND HANNIBAL HAMLIN.
Columbus: Follett, Foster, 1860.
The life of Hamlin by J.L. Hayes.

9546. VENETIAN LIFE. Lon: Trübner, 1866.

9547. VENETIAN LIFE. NY: Hurd & Houghton, 1866.
Extended editions published in 1867 (No. 9550), 1872 (No. 9562) & 1907 (No.
9784).

9551. ITALIAN JOURNEYS. NY: Hurd & Houghton, 1867.
Extended edition published in 1872 (No. 9560) & revised in 1901 (Nos. 9742 &
9743).

9552. NO LOVE LOST A ROMANCE OF TRAVEL. NY: Putnam & Son, 1869.

*9555. SUBURBAN SKETCHES. NY: Hurd & Houghton, 1871.
Extended edition published in 1872 (No. 9561).

*9558. THEIR WEDDING JOURNEY. Bos: Osgood, 1872.
Reprinted in 1887 (No. 9632) with the addition "Niagara Revisited," see No. 9615
below.

9566. A CHANCE ACQUAINTANCE. Bos: Osgood, 1873.

9567. POEMS. Bos: Osgood, 1873.
Extended edition published in 1886 (No. 9622).

*9568. A FOREGONE CONCLUSION. Bos: Osgood, 1875.

9572. SKETCH OF THE LIFE AND CHARACTER OF RUTHERFORD B. HAYES …
ALSO A BIOGRAPHICAL SKETCH OF WILLIAM A. WHEELER. NY: Hurd
& Houghton, 1876.

9574. THE PARLOR CAR. FARCE. Bos: Osgood, 1876.

9575. OUT OF THE QUESTION. A COMEDY. Bos: Osgood, 1877.

9577. A COUNTERFEIT PRESENTMENT. COMEDY. Bos: Osgood, 1877.

WILLIAM DEAN HOWELLS (cont.)

*9584. THE LADY OF THE AROOSTOOK. Bos: Houghton, Osgood, 1879.

*9589. THE UNDISCOVERED COUNTRY. Bos: Houghton, Mifflin, 1880.

9591. A FEARFUL RESPONSIBILITY AND OTHER STORIES. Bos: Osgood, 1881.

9594. DOCTOR BREEN'S PRACTICE A NOVEL. Bos: Osgood, 1881.
A partial copyright printing was also produced in 1881 (No. 9591A).

9601. A MODERN INSTANCE A NOVEL. Edinburgh: Douglas, 1882.
2v. A copyright printing was also produced in 1882 (No. 9597).

*9602. A MODERN INSTANCE A NOVEL. Bos: Osgood, 1882.

9609. THE SLEEPING-CAR A FARCE. Bos: Osgood, 1883.

9610. A WOMAN'S REASON A NOVEL. Bos: Osgood, 1883.
A partial copyright printing was also produced in 1883 (No. 9607A).

*9612. A LITTLE GIRL AMONG THE OLD MASTERS. Bos: Osgood, 1884.
Drawings by Mildred Howells, with "introduction and comment" by W.D. Howells.

9613. THE REGISTER FARCE. Bos: Osgood, 1884.

9614. THREE VILLAGES. Bos: Osgood, 1884.

9615. NIAGARA REVISITED. Chi: Dalziel, <n.d., 1884?>.
For comment see No. 9558 above.

9617. THE ELEVATOR FARCE. Bos: Osgood, 1885.

*9619. THE RISE OF SILAS LAPHAM. Bos: Ticknor, 1885.
A copyright printing was also produced in 1885 (No. 9614A).

9620. TUSCAN CITIES. Bos: Ticknor, 1886.

9623. THE GARROTERS FARCE. NY: Harper & Bros., 1886.

9624. INDIAN SUMMER. Bos: Ticknor, 1886.
A copyright printing was produced in 1885 (No. 9618).

9626. THE MINISTER'S CHARGE OR THE APPRENTICESHIP OF LEMUEL BARKER.
Edinburgh: Douglas, 1886.

9627. THE MINISTER'S CHARGE OR THE APPRENTICESHIP OF LEMUEL BARKER.
Bos: Ticknor, 1887.

9629. MODERN ITALIAN POETS ESSAYS AND VERSIONS. NY: Harper & Bros.,
1887.

9630. APRIL HOPES A NOVEL. Edinburgh: Douglas, 1887.

9634. APRIL HOPES. NY: Harper & Bros., 1888.

9638. A SEA-CHANGE OR LOVE'S STOWAWAY A LYRICATED FARCE. Bos:
Ticknor, 1888.
Also published with music by George Henschel as a libretto in 1888, but with
copyright notice dated 1884, by Arthur P. Schmidt, Boston.

9639. ANNIE KILBURN A NOVEL. Edinburgh: Douglas, 1888.
A copyright printing was also produced in 1888 (No. 9637A).

9641. ANNIE KILBURN A NOVEL. NY: Harper & Bros., 1889.

9642. THE MOUSE-TRAP AND OTHER FARCES. NY: Harper & Bros., 1889.

WILLIAM DEAN HOWELLS (cont.)

*9646. A HAZARD OF NEW FORTUNES A NOVEL. NY: Harper & Bros., 1890 <i.e. 1889>.
Harper's Franklin Square Library, New Series, No. 661, Nov. 1889. A copyright printing was also produced in 1889 (No. 9641A).

9650. THE SHADOW OF A DREAM A NOVEL. Edinburgh: Douglas, 1890.

9651. THE SHADOW OF A DREAM A STORY. NY: Harper & Bros., 1890.
Cloth; and paper wrapper of *Harper's Franklin Square Library, New Series,* No. 672, May, 1890.

*9654. A BOY'S TOWN. NY: Harper & Bros., 1890.

9656. CRITICISM AND FICTION. NY: Harper & Bros., 1891.

*9658. THE ALBANY DEPOT. NY: Harper & Bros., 1892.
A private printing for professional use was also produced, presumably in 1891 (No. 9657).

*9659. AN IMPERATIVE DUTY. A NOVEL. NY: Harper & Bros., 1892 <i.e. 1891>.

9665. MERCY A NOVEL. Edinburgh: Douglas, 1892.
For U.S. edition see next entry.

*9666. THE QUALITY OF MERCY A NOVEL. NY: Harper & Bros., 1892.

9667. A LETTER OF INTRODUCTION FARCE. NY: Harper & Bros., 1892.

9669. A LITTLE SWISS SOJOURN. NY: Harper & Bros., 1892.

9671. CHRISTMAS EVERY DAY AND OTHER STORIES TOLD FOR CHILDREN. NY: Harper & Bros., 1893.

9672. THE WORLD OF CHANCE A NOVEL. Edinburgh: Douglas, 1893.

9673. THE WORLD OF CHANCE A NOVEL. NY: Harper & Bros., 1893.
Cloth; and paper wrapper of *Harper's Franklin Square Library, New Series,* No. 736, July, 1893.

9674. THE UNEXPECTED GUESTS A FARCE. NY: Harper & Bros., 1893.

9676. MY YEAR IN A LOG CABIN. NY: Harper & Bros., 1893.

9677. EVENING DRESS FARCE. NY: Harper & Bros., 1893.

9679. THE COAST OF BOHEMIA A NOVEL. NY: Harper & Bros., 1893.

9685. A TRAVELER FROM ALTRURIA ROMANCE. NY: Harper & Bros., 1894.
For comment see No. 9882A below.

9694. MY LITERARY PASSIONS. NY: Harper & Bros., 1895.

*9697. STOPS OF VARIOUS QVILLS. NY: Harper & Bros., 1895.

9703. THE DAY OF THEIR WEDDING A NOVEL. NY: Harper & Bros., 1896.
Published in the U.K. with *A Parting and a Meeting,* see next entry, in 1896 as *Idyls in Drab* (No. 9708).

9704. A PARTING AND A MEETING STORY. NY: Harper & Bros., 1896.
For comment see preceding entry.

9706. IMPRESSIONS AND EXPERIENCES. NY: Harper & Bros., 1896.

9711. A PREVIOUS ENGAGEMENT COMEDY. NY: Harper & Bros., 1897.

WILLIAM DEAN HOWELLS (cont.)

9713. THE LANDLORD AT LION'S HEAD. Edinburgh: Douglas, 1897.

*9714. THE LANDLORD AT LION'S HEAD A NOVEL. NY: Harper & Bros., 1897.

9715. AN OPEN-EYED CONSPIRACY AN IDYL OF SARATOGA. NY & Lon: Harper & Bros., 1897.

9716. STORIES OF OHIO. NY, Cinc, &c.: American Book Co., 1897.

9719. THE STORY OF A PLAY A NOVEL. NY & Lon: Harper & Bros., 1898.

9723. RAGGED LADY A NOVEL. NY & Lon: Harper & Bros., 1899.

9726. THEIR SILVER WEDDING JOURNEY. NY & Lon: Harper & Bros., 1899. 2v.

9731. BRIDE ROSES A SCENE. Bos & NY: Houghton, Mifflin, 1900.

9732. ROOM FORTY-FIVE A FARCE. Bos & NY: Houghton, Mifflin, 1900.

*9733. AN INDIAN GIVER A COMEDY. Bos & NY: Houghton, Mifflin, 1900.

*9734. THE SMOKING CAR A FARCE. Bos & NY: Houghton, Mifflin, 1900.

*9736. LITERARY FRIENDS AND ACQUAINTANCE. NY & Lon: Harper & Bros., 1900.
Extended edition published in 1911 (No. 9811).

*9739. A PAIR OF PATIENT LOVERS. NY & Lon: Harper & Bros., 1901.
Harper's Portrait Collection of Short Stories, Vol. 1.

9741. HEROINES OF FICTION. NY & Lon: Harper & Bros., 1901. 2v.

*9747. THE KENTONS A NOVEL. NY & Lon: Harper & Bros., 1902.

9748. THE FLIGHT OF PONY BAKER A BOY'S TOWN STORY. NY & Lon: Harper & Bros., 1902.

9749. LITERATURE AND LIFE STUDIES. NY & Lon: Harper & Bros., 1902.

9752. QUESTIONABLE SHAPES. NY & Lon: Harper & Bros., 1903.

9753. LETTERS HOME. NY & Lon: Harper & Bros., 1903.

9758. THE SON OF ROYAL LANGBRITH A NOVEL. NY & Lon: Harper & Bros., 1904.

9760. MISS BELLARD'S INSPIRATION A NOVEL. NY & Lon: Harper & Bros., 1905.

9762. LONDON FILMS. NY & Lon: Harper & Bros., 1905.

*9774. CERTAIN DELIGHTFUL ENGLISH TOWNS WITH GLIMPSES OF THE PLEASANT COUNTRY BETWEEN. NY & Lon: Harper & Bros., 1906.

9779. THROUGH THE EYE OF THE NEEDLE A ROMANCE. NY & Lon: Harper & Bros., 1907.

9783. BETWEEN THE DARK AND THE DAYLIGHT ROMANCES. NY & Lon: Harper & Bros., 1907.

9787. FENNEL AND RUE A NOVEL. NY & Lon: Harper & Bros., 1908.

*9791. ROMAN HOLIDAYS AND OTHERS. NY & Lon: Harper & Bros., 1908.

9793. THE MOTHER AND THE FATHER DRAMATIC PASSAGES. NY & Lon: Harper & Bros., 1909.

WILLIAM DEAN HOWELLS (cont.)

9795.   SEVEN ENGLISH CITIES. NY & Lon: Harper & Bros., 1909.

9803.   MY MARK TWAIN REMINISCENCES AND CRITICISMS. NY & Lon: Harper & Bros., 1910.

9804.   IMAGINARY INTERVIEWS. NY & Lon: Harper & Bros., 1910.

9808.   PARTING FRIENDS A FARCE. NY & Lon: Harper & Bros., 1911.

*9825. NEW LEAF MILLS A CHRONICLE. NY & Lon: Harper & Bros., 1913.

9826.   FAMILIAR SPANISH TRAVELS. NY & Lon: Harper & Bros., 1913.

9829.   THE SEEN AND UNSEEN AT STRATFORD-ON-AVON A FANTASY. NY & Lon: Harper & Bros., 1914.

9837.   THE DAUGHTER OF THE STORAGE AND OTHER THINGS IN PROSE AND VERSE. NY & Lon: Harper & Bros., <1916>.

9840.   THE LEATHERWOOD GOD. NY: Century Co., 1916.

*9841. YEARS OF MY YOUTH. NY & Lon: Harper & Bros., <1916>.

*9862. THE VACATION OF THE KELWYNS AN IDYL OF THE MIDDLE EIGHTEEN-SEVENTIES. NY & Lon: Harper & Bros., <1920>.

9864.   MRS. FARRELL A NOVEL. NY & Lon: Harper & Bros. <1921>.

9870.   LIFE IN LETTERS OF WILLIAM DEAN HOWELLS. Garden City NY: Doubleday, Doran, 1928.
2v. Ed. Mildred Howells.

9880.   CRITICISM AND FICTION AND OTHER ESSAYS. <NY>: New York U PR, 1959.
Ed. Clara Marburg Kirk & Rudolf Kirk.

9881.   MARK TWAIN—HOWELLS LETTERS THE CORRESPONDENCE OF SAMUEL L. CLEMENS AND WILLIAM D. HOWELLS 1872-1910. Cambridge: Harvard U PR, 1960.
2v. Ed. Henry Nash Smith & William M. Gibson.

9882.   THE COMPLETE PLAYS OF WILLIAM DEAN HOWELLS. <NY>: New York U PR, 1960.
Ed. Walter J. Meserve.

9882A. LETTERS OF AN ALTRURIAN TRAVELLER (1893-94). Gainesville: Scholars' Facsimiles & Reprints, 1961.
Facsimile reproduction from *The Cosmopolitan* magazine, where it continued *A Traveler from Altruria*, No. 9685 above. Much of this material was revised & published in Nos. 9706 & 9779 above.

9882B. DISCOVERY OF A GENIUS WILLIAM DEAN HOWELLS AND HENRY JAMES. NY: Twayne, 1961.
Ed. Albert Mordell.

James Gibbons Huneker
1857–1921

9883. MEZZOTINTS IN MODERN MUSIC. NY: Scribner's Sons, 1899.

9886. CHOPIN THE MAN AND HIS MUSIC. NY: Scribner's Sons, 1900.

9888. MELOMANIACS. NY: Scribner's Sons, 1902.

*9891. OVERTONES A BOOK OF TEMPERAMENTS. NY: Scribner's Sons, 1904.

*9892. ICONOCLASTS A BOOK OF DRAMATISTS. NY: Scribner's Sons, 1905.

9893. VISIONARIES. NY: Scribner's Sons, 1905.

9897. EGOISTS A BOOK OF SUPERMEN. NY: Scribner's Sons, 1909.

9899. PROMENADES OF AN IMPRESSIONIST. NY: Scribner's Sons, 1910.

9902. FRANZ LISZT. NY: Scribner's Sons, 1911.

*9905. THE PATHOS OF DISTANCE A BOOK OF A THOUSAND AND ONE MOMENTS. NY: Scribner's Sons, 1913.

9906. OLD FOGY HIS MUSICAL OPINIONS AND GROTESQUES. Phila: Presser, <1913>.

9908. NEW COSMOPOLIS A BOOK OF IMAGES. NY: Scribner's Sons, 1915.

9910. IVORY APES AND PEACOCKS. NY: Scribner's Sons, 1915.

9912. UNICORNS. NY: Scribner's Sons, 1917.

9915. THE PHILHARMONIC SOCIETY OF NEW YORK AND ITS SEVENTY-FIFTH ANNIVERSARY A RETROSPECT. <n.p., n.d.; NY, 1917? 1918?>.

9919. BEDOUINS. NY: Scribner's Sons, 1920.

9920. STEEPLEJACK. NY: Scribner's Sons, 1920.
2v.

*9921. PAINTED VEILS. NY: Boni & Liveright, <1920>.

9922. VARIATIONS. NY: Scribner's Sons, 1921.

*9923. LETTERS OF JAMES GIBBONS HUNEKER. NY: Scribner's Sons, 1922.
Ed. Josephine Huneker.

9924. INTIMATE LETTERS OF JAMES GIBBONS HUNEKER. <NY>: Boni & Liveright, 1924.
"Issued for subscribers only." Ed. Josephine Huneker.

Joseph Holt Ingraham
1809–1860

Note: After Ingraham's death, many of his works were thoroughly altered & revised by his son, Col. Prentiss Ingraham, and published under new titles. Other posthumous works may be falsely attributed to Ingraham. Also, the sheets of *The Dancing Star,* 1857 (No. 10051) and *The Lady Imogen,* 1861 (No. 10057) were removed from *The Weekly Novelette* and issued in paper wrapper with cover-title; these two works were not otherwise published in book form.

9929. THE SOUTH-WEST. By a Yankee. NY: Harper & Bros., 1835.
2v.

*9930. LAFITTE: THE PIRATE OF THE GULF. NY: Harper & Bros., 1836.
2v. Anon. Revised "second edition" also published in 1836 (No. 9931). Published in the U.K. in 1837 as *The Pirate of the Gulf* & in 1839 as *The Pirate* (No. 9941).

*9934. BURTON; OR, THE SIEGES. A ROMANCE. NY: Harper & Bros., 1838.
2v. Anon. Published in the U.K. in 1839 <i.e. Nov. 1838> as *Quebec and New York* (No. 9942).

9937. CAPTAIN KYD; OR, THE WIZARD OF THE SEA. A ROMANCE. NY: Harper & Bros., 1839.
2v. Anon. Published in the U.K. in 1839 as *Kyd the Buccanier* (No. 9938).

9939. THE AMERICAN LOUNGER; OR, TALES, SKETCHES, AND LEGENDS GATHERED IN SUNDRY JOURNEYINGS. Phila: Lea & Blanchard, 1839.
Anon.

9943. THE QUADROONE: OR, ST. MICHAEL'S DAY. Lon: Bentley, 1840.
3v. Anon.

9946. THE QUADROONE; OR, ST. MICHAEL'S DAY. NY: Harper & Bros., 1841.
2v. Anon.

*9947. THE DANCING FEATHER, OR THE AMATEUR FREEBOOTERS. A ROMANCE OF NEW YORK. Bos: G. Roberts, 1842.
A truncated version was also published in 1842 (No. 9948). Reprinted in 1877 as *The Pirate Schooner* (No. 10078); see also No. 9954 below.

9949. EDWARD AUSTIN: OR, THE HUNTING FLASK. A TALE OF THE FOREST AND TOWN. Bos: Gleason, 1842.

9951. THE GIPSY OF THE HIGHLANDS OR, THE JEW AND THE HEIR. Bos: Redding, 1843.

9952. JEMMY DAILY: OR, THE LITTLE NEWS VENDER. Bos: Brainard, 1843.

*9954. MORRIS GRÆME: OR, THE CRUISE OF THE SEA-SLIPPER. Bos: E.P. Williams, 1843.
Sequel to *The Dancing Feather.* The 2 works were abridged & published in 1880 as *The Sea Slipper* (No. 10084).

*9955. FANNY H___. OR, THE HUNCHBACK AND THE ROUÉ. Bos: E.P. Williams, 1843.

JOSEPH HOLT INGRAHAM (cont.)

9956.   MARK MANLY: OR, THE SKIPPER'S LAD. Bos: E.P. Williams, 1843.
Another version published in 1887 as *The Flying Fish* (No. 10087).

9957.   FRANK RIVERS: OR, THE DANGERS OF THE TOWN. Bos: E.P. Williams, 1843.

9958.   THE YOUNG GENIUS; OR, TRIALS AND TRIUMPHS. Bos: E.P. Williams, 1843.

9959.   HOWARD: OR, THE MYSTERIOUS DISAPPEARANCE. Bos: E.P. Williams, 1843.

9960.   BLACK RALPH: OR, THE HELMSMAN OF HURLGATE. Bos: E.P. Williams, 1844.

9961.   THEODORE; OR, THE 'CHILD OF THE SEA.' Bos: E.P. Williams, 1844.
Sequel to *Lafitte*. Another version published in 1884 as *Lafitte's Lieutenant* (No. 10086).

9962.   RODOLPHE IN BOSTON! A TALE. Bos: E.P. Williams, 1844.

9963.   BIDDY WOODHULL; OR, THE PRETTY HAYMAKER. Bos: E.P. Williams, 1844.

9964.   THE CORSAIR OF CASCO BAY OR THE PILOT'S DAUGHTER. Gardiner ME: Atwood, 1844.

9965.   ELLEN HART: OR, THE FORGER'S DAUGHTER. Bos: Yankee Office, 1844.

9966.   THE MISERIES OF NEW YORK. OR THE BURGLAR AND COUNSELLOR. Bos: Yankee Office, 1844.
Reprinted in 1870 as *Jeannette Wetmore* (No. 10072).

*9967. STEEL BELT; OR THE THREE MASTED GOLETA. Bos: Yankee Office, 1844.
Another version published in 1887 as *The Patriot Cruiser* (No. 10088).

9968.   ARNOLD: OR THE BRITISH SPY! Bos: Yankee Office, 1844.
Reprinted in 1847 as *The Treason of Arnold* (No. 10037).

9969.   THE MIDSHIPMAN, OR THE CORVETTE AND BRIGANTINE. Bos: Gleason, 1844.

*9970. LA BONITA CIGARERA; OR THE BEAUTIFUL CIGAR VENDER! A TALE OF NEW YORK. Bos: Yankee Office, 1844.
Reprinted with other material in 1849 as *The Beautiful Cigar Vender* (No. 10041).
Another version published in 1881 as *The Burglar Captain* (No. 10085).

9971.   THE SPANISH GALLEON, OR THE PIRATE OF THE MEDITERRANEAN. Bos: Gleason, 1844.

9972.   ESTELLE: OR, THE CONSPIRATOR OF THE ISLE. Bos: Yankee Office, 1844.

*9973. THE SILVER BOTTLE: OR, THE ADVENTURES OF "LITTLE MARLBORO'" IN SEARCH OF HIS FATHER. Bos: Yankee Office, 1844.
2 parts. Another version published in 1868 as *The Eagle Crest* (No. 10060).

9974.   HERMAN DE RUYTER: OR, THE MYSTERY UNVEILED. Bos: Yankee Office, 1844.
Sequel to *The Beautiful Cigar Vender* <i.e. *La Bonita Cigarera*>.

JOSEPH HOLT INGRAHAM (cont.)

9975.   THE DIARY OF A HACKNEY COACHMAN. <Bos: Yankee Office, 1844>.

*9976. SANTA CLAUS. OR, THE MERRY KING OF CHRISTMAS. Bos: H.L. Williams, 1844.

9977.   CAROLINE ARCHER; OR, THE MILINER'S <sic> APPRENTICE. Bos: E.P. Williams, <1844>.

9978.   ELEANOR SHERWOOD, THE BEAUTIFUL TEMPTRESS! <Bos: Yankee Office, 1844>.

9979.   THE CLIPPER-YACHT; OR, MOLOCH, THE MONEY-LENDER! Bos: H.L. Williams, 1845.
        Reprinted in 1869 as *Moloch, the Money-Lender* (No. 10064).

*9980. MARIE: OR, THE FUGITIVE! Bos: Yankee Office, <1845>.

*9981. FREEMANTLE: OR, THE PRIVATEERSMAN! Bos: Redding, <1845>.

9982.   SCARLET FEATHER, OR THE YOUNG CHIEF OF THE ABENAQUIES. Bos: Gleason, 1845.

*9983. FORRESTAL: OR THE LIGHT OF THE REEF. Bos: H.L. Williams, 1845.

*9984. RAFAEL. Bos: H.L. Williams, 1845.

9985.   THE KNIGHTS OF SEVEN LANDS. Bos: Gleason, 1845.
        Another edition, omitting 1 tale, was also published in 1845 by H.L. Williams as *The Seven Knights* (No. 9986); sequence not established.

*9987. MONTEZUMA, THE SERF, OR THE REVOLT OF THE MEXITILI. Bos: H.L. Williams, 1845.
        2v. in 5 parts. These sheets reissued in 1v. by Burgess, Stringer, New York.

9988.   WILL TERRIL: OR, THE ADVENTURES OF A YOUNG GENTLEMAN BORN IN A CELLAR. Bos: Yankee Office, 1845.

9989.   NORMAN; OR, THE PRIVATEERSMAN'S BRIDE. Bos: Yankee Office, 1845.
        Sequel to *Freemantle.*

9990.   NEAL NELSON; OR, THE SEIGE< sic > OF BOSTON. Bos: H.L. Williams, 1845.
        Reprinted in 1887 as *Sons of Liberty* (No. 10089).

*9991. A ROMANCE OF THE SUNNY SOUTH. OR FEATHERS FROM A TRAVELLER'S WING. Bos: H.L. Williams, 1845.
        Cover-title: *The Southern Belle.*

9992.   PAUL DEVERELL, OR TWO JUDGMENTS FOR ONE CRIME. Bos: H.L. Williams, 1845.

9993.   PART II. PAUL DEVERELL: OR, TWO JUDGMENTS FOR ONE CRIME. Bos: H.L. Williams, 1845.
        Reprinted, both parts in 1v., in 1845.

9994.   PAUL PERRIL, THE MERCHANT'S SON ... PART FIRST. Bos: Williams & Bros., <n.d., 1845?>.
        For Part 2 see No. 10018 below.

9995.   THE ADVENTURES OF WILL WIZARD! CORPORAL OF THE SACCARAPA VOLUNTEERS. Bos: H.L. Williams, 1845.

JOSEPH HOLT INGRAHAM (cont.)

9996. ALICE MAY, AND BRUISING BILL. Bos: Gleason, 1845.
"Alice May" was also published separately in 1845 by H.L. Williams (No. 9997); sequence not established.

9998. BERTRAND, OR, THE STORY OF MARIE DE HEYWODE. Bos: H.L. Williams, 1845.
Sequel to *Marie: or, The Fugitive*, 1845.

*9999. CHARLES BLACKFORD. OR, THE ADVENTURES OF A STUDENT IN SEARCH OF A PROFESSION. Bos: Yankee Office, 1845.
Another edition published in 1845 by G.W. Redding, Boston; sequence not established.

10000. THE CRUISER OF THE MIST. NY: Burgess, Stringer, 1845.

10001. FLEMING FIELD; OR THE YOUNG ARTISAN. NY: Burgess, Stringer, 1845.

*10002. GRACE WELDON, OR FREDERICA, THE BONNET-GIRL. Bos: H.L. Williams, 1845.

*10003. HARRY HAREFOOT; OR, THE THREE TEMPTATIONS. Bos: Yankee Office, 1845.

10004. HENRY HOWARD; OR, TWO NOES MAKE ONE YES. Bos: H.L. Williams, 1845.

10005. MARY WILBUR: OR, THE DEACON AND THE WIDOW'S DAUGHTER. Bos: Yankee Office, <1845>.

10006. THE MAST-SHIP: OR, THE BOMBARDMENT OF FALMOUTH. Bos: H.L. Williams, 1845.

10007. THE WING OF THE WIND. A NOUVELETTE OF THE SEA. NY: Burgess, Stringer, 1845.

10010. ARTHUR DENWOOD: OR THE MAIDEN OF THE INN. Bos: H.L. Williams, 1846.
Another version published in 1888 as *The Kennebec Cruiser* (No. 10091).

*10011. THE LADY OF THE GULF. A ROMANCE OF THE CITY AND THE SEAS. Bos & NY: H.L. Williams, 1846.
Reprinted in 1853 (?) as *Josephene* (No. 10044); another version published in 1877 as *Josephine* (No. 10076).

10012. LEISLER: OR THE REBEL AND THE KING'S MAN. Bos & NY: H.L. Williams, 1846.

10013. RAMERO: OR, THE PRINCE AND THE PRISONER! Bos & NY: H.L. Williams, 1846.
Truncated version published in 1869 as *The Fair Joceline* (No. 10065).

10014. WINWOOD: OR, THE FUGITIVE OF THE SEAS. NY & Bos: H.L. Williams, 1846.
Two truncated versions published in 1870: *The Red Arrow* (No. 10073) & *The Ocean Bloodhound* (No. 10074); the former reprinted in 1889 as *The Hunted Slaver* (No. 10093).

10015. BONFIELD: OR, THE OUTLAW OF THE BERMUDAS. NY & Bos: H.L. Williams, 1846.

JOSEPH HOLT INGRAHAM (cont.)

10017. THE SILVER SHIP OF MEXICO. A TALE OF THE SPANISH MAIN. NY & Bos: H.L. Williams, 1846.

10018. PAUL PERRIL, THE MERCHANT'S SON ... PART SECOND. Bos: Williams & Bros., <n.d., 1846?>.
For Part 1 see No. 9994 above.

10019. BERKELEY: OR, THE LOST AND REDEEMED. Bos: H.L. Williams, 1846.

10020. MATE BURKE; OR, THE FOUNDLINGS OF THE SEA. NY: Burgess, Stringer, 1846.

10021. THE MYSTERIOUS STATE-ROOM; A TALE OF THE MISSISSIPPI. Bos: Gleason, 1846.

10022. THE ODD FELLOW, OR, THE SECRET ASSOCIATION, AND FORAGING PETER. Bos: United States Pub. Co., 1846.
Originally published in 1843 as sheets of *The Boston Notion* issued in a paper wrapper with cover-title *Lame Davy's Son ...* (No. 9953).

10023. PIERCE FENNING, OR, THE LUGGER'S CHASE. Bos & NY: H.L. Williams, 1846.
Another version published in 1867 as *The Rebel Coaster* (No. 10059).

*10024. THE RINGDOVE; OR, THE PRIVATEER AND THE CUTTER. Bos: H.L. Williams, 1846.
Not located. Reprinted in 1888 as *A Yankee Blue-Jacket* (No. 10090).

10025. THE SLAVE KING; OR THE TRIUMPH OF LIBERTY. <Bos>: H.L. Williams, 1846.
2v.

10026. THE SPECTRE STEAMER, AND OTHER TALES. Bos: United States Pub. Co., 1846.

10027. THE YOUNG ARTIST, AND THE BOLD INSURGENT. Bos: United States Pub. Co., 1846.

10028. THE SURF SKIFF: OR, THE HEROINE OF THE KENNEBEC. NY & Bos: Williams Bros., 1847.

10029. THE TRUCE: OR ON AND OFF SOUNDINGS. NY & Bos: Williams Bros., 1847.
Another version published in 1871 as *Nick's Mate* (No. 10075) & reprinted in 1889 as *The Hunted Sloop* (No. 10092).

10030. BLANCHE TALBOT: OR, THE MAIDEN'S HAND. NY & Bos: Williams Bros., 1847.

10031. THE BRIGANTINE: OR, GUITIERRO AND THE CASTILIAN. NY & Bos: Williams Bros., 1847.

10032. EDWARD MANNING: OR, THE BRIDE AND THE MAIDEN. NY & Bos: Williams Bros., 1847.

*10033. BEATRICE, THE GOLDSMITH'S DAUGHTER. NY & Bos: Williams Bros., 1847.

10034. RINGOLD GRIFFITT: OR, THE RAFTSMAN OF THE SUSQUEHANNAH. Bos: Gleason, 1847.

JOSEPH HOLT INGRAHAM (cont.)

10035. THE FREE-TRADER: OR, THE CRUISER OF NARRAGANSETT BAY. NY: Williams Bros., 1847.

10036. THE TEXAN RANGER; OR THE MAID OF MATAMORAS. NY: Williams Bros., 1847.
Two truncated versions published in 1870: *The Texan Ranger* (No. 10070) & *The Mexican Bravo* (No. 10071).

10038. WILDASH; OR, THE CRUISER OF THE CAPES. NY: Williams Bros., 1847.

10039. JENNETTE ALISON: OR THE YOUNG STRAWBERRY GIRL. Bos: Gleason, 1848.

10042. NOBODY'S SON; OR, THE LIFE AND ADVENTURES OF PERCIVAL MAYBERRY. Phila: Hart, 1851.
Anon. Reprinted in 1854 as *The Life and Adventures of Percival Mayberry* (No. 10045).

10046. PAMPHLETS FOR THE PEOPLE. IN ILLUSTRATION OF THE CLAIMS OF THE CHURCH AND METHODISM. By a Presbyter of Mississippi. Phila: Hooker, 1854.
Revised "third edition" published in 1857.

10047. THE ARROW OF GOLD: OR, THE SHELL GATHERER. NY: French <n.d., 1854–57>.
Anon.

10048. THE PRINCE OF THE HOUSE OF DAVID; OR THREE YEARS IN THE HOLY CITY. NY: Pudney & Russell, 1855.
Revised editions published in 1856 (No. 10050) & 1859 (No. 10052).

10049. RIVINGSTONE; OR, THE YOUNG RANGER HUSSAR. NY: De Witt & Davenport, 1855.

*10053. THE PILLAR OF FIRE; OR, ISRAEL IN BONDAGE. NY: Pudney & Russell, 1859.

*10054. THE THRONE OF DAVID. Phila: G.G. Evans, 1860.

*10055. THE SUNNY SOUTH; OR, THE SOUTHERNER AT HOME. Phila: G.G. Evans, 1860.
Reprinted, omitting the final lines, in 1880 as *Not "A Fool's Errand"* (No. 10083) & in 1891 as *Kate's Experiences* (No. 10094).

10058. MORTIMER; OR, THE BANKRUPT'S HEIRESS. NY: Brady, <1865>.
Reprinted in 1870 as *Annie Temple* (No. 10069).

10061. WILDBIRD: OR, THE THREE CHANCES. NY: De Witt, 1869.
De Witt's Ten Cent Romances, No. 33.

*10062. THE RED WING; OR, BELMONT, THE BUCCANEER OF THE BAY. NY: De Witt, 1869.
Not located.

10063. THE AVENGING BROTHER; OR, THE TWO MAIDENS. NY: De Witt, 1869.
De Witt's Ten Cent Romances, No. 37. Sequel to *The Red Wing*.

10068. THE PIRATE CHIEF; OR, THE CUTTER OF THE OCEAN. NY: Dick & Fitzgerald, <n.d., *ca.* 1870?>.
Anon.

Washington Irving
(Geoffrey Crayon, Diedrich Knickerbocker,
Jonathan Oldstyle)
1783–1859

Note: Omitted from this list are dramatic works adapted from the French by John Howard Payne in collaboration with Irving; for details and comment see BAL (No. 10222) and the Payne list below.

*10096. A VOYAGE TO THE EASTERN PART OF TERRA FIRMA, OR THE SPANISH MAIN, IN SOUTH-AMERICA, DURING THE YEARS 1801, 1802, 1803, AND 1804. Translated by an American Gentleman. NY: I. Riley, 1806.
> 3v. By F. Depons; translation by Irving, his brother Peter Irving, & George Caines. A prospectus was also issued in 1806 (No. 10095).

*10097. SALMAGUNDI; OR, THE WHIM-WHAMS AND OPINIONS OF LAUNCELOT LANGSTAFF, ESQ. AND OTHERS. NY: D. Longworth, 1807–08.
> 2v. in 20 parts. Anon. Joint production by Irving, his brother William Irving, & James Kirke Paulding; see No. 15685 below. Revised editions by Irving published in 1814 (No. 10102) & 1824 (No. 10113); critical edition published in 1977 (No. 15757).

10098. A HISTORY OF NEW YORK, FROM THE BEGINNING OF THE WORLD TO THE END OF THE DUTCH DYNASTY. By Diedrich Knickerbocker. NY: Inskeep & Bradford, 1809.
> 2v. Revised editions published in 1812 (No. 10100), 1848 (No. 10164), 1849 (No. 10174) & 1886 (No. 10203).

*10106. THE SKETCH BOOK OF GEOFFREY CRAYON, GENT. NY: Van Winkle, 1819–20.
> 7 parts. The U.K. edition published in 1820 (Nos. 10107 & 10108) is revised & extended. Further extended editions published in 1824 (No. 10117) & 1848 (No. 10165). See also No. 10213 below.

*10109. BRACEBRIDGE HALL, OR THE HUMOURISTS. A MEDLEY. By Geoffrey Crayon. NY: Van Winkle, 1822.
> 2v. The U.K. edition published in 1822 (No. 10110) contains 5 pieces not in this edition, but included in the second U.S. edition of 1822 (No. 10111). Revised edition published in 1849 (No. 10167).

10112. LETTERS OF JONATHAN OLDSTYLE, GENT. NY: Clayton, 1824.
> Anon.

*10115. TALES OF A TRAVELLER. By Geoffrey Crayon, Gent. Lon: Murray, 1824.
> 2v. Contains 5 pieces not in the first U.S. edition.

*10116. TALES OF A TRAVELLER. By Geoffrey Crayon. Phila: Carey & Lea, 1824.
> 4 parts. The revised & extended "second American edition" published in 1825 (No. 10119) contains the 5 additional pieces from the first U.K. edition. Further revised edition published in 1849 (No. 10168).

WASHINGTON IRVING (cont.)

*10123. A HISTORY OF THE LIFE AND VOYAGES OF CHRISTOPHER COLUMBUS. Lon: Murray, 1828.
4v.

10124. A HISTORY OF THE LIFE AND VOYAGES OF CHRISTOPHER COLUMBUS. NY: G. & C. Carvill, 1828.
3v. Revised editions published in 1831 (No. 10131) & 1848 (No. 10166). Abridged edition first published in 1829 (No. 10127).

*10125. A CHRONICLE OF THE CONQUEST OF GRANADA. By Fray Antonio Agapida. Phila: Carey, Lea & Carey, 1829.
2v. Revised edition published in 1850 (No. 10177).

10132. VOYAGES AND DISCOVERIES OF THE COMPANIONS OF COLUMBUS. Lon: Murray, 1831.
Some copies issued in *The Family Library* series.

10133. VOYAGES AND DISCOVERIES OF THE COMPANIONS OF COLUMBUS. Phila: Carey & Lea, 1831.
Revised edition published in 1848–49 (No. 10166).

10135. THE ALHAMBRA. By Geoffrey Crayon. Lon: Colburn & Bentley, 1832.
2v.

10136. THE ALHAMBRA: A SERIES OF TALES AND SKETCHES. Phila: Carey & Lea, 1832.
2v. Anon. Revised edition published in 1851 (Nos. 10180 & 10181).

*10139. A TOUR ON THE PRAIRIES. Lon: Murray, 1835.
Anon. *Miscellanies*, No. 1.

*10140. A TOUR ON THE PRAIRIES. Phila: Carey, Lea, & Blanchard, 1835.
Anon. *The Crayon Miscellany*, No. 1. Revised edition published in 1849 (No. 10171).

10141. ABBOTSFORD, AND NEWSTEAD ABBEY. Lon: Murray, 1835.
Anon. *Miscellanies*, No. 2.

*10142. ABBOTSFORD AND NEWSTEAD ABBEY. Phila: Carey, Lea & Blanchard, 1835.
Anon. *The Crayon Miscellany*, No. 2. Revised edition published in 1849 (No. 10171).

*10144. LEGENDS OF THE CONQUEST OF SPAIN. Phila: Carey, Lea & Blanchard, 1835.
Anon. *The Crayon Miscellany*, No. 3.

*10148. ASTORIA, OR ANECDOTES OF AN ENTERPRISE BEYOND THE ROCKY MOUNTAINS. Phila: Carey, Lea, & Blanchard, 1836.
2v. Revised edition published in 1849 (No. 10169).

*10156. THE LIFE OF OLIVER GOLDSMITH, WITH SELECTIONS FROM HIS WRITINGS. NY: Harper & Bros., 1840.
2v. *Family Library*, Nos. 121–22. Earlier version published in *The Miscellaneous Works of Oliver Goldsmith*, Paris, 1825 (No. 10118); an extended edition published in 1849 as *Oliver Goldsmith: A Biography*, (No. 10173).

WASHINGTON IRVING (cont.)

10159. BIOGRAPHY AND POETICAL REMAINS OF THE LATE MARGARET MILLER DAVIDSON. Phila: Lea & Blanchard, 1841.

*10175. MAHOMET AND HIS SUCCESSORS. NY: Putnam, 1850.
2v.

*10187. CHRONICLES OF WOLFERT'S ROOST AND OTHER PAPERS. Edinburgh: Constable, 1855.
Constable's Miscellany of Foreign Literature, Vol. 4.

*10188. WOLFERT'S ROOST AND OTHER PAPERS. NY: Putnam, 1855.

*10192. LIFE OF GEORGE WASHINGTON. NY: Putnam, 1855–59.
5v. or 68 parts. Originally announced in 3v. Published in the U.S. in 6 formats & in a simultaneous U.K. edition.

*10198. THE LIFE AND LETTERS OF WASHINGTON IRVING. NY: Putnam, 1862–64.
4v. By Pierre M. Irving. Published in 5 formats.

10201. SPANISH PAPERS AND OTHER MISCELLANIES. NY: Putnam, 1866.
2v. Ed. Pierre M. Irving.

10205. THE LETTERS OF WASHINGTON IRVING TO HENRY BREVOORT. NY: Putnam's Sons, 1915.
2v. Ed. George S. Hellman. Limited edition; the trade edition was published in 1918 (No. 10409).

*10206. THE JOURNALS OF WASHINGTON IRVING. Bos: Bibliophile Soc'y, 1919.
3v. Ed. William P. Trent & George S. Hellman. Newly edited & published in 1944 as The Western Journals of Washington Irving (No. 10223).

10207. NOTES AND JOURNAL OF TRAVEL IN EUROPE 1804–1805. NY: Grolier Club, 1921.
3v.

10209. ABU HASSAN. Bos: Bibliophile Soc'y, 1924.

10212. WASHINGTON IRVING DIARY SPAIN 1828–1829. NY: Hispanic Soc'y of America, 1926.
Ed. Clara Louisa Penney.

10213. NOTES WHILE PREPARING SKETCH BOOK ... 1817. New Haven: Yale U PR, 1927.
Ed. Stanley T. Williams.

10214. TOUR IN SCOTLAND 1817 AND OTHER MANUSCRIPT NOTES. New Haven: Yale U PR, 1927.
Ed. Stanley T. Williams.

10215. LETTERS FROM SUNNYSIDE AND SPAIN. New Haven: Yale U PR, 1928.
Ed. Stanley T. Williams.

10216. JOURNAL OF WASHINGTON IRVING (1823–1824). Cambridge: Harvard U PR, 1931.
Ed. Stanley T. Williams.

WASHINGTON IRVING (cont.)
10218. WASHINGTON IRVING AND THE STORROWS LETTERS FROM ENGLAND AND THE CONTINENT 1821–1828. Cambridge: Harvard U PR, 1933.
Ed. Stanley T. Williams.

10219. JOURNAL, 1803. Lon & NY: Oxford U PR, 1934.
Ed. Stanley T. Williams.

10221. JOURNAL OF WASHINGTON IRVING 1828 AND MISCELLANEOUS NOTES ON MOORISH LEGEND AND HISTORY. NY: American Book Co., 1937.
Ed. Stanley T. Williams.

Helen Hunt Jackson
(H.H.)
1830–1885

10413. VERSES. By H.H. Bos: Fields, Osgood, 1870.
Extended edition published in 1871 (No. 10415). See also No. 10422 below.

*10418. BITS OF TRAVEL. By H.H. Bos: Osgood, 1872.
The U.K. edition (No. 10416) possibly precedes this edition. Slightly revised edition published in 1873 (No. 10420).

10419. BITS OF TALK ABOUT HOME MATTERS. By H.H. Bos: Roberts Bros., 1873.

10421. SAXE HOLM'S STORIES. NY: Scribner, Armstrong, 1874.
Anon.

10422. VERSES. By H.H. Bos: Roberts Bros., 1874.
"New and enlarged edition."

10424. THE STORY OF BOON. By H.H. Bos: Roberts Bros., 1874.

10427. MERCY PHILBRICK'S CHOICE. Bos: Roberts Bros., 1876.
Anon. *No Name Series.*

10428. BITS OF TALK, IN VERSE AND PROSE, FOR YOUNG FOLKS. By H.H. Bos: Roberts Bros., 1876.

*10431. HETTY'S STRANGE HISTORY. Bos: Roberts Bros., 1877.
Anon. *No Name Series.*

*10434. BITS OF TRAVEL AT HOME. By H.H. Bos: Roberts Bros., 1878.

10435. SAXE HOLM'S STORIES SECOND SERIES. NY: Scribner's Sons, 1878.
Anon.

10436. NELLY'S SILVER MINE. A STORY OF COLORADO LIFE. By H.H. Bos: Roberts Bros., 1878.

10444. A CENTURY OF DISHONOR A SKETCH OF THE UNITED STATES GOVERNMENT'S DEALINGS WITH SOME OF THE INDIAN TRIBES. By H.H. NY: Harper & Bros., 1881.
Extended edition published in 1885 (No. 10496) containing *Report on the Condition and Needs of the Mission Indians of California,* 1883 (No. 10453).

HELEN HUNT JACKSON (cont.)

*10446. MAMMY TITTLEBACK AND HER FAMILY. A TRUE STORY OF SEVENTEEN CATS. By H.H. Bos: Roberts Bros., 1881.

*10455. THE HUNTER CATS OF CONNORLOA. Bos: Roberts Bros., 1884.

10456. RAMONA. A STORY. Bos: Roberts Bros., 1884.

10457. EASTER BELLS AN ORIGINAL POEM. NY: White, Stokes, & Allen, <1884>.

10460. ZEPH. A POSTHUMOUS STORY. Bos: Roberts Bros., 1885.

10462. GLIMPSES OF THREE COASTS. Bos: Roberts Bros., 1886.

10470. SONNETS AND LYRICS. Bos: Roberts Bros., 1886.
An extended edition dated 1889 (No. 10477) was issued with sheets of an 1890 printing of *Verses* with binder's title *Helen Jackson's Poems* (No. 10506). Another collected edition of her poetry published in 1892 as *Poems* (No. 10511).

10471. BETWEEN WHILES. Bos: Roberts Bros., 1887.

*10482. PANSY BILLINGS AND POPSY TWO STORIES OF GIRL LIFE. Bos: Lothrop, <1898>.

Henry James
1843–1916

10529. A PASSIONATE PILGRIM, AND OTHER TALES. Bos: Osgood, 1875.

10530. TRANSATLANTIC SKETCHES. Bos: Osgood, 1875.

10531. RODERICK HUDSON. Bos: Osgood, 1876.
Revised editions published in 1879 (No. 10542) & 1882 (No. 10555).

10532. THE AMERICAN. Bos: Osgood, 1877.
A dramatization by James was privately printed in 1891 (No. 10595).

10534. FRENCH POETS AND NOVELISTS. Lon: Macmillan, 1878.

*10535. WATCH AND WARD. Bos: Houghton, Osgood, 1878.

*10536. THE EUROPEANS. A SKETCH. Lon: Macmillan, 1878.
2v.

*10537. THE EUROPEANS. A SKETCH. Bos: Houghton, Osgood, 1879.

10538. DAISY MILLER A STUDY. NY: Harper & Bros., 1879.
Harper's Half-Hour Series, No. 82. The U.K. 1879 edition (No. 10540) also contains "An International Episode" and "Four Meetings." For a dramatization see No. 10560 below.

*10539. AN INTERNATIONAL EPISODE. NY: Harper & Bros., 1879.
Harper's Half-Hour Series, No. 91. For comment see preceding entry.

10543. THE MADONNA OF THE FUTURE AND OTHER TALES. Lon: Macmillan, 1879.
2v.

10544. HAWTHORNE. Lon: Macmillan, 1879.
English Men of Letters series.

HENRY JAMES (cont.)

10546. CONFIDENCE. Lon: Chatto & Windus, 1880.
2v.

10547. HAWTHORNE. NY: Harper & Bros., 1880.

10548. A BUNDLE OF LETTERS. Bos: Loring, <n.d., 1880>.
"Reprinted from The Parisian."

10549. CONFIDENCE. Bos: Houghton, Osgood, 1880.
Another edition, newly edited, published in 1962 (No. 10749).

10550. THE DIARY OF A MAN OF FIFTY AND A BUNDLE OF LETTERS. NY: Harper
& Bros., 1880.
Harper's Half-Hour Series, No. 135.

10551. WASHINGTON SQUARE. NY: Harper & Bros., 1881.
The U.K. 1881 edition (No. 10552) also contains "The Pension Beaurepas" and
"A Bundle of Letters."

10553. THE PORTRAIT OF A LADY. Lon: Macmillan, 1881.
3v.

*10554. THE PORTRAIT OF A LADY. Bos & NY: Houghton, Mifflin, 1882.

10558. THE SIEGE OF LONDON, THE PENSION BEAUREPAS, AND THE POINT
OF VIEW. Bos: Osgood, 1883.
"The Point of View" was also privately printed in the U.K. in 1882 (No. 10557).

10560. DAISY MILLER A COMEDY. Bos: Osgood, 1883.
Also privately printed in the U.K. in 1882 (No. 10556).

10562. PORTRAITS OF PLACES. Lon: Macmillan, 1883.

10563. PORTRAITS OF PLACES. Bos: Osgood, 1884.

10569. TALES OF THREE CITIES. Bos: Osgood, 1884.
A copyright printing was also produced in 1883–84.

10570. A LITTLE TOUR IN FRANCE. Bos: Osgood, 1885.
Revised edition published in 1900 (No. 10642).

10571. THE AUTHOR OF BELTRAFFIO PANDORA GEORGINA'S REASONS THE
PATH OF DUTY FOUR MEETINGS. Bos: Osgood, 1885.

10572. THE ART OF FICTION. Bos: Cupples, Upham, 1885.
With Walter Besant, whose name appears alone on the title-page.

10573. STORIES REVIVED. Lon: Macmillan, 1885.
3v.

10575. THE BOSTONIANS A NOVEL. Lon: Macmillan, 1886.
3v.

10576. THE BOSTONIANS A NOVEL. Lon & NY: Macmillan, 1886.
1v. First U.S. edition.

10577. THE PRINCESS CASAMASSIMA A NOVEL. Lon & NY: Macmillan, 1886.
3v.

10578. THE PRINCESS CASAMASSIMA A NOVEL. Lon & NY: Macmillan, 1886.
1v. First U.S. edition.

HENRY JAMES (cont.)

10581. PARTIAL PORTRAITS. Lon & NY: Macmillan, 1888.
Distributed in both the U.K. & the U.S.

10582. THE REVERBERATOR. Lon & NY: Macmillan, 1888.
2v.

*10583. THE REVERBERATOR. Lon & NY: Macmillan, 1888.
1v. First U.S. edition.

10584. THE ASPERN PAPERS LOUISA PALLANT THE MODERN WARNING. Lon
& NY: Macmillan, 1888.
2v.

10585. THE ASPERN PAPERS LOUISA PALLANT THE MODERN WARNING. Lon
& NY: Macmillan, 1888.
1v. First U.S. edition.

10586. A LONDON LIFE THE PATAGONIA THE LIAR MRS. TEMPERLY. Lon &
NY: Macmillan, 1889.
2v.

10587. A LONDON LIFE THE PATAGONIA THE LIAR MRS. TEMPERLY. Lon &
NY: Macmillan, 1889.
1v. First U.S. edition.

*10590. THE TRAGIC MUSE. Bos & NY: Houghton, Mifflin, 1890.
2v.

10596. THE LESSON OF THE MASTER   THE MARRIAGES   THE PUPIL
BROOKSMITH   THE SOLUTION   SIR EDMUND ORME. NY & Lon:
Macmillan, 1892.
Also a simultaneous U.K. edition.

*10600. THE REAL THING AND OTHER TALES. NY & Lon: Macmillan, 1893.
Also a simultaneous (?) U.K. edition.

10601. PICTURE AND TEXT. NY: Harper & Bros., 1893.

10602. THE PRIVATE LIFE THE WHEEL OF TIME LORD BEAUPRE THE VISITS
COLLABORATION OWEN WINGRAVE. Lon: Osgood, McIlvaine, 1893.
For U.S. publication see Nos. 10604 & 10606 below.

10603. ESSAYS IN LONDON AND ELSEWHERE. Lon: Osgood, McIlvaine, 1893.

10604. THE PRIVATE LIFE LORD BEAUPRE THE VISITS. NY: Harper & Bros.,
1893.

10605. ESSAYS IN LONDON AND ELSEWHERE. NY: Harper & Bros., 1893.

10606. THE WHEEL OF TIME COLLABORATION OWEN WINGRAVE. NY: Harper
& Bros., 1893.

10607. THEATRICALS TWO COMEDIES TENANTS DISENGAGED. Lon: Osgood,
McIlvaine, 1894.

10608. THEATRICALS TWO COMEDIES TENANTS DISENGAGED. NY: Harper
& Bros., 1894.

10610. THEATRICALS SECOND SERIES THE ALBUM THE REPROBATE. Lon:
Osgood, McIlvaine, 1895.

HENRY JAMES (cont.)

10611. THEATRICALS SECOND SERIES THE ALBUM THE REPROBATE. NY: Harper & Bros., 1895.

*10614. TERMINATIONS THE DEATH OF THE LION THE COXON FUND THE MIDDLE YEARS THE ALTAR OF THE DEAD. Lon: Heinemann, 1895.

10615. TERMINATIONS THE DEATH OF THE LION THE COXON FUND THE MIDDLE YEARS THE ALTAR OF THE DEAD. NY: Harper & Bros., 1895.
A copyright printing was also produced in 1895 (No. 10613).

*10617. EMBARRASSMENTS THE FIGURE IN THE CARPET GLASSES THE NEXT TIME THE WAY IT CAME. Lon: Heinemann, 1896.

10618. EMBARRASSMENTS. NY & Lon: Macmillan, 1896.
A copyright printing was also produced in 1896 (No. 10616).

10620. THE OTHER HOUSE. Lon: Heinemann, 1896.
2v.

10621. THE OTHER HOUSE. NY & Lon: Macmillan, 1896.
A copyright printing was also produced in 1896 (No. 10619).

*10622. THE SPOILS OF POYNTON. Lon: Heinemann, 1897.

10623. THE SPOILS OF POYNTON. Bos & NY: Houghton, Mifflin, 1897.

*10625. WHAT MAISIE KNEW. Lon: Heinemann, 1898 <i.e. 1897>.

10627. WHAT MAISIE KNEW. Chi & NY: Stone, 1897.

10630. IN THE CAGE. Chi & NY: Stone, 1898.
Also a simultaneous (?) U.K. edition (No. 10631).

10633. THE TWO MAGICS THE TURN OF THE SCREW COVERING END. Lon: Heinemann, 1898.
A U.K. copyright printing of "The Turn of the Screw" was also produced in 1898 (No. 10629).

10634. THE TWO MAGICS THE TURN OF THE SCREW COVERING END. NY & Lon: Macmillan, 1898.
A U.S. copyright printing of these works was also produced in 1898 (No. 10632).

*10636. THE AWKWARD AGE A NOVEL. NY & Lon: Harper & Bros., 1899.
Also a simultaneous (?) U.K. edition (No. 10637).

10639. THE SOFT SIDE. NY & Lon: Macmillan, 1900.
Also a simultaneous (?) U.K. edition (No. 10640).

*10644. THE SACRED FOUNT. NY: Scribner's Sons, 1901.

10647. THE WINGS OF THE DOVE. NY: Scribner's Sons, 1902.
2v.

*10652. THE BETTER SORT. NY: Scribner's Sons, 1903.
Also a simultaneous U.K. edition.

10653. THE AMBASSADORS. Lon: Methuen, 1903.

*10655. WILLIAM WETMORE STORY AND HIS FRIENDS FROM LETTERS, DIARIES, AND RECOLLECTIONS. Bos: Houghton, Mifflin, 1903.
2v. These sheets issued simultaneously in the U.K. by Blackwood.

HENRY JAMES (cont.)

10656. THE AMBASSADORS A NOVEL. NY & Lon: Harper & Bros., 1903.
A copyright printing was also produced in 1903 (No. 10651).

10659. THE GOLDEN BOWL. NY: Scribner's Sons, 1904.
2v.

*10660. THE QUESTION OF OUR SPEECH THE LESSON OF BALZAC TWO LECTURES. Bos & NY: Houghton, Mifflin, 1905.

10661. ENGLISH HOURS. Lon: Heinemann, 1905.

*10662. ENGLISH HOURS. Bos & NY: Houghton, Mifflin, 1905.

*10663. THE AMERICAN SCENE. NY & Lon: Harper & Bros., 1907.
Published simultaneously in London and the British colonies with an additional Section VII at the end of the final chapter.

*10665. THE NOVELS AND TALES OF HENRY JAMES NEW YORK EDITION. NY: Scribner's Sons, 1907–17.
26v. Revised texts with new critical prefaces; some of the prefatory material was collected in 1934 as *The Art of the Novel* (No. 10802).

*10666. VIEWS AND REVIEWS. Bos: Ball Pub. Co., 1908.

10668. ITALIAN HOURS. Lon: Heinemann, 1909.

10669. ITALIAN HOURS. Bos & NY: Houghton Mifflin, 1909.

10671. THE FINER GRAIN. NY: Scribner's Sons, 1910.

10673. THE OUTCRY. Lon: Methuen, <1911>.

10674. THE OUTCRY. NY: Scribner's Sons, 1911.

*10677. A SMALL BOY AND OTHERS. NY: Scribner's Sons, 1913.
Also a simultaneous (?) U.K. edition.

10679. NOTES OF A SON AND BROTHER. NY: Scribner's Sons, 1914.

10680. NOTES ON NOVELISTS WITH SOME OTHER NOTES. <n.p., Lon>: Dent, 1914.

10681. NOTES ON NOVELISTS WITH SOME OTHER NOTES. NY: Scribner's Sons, 1914.

10694. THE IVORY TOWER. Lon, Glasgow, &c.: Collins Sons, <1917>.
Ed. Percy Lubbock.

10695. THE SENSE OF THE PAST. Lon, Glasgow, &c.: Collins Sons, <1917>.
Ed. Percy Lubbock.

10697. THE IVORY TOWER. NY: Scribner's Sons, 1917.
Ed. Percy Lubbock. Also issued simultaneously (?) as *The Novels and Tales*, Vol. 25, see No. 10665 above.

10698. THE SENSE OF THE PAST. NY: Scribner's Sons, 1917.
Ed. Percy Lubbock. Also issued simultaneously (?) as *The Novels and Tales*, Vol. 26, see No. 10665 above.

10699. THE MIDDLE YEARS. Lon, Glasgow, &c.: Collins Sons, <1917>.
Ed. Percy Lubbock.

10700. THE MIDDLE YEARS. NY: Scribner's Sons, 1917.
Ed. Percy Lubbock.

HENRY JAMES (cont.)
10701. GABRIELLE DE BERGERAC. NY: Boni & Liveright, 1918.
Ed. Albert Mordell.

10702. WITHIN THE RIM AND OTHER ESSAYS 1914–15. Lon, Glasgow, &c.:
Collins Sons, <1918, i.e. 1919>.

10703. TRAVELLING COMPANIONS. NY: Boni & Liveright, 1919.
Ed. Albert Mordell.

*10704. A LANDSCAPE PAINTER. NY: Scott & Seltzer, 1919.
Ed. Albert Mordell.

10705. THE LETTERS OF HENRY JAMES. Lon: Macmillan, 1920.
2v. Ed. Percy Lubbock.

10706. THE LETTERS OF HENRY JAMES. NY: Scribner's Sons, 1920.
2v. Ed. Percy Lubbock.

*10707. MASTER EUSTACE. NY: Seltzer, 1920.

*10708. NOTES AND REVIEWS A SERIES OF TWENTY-FIVE PAPERS. Cambridge:
Dunster House, 1921.

*10713. LETTERS OF HENRY JAMES TO WALTER BERRY. Paris: Black Sun PR,
1928.

10714. LETTERS TO A.C. BENSON AND AUGUSTE MONOD. Lon: Mathews &
Marrot, 1930.
Ed. E.F. Benson.

10715. THEATRE AND FRIENDSHIP SOME HENRY JAMES LETTERS. Lon: Cape,
<1932>.

10717. THEATRE AND FRIENDSHIP SOME HENRY JAMES LETTERS. NY:
Putnam's Sons, 1932.

10723. THE NOTEBOOKS OF HENRY JAMES. NY: Oxford U PR, 1947.
Ed. F.O. Matthiessen & Kenneth B. Murdock.

10725. THE SCENIC ART NOTES ON ACTING & THE DRAMA: 1872–1901. New
Brunswick: Rutgers U PR, 1948.
Ed. Allan Wade.

10728. THE COMPLETE PLAYS OF HENRY JAMES. Phila: Lippincott, <1949>.
Ed. Leon Edel. "Guy Domville," here collected, was printed privately in 1894
(No. 10609).

10729. EIGHT UNCOLLECTED TALES. New Brunswick: Rutgers U PR, 1950.
Ed. Edna Kenton.

10734. THE SELECTED LETTERS OF HENRY JAMES. NY: Farrar, Straus &
Cudahy, <1955>.
Ed. Leon Edel.

10736. THE AMERICAN ESSAYS. NY: Vintage Books, 1956.
Ed. Leon Edel.

10739. THE PAINTER'S EYE NOTES AND ESSAYS ON THE PICTORIAL ARTS.
Lon: Hart-Davis, 1956.
Ed. John L. Sweeney.

HENRY JAMES (cont.)

10740. THE PAINTER'S EYE NOTES AND ESSAYS ON THE PICTORIAL ARTS. Cambridge: Harvard U PR, 1956.
Ed. John L. Sweeney.

10742. PARISIAN SKETCHES. LETTERS TO THE NEW YORK TRIBUNE 1875–1876. NY: New York U PR, 1957.
Ed. Leon Edel & Ilse Dusior Lind.

10744. LITERARY REVIEWS AND ESSAYS ... ON AMERICAN, ENGLISH, AND FRENCH LITERATURE. NY: Twayne, <1957>.
Ed. Albert Mordell.

10748. FRENCH WRITERS AND AMERICAN WOMEN ESSAYS. Branford CT: Compass Pub. Co., 1960.
Ed. Peter Buitenhuis.

Thomas Allibone Janvier
1849–1913

10833. COLOR STUDIES. NY: Scribner's Sons, 1885.
For an extended edition see No. 10843 below.

10834. THE MEXICAN GUIDE. NY: Scribner's Sons, 1886.
Revised & extended editions published in 1887 (No. 10835), 1888 (No. 10836), 1889 (No. 10837), 1890 (No. 10839) & 1895 (No. 10851)

10841. THE AZTEC TREASURE-HOUSE A ROMANCE OF CONTEMPORANEOUS ANTIQUITY. NY: Harper & Bros., 1890.

10842. STORIES OF OLD NEW SPAIN. NY: Appleton, 1891.
Cloth; and, paper wrapper of *Appletons' Town and Country Library*, No. 71.

*10843. COLOR STUDIES AND A MEXICAN CAMPAIGN. NY: Scribner's Sons, 1891.

10844. THE UNCLE OF AN ANGEL AND OTHER STORIES. NY: Harper & Bros., 1891.

10847. AN EMBASSY TO PROVENCE. NY: Century Co., 1893.

10848. THE WOMEN'S CONQUEST OF NEW-YORK. By a Member of the Committee of Safety of 1908. NY: Harper & Bros., 1953 <i.e. 1894>.
Harper's Franklin Square Library extra, No. 750, June 1894.

10849. IN OLD NEW YORK. NY: Harper & Bros., 1894.

10854. IN THE SARGASSO SEA A NOVEL. NY & Lon: Harper & Bros., 1898.
These sheets issued simultaneously (?) in the U.K.

10856. THE PASSING OF THOMAS IN THE ST. PETER'S SET AT THE GRAND HÔTEL DU PARADIS THE FISH OF MONSIEUR QUISSARD LE BON ONCLE D'AMÉRICQUE FIVE STORIES. NY & Lon: Harper & Bros., 1900.

10857. IN GREAT WATERS FOUR STORIES. NY & Lon: Harper & Bros., 1901.

10858. THE CHRISTMAS KALENDS OF PROVENCE AND SOME OTHER PROVENÇAL FESTIVALS. NY & Lon: Harper & Bros., 1902.

THOMAS A. JANVIER (cont.)
10859. THE DUTCH FOUNDING OF NEW YORK. NY & Lon: Harper & Bros.,
1903.
*10864. SANTA FÉ'S PARTNER. NY & Lon: Harper & Bros., 1907.
10865. HENRY HUDSON A BRIEF STATEMENT OF HIS AIMS AND HIS ACHIEVE-
MENTS. NY & Lon: Harper & Bros., 1909.
10866. LEGENDS OF THE CITY OF MEXICO. NY & Lon: Harper & Bros., 1910.
10867. FROM THE SOUTH OF FRANCE THE ROSES OF MONSIEUR ALPHONSE
THE POODLE OF MONSIEUR GÁILLARD THE RECRUDESCENCE OF MA-
DAME VIC MADAME JOLICOEUR'S CAT A CONSOLATE GIANTESS. NY &
Lon: Harper & Bros., 1912.
10868. AT THE CASA NAPOLEON. NY & Lon: Harper & Bros., 1914.

Sarah Orne Jewett
1849–1909

*10871. DEEPHAVEN. Bos: Osgood, 1877.
Illustrated edition with new preface published in 1894 (No. 10904).

10874. PLAY DAYS. A BOOK OF STORIES FOR CHILDREN. Bos: Houghton,
Osgood, 1878.
*10876. OLD FRIENDS AND NEW. Bos: Houghton, Osgood, 1879.
10878. COUNTRY BY-WAYS. Bos: Houghton, Mifflin, 1881.
10881. THE MATE OF THE DAYLIGHT AND FRIENDS ASHORE. Bos & NY:
Houghton, Mifflin, 1884.
10882. A COUNTRY DOCTOR. Bos & NY: Houghton, Mifflin, 1884.
*10885. A MARSH ISLAND. Bos & NY: Houghton, Mifflin, 1885.
*10887. A WHITE HERON AND OTHER STORIES. Bos & NY: Houghton, Mifflin,
1886.
10888. THE STORY OF THE NORMANS TOLD CHIEFLY IN RELATION TO THEIR
CONQUEST OF ENGLAND. NY & Lon: Putnam's Sons, 1887.
The Story of the Nations series. Reprinted in 1898 as The Normans (No. 10939).
10890. THE KING OF FOLLY ISLAND AND OTHER PEOPLE. Bos & NY:
Houghton, Mifflin, 1888.
*10895. BETTY LEICESTER A STORY FOR GIRLS. Bos & NY: Houghton,
Mifflin, 1890.
10898. STRANGERS AND WAYFARERS. Bos & NY: Houghton, Mifflin, 1890.
10902. A NATIVE OF WINBY AND OTHER TALES. Bos & NY: Houghton,
Mifflin, 1893.
10906. THE LIFE OF NANCY. Bos & NY: Houghton, Mifflin, 1895.
*10910. THE COUNTRY OF THE POINTED FIRS. Bos & NY: Houghton Mifflin,
1896.
Extended edition published in 1910 as part of the uniform edition of Jewett's
Stories and Tales, see No. 10921 below.

SARAH ORNE JEWETT (cont.)

10912. BETTY LEICESTER'S CHRISTMAS. Bos & NY: Houghton, Mifflin, 1899.
Revised. Originally printed privately in 1894 for the Bryn Mawr School, Baltimore, as *Betty Leicester's English Xmas* (No. 10905).

10913. THE QUEEN'S TWIN AND OTHER STORIES. Bos & NY: Houghton, Mifflin, 1899.

*10914. THE TORY LOVER. Bos & NY: Houghton, Mifflin, 1901.

10919. AN EMPTY PURSE A CHRISTMAS STORY. Bos, 1905.
"Privately printed."

10921. STORIES AND TALES. Bos & NY: Houghton Mifflin, <1884–1910, i.e. 1910>.
7v. Not identified as part of a set; the designation *Stories and Tales* is taken from contemporary notices & advertisements. Contains 1 new story added to *The Country of the Pointed Firs.*

10922. LETTERS OF SARAH ORNE JEWETT. Bos & NY: Houghton Mifflin, 1911.
Ed. Annie Fields.

10924. VERSES. Bos, 1916.
"Printed for Her Friends." Ed. M.A. DeWolfe Howe.

10928. SARAH ORNE JEWETT LETTERS. Waterville ME: Colby College PR, 1956.
Ed. Richard Cary. An earlier edition of her letters in the Colby College Library was published in 1947 (No. 10926).

Richard Malcolm Johnston
1822–1898

10950. THE ENGLISH CLASSICS: A HISTORICAL SKETCH OF THE LITERATURE OF ENGLAND ... TO THE ACCESSION OF KING GEORGE III. Phila: Lippincott, 1860.
Enlarged editon, written with William Hand Browne, published in 1873 as *English Literature* (No. 10956).

10952. GEORGIA SKETCHES ... FROM RECOLLECTIONS OF AN OLD MAN. By Philemon Perch. <Augusta GA>: Stockton, 1864.
These sketches revised & collected in *Dukesborough Tales,* see next entry.

10955. DUKESBOROUGH TALES. By Philemon Perch. Baltimore: Turnbull Bros., 1871.
Extended editions published in 1874 (No. 10957) & 1883 (No. 10961); selected & revised edition in 1892 (No. 10974).

10959. LIFE OF ALEXANDER H. STEPHENS. Phila: Lippincott, 1878.
With William Hand Browne. Revised & extended editions published in 1883 (No. 10963) & 1884 (No. 10966).

RICHARD MALCOLM JOHNSTON (cont.)
10964. OLD MARK LANGSTON A TALE OF DUKE'S CREEK. NY: Harper & Bros., 1884.

10967. TWO GRAY TOURISTS. Baltimore: Baltimore Pub. Co., <1885>.
"From Papers of Mr. Philemon Perch."

10968. MR. ABSALOM BILLINGSLEA AND OTHER GEORGIA FOLK. NY: Harper & Bros., 1888.

10969. OGEECHEE CROSS-FIRINGS A NOVEL. NY: Harper & Bros., 1889.
Harper's Franklin Square Library, New Series, No. 656, Sept. 1889.

10970. WIDOW GUTHRIE A NOVEL. NY: Appleton, 1890.

*10971. THE PRIMES AND THEIR NEIGHBORS TEN TALES OF MIDDLE GEORGIA. NY: Appleton, 1891.
Published in 3 formats, including some copies as *Appletons' Town and Country Library,* No. 69.

10972. STUDIES, LITERARY AND SOCIAL ... FIRST SERIES. Indianapolis: Bowen-Merrill, 1891.

10975. MR. FORTNER'S MARITAL CLAIMS AND OTHER STORIES. NY: Appleton, 1892.

10976. MR. BILLY DOWNS AND HIS LIKES. NY: Webster, 1892.

10978. STUDIES, LITERARY AND SOCIAL ... SECOND SERIES. Indianapolis: Bowen-Merrill, 1892.

10979. LITTLE IKE TEMPLIN AND OTHER STORIES. Bos: Lothrop, 1894.

10982. OLD TIMES IN MIDDLE GEORGIA. NY: Macmillan, 1897.

10983. LECTURES ON LITERATURE ENGLISH, FRENCH AND SPANISH. Akron OH: McBride, 1897.
Catholic Summer and Winter School Library.

10986. PEARCE AMERSON'S WILL. Chi: Way & Williams, 1898.
Originally published as the Dec. 1892 issue of *Lippincott's Monthly Magazine* (No. 10977).

10988. AUTOBIOGRAPHY OF COL. RICHARD MALCOLM JOHNSTON. Wash DC: Neale, 1900.

John Beauchamp Jones
1810–1866

10989. WILD WESTERN SCENES; A NARRATIVE OF ADVENTURES IN THE WESTERN WILDERNESS, FORTY YEARS AGO. NY: Colman, 1841.
Originally published in parts. First 1v. edition published in 1849 (No. 10993); revised editions published in 1852 (No. 10997) & 1856 (No. 11004). For *Second Series* and *New Series,* see Nos. 11003 & 11006 below.

10990. THE BOOK OF VISIONS ... THE SECRET THOUGHTS OF A VARIETY OF INDIVIDUALS WHILE ATTENDING CHURCH. Phila: J.W. Moore, 1847.
Anon.

JOHN B. JONES (cont.)

10991. RURAL SPORTS; A TALE. Phila: Marshall, 1849.

10992. THE WESTERN MERCHANT. A NARRATIVE. By Luke Shortfield. Phila: Grigg, Elliot, 1849.

10994. THE CITY MERCHANT; OR, THE MYSTERIOUS FAILURE. Phila: Lippincott, Grambo, 1851.

10995. ADVENTURES OF COL. GRACCHUS VANDERBOMB, OF SLOUGHCREEK, IN PURSUIT OF THE PRESIDENCY: ALSO, THE EXPLOITS OF MR. NUMERIUS PLUTARCH KIPPS, HIS PRIVATE SECRETARY. Phila: Hart, 1852.
Library of Humorous American Works.

10996. THE SPANGLERS AND TINGLES; OR, THE RIVAL BELLES. A TALE. Phila: Hart, 1852.
Library of Humorous American Works. Reprinted in 1864 as *The Rival Belles* (No. 11014).

10998. THE MONARCHIST: AN HISTORICAL NOVEL. Phila: Hart, 1853.

10999. LIFE AND ADVENTURES OF A COUNTRY MERCHANT. A NARRATIVE. Phila: Lippincott, Grambo, 1854.

11001. FREAKS OF FORTUNE: OR, THE HISTORY AND ADVENTURES OF NED LORN. Phila: Peterson, <1854>.

*11002. THE WINKLES; OR, THE MERRY MONOMANIACS. AN AMERICAN PICTURE. NY & Lon: Appleton, 1855.
1v. in cloth or 2v. in wrappers.

11003. WILD WESTERN SCENES—SECOND SERIES. THE WAR PATH: A NARRATIVE OF ADVENTURES IN THE WILDERNESS. Phila: Lippincott, 1856.

11005. BORDER WAR; A TALE OF DISUNION. NY: Rudd & Carleton, 1859.
Reprinted in 1859 as *Wild Southern Scenes* (No. 11011) & in 1861 as *Secession, Coercion, and Civil War* (No. 11012).

11006. WILD WESTERN SCENES; OR, THE WHITE SPIRIT OF THE WILDERNESS ... [NEW SERIES]. Richmond: Malsby, 1863.
Apparently only 1v. of a projected 2v. edition was published.

11007. LOVE AND MONEY. Phila: Peterson & Bros., <1865>.

11008. A REBEL WAR CLERK'S DIARY AT THE CONFEDERATE STATES CAPITAL. Phila: Lippincott, 1866.
2v.

Samuel Benjamin Helbert Judah
1804–1876

11016. THE MOUNTAIN TORRENT, A GRAND MELO-DRAMA. NY: T. Longworth, 1820.

11017. ODOFRIEDE; THE OUTCAST; A DRAMATIC POEM. NY: Wiley & Halsted, 1822.

S. B. H. JUDAH (cont.)

*11018. THE ROSE OF ARRAGON; OR, THE VIGIL OF ST. MARK: A MELO-DRAMA.
NY: King, 1822.

11019. A TALE OF LEXINGTON: A NATIONAL COMEDY. NY: Dramatic Repository, 1823.

11020. GOTHAM AND THE GOTHAMITES, A MEDLEY. NY: The Author, 1823.
Anon.

*11021. THE BUCCANEERS; A ROMANCE OF OUR OWN COUNTRY, IN ITS AN-
CIENT DAY. By Terentius Phlogobombos. Bos: Munroe & Francis,
1827.
2v.

Sylvester Judd
1813–1853

11022. A YOUNG MAN'S ACCOUNT OF HIS CONVERSION FROM CALVINISM. A
STATEMENT OF FACTS. Bos: Munroe, 1838.
Anon. At head of title: *1st Series, No. 128.*

11027. MARGARET. A TALE OF THE REAL AND IDEAL. Bos: Jordan & Wiley,
1845.
Anon. Revised edition published in 1851 (No. 11032)

11029. PHILO: AN EVANGELIAD. Bos: Phillips, Sampson, 1850.
Anon.

11031. RICHARD EDNEY AND THE GOVERNOR'S FAMILY. A RUS-URBAN TALE.
Bos: Phillips, Sampson, 1850.
Anon.

11034. THE CHURCH: IN A SERIES OF DISCOURSES. Bos: Crosby, Nichols,
1854.
Ed. Joseph H. Williams. See BAL for the original publication of many of Judd's
sermons and religious works.

John Pendleton Kennedy
1795–1870

*11036. THE RED BOOK. Baltimore: Ptd by J. Robinson, <1819–21>.
10 parts. Anon. Joint production with Peter Hoffman Cruse. Slightly revised
"second edition" published in 2v. in 1821 (No. 11037).

11040. SWALLOW BARN, OR A SOJOURN IN THE OLD DOMINION. Phila: Carey
& Lea, 1832.
2v. Anon, but prefatory material signed *Mark Littleton.* Revised edition published
in 1851 (No. 11058).

11044. HORSE SHOE ROBINSON; A TALE OF THE TORY ASCENDENCY. Phila:
Carey, Lea & Blanchard, 1835.
2v. Anon, but prefatory material signed *Mark Littleton.* Revised editions published in 1836 (No. 11046) & 1852 (No. 11060).

J. P. KENNEDY (cont.)

11047. ROB OF THE BOWL: A LEGEND OF ST. INIGOE'S. Phila: Lea & Blanchard, 1838.
2v. Anon. Revised edition published in 1854 (No. 11061).

11050. QUODLIBET: CONTAINING SOME ANNALS THEREOF. Edited by Solomon Secondthoughts, Schoolmaster. Phila: Lea & Blanchard, 1840.

11056. MEMOIRS OF THE LIFE OF WILLIAM WIRT. Phila: Lea & Blanchard, 1849.
2v. Revised edition published in 1850 (No. 11057).

11073. MR. AMBROSE'S LETTERS ON THE REBELLION. NY: Hurd & Houghton, 1865.
Letter VII, dated Jan. 1864, was also printed separately, probably in 1864 (No. 11072).

*11076. COLLECTED WORKS. NY: Putnam & Sons, 1871–72.
10v. Made up of separately issued volumes. These include *Political and Official Papers,* 1872 (No. 11077) & *Occasional Addresses,* 1872 (No. 11079); see BAL for the original publication of much of the material collected in these two volumes. See also next entry.

11078. AT HOME AND ABROAD: A SERIES OF ESSAYS: WITH A JOURNAL IN EUROPE IN 1867–8. <NY>: Putnam & Sons, 1872.
Issued as part of the *Collected Works,* see preceding entry.

Francis Scott Key
1779–1843

*11081. THE STAR SPANGLED BANNER. 1814.
The earliest appearances of this poem were published anonymously under the title "Defence of Fort M'Henry." The first known publication was in the *Baltimore Patriot and Evening Advertiser,* 20 Sept. 1814. BAL lists the following: early dated periodical appearances, separate printings (exclusive of sheet music), appearances in books, and sheet music. Collected in *Poems,* 1857, see next entry.

11093. POEMS. NY: Carter & Bros., 1857.
Ed. Henry V.D. Johns.

Alfred Joyce Kilmer
1886–1918

11096. SUMMER OF LOVE. NY: Baker & Taylor, 1911.

*11104. TREES AND OTHER POEMS. NY: Doran, <1914>.

11108. THE CIRCUS AND OTHER ESSAYS. NY: Gomme, 1916.
These sheets reissued by Mitchell Kennerley, New York. For extended edition see No. 11122 below.

JOYCE KILMER (cont.)

11111. LITERATURE IN THE MAKING BY SOME OF ITS MAKERS. NY & Lon: Harper & Bros., <1917>.

*11114. MAIN STREET AND OTHER POEMS. NY: Doran, <1917>.

*11118. JOYCE KILMER. NY: Doran, <1918>.
2v.: *Memoir and Poems* and *Prose Works*. Ed. Robert Cortes Holliday.

11122. THE CIRCUS AND OTHER ESSAYS AND FUGITIVE PIECES. NY: Doran, <1921>.
Ed. Robert Cortes Holliday.

Caroline Matilda Stansbury Kirkland
1801–1864

11139. A NEW HOME—WHO'LL FOLLOW? OR, GLIMPSES OF WESTERN LIFE. By Mrs. Mary Clavers. NY: C.S. Francis, 1839.
Revised edition published in 1850 (No. 11161) & reprinted in 1872 as *Our New Home in the West* (No. 11189). Published in the U.K. in 1840 as *Montacute* (No. 11140) & in 1845 as *The Settler's New Home* (No. 11150).

*11143. FOREST LIFE. NY: C.S. Francis, 1842.
2v. Anon.

11149. WESTERN CLEARINGS. NY: Wiley & Putnam, 1845.
Library of American Books, No. 7.

11159. HOLIDAYS ABROAD; OR EUROPE FROM THE WEST. NY: Baker & Scribner, 1849.
2v.

11166. THE EVENING BOOK: OR, FIRESIDE TALK ON MORALS AND MANNERS, WITH SKETCHES OF WESTERN LIFE. NY: Scribner, 1852.

*11167. THE BOOK OF HOME BEAUTY. NY: Putnam, 1852.

11170. A BOOK FOR THE HOME CIRCLE ... A COMPANION FOR THE EVENING BOOK. NY: Scribner, 1853.

11173. THE HELPING HAND: COMPRISING AN ACCOUNT OF THE HOME, FOR DISCHARGED FEMALE CONVICTS. NY: Scribner, 1853.
"Sold for the benefit of the institution."

11175. AUTUMN HOURS, AND FIRESIDE READING. NY: Scribner, 1854.

11180. MEMOIRS OF WASHINGTON. NY & Lon: Appleton, 1857.

Joseph Kirkland
1830–1894

11194. ZURY: THE MEANEST MAN IN SPRING COUNTY. Bos & NY: Houghton, Mifflin, 1887.
Revised edition published in 1888 (No. 11195).

11196. THE McVEYS (AN EPISODE). Bos & NY: Houghton, Mifflin, 1888.

JOSEPH KIRKLAND (cont.)

11198. THE CAPTAIN OF COMPANY K. Chi: Dibble, 1891.
At head of title: *"Detroit Free-Press" Competition, First-Prize Story.*

11199. THE STORY OF CHICAGO. Chi: Dibble, 1892.
Extended "second edition" also published in 1892 (No. 11200).

11204. THE STORY OF CHICAGO ... VOL. II. Chi: Dibble, 1894.
Completed by Caroline Kirkland, Kirkland's daughter.

Melville De Lancey Landon
(Eli Perkins)
1839–1910

11208. THE FRANCO-PRUSSIAN WAR IN A NUTSHELL. A DAILY DIARY. NY: Carleton, 1871.

11209. SARATOGA IN 1901. By Eli Perkins. NY: Sheldon, 1872.

11213. ELI PERKINS (AT LARGE): HIS SAYINGS AND DOINGS. NY: Ford, 1875.
Extended & altered edition in 1883 as *Eli Perkins Wit, Humour and Pathos* (No. 11219).

11217. ELI PERKINS, HIS LAST JOKES. NY: A.J. Fisher, <n.d., 1879–80?>.

11225. KINGS OF THE PLATFORM AND PULPIT. Chi: Smedlcy, 1890.
Compiled by Landon. For full entry see BAL, Vol. 2, p. 249. Reprinted, not before 1898, as *American Lecturers and Humorists* (No. 11228).

11226. ELI PERKINS THIRTY YEARS OF WIT AND REMINISCENCES OF WITTY, WISE AND ELOQUENT MEN. NY: Cassell, <1891>.

11227. MONEY GOLD, SILVER OR BIMETALLISM. Chi: Kerr, 1895.
American Politics, No. 2, June 1895.

Sidney Clopton Lanier
1842–1881

*11241. TIGER-LILIES. A NOVEL. NY: Hurd & Houghton, 1867.

*11247. FLORIDA ... WITH AN ACCOUNT OF CHARLESTON, SAVANNAH, AUGUSTA, AND AIKEN. Phila: Lippincott, 1876.

11249. POEMS. Phila & Lon: Lippincott, 1877.

11259. THE SCIENCE OF ENGLISH VERSE. NY: Scribner's Sons, 1880.

11269. THE ENGLISH NOVEL AND THE PRINCIPLE OF ITS DEVELOPMENT. NY: Scribner's Sons, 1883.
Ed. William Hand Browne. Revised edition, ed. Mary Day Lanier, published in 1897 (No. 11275).

11270. POEMS. NY: Scribner's Sons, 1884.
Ed. Lanier's wife. Extended editions published in 1891 (No. 11273) & 1916 (No. 11284).

SIDNEY LANIER (cont.)
11276. MUSIC AND POETRY ESSAYS. NY: Scribner's Sons, 1898.
Ed. Henry Wysham Lanier.

11277. RETROSPECTS AND PROSPECTS DESCRIPTIVE AND HISTORICAL ESSAYS. NY: Scribner's Sons, 1899.
Ed. Henry Wysham Lanier.

11278. LETTERS OF SIDNEY LANIER SELECTIONS ... 1866–1881. NY: Scribner's Sons, 1899.
Ed. Henry Wysham Lanier.

11279. BOB THE STORY OF OUR MOCKING-BIRD. NY: Scribner's Sons, 1899.

*11280. SHAKSPERE AND HIS FORERUNNERS   STUDIES IN ELIZABETHAN POETRY. NY: Doubleday, Page, 1902.
2v. Ed. Henry Wysham Lanier.

11283. POEM OUTLINES. NY: Scribner's Sons, 1908.

11289. WORKS CENTENNIAL EDITION. Baltimore: Johns Hopkins PR, 1945.
10v. Ed. Charles R. Anderson et al.

Lucy Larcom
1824–1893

11302. SIMILITUDES. Bos: Jewett, 1854.

11309. LOTTIE'S THOUGHT-BOOK. Phila: American Sunday-School Union, <1858>.
Anon.

11311. SHIPS IN THE MIST; AND OTHER STORIES. Bos: Hoyt, <1860>.

11314. LEILA AMONG THE MOUNTAINS. Bos: Hoyt, <1861>.
Anon. Attribution to Larcom unverified.

*11327. POEMS. Bos: Fields, Osgood, 1869.

11335. CHILDHOOD SONGS. Bos: Osgood, 1875.

11337. AN IDYL OF WORK. Bos: Osgood, 1875.

11358. WILD ROSES OF CAPE ANN, AND OTHER POEMS. Bos: Houghton, Mifflin, 1881.

*11368. THE POETICAL WORKS ... HOUSEHOLD EDITION. Bos & NY: Houghton, Mifflin, 1885.

*11371. WHEATON SEMINARY; A SEMI-CENTENNIAL SKETCH. Cambridge: Riverside PR, 1885.

*11373. EASTER MESSENGERS A NEW POEM OF THE FLOWERS. NY: White, Stokes, & Allen, 1886.

11381. A NEW ENGLAND GIRLHOOD OUTLINED FROM MEMORY. Bos & NY: Houghton, Mifflin, 1889.
The Riverside Library for Young People, No. 6.

11382. EASTER GLEAMS. Bos & NY: Houghton, Mifflin, 1890.

LUCY LARCOM (cont.)

*11385. AS IT IS IN HEAVEN. Bos & NY: Houghton, Mifflin, 1891.

 11386. THE UNSEEN FRIEND. Bos & NY: Houghton, Mifflin, 1892.

*11389. AT THE BEAUTIFUL GATE AND OTHER SONGS OF FAITH. Bos & NY: Houghton, Mifflin, 1892.

 11394. LUCY LARCOM LIFE, LETTERS, AND DIARY. Bos & NY: Houghton, Mifflin, 1894.
 By Daniel Dulany Addison.

George Parsons Lathrop
1851–1898

 11416. ROSE AND ROOF-TREE: POEMS. Bos: Osgood, 1875.

 11418. A STUDY OF HAWTHORNE. Bos: Osgood, 1876.

*11420. AFTERGLOW. Bos: Roberts Bros., 1877.
 Anon. *No Name Series.*

 11422. SOMEBODY ELSE. Bos: Roberts Bros., 1878.

*11423. A MASQUE OF POETS. Bos: Roberts Bros., 1878.
 Anon. *No Name Series.* Edited, with contributions, by Lathrop. For full entry see BAL. (No. 118).

 11427. PRESIDENTIAL PILLS ... CONCERNING GENERALS HANFIELD AND GARCOCK. Bos: A. Williams, 1880.

 11430. IN THE DISTANCE. AN AMERICAN STORY. Lon: Low, Marston, et al, 1882.
 2v.

 11431. IN THE DISTANCE A NOVEL. Bos: Osgood, 1882.

 11432. AN ECHO OF PASSION. Bos & NY: Houghton, Mifflin, 1882.

 11438. SPANISH VISTAS. NY: Harper & Bros., 1883.

 11441. HISTORY OF THE UNION LEAGUE OF PHILADELPHIA. Phila: Lippincott, 1884.

*11442. NEWPORT. NY: Scribner's Sons, 1884.

*11444. TRUE AND OTHER STORIES. NY & Lon: Funk & Wagnalls, 1884.
 Standard Library series.

 11449. "BEHIND TIME." NY: Cassell, <1886>.

*11455. GETTYSBURG: A BATTLE ODE. NY: Scribner's Sons, 1888.
 Read before the Society of the Army of the Potomac at Gettysburg, 3 July 1888.

 11457. TWO SIDES OF A STORY OLEY GROW'S DAUGHTER.—MRS. WINTERROWD'S MUSICALE.—"UNFINISHED."—MARCH AND APRIL.—RAISING CAIN. NY: Cassell, <1889>.
 Cassell's Sunshine Series of Choice Fiction, Vol. 1, No. 33, 1 Aug. 1889.

 11458. WOULD YOU KILL HIM? A NOVEL. NY: Harper & Bros., 1890.

 11463. THE LETTER OF CREDIT A NOVEL. NY: Collier, 1890.
 With William H. Rideing. *Once a Week Library*, Vol. 1, No. 26, 25 Aug. 1890.

GEORGE PARSONS LATHROP (cont.)

11470. DREAMS AND DAYS POEMS. NY: Scribner's Sons, 1892.

11471. GOLD OF PLEASURE. Phila: Lippincott, 1892.
Originally published as the June 1891 issue of *Lippincott's Monthly Magazine* (No. 11466).

*11475. A STORY OF COURAGE ANNALS OF THE GEORGETOWN CONVENT OF THE VISITATION OF THE BLESSED VIRGIN MARY. Bos & NY: Houghton, Mifflin, 1894.
With Rose Hawthorne Lathrop.

11477. THE SCARLET LETTER DRAMATIC POEM. <Bos, 1895>.
Music by Walter Damrosch. Based on Hawthorne's *Scarlet Letter.*

Emma Lazarus
1849–1887

11484. POEMS AND TRANSLATIONS ... WRITTEN BETWEEN THE AGES OF FOUR-TEEN AND SEVENTEEN. NY: Hurd & Houghton, 1867.
An earlier collection "written between the ages of fourteen and sixteen" was printed for private circulation in 1866 (No. 11483).

11485. ADMETUS AND OTHER POEMS. NY: Hurd & Houghton, 1871.

*11486. ALIDE: AN EPISODE OF GOETHE'S LIFE. Phila: Lippincott, 1874.

11487. THE SPAGNOLETTO. <n.p.>, 1876.
"Unpublished manuscript."

11488. POEMS AND BALLADS OF HEINRICH HEINE. NY: Worthington, 1881.
Translation.

11489. SONGS OF A SEMITE: THE DANCE TO DEATH, AND OTHER POEMS. NY: Office of "The American Hebrew," 1882.

11503. THE POEMS. Bos & NY: Houghton, Mifflin, 1889.
2v.: *Narrative, Lyric, and Dramatic* and *Jewish Poems: Translations.*

11507. AN EPISTLE TO THE HEBREWS. NY: Cowen, 1900.
At head of title: *Publications of the Federation of American Zionists No. 6.*

11509. EMMA LAZARUS SELECTIONS FROM HER POETRY AND PROSE. NY: Cooperative Book League, <1944>.
Ed. Morris U. Schappes. Revised & enlarged edition published in 1947 (No. 11510).

11512. THE LETTERS OF EMMA LAZARUS 1868–1885. NY: NY Public Library, 1949.
Ed. Morris U. Schappes.

Charles Godfrey Leland
(Hans Breitmann)
1824–1903

Note: Leland's many translations from the German and other languages are here omitted, as are his arts and handicrafts manuals. The publication history, especially in the U.K., of Leland's "Breitmann Ballads" is complicated, and many of the titles listed here contain chiefly reprinted material. The only U.K. editions included are those of Leland's authorized publisher, Trübner. For further details see BAL, especially the note preceding No. 11554 and Nos. 11563 & 11566.

11525. MEISTER KARL'S SKETCH-BOOK. Phila: Parry & McMillan, 1855.
Revised editon published in 1872 (No. 11581).

11527. THE POETRY AND MYSTERY OF DREAMS. Phila: Butler, 1856.
Compiled, with contributions & translations, by Leland.

11533. SUNSHINE IN THOUGHT. NY: C.T. Evans, 1862.

11537. YE BOOK OF COPPERHEADS. Phila: Leypoldt, 1863.
Anon. Joint publication with H.P. Leland and others.

11541. LEGENDS OF THE BIRDS. Phila: Leypoldt, 1864.

11542. MOTHER PITCHER'S POEMS FOR LITTLE PEOPLE. Phila: Leypoldt, 1864.
Anon.

*11548. THE ART OF CONVERSATION, WITH DIRECTIONS FOR SELF EDUCATION. NY: Carleton, 1864.
Anon.

11552. THE UNION PACIFIC RAILWAY, EASTERN DIVISION, OR, THREE THOUSAND MILES IN A RAILWAY CAR. Phila: Ringwalt & Brown, 1867.

11554. HANS BREITMANN'S PARTY. WITH OTHER BALLADS. Phila: Peterson & Bros., <1868>.
Extended edition published in 1869 (No. 11556). The U.K. Trübner editions of 1868 (No. 11555) & 1869 (No. 11564) are slightly altered & extended.

11557. HANS BREITMANN'S CHRISTMAS. WITH OTHER BALLADS. Lon: Trübner, 1869.

11558. HANS BREITMANN AS A POLITICIAN. Lon: Trübner, 1869.
For U.S. edition see No. 11562 below. Trübner's 1870 "third edition" (No. 11571) is slightly extended.

11561. HANS BREITMANN UND HIS PHILOSOPEDE. NY: Haney, 1869.

11562. HANS BREITMANN IN POLITICS. Phila: Lippincott, 1869.
"Reprinted from Lippincott's Magazine."

11565. HANS BREITMANN ABOUT TOWN. AND OTHER NEW BALLADS. Phila: Peterson & Bros., <1869>.
"Second series of the Breitmann Ballads."

CHARLES G. LELAND (cont.)

*11567. HANS BREITMANN IN CHURCH. WITH OTHER BALLADS. Lon: Trübner, 1870.

11568. HANS BREITMANN IN CHURCH. WITH OTHER NEW BALLADS. Phila: Peterson & Bros., <1870>.
"Third series of the Breitmann Ballads."

11572. BREITMANN AS AN UHLAN. Lon: Trübner, 1871.

11573. HANS BREITMANN AS AN UHLAN. WITH OTHER NEW BALLADS. Phila: Peterson & Bros., <1871>.
"Fourth series of the Breitmann Ballads."

11574. THE BREITMANN BALLADS ... COMPLETE EDITION. Lon: Trübner, 1871.
Extended edition published in 1889 (No. 11643); selected edition in 1902 (No. 11694).

*11577. HANS BREITMANN'S BALLADS ... COMPLETE EDITION. Phila: Peterson & Bros., <1871>.
1v. Also published in 2v. in 1870–71 (Nos. 11713 & 11575).

11578. THE MUSIC-LESSON OF CONFUCIUS, AND OTHER POEMS. Lon: Trübner, 1872.

11579. THE MUSIC-LESSON OF CONFUCIUS, AND OTHER POEMS. Bos: Osgood, 1872.

11584. THE EGYPTIAN SKETCH-BOOK. Lon: Strahan, 1873.

11585. THE ENGLISH GIPSIES AND THEIR LANGUAGE. Lon: Trübner, 1873.

11586. THE ENGLISH GIPSIES AND THEIR LANGUAGE. NY: Hurd & Houghton, 1873.

11587. THE EGYPTIAN SKETCH BOOK. NY: Hurd & Houghton, 1874.

11596. PIDGIN-ENGLISH SING-SONG OR SONGS AND STORIES IN THE CHINA-ENGLISH DIALECT. Lon: Trübner, 1876.

11597. PIDGIN-ENGLISH SING-SONG OR SONGS AND STORIES IN THE CHINA-ENGLISH DIALECT. Phila: Lippincott, 1876.

*11598. JOHNNYKIN AND THE GOBLINS. Lon: Macmillan, 1877 <i.e. 1876>.

11599. JOHNNYKIN AND THE GOBLINS. NY: Macmillan, 1876.

11601. ABRAHAM LINCOLN. Lon: Ward, 1879.
New Plutarch series, No. 4.

11602. ABRAHAM LINCOLN AND THE ABOLITION OF SLAVERY IN THE UNITED STATES. NY: Putnam's Sons, 1879.
New Plutarch series. Corrected & extended edition also published in 1879 (No. 11604).

11614. THE GYPSIES. Bos & NY: Houghton, Mifflin, 1882.

11623. THE ALGONQUIN LEGENDS OF NEW ENGLAND OR MYTHS AND FOLK LORE OF THE MICMAC, PASSAMAQUODDY, AND PENOBSCOT TRIBES. Bos & NY: Houghton, Mifflin, 1884.
Second edition, slightly revised, published in 1885 (No. 11626).

CHARLES G. LELAND (cont.)

11628. BRAND-NEW BALLADS. Lon: "Fun" Office, 1885.

11629. SNOOPING ... COMIC ANECDOTES ABOUT PEOPLE WHO PEEP OVER OTHER PEOPLE'S SHOULDERS. Lon: "Fun" Office, <n.d., 1885>.

11649. GYPSY SORCERY AND FORTUNE TELLING. NY: Scribner's Sons, 1891.

*11658. ETRUSCAN ROMAN REMAINS IN POPULAR TRADITION. Lon: Unwin, 1892.

*11659. THE HUNDRED RIDDLES OF THE FAIRY BELLARIA. Lon: Unwin, 1892.

11660. ETRUSCAN ROMAN REMAINS IN POPULAR TRADITION. NY: Scribner's Sons, 1892.

11668. MEMOIRS. Lon: Heinemann, 1893.
2v.

11669. MEMOIRS. NY: Appleton, 1893.

11672. SONGS OF THE SEA AND LAYS OF THE LAND. Lon: A. & C. Black, 1895.

*11673. HANS BREITMANN IN GERMANY TYROL. Lon: Unwin, <n.d., 1895>.

11674. LEGENDS OF FLORENCE ... FIRST SERIES. Lon: Nutt, 1895.
Revised edition published in 1896 (No. 11677).

11675. LEGENDS OF FLORENCE ... FIRST SERIES. NY: Macmillan, 1895.

11676. LEGENDS OF FLORENCE ... SECOND SERIES. Lon: Nutt, 1896.

11678. LEGENDS OF FLORENCE ... SECOND SERIES. NY: Macmillan, 1896.

*11685. HAVE YOU A STRONG WILL? OR HOW TO DEVELOPE< sic > WILL-POWER. Lon: Redway, 1899.
Revised and enlarged editions published in 1902 (No. 11693) & 1903 (No. 11697).
For U.S. edition see No. 11701 below.

11686. ARADIA OR THE GOSPEL OF THE WITCHES. Lon: Nutt, 1899.

11695. FLAXIUS LEAVES FROM THE LIFE OF AN IMMORTAL. Lon: Wellby, 1902.

11699. THE ALTERNATE SEX OR THE FEMALE INTELLECT IN MAN, AND THE MASCULINE IN WOMAN. Lon: Wellby, 1904.
A presumed copyright printing was also produced in 1904 (No. 11698).

11700. THE ALTERNATE SEX OR THE FEMALE INTELLECT IN MAN, AND THE MASCULINE IN WOMAN. NY: Funk & Wagnalls, 1904.

11701. THE MYSTIC WILL A METHOD OF DEVELOPING AND STRENGTHENING THE FACULTIES OF THE MIND. Chi: Atkinson, 1907.
First U.S. edition (omitting chap. 11) of *Have You a Strong Will?*, 1899. A U.S. copyright printing of chap. 11 was produced in 1899 (No. 11689).

Alfred Henry Lewis
1857–1914

11743. WOLFVILLE. NY: Stokes, <1897>.

11744. SANDBURRS. NY: Stokes, <1900>.

*11745. RICHARD CROKER. NY: Life Pub. Co., 1901.

ALFRED HENRY LEWIS (cont.)

11747. WOLFVILLE DAYS. NY: Stokes, <1902>.

*11748. WOLFVILLE NIGHTS. NY: Stokes, <1902>.

11749. THE BLACK LION INN. NY: Russell, 1903.

*11750. PEGGY O'NEAL. Phila: D. Biddle, <1903>.

11751. THE BOSS AND HOW HE CAME TO RULE NEW YORK. NY: Barnes, 1903.

*11752. THE PRESIDENT A NOVEL. NY: Barnes, 1904.

11754. THE SUNSET TRAIL. NY: Barnes, 1905.

11755. THE THROWBACK A ROMANCE OF THE SOUTHWEST. NY: Outing Pub. Co., 1906.

*11756. THE STORY OF PAUL JONES AN HISTORICAL ROMANCE. NY: G.W. Dillingham, <1906>.

11757. CONFESSIONS OF A DETECTIVE. NY: Barnes, 1906.

11760. WHEN MEN GREW TALL OR THE STORY OF ANDREW JACKSON. NY: Appleton, 1907.

11761. AN AMERICAN PATRICIAN OR THE STORY OF AARON BURR. NY: Appleton, 1908.

11762. WOLFVILLE FOLKS. NY: Appleton, 1908.

11763. THE APACHES OF NEW YORK. NY: G.W. Dillingham, <1912>.

*11764. FARO NELL AND HER FRIENDS WOLFVILLE STORIES. NY: G.W. Dillingham, <1913>.

11765. NATION-FAMOUS NEW YORK MURDERS. NY: G.W. Dillingham, <1914>.

George Lippard
1822–1854

11769. ADRIAN, THE NEOPHYTE. Phila: I.R. & A.H. Diller, 1843.

11770. THE BATTLE-DAY OF GERMANTOWN. Phila: A.H. Diller, 1843.

11771. THE LADYE ANNABEL; OR, THE DOOM OF THE POISONER. By an Unknown Author. Phila: Berford, 1844.
Extended edition published in 1849 (No. 11785); reprinted in 1859 as *The Ladye of Albarone* (No. 11806) & in 1864 as *The Mysteries of Florence* (No. 11809).

11772. HERBERT TRACY, OR THE LEGEND OF THE BLACK RANGERS. Phila: Berford, 1844.

11773. THE QUAKER CITY; OR, THE MONKS OF MONK-HALL. Phila: Zieber, 1844.
Anon. 10 parts. Published in the U.K. in 1848 as *Dora Livingstone, the Adultress* (No. 11799).

11776. THE NAZARENE; OR, THE LAST OF THE WASHINGTONS. Phila: Lippard, 1846.
5 parts.

GEORGE LIPPARD (cont.)

11777. BLANCHE OF BRANDYWINE; OR, SEPTEMBER THE ELEVENTH, 1777. Phila: Zieber, 1846.
3 parts.

11778. WASHINGTON AND HIS GENERALS: OR, LEGENDS OF THE REVOLUTION. Phila: Zieber, 1847.
4 parts in three. Reprinted, not before 1858, as *Legends of the American Revolution* (No. 11800).

11780. THE ROSE OF WISSAHIKON, OR, THE FOURTH OF JULY, 1776. Phila: Zieber, 1847.
Reprinted in 1849 as *The Fourth of July, 1776* (No. 11801).

11781. LEGENDS OF MEXICO. Phila: Peterson, 1847.

11783. 'BEL OF PRAIRIE EDEN. A ROMANCE OF MEXICO. Bos: Hotchkiss, 1848.

*11784. PAUL ARDENHEIM, THE MONK OF WISSAHIKON. Phila: Peterson, <1848>.

11787. MEMOIRS OF A PREACHER, A REVELATION OF THE CHURCH AND THE HOME. Phila: Severns, <1849>.
Reprinted in 1851 as *Mysteries of the Pulpit* (No. 11804).

11789. THE MAN WITH THE MASK; A SEQUEL TO THE MEMOIRS OF A PREACHER. Phila: Severns, <n.d., 1849>.

11790. THE ENTRANCED; OR, THE WANDERER OF EIGHTEEN CENTURIES. Phila: Severns, 1849.

11791. WASHINGTON AND HIS MEN: A NEW SERIES OF LEGENDS OF THE REVOLUTION. Phila: Severns, <1849>.

11792. THE EMPIRE CITY OR NEW YORK BY NIGHT AND DAY. NY: Stringer & Townsend, 1850.
2v. Part 1 apparently published separately in 1849 (No. 11788).

11793. THE KILLERS. A NARRATIVE OF REAL LIFE IN PHILADELPHIA. By a Member of the Philadelphia Bar. Phila: Hankinson & Bartholomew, 1850.
Anon. Reprinted in 1851 as *The Bank Director's Son* (No. 11803).

11796. NEW YORK: ITS UPPER TEN AND LOWER MILLION. Cincinnati: Rulison, 1853.

*11797 THE MIDNIGHT QUEEN; OR, LEAVES FROM NEW-YORK LIFE. NY: Garrett, <1853>.

David Ross Locke
(Petroleum Vesuvius Nasby)
1833–1888

*11815. THE NASBY PAPERS. LETTERS AND SERMONS. By Petroleum V. Nasby. Indianapolis: Perrine, 1864.

11817. NASBY. DIVERS VIEWS, OPINIONS AND PROPHECIES. By Petroleum V. Nasby. Cincinnati: Carroll, 1866.

*11819. SWINGING ROUND THE CIRCLE; OR, ANDY'S TRIP TO THE WEST, TOGETHER WITH A LIFE OF ITS HERO. By Petroleum V. Nasby. NY: Haney, 1866.
Not to be confused with the next entry. Reprints published as *Andy's Trip to the West* and *Nasby's Life of Andy Jonsun* (No. 11861).

11820. "SWINGIN ROUND THE CIRKLE." ... IDEAS OF MEN, POLITICS, AND THINGS. By Petroleum V. Nasby. Bos: Lee & Shepard, 1867.

11821. EKKOES FROM KENTUCKY. By Petroleum V. Nasby. Bos: Lee & Shepard, 1868.

*11822. THE IMPENDIN CRISIS UV THE DIMOCRACY. By Petroleum V. Nasby. Toledo: Miller, Locke, 1868.

*11826. THE STRUGGLES (SOCIAL, FINANCIAL AND POLITICAL) OF PETROLEUM V. NASBY. Bos: Richardson, 1872.
Reprinted in 1874 as *The Moral History of America's Life-Struggle* (No. 11862).

11828. EASTERN FRUIT ON WESTERN DISHES. By Petroleum V. Nasby. Lon: Routledge & Sons, <1875>.

11829. EASTERN FRUIT ON WESTERN DISHES. THE MORALS OF ABOU BEN ADHEM. Ed. D.R. Locke. Bos: Lee & Shepard, 1875.

11831. INFLATION AT THE CROSS ROADS. By Petroleum V. Nasby. NY: American News Co., 1875.
Extended edition published in 1875 as *Nasby on Inflation* (No. 11832).

11834. THE PRESIDENT'S POLICY BEING AN EXPOSITION OF THE SAME FROM THE STAND-POINT OF THE CONFEDERIT X ROADS. By Petroleum V. Nasby. Toledo: Blade Co., 1877.

11837. A PAPER CITY. Bos: Lee & Shepard, 1879.

11839. THE DEMOCRATIC JOHN BUNYAN. By Petroleum V. Nasby. Toledo: Toledo Blade Co., 1880.

11840. THE DIARY OF AN OFFICE SEEKER BEING A RECORD OF THE EXPERIENCE OF THOMAS JEFFERSON WATKINS. Ed. D.R. Locke. Toledo: Blade Co., 1881.

11841. HANNAH JANE. Bos: Lee & Shepard, 1882.

*11842. NASBY IN EXILE: OR, SIX MONTHS OF TRAVEL. Toledo & Bos: Locke Pub. Co., 1882.

11849. THE DEMAGOGUE A POLITICAL NOVEL. Bos: Lee & Shepard, 1891.

*11851. THE NASBY LETTERS. Toledo: Toledo Blade Co., <1893>.

Jack London
1876–1916

*11869. THE SON OF THE WOLF TALES OF THE FAR NORTH. Bos & NY: Houghton, Mifflin, 1900.

11870. THE GOD OF HIS FATHERS & OTHER STORIES. NY: McClure, Phillips, 1901.

11872. THE CRUISE OF THE DAZZLER. NY: Century Co., 1902.
St. Nicholas Books.

11873. CHILDREN OF THE FROST. NY: Macmillan, 1902.
A copyright printing was also produced in 1902 (No. 11871).

11874. A DAUGHTER OF THE SNOWS. Phila: Lippincott, 1902.

11875. THE KEMPTON-WACE LETTERS. NY: Macmillan, 1903.
Anon. With Anna Strunsky.

11876. THE CALL OF THE WILD. NY: Macmillan, 1903.

11877. THE PEOPLE OF THE ABYSS. NY: Macmillan, 1903.

11878. THE FAITH OF MEN AND OTHER STORIES. NY: Macmillan, 1904.

*11882. THE SEA-WOLF. NY: Macmillan, 1904.

11885. WAR OF THE CLASSES. NY: Macmillan, 1905.
"The Tramp" & "The Scab," both here collected, were published separately in 1904 (No. 11880) & 1905 (No. 11884) respectively.

11886. THE GAME. NY: Macmillan, 1905.

11887. TALES OF THE FISH PATROL. NY: Macmillan, 1905.

11895. MOON-FACE AND OTHER STORIES. NY: Macmillan, 1906.
A copyright printing was also produced in 1906 (No. 11894).

*11896. WHITE FANG. NY: Macmillan, 1906.
A copyright printing was produced in 1905 (No. 11888).

11898. SCORN OF WOMEN IN THREE ACTS. NY: Macmillan, 1906.

11903. BEFORE ADAM. NY: Macmillan, 1907.
A copyright printing was produced in 1906 (No. 11894B).

11904. LOVE OF LIFE AND OTHER STORIES. NY: Macmillan, 1907.
A copyright printing was produced in 1906 (No. 11894A).

11906. THE ROAD. NY: Macmillan, 1907.

11908. THE IRON HEEL. NY: Macmillan, 1908.
A copyright printing was produced in 1907 (No. 11902).

11912. MARTIN EDEN. NY: Macmillan, 1909.
A copyright printing was produced in 1908 (No. 11909).

11915. LOST FACE. NY: Macmillan, 1910.

11916. REVOLUTION AND OTHER ESSAYS. NY: Macmillan, 1910.
"Revolution" & "What Life Means to Me," both here collected, were published separately in 1909 (No. 11913) & 1906 (No. 11900) respectively.

*11918. BURNING DAYLIGHT. NY: Macmillan, 1910.

JACK LONDON (cont.)

11919. THEFT A PLAY. NY: Macmillan, 1910.

11926. WHEN GOD LAUGHS AND OTHER STORIES. NY: Macmillan, 1911.
"The Apostate A Parable of Child Labor," here collected, was published separately in 1906 (No. 11897).

11927. ADVENTURE. Lon, Edinburgh, &c.: Nelson & Sons, <1911>.

11928. ADVENTURE. NY: Macmillan, 1911.

11929. THE CRUISE OF THE SNARK. NY: Macmillan, 1911.

11932. SOUTH SEA TALES. NY: Macmillan, 1911.

11936. THE HOUSE OF PRIDE AND OTHER TALES OF HAWAII. NY: Macmillan, 1912.

11937. A SON OF THE SUN. Garden City NY: Doubleday, Page, 1912.

11939. SMOKE BELLEW. NY: Century Co., 1912.
"Wonder of Woman," one of the *Smoke Bellew* stories, was also published separately in 1912 (No. 11938).

*11942. THE NIGHT-BORN. NY: Century Co., 1913.

11945. THE ABYSMAL BRUTE. NY: Century Co., 1913.

*11946. JOHN BARLEYCORN. NY: Century Co., 1913.
A partial text of the 1st installment was also published in 1913 as a leaflet entitled *How Will Your Vote Effect This Boy?* (No. 11943).

11947. THE VALLEY OF THE MOON. NY: Macmillan, 1913.
A partial text was also published in 1913 (No. 11944).

11955. THE STRENGTH OF THE STRONG. NY: Macmillan, 1914.
"The Strength of the Strong" & "The Dream of Debs," both here collected, were published separately in 1911 (No. 11931) & not before 1912 (No. 11941) respectively.

11956. THE MUTINY OF THE ELSINORE. NY: Macmillan, 1914.

11960. THE SCARLET PLAGUE. NY: Macmillan, 1915.
A copyright printing was produced in 1912 (No. 11940).

11962. THE JACKET (THE STAR ROVER). Lon: Mills & Boon, <1915>.
For U.S. edition see next entry.

11963. THE STAR ROVER. NY: Macmillan, 1915.

11964. THE ACORN-PLANTER A CALIFORNIA FOREST PLAY. NY: Macmillan, 1916.

11966. THE LITTLE LADY OF THE BIG HOUSE. NY: Macmillan, 1916.

11968. THE TURTLES OF TASMAN. NY: Macmillan, 1916.

11972. THE HUMAN DRIFT. NY: Macmillan, 1917.

11973. JERRY OF THE ISLANDS. NY: Macmillan, 1917.

11974. MICHAEL BROTHER OF JERRY. NY: Macmillan, 1917.

11977. THE RED ONE. NY: Macmillan, 1918.

11978. HEARTS OF THREE. Lon: Mills & Boon, <n.d., 1918>.

JACK LONDON (cont.)

11981. ON THE MAKALOA MAT. NY: Macmillan, 1919.

11982. HEARTS OF THREE. NY: Macmillan, 1920.

11985. DUTCH COURAGE AND OTHER STORIES. NY: Macmillan, 1922.
Some of these stories were also published in 1922 in *Stories of Ships and the Sea* (No. 11986) as *Little Blue Book*, No. 1169.

11997. THE ASSASSINATION BUREAU, LTD. NY: McGraw-Hill, <1963>.
"Completed by Robert L. Fish from notes by Jack London."

11998. LETTERS FROM JACK LONDON CONTAINING AN UNPUBLISHED CORRESPONDENCE BETWEEN LONDON AND SINCLAIR LEWIS. NY: Odyssey PR, <1965>.
Ed. King Hendricks & Irving Shepard.

Henry Wadsworth Longfellow
1807–1882

*12053. OUTRE-MER; A PILGRIMAGE BEYOND THE SEA. NO. I. Bos: Hilliard, Gray, 1833.
Anon. For an extended edition see below under 1835.

12056. OUTRE-MER; A PILGRIMAGE BEYOND THE SEA. NO. II. Bos: Lilly, Wait, 1834.
Anon. For an extended edition see next entry.

*12059. OUTRE-MER; A PILGRIMAGE BEYOND THE SEA. NY: Harper & Bros., 1835.
2v. Anon. The U.K. 1835 edition (No. 12060) contains 1 piece not otherwise located in Longfellow's works. Revised edition published in 1846 (No. 12085); extended edition in 1851 (No. 12101).

*12064. HYPERION, A ROMANCE. NY: Colman, 1839.
2v. Anon. Frequently revised, first in 1845 (No. 12080) & finally in 1869 (No. 12152).

*12065. VOICES OF THE NIGHT. Cambridge: Owen, 1839.

12068. POEMS ON SLAVERY. Cambridge: Owen, 1842.

12070. BALLADS AND OTHER POEMS. Cambridge: Owen, 1842.

12071. THE SPANISH STUDENT. A PLAY. Cambridge: Owen, 1843.

12079. POEMS. Phila: Carey & Hart, 1845.

12083. THE BELFRY OF BRUGES AND OTHER POEMS. Cambridge: Owen, 1846.

12089. EVANGELINE, A TALE OF ACADIE. Bos: Ticknor, 1847.

*12096. KAVANAGH, A TALE. Bos: Ticknor, Reed, & Fields, 1849.

*12099. THE SEASIDE AND THE FIRESIDE. Bos: Ticknor, Reed, & Fields, 1850.
Also a simultaneous (?) U.K. edition (No. 12100).

HENRY WADSWORTH LONGFELLOW (cont.)

*12102. THE GOLDEN LEGEND. Bos: Ticknor, Reed, & Fields, 1851.
Also a simultaneous U.K. edition (No. 12103). Longfellow added notes in 1854.
Later published as part of *Christus A Mystery*, 1872 (No. 12160).

*12111. THE SONG OF HIAWATHA. Lon: Bogue, 1855.
Published in 2 formats.

*12112. THE SONG OF HIAWATHA. Bos: Ticknor & Fields, 1855.

*12116. PROSE WORKS. Bos: Ticknor & Fields, 1857.
2v. *Blue & Gold* edition.

*12121. THE COURTSHIP OF MILES STANDISH, AND OTHER POEMS. Lon:
Kent, 1858.
Published in 2 formats.

*12122. THE COURTSHIP OF MILES STANDISH, AND OTHER POEMS. Bos:
Ticknor & Fields, 1858.

*12135. TALES OF A WAYSIDE INN. Lon: Routledge, Warne, et al, 1864
<i.e. 1863>.

*12136. TALES OF A WAYSIDE INN. Bos: Ticknor & Fields, 1863.

*12141. THE COMPLETE WORKS OF HENRY WADSWORTH LONGFELLOW RE-
VISED EDITION. Bos: Ticknor & Fields, 1866.
7v.

12143. FLOWER-DE-LUCE. Lon: Routledge & Sons, 1867.

12144. FLOWER-DE-LUCE. Bos: Ticknor & Fields, 1867.
"Noël," here collected, was printed separately for private distribution in 1864
(No. 12137).

*12146. THE DIVINE COMEDY OF DANTE ALIGHIERI. Bos: Ticknor & Fields,
1867.
3v. Trans. by Longfellow. Also a simultaneous U.K. edition. An earlier text was
privately printed in 1865–67 (No. 12139).

*12150. THE NEW ENGLAND TRAGEDIES ... I. JOHN ENDICOTT. II. GILES COREY
OF THE SALEM FARMS. Bos: Ticknor & Fields, 1868.
Also simultaneous U.K. & Tauchnitz editions. A privately printed edition, with
"John Endicott" entitled "Wenlock Christison," was also produced in 1868 (No.
12148); an earlier prose version of "John Endicott" was privately printed in 1860
as *The New England Tragedy* (No. 12127). Later published as part of *Christus A
Mystery*, 1872 (No. 12160).

*12157. THE DIVINE TRAGEDY. Bos: Osgood, 1871.
Published in 2 formats. Later published as part of *Christus A Mystery*, 1872 (No.
12160).

12159. THREE BOOKS OF SONG. Bos: Osgood, 1872.
"The Alarm-Bell of Atri," here collected, was published separately in 1871 (No.
12156).

*12164. AFTERMATH. Bos: Osgood, 1873.
Also a simultaneous (?) U.K. edition.

HENRY WADSWORTH LONGFELLOW (cont.)

*12166. THE HANGING OF THE CRANE. Bos: Osgood, 1875.
Both U.S. & U.K. copyright printings were produced in 1874.

*12170. THE MASQUE OF PANDORA AND OTHER POEMS. Bos: Osgood, 1875.
Also a simultaneous (?) U.K. edition (No. 12171). Earlier versions of "Morituri Salutamus," here collected, were also privately printed in 1875 (No. 12168). A dramatization of "The Masque of Pandora," apparently prepared with Longfellow's assistance, was published in 1881 (No. 12225).

12199. KÉRAMOS AND OTHER POEMS. Bos: Houghton, Osgood, 1878.
Also a simultaneous (?) U.K. edition. The title poem was privately printed in 1877 (No. 12189); "A Ballad of the French Fleet October 1746," here collected, was also published separately, probably in 1877 (No. 12194).

12222. ULTIMA THULE. Lon: Routledge & Sons, 1880.

12223. ULTIMA THULE. Bos: Houghton, Mifflin, 1880.
Many of these pieces were privately printed in 1879–80 (Nos. 12210, 12212, 12218 & 12220).

*12239. IN THE HARBOR ULTIMA THULE.—PART II. Bos & NY: Houghton, Mifflin, 1882.
Also a simultaneous (?) U.K. edition (No. 12240).

*12250. MICHAEL ANGELO A DRAMATIC POEM. Bos & NY: Houghton, Mifflin, 1884.
These sheets issued simultaneously (?) in the U.K. A printing in 3 parts was produced in 1882–83 for U.K. copyright purposes. The text was first published in the U.S. in several collected editions of Longfellow's poetical works printed in 1883.

*12258. LIFE OF HENRY WADSWORTH LONGFELLOW WITH EXTRACTS FROM HIS JOURNALS AND CORRESPONDENCE. Bos: Ticknor, 1886.
2v. Ed. Samuel Longfellow.

*12259. WORKS. Bos & NY: Houghton, Mifflin, 1886.
11v. Ed. Horace E. Scudder. A later *Works of Longfellow* in 10v., ed. Charles Welsh & collecting a few additional fugitive pieces, was published by subscription in 1909 (No. 12268).

*12260. FINAL MEMORIALS OF HENRY WADSWORTH LONGFELLOW. Bos: Ticknor, 1887.
Ed. Samuel Longfellow.

Augustus Baldwin Longstreet
1790–1870

12946. GEORGIA SCENES, CHARACTERS, INCIDENTS, &C. IN THE FIRST HALF CENTURY OF THE REPUBLIC. By a Native Georgian. Augusta GA: S.R. Sentinel Office, 1835.
The "second edition," first published by Harper & Bros. in 1840, is a reprint.

A. B. LONGSTREET (cont.)

12956. MASTER WILLIAM MITTEN: OR, A YOUTH OF BRILLIANT TALENTS, WHO WAS RUINED BY BAD LUCK. Macon GA: Burke, Boykin, 1864.
Anon.

12959. STORIES WITH A MORAL HUMOROUS AND DESCRIPTIVE OF SOUTH-ERN LIFE A CENTURY AGO. Phila: Winston, 1912.
Ed. Fitz R. Longstreet.

Amy Lowell
1874–1925

12960. DREAM DROPS OR STORIES FROM FAIRY LAND. By a Dreamer. Bos: The Author, <n.d., 1887>.
With Katherine Bigelow Lawrence Lowell & Elizabeth Lowell.

12963. A DOME OF MANY-COLOURED GLASS. Bos & NY: Houghton Mifflin, 1912.

12967. SWORD BLADES AND POPPY SEED. NY: Macmillan, 1914.

12969. SIX FRENCH POETS STUDIES IN CONTEMPORARY LITERATURE. NY: Macmillan, 1915.

12972. MEN, WOMEN AND GHOSTS. NY: Macmillan, 1916.

12974. TENDENCIES IN MODERN AMERICAN POETRY. NY: Macmillan, 1917.

12979. CAN GRANDE'S CASTLE. NY: Macmillan, 1918.

12982. PICTURES OF THE FLOATING WORLD. NY: Macmillan, 1919.

*12989. LEGENDS. Bos & NY: Houghton Mifflin, 1921.

12996. A CRITICAL FABLE ... A SEQUEL TO THE "FABLE FOR CRITICS". By a Poker of Fun. Bos & NY: Houghton Mifflin, 1922.

13006. JOHN KEATS. Bos & NY: Houghton Mifflin, 1925.
2v.

13007. WHAT'S O'CLOCK. Bos & NY: Houghton Mifflin, 1925.
Ed. Ada Dwyer Russell.

13011. EAST WIND. Bos & NY: Houghton Mifflin, 1926.
Ed. Ada Dwyer Russell.

13013. BALLADS FOR SALE. Bos & NY: Houghton Mifflin, 1927.
Ed. Ada Dwyer Russell. Some of this material was published in 1913–14 (?) as *Sunwise Turn Broadside,* No. 1 (No. 12964); "The Madonna of Carthagena," here collected, was also privately printed in 1927 (No. 13012).

13015. POETRY AND POETS ESSAYS. Bos & NY: Houghton Mifflin, 1930.
Ed. Ferris Greenslet.

13017. FLORENCE AYSCOUGH & AMY LOWELL CORRESPONDENCE OF A FRIENDSHIP. Chi: U of Chicago PR, <1945, i.e. 1946>.
Ed. Harley Farnsworth MacNair. Lowell & Ayscough collaborated on *Fir-Flower Tablets,* 1921 (No. 12993), a collection of poems translated from the Chinese.

13018. THE COMPLETE POETICAL WORKS OF AMY LOWELL. Bos: Houghton Mifflin, 1955.

James Russell Lowell
1819–1891

13036. CLASS POEM. <Cambridge: Metcalf, Torry & Ballou>, 1838.
Anon.

13037. A YEAR'S LIFE. Bos: Little & Brown, 1841.

*13045. POEMS. Cambridge: Owen, 1844.

13049. CONVERSATIONS ON SOME OF THE OLD POETS. Cambridge: Owen, 1845.
Slightly revised "second edition" published in 1846 (No. 13054); "third edition enlarged" in 1893 (No. 13226).

*13062. A FABLE FOR CRITICS. By a Wonderful Quiz. <NY>: Putnam, <18>48.
Two corrected editions also published in 1848 (Nos. 13063 & 13064).

13066. POEMS ... SECOND SERIES. Cambridge: Nichols, 1848.

13068. THE BIGLOW PAPERS. Edited by Homer Wilbur. Cambridge: Nichols, 1848.

13069. THE VISION OF SIR LAUNFAL. Cambridge: Nichols, 1848.

13073. POEMS. Bos: Ticknor, Reed, & Fields, 1849.
2v. Later collected editions of Lowell's verse containing new material, most with title *The Poetical Works*, were published in 1858 (No. 13090), 1869 (No. 13131), 1890 (Nos. 13218 & 13219), *ca.* 1895 (No. 13231), 1896 (No. 13233) & 1917 (No. 13248).

13104. THE BIGLOW PAPERS ... SECOND SERIES. Lon: Trübner, 1862.
Part 1 of three.

13106. THE BIGLOW PAPERS ... SECOND SERIES. Lon: Trübner, 1862.
Part 2 of three.

13108. THE BIGLOW PAPERS ... SECOND SERIES. Lon: Trübner, 1862.
Part 3 of three. Sheets of all 3 parts reissued with additional material in 1864 (No. 13116); a further extended edition published in 1865 (No. 13121). For U.S. edition see No. 13126 below.

13117. FIRESIDE TRAVELS. Bos: Ticknor & Fields, 1864.

13120. ODE RECITED AT THE COMMEMORATION OF THE LIVING AND DEAD SOLDIERS OF HARVARD UNIVERSITY, JULY 21, 1865. Cambridge, 1865.
"Privately printed."

*13126. THE BIGLOW PAPERS. SECOND SERIES. Bos: Ticknor & Fields, 1867.
Anon. For comment on the U.K. editions see No. 13108 above.

*13129. UNDER THE WILLOWS AND OTHER POEMS. Bos: Fields, Osgood, 1869.

13135. THE CATHEDRAL. Bos: Fields, Osgood, 1870.

*13136. AMONG MY BOOKS. Bos: Fields, Osgood, 1870.

*13139. MY STUDY WINDOWS. Bos: Osgood, 1871.

*13152. AMONG MY BOOKS. SECOND SERIES. Bos: Osgood, 1876.

13154. THREE MEMORIAL POEMS. Bos: Osgood, 1877.

JAMES RUSSELL LOWELL (cont.)

*13187. DEMOCRACY AND OTHER ADDRESSES. Bos & NY: Houghton, Mifflin, 1887.
The title piece, "On Democracy," was first privately printed and later published separately, both in 1884 (No. 13171).

13191. EARLY POEMS. NY: Alden, 1887.

*13194. HEARTSEASE AND RUE. Bos & NY: Houghton, Mifflin, 1888.

*13198. POLITICAL ESSAYS. Bos & NY: Houghton, Mifflin, 1888.
"The Independent in Politics," here collected, was also published separately in 1888 (No. 13199).

*13212. THE WRITINGS OF JAMES RUSSELL LOWELL. Bos & NY: Houghton, Mifflin, 1890–92.
12v. A later collected edition in 16v., *The Complete Writings*, 1904 (No. 13245), contains no new Lowell material save for letters.

*13223. LATEST LITERARY ESSAYS AND ADDRESSES. Bos & NY: Houghton, Mifflin, 1892 <i.e. 1891>.
Ed. Charles Eliot Norton. *The Writings*, Vol. 11.

13224. AMERICAN IDEAS FOR ENGLISH READERS. Bos: Cupples, <1892>.

*13225. THE OLD ENGLISH DRAMATISTS. Bos & NY: Houghton, Mifflin, 1892.
Ed. Charles Eliot Norton. *The Writings*, Vol. 12.

13227. LETTERS. Lon: Osgood, McIlvaine, 1894.
2v. Ed. Charles Eliot Norton.

13228. LETTERS. NY: Harper & Bros., 1894.
2v. Ed. Charles Eliot Norton. Additional letters were included in Vols. 14–16 of *The Complete Writings*, 1904 (No. 13245); see also Nos. 13251 & 13254 below.

13230. LAST POEMS. Bos & NY: Houghton, Mifflin, 1895.
Ed. Charles Eliot Norton.

13235. LECTURES ON ENGLISH POETS. Cleveland: Rowfant Club, 1897.
Ed. S.A. Jones.

*13238. IMPRESSIONS OF SPAIN. Bos & NY: Houghton, Mifflin, 1899.
Ed. Joseph B. Gilder.

13243. EARLY PROSE WRITINGS. Lon & NY: Lane, <1902>.

13244. THE ANTI-SLAVERY PAPERS OF JAMES RUSSELL LOWELL. Bos & NY: Houghton Mifflin, 1902.
2v. Ed. William Belmont Parker.

13247. THE ROUND TABLE. Bos: Badger, <1913>.

13250. THE FUNCTION OF THE POET AND OTHER ESSAYS. Bos & NY: Houghton Mifflin, 1920.
Ed. Albert Mordell.

13251. NEW LETTERS. NY & Lon: Harper & Bros., 1932.
Ed. M.A. DeWolfe Howe.

13253. UNCOLLECTED POEMS. Phila: U of Pennsylvania PR, 1950.
Ed. Thelma M. Smith.

JAMES RUSSELL LOWELL (cont.)

13254. THE SCHOLAR-FRIENDS. Cambridge: Harvard U PR, 1952.
Letters of Francis James Child & Lowell. Ed. M.A. DeWolfe Howe & G.W.
Cottrell, Jr.

13255. UNDERGRADUATE VERSES. Hartford: Trinity College, 1956.
"Rhymed minutes of the Hasty Pudding Club." Ed. Kenneth Walter Cameron.

Robert Traill Spence Lowell
1816–1891

13478. THE NEW PRIEST IN CONCEPTION BAY. Bos: Phillips, Sampson, 1858.
2v. Anon. Revised edition published in 1889 (No. 13496). Truncated edition
published in 1864 as *The Story of the New Priest in Conception Bay* (No. 13487).

13480. FRESH HEARTS THAT FAILED THREE THOUSAND YEARS AGO; WITH
OTHER THINGS. Bos: Ticknor & Fields, 1860.
Anon.

13486. THE POEMS ... A NEW EDITION. Bos: Dutton, 1864.

13491. ANTONY BRADE. Bos: Roberts Bros., 1874.

13492. BURGOYNE'S LAST MARCH. POEM. <Newark: Ptd by L.J. Hardham>,
1878.
For the celebration of the 100th year of Bemis Heights, Saratoga, 19 Sept. 1877.

13493. A STORY OR TWO FROM AN OLD DUTCH TOWN. Bos: Roberts Bros.,
1878.

George Barr McCutcheon
1866–1928

13499. SEVERAL SHORT ONES, FOUND ... DURING FLIGHTS OF IMAGINATION.
<n.p., Lafayette IN>: Morning Journal Print, <n.d., *ca.* 1886–90>.

*13501. GRAUSTARK THE STORY OF A LOVE BEHIND A THRONE. Chi: Stone,
1901.

*13502. CASTLE CRANEYCROW. Chi: Stone, 1902.

*13504. BREWSTER'S MILLIONS. By Richard Greaves. Chi: Stone, 1903.

*13505. THE SHERRODS. NY: Dodd, Mead, 1903.

*13506. THE DAY OF THE DOG. NY: Dodd Mead, 1904.

*13507. BEVERLY OF GRAUSTARK. NY: Dodd, Mead, 1904.

*13508. THE PURPLE PARASOL. NY: Dodd, Mead, 1905.

*13509. NEDRA. NY: Dodd, Mead, 1905.

*13511. COWARDICE COURT. NY: Dodd Mead, 1906.

13512. JANE CABLE. NY: Dodd, Mead, 1906.

13514. THE FLYERS. NY: Dodd Mead, 1907.

13515. THE DAUGHTER OF ANDERSON CROW. NY: Dodd, Mead, 1907.

GEORGE BARR McCUTCHEON (cont.)

13516. THE HUSBANDS OF EDITH. NY: Dodd, Mead, 1908.

13517. THE MAN FROM BRODNEY'S. NY: Dodd, Mead, 1908.

13519. THE ALTERNATIVE. NY: Dodd, Mead, 1909.

*13520. TRUXTON KING A STORY OF GRAUSTARK. NY: Dodd, Mead, 1909.

13521. THE BUTTERFLY MAN. NY: Dodd, Mead, 1910.

13522. THE ROSE IN THE RING. NY: Dodd, Mead, 1910.

13523. BROOD HOUSE A PLAY. NY, 1910.
"Privately printed."

*13525. WHAT'S-HIS-NAME. NY: Dodd, Mead, 1911.
Also published serially as a "Special Fiction Section" of *The New York Herald,* 1910–
11 (No. 13524).

13526. MARY MIDTHORNE. NY: Dodd, Mead, 1911.

13528. HER WEIGHT IN GOLD. NY: Dodd, Mead, 1912.
Also printed in 1911 by the Bobbs-Merrill Co (No. 13527).; some copies of this
printing were distributed as Vol. 5 of the 12v. *Hoosier Set* at the Indiana Society of
Chicago annual dinner, 9 Dec. 1911.

*13529. THE HOLLOW OF HER HAND. NY: Dodd, Mead, 1912.

*13532. A FOOL AND HIS MONEY. NY: Dodd, Mead, 1913.

13533. BLACK IS WHITE. NY: Dodd, Mead, 1914.

*13534. THE PRINCE OF GRAUSTARK. NY: Dodd, Mead, 1914.

13535. MR. BINGLE. NY: Dodd, Mead, 1915.

13536. THE LIGHT THAT LIES. NY: Dodd, Mead, 1916.

13537. FROM THE HOUSETOPS. NY: Dodd, Mead, 1916.

13540. GREEN FANCY. NY: Dodd, Mead, 1917.

13544. SHOT WITH CRIMSON. NY: Dodd, Mead, 1918.

13546. THE CITY OF MASKS. NY: Dodd, Mead, 1918.
The U.K. edition published in 1919 <i.e. 1920> as *The Court of New York* (No.
13550).

13548. ONE SCORE AND TEN A COMEDY. NY: The Author, 1919.
"Printed, but not published. "

13549. SHERRY. NY: Dodd, Mead, 1919.

13551. ANDERSON CROW DETECTIVE. NY: Dodd, Mead, 1920.

*13552. WEST WIND DRIFT. NY: Dodd, Mead, 1920.

13553. QUILL'S WINDOW. NY: Dodd, Mead, 1921.

13556. YOLLOP. NY: Dodd, Mead, 1922.

*13557. VIOLA GWYN. NY: Dodd, Mead, 1922.

13559. OLIVER OCTOBER. NY: Dodd, Mead, 1923.

13561. EAST OF THE SETTING SUN A STORY OF GRAUSTARK. NY: Dodd, Mead,
1924.

GEORGE BARR McCUTCHEON (cont.)

13563. ROMEO IN MOON VILLAGE. NY: Dodd, Mead, 1925.

*13564. KINDLING AND ASHES OR, THE HEART OF BARBARA WAYNE. NY: Dodd, Mead, 1926.

13565. THE INN OF THE HAWK AND RAVEN A TALE OF OLD GRAUSTARK. NY: Dodd, Mead, 1927.

13566. BLADES. NY: Dodd, Mead, 1928.

13567. THE MERIVALES. NY: Dodd, Mead, 1929.

13568. BOOKS ONCE WERE MEN AN ESSAY FOR BOOKLOVERS. NY: Dodd, Mead, 1931.

James McHenry
1785–1845

13569. THE BARD OF ERIN, AND OTHER POEMS MOSTLY NATIONAL. Belfast: Ptd by Smyth & Lyons, 1808.

13570. PATRICK: A POETICAL TALE. Glasgow: Ptd by D. M'Kenzie, 1810.

13571. THE PLEASURES OF FRIENDSHIP, A POEM, IN TWO PARTS; TO WHICH ARE ADDED A FEW ORIGINAL IRISH MELODIES. Pittsburgh: The Author, 1822.
Later editions with additional poems published in 1825 (No. 13577), 1828 (No. 13583), 1830 (Nos. 13588) & 1836 (No. 13595). The U.K. edition published in 1825 as *The Blessings of Friendship* (No. 13579) also contains new material.

13572. WALTHAM: AN AMERICAN REVOLUTIONARY TALE. NY: Bliss & White, 1823.

13573. THE WILDERNESS; OR BRADDOCK'S TIMES. NY: Bliss & White, 1823.
2v. Anon.

13575. THE SPECTRE OF THE FOREST, OR, ANNALS OF THE HOUSATONIC. NY: Bliss & White, 1823.
2v. Anon.

13576. O'HALLORAN; OR, THE INSURGENT CHIEF. Phila: Carey & Lea, 1824.
2v. Anon. Revised edition published in Glasgow in 1848 as *The Insurgent Chief* (No. 13602).

13578. THE HEARTS OF STEEL, AN IRISH HISTORICAL TALE. Lon: Wightman & Cramp, 1825.
3v. Anon.

13580. THE HEARTS OF STEEL. AN IRISH HISTORICAL TALE. Phila: Poole, 1825.
2v. Anon.

13586. THE USURPER, AN HISTORICAL TRAGEDY. Phila: Harding, 1829.

*13589. THE BETROTHED OF WYOMING AN HISTORICAL TALE. Phila, NY, &c.: The Principal Booksellers, 1830.
Anon. Presumably by McHenry.

JAMES McHENRY (cont.)

13590. THE FEELINGS OF AGE, TO WHICH IS ADDED THE STAR OF LOVE: POEMS ... SECOND EDITION. Phila: Banks & Bro., 1830.
These poems are also in the "fourth American edition" of *Pleasures of Friendship*, 1830 (No. 13588).

13593. MEREDITH; OR, THE MYSTERY OF THE MESCHIANZA. Phila, NY, &c.: The Principal Booksellers, 1831.
Anon. By the author of "The Betrothed of Wyoming"; presumably McHenry.

13596. THE ANTEDILUVIANS, OR, THE WORLD DESTROYED; A NARRATIVE POEM. Lon: Cradock, 1839.

13597. TO BRITANNIA: AN ODE. Lon: Stephenson, <1839>.
"Dedicated to the Members of the Literary Fund Society."

13598. THE ANTEDILUVIANS, OR THE WORLD DESTROYED; A NARRATIVE POEM. Phila: Lippincott, 1840.

Charles Major
1856–1913

13605. WHEN KNIGHTHOOD WAS IN FLOWER OR THE LOVE STORY OF CHARLES BRANDON AND MARY TUDOR. By Edwin Caskoden. Indianapolis & Kansas City: Bowen-Merrill, 1898.
"Rewritten and rendered into modern English from Sir Edwin Caskoden's Memoir."

13606. THE BEARS OF BLUE RIVER. NY: Doubleday & McClure, 1901.

*13607. DOROTHY VERNON OF HADDON HALL. NY: Macmillan, 1902.
A copyright printing was also produced in 1902.

13609. A FOREST HEARTH A ROMANCE OF INDIANA IN THE THIRTIES. NY: Macmillan, 1903.

*13610. YOLANDA MAID OF BURGUNDY. NY: Macmillan, 1905.

13612. UNCLE TOM ANDY BILL A STORY OF BEARS AND INDIAN TREASURE. NY: Macmillan, 1908.

13613. A GENTLE KNIGHT OF OLD BRANDENBURG. NY: Macmillan, 1909.

13615. THE LITTLE KING A STORY OF THE CHILDHOOD OF LOUIS XIV. NY: Macmillan, 1910.

*13616. SWEET ALYSSUM. Indianapolis: Bobbs-Merrill, <1911>.

13617. THE TOUCHSTONE OF FORTUNE BEING THE MEMOIR OF BARON CLYDE. NY: Macmillan, 1912.

13619. ROSALIE. NY: Macmillan, 1925.

Cornelius Mathews
1817–1889

13620. THE MOTLEY BOOK: A SERIES OF TALES AND SKETCHES. By the Late Ben. Smith. NY: Turney, 1838.
> 7 parts. The "new edition" in 1v. also published in 1838 (No. 13621) is probably a reprint; an extended edition published in 1840 (No. 13624).

*13622. BEHEMOTH: A LEGEND OF THE MOUND-BUILDERS. NY: J. & H.G. Langley, 1839.
> Anon.

*13625. THE POLITICIANS: A COMEDY. NY: Trevett, 1840.
> Also privately printed in 1840 for the use of the actors.

*13626. WAKONDAH; THE MASTER OF LIFE. A POEM. NY: Curry, 1841.
> Anon.

13630. THE CAREER OF PUFFER HOPKINS. NY: Appleton, 1842.
> The first 10 chapters published in 1841 as a supplement to *Arcturus* (No. 13627); the entire work also published as a supplement to *Brother Jonathan,* 26 Nov. 1842.

*13632. THE VARIOUS WRITINGS OF CORNELIUS MATHEWS. NY: Harper & Bros., 1863 <i.e. 1843>.
> 1v. Originally issued in 8 parts?

13633. POEMS ON MAN, IN HIS VARIOUS ASPECTS UNDER THE AMERICAN REPUBLIC. NY: Wiley & Putnam, 1843.
> Revised edition published in 1846 as *Man in the Republic* (No. 13639).

*13637. BIG ABEL, AND LITTLE MANHATTAN. NY: Wiley & Putnam, 1845.
> *Library of American Books,* No. 5.

*13640. MONEYPENNY, OR, THE HEART OF THE WORLD. A ROMANCE OF THE PRESENT DAY. NY: DeWitt & Davenport, 1849–50.
> Anon. 2 parts or 1v. (dated 1849).

13642. CHANTICLEER: A THANKSGIVING STORY OF THE PEABODY FAMILY. Bos: Mussey, 1850.
> Anon.

13643. WITCHCRAFT: A TRAGEDY. Lon: Bogue, 1852.

13644. WITCHCRAFT: A TRAGEDY. NY: French, 1852.

13645. CALMSTORM, THE REFORMER. A DRAMATIC COMMENT. NY: Tinson, 1853.
> Anon. Presumably by Mathews.

13646. A PEN-AND-INK PANORAMA OF NEW-YORK CITY. NY: J.S. Taylor, 1853.

13647. FALSE PRETENCES; OR, BOTH SIDES OF GOOD SOCIETY. NY, 1856.
> "Each copy of this play is the private property of the author."

CORNELIUS MATHEWS (cont.)

13648. THE INDIAN FAIRY BOOK. FROM THE ORIGINAL LEGENDS. NY: Mason Bros., 1856.

Edited anonymously by Mathews. Reprinted in 1877 as *The Enchanted Moccasins and Other Legends* (No. 13650); slightly revised & extended edition published in the U.K. in 1882 as *Hiawatha and Other Legends* (No. 13651).

Herman Melville
1819–1891

*13652. NARRATIVE OF A FOUR MONTHS' RESIDENCE AMONG THE NATIVES OF A VALLEY OF THE MARQUESAS ISLANDS; OR, A PEEP AT POLYNESIAN LIFE. Lon: Murray, 1846.

2 parts or 1v. *Home and Colonial Library*, Nos. 30–31 or No. 15. A sequel, "The Story of Toby," was printed in 1846 & issued separately (No. 13718) or with this work (No. 13719). Reprinted in 1847 as *Typee* (Nos. 13720–22). For U.S. edition see next entry.

*13653. TYPEE: A PEEP AT POLYNESIAN LIFE. DURING A FOUR MONTHS' RESIDENCE IN A VALLEY OF THE MARQUESAS. NY: Wiley & Putnam, 1846.

2v. or 2v. in one. *Library of American Books*, Nos. 13–14. Revised edition, extended by the addition of "The Story of Toby," also published in 1846 (No. 13654); critical edition in 1968 (No. 13713).

13655. OMOO: A NARRATIVE OF ADVENTURES IN THE SOUTH SEAS. Lon: Murray, 1847.

2 parts or 1v. *Home and Colonial Library*, No. 22.

13656. OMOO: A NARRATIVE OF ADVENTURES IN THE SOUTH SEAS. NY: Harper & Bros., 1847.

2 parts or 1v. Critical edition published in 1968 (No. 13714).

13657. MARDI: AND A VOYAGE THITHER. Lon: Bentley, 1849.

3v.

13658. MARDI: AND A VOYAGE THITHER. NY: Harper & Bros., 1849.

2v. Critical edition published in 1970 (No. 13716).

13659. REDBURN: HIS FIRST VOYAGE. Lon: Bentley, 1849.

2v. These sheets reissued in 1853, 2v. in one.

*13660. REDBURN: HIS FIRST VOYAGE. NY: Harper & Bros., 1849.

Critical edition published in 1969 (No. 13715).

13661. WHITE JACKET; OR, THE WORLD IN A MAN-OF-WAR. Lon: Bentley, 1850.

2v. These sheets reissued in 1853, 2v. in one.

*13662. WHITE-JACKET; OR THE WORLD IN A MAN-OF-WAR. NY: Harper & Bros., 1850.

2 parts or 1v. Critical editions published in 1967 (No. 13712) & 1970 (No. 13717).

13663. THE WHALE. Lon: Bentley, 1851.

3v. For U.S. edition see next entry.

HERMAN MELVILLE (cont.)

13664. MOBY-DICK; OR, THE WHALE. NY: Harper & Bros., 1851.
Critical edition published in 1967 (No. 13711).

13666. PIERRE; OR, THE AMBIGUITIES. NY: Harper & Bros., 1852.

*13667. ISRAEL POTTER: HIS FIFTY YEARS OF EXILE. NY: Putnam, 1855.
Reprinted in 1865 as *The Refugee* (No. 13724).

13669. THE PIAZZA TALES. NY: Dix & Edwards, 1856.

13670. THE CONFIDENCE-MAN: HIS MASQUERADE. NY: Dix, Edwards, 1857.
Also a simultaneous (?) U.K. edition (No. 13671).

13673. BATTLE-PIECES AND ASPECTS OF THE WAR. NY: Harper & Bros., 1866.

13674. CLAREL A POEM AND A PILGRIMAGE IN THE HOLYLAND. NY: Putnam's
Sons, 1876.
2v. Revised & corrected edition published in 1960 (No. 13703).

13676. JOHN MARR AND OTHER SAILORS WITH SOME SEA-PIECES. NY: De
Vinne PR, 1888.
Anon. Privately printed.

13677. TIMOLEON ETC. NY: Caxton PR, 1891.
Anon. Privately printed.

13680. THE WORKS OF HERMAN MELVILLE STANDARD EDITION. Lon,
Bombay, &c.: Constable, 1922–24.
16v. Reprinted in the U.S. in 1963 (No. 13707).

*13681. THE APPLE-TREE TABLE AND OTHER SKETCHES. Princeton: Princeton
U PR, 1922 <i.e. 1923?>.

13682. BILLY-BUDD AND OTHER PROSE PIECES. Lon, Bombay, &c.: Con-
stable, 1924.
The Works ... Standard Edition, Vol. 13. Ed. Raymond M. Weaver. Reprinted in the
U.S. in 1963 (No. 13708). Contains the first publication of "Billy Budd,
Foretopman," which is here adapted from Melville's unfinished manuscript; for
a critical edition see No. 13705 below.

13683. POEMS ... BATTLE-PIECES JOHN MARR AND OTHER SAILORS TIMOLEON
AND OTHER MISCELLANEOUS POEMS. Lon, Bombay, &c.: Constable,
1924.
The Works ... Standard Edition, Vol. 16. Ed. Michael Sadleir & Raymond M. Weaver.
Reprinted in the U.S. in 1963 (No. 13709).

13690. JOURNAL UP THE STRAITS OCTOBER 11, 1856—MAY 5, 1857. NY: The
Colophon, 1935.
Ed. Raymond Weaver. Another edition published in 1955 as *Journal of a Visit to
Europe and the Levant* (No. 13701).

13695. JOURNAL OF A VISIT TO LONDON AND THE CONTINENT ... 1849–1850.
Cambridge: Harvard U PR, 1948.
Ed. Eleanor Melville Metcalf.

13704. THE LETTERS OF HERMAN MELVILLE. New Haven: Yale U PR, 1960.
Ed. Merrell R. Davis & William H. Gilman.

HERMAN MELVILLE (cont.)

13705. BILLY BUDD SAILOR (AN INSIDE NARRATIVE). <Chi>: U of Chicago PR, <1962>.
Ed. Harrison Hayford & Merton M. Sealts, Jr. Originally published as "Billy Budd, Foretopman," see No. 13682 above. An earlier critical edition by F. Barron Freeman was published in 1948 in *Melville's Billy Budd* (No. 13969).

Joaquin Miller
(Cincinnatus Hiner Miller)
1837–1913

13746. SPECIMENS. <Canyon City OH, 1868>.
Anon. Preface signed at end: *C. H. Miller.*

13747. JOAQUIN, ET AL., By Cincinnatus H Miller. Portland OR: McCormick, 1869.
Reprinted in London in 1872 (No. 13887); altered copies of this edition may be confused with the genuine first edition.

13749. PACIFIC POEMS. Lon: Whittingham & Wilkins, 1871.
For revised & extended edition see next entry.

13750. SONGS OF THE SIERRAS. Lon: Longmans, Green, et al, 1871.
These sheets were issued in the U.S. for copyright purposes only.

*13751. SONGS OF THE SIERRAS. Bos: Roberts Bros., 1871.
The text varies considerably from the U.K. edition; the U.S. sheets were issued in the U.K. in 1872 (No. 13886). Revised edition published as part of *Songs of the Sierras and Sunlands* in 1878 (No. 13775) & 1892 (No. 13826).

*13754. SONGS OF THE SUN-LANDS. Lon: Longmans, Green, et al, 1873.

13755. LIFE AMONGST THE MODOCS: UNWRITTEN HISTORY. Lon: Bentley & Son, 1873.
For U.S. edition see No. 13757 below.

13756. SONGS OF THE SUN-LANDS. Bos: Roberts Bros., 1873.
Revised edition published as part of *Songs of the Sierras and Sunlands* in 1878 (No. 13775) & 1892 (No. 13826).

*13757. UNWRITTEN HISTORY: LIFE AMONGST THE MODOCS. Hartford: American Pub. Co., 1874.
"Sold by subscription only." Reprinted in 1881 as *Paquita* (No. 13891). Revised edition published in 1890 as *My Own Story* (No. 13820); reprinted in 1890 (?) as *Joaquin Miller's Romantic Life amongst the Red Indians* (No. 13898) & in 1892 as *My Life among the Indians* (No. 13899).

13758. FIRST FAM'LIES IN THE SIERRAS. Lon: Routledge & Sons, 1875.

13759. THE SHIP IN THE DESERT. Lon: Chapman & Hall, 1875.

13760. THE SHIP IN THE DESERT. Bos: Roberts Bros., 1875.

13764. THE ONE FAIR WOMAN. Lon: Chapman & Hall, 1876.
3v.

JOAQUIN MILLER (cont.)

13765. FIRST FAM'LIES OF THE SIERRAS. Chi: Jansen, McClurg, 1876.
Much revised from the U.K. 1875 edition. Later revisions published as *The Danites in the Sierras* in 1881 (No. 13779) & 1889 (No. 13818). For a dramatization under the latter title see No. 13784 below.

*13766. THE ONE FAIR WOMAN. NY: Carleton, 1876.
3v. in one.

13771. THE BARONESS OF NEW YORK. NY: Carleton, 1877.

13773. SONGS OF ITALY. Bos: Roberts Bros., 1878.

13774. SONGS OF FAR-AWAY LANDS. Lon: Longmans, Green, et al, 1878.

*13778. SHADOWS OF SHASTA. Chi: Janson, McClurg, 1881.

*13784. FORTY-NINE: A CALIFORNIA DRAMA <and> DANITES IN THE SIERRAS: A DRAMA. SF: California Pub. Co., 1882.
The sheets of each play were also issued separately.

13786. THE SILENT MAN: A COMEDY-DRAMA. <n.p.>, 1883.
Presumably printed for copyright purposes only.

13788. "TALLY-HO!" A MUSICAL DRAMA. <n.p.>, 1883.
Presumably printed for copyright purposes only.

*13795. MEMORIE AND RIME. NY: Funk & Wagnalls, 1884.
Standard Library series, No. 108 (paper) & No. 3 (cloth).

*13799. '49 THE GOLD-SEEKER OF THE SIERRAS. NY & Lon: Funk & Wagnalls, 1884.
Standard Library series, No. 123 (paper) & No. 18 (cloth).

13808. THE DESTRUCTION OF GOTHAM. NY & Lon: Funk & Wagnalls, 1886.
Cloth; and paper wrapper of the *Standard Library* series, No. 139.

*13812. SONGS OF THE MEXICAN SEAS. Bos: Roberts Bros., 1887.

13821. IN CLASSIC SHADES AND OTHER POEMS. Chi: Belford-Clarke, 1890.

*13830. THE BUILDING OF THE CITY BEAUTIFUL. Cambridge & Chi: Stone & Kimball, 1893.
Revised edition published in 1905 (No. 13860).

13835. AN ILLUSTRATED HISTORY OF THE STATE OF MONTANA. Chi: Lewis Pub. Co., 1894.
2v.

*13838. SONGS OF THE SOUL. SF: Whitaker & Ray, 1896.

13841. THE COMPLETE POETICAL WORKS. SF: Whitaker & Ray, 1897.
Extended edition published in 1902 (No. 13853).

13847. CHANTS FOR THE BOER. SF: Whitaker & Ray, 1900.

*13848. TRUE BEAR STORIES. Chi & NY: Rand, McNally, <1900>.

13855. AS IT WAS IN THE BEGINNING. A POEM. <SF: Robertson, 1903>.

13859. JAPAN OF SWORD AND LOVE. Tokyo: Kanao Bunyendo, 1905.
With Yone Noguchi.

13861. LIGHT A NARRATIVE POEM. Bos: Turner, 1907.

JOAQUIN MILLER (cont.)
*13864. COLLECTED WORKS. SF: Whitaker & Ray, 1909–10.
6v. A version of Miller's "An Introduction" in Vol. 1 was published separately in 1930 as *Overland in a Covered Wagon. An Autobiography* (No. 13879).

13883. JOAQUIN MILLER HIS CALIFORNIA DIARY BEGINNING IN 1855 & END-ING IN 1857. Seattle: McCaffrey, 1936.
Ed. John S. Richards.

Donald Grant Mitchell
(Ik. Marvel)
1822–1908

*13920. THE DIGNITY OF LEARNING. A VALEDICTORY ORATION. New Haven: Ptd by Hamlen, 1841.
"Published by request of the class." Pronounced before the senior class of Yale College, 7 July 1841. Also published with *Poem* by Guy Bryan Scott.

*13922. FRESH GLEANINGS; OR, A NEW SHEAF FROM THE OLD FIELDS OF CONTINENTAL EUROPE. By Ik. Marvel. NY: Harper & Bros., 1847.
2 parts or 1v.

*13924. THE BATTLE SUMMER: BEING TRANSCRIPTS FROM PERSONAL OBSERVATION IN PARIS, DURING THE YEAR 1848. By Ik. Marvel. NY: Baker & Scribner, 1850.

*13925. THE LORGNETTE OR STUDIES OF THE TOWN. By an Opera Goer. NY: Kernott, 1850.
24 parts. Revised "second edition" published in 2v. in 1850 (No. 13926); these sheets issued in the U.K. in 1852 as *The Opera Goer* (No. 13992).

13927. REVERIES OF A BACHELOR: OR A BOOK OF THE HEART. By Ik. Marvel. NY: Baker & Scribner, 1850.
Slightly revised edition published in 1884 (No. 13961). A private printing of some of this material was also produced in 1850 as *A Bachelor's Reverie* (No. 13928). An additional piece, entitled *A New Reverie*, was distributed for periodical syndi-cation in 1895 (No. 13979).

*13931. DREAM LIFE: A FABLE OF THE SEASONS. By Ik. Marvel. NY: Scribner, 1851.

13933. FUDGE DOINGS: BEING TONY FUDGE'S RECORD OF THE SAME. By Ik. Marvel. NY: Scribner, 1855.
2v.

*13937. MY FARM OF EDGEWOOD: A COUNTRY BOOK. NY: Scribner, 1863.
Anon.

13941. SEVEN STORIES, WITH BASEMENT AND ATTIC. NY: Scribner, 1864.
Anon.

13942. WET DAYS AT EDGEWOOD: WITH OLD FARMERS, OLD GARDENERS, AND OLD PASTORALS. NY: Scribner, 1865.
Anon.

D. G. MITCHELL (cont.)

13943. DOCTOR JOHNS: BEING A NARRATIVE OF CERTAIN EVENTS IN THE LIFE OF AN ORTHODOX MINISTER OF CONNECTICUT. NY: Scribner, 1866.
2v. Anon. A "new and revised" edition published in 1884 (Nos. 13964 & 13965).

*13944. RURAL STUDIES WITH HINTS FOR COUNTRY PLACES. NY: Scribner, 1867.
Anon. Reprinted, with new preface, in 1884 as *Out-of-Town Places* (No. 13967).

13947. PICTURES OF EDGEWOOD. NY: Scribner, 1869.
Anon. Illustrated with photographs by Rockwood.

*13954. ABOUT OLD STORY-TELLERS: OF HOW AND WHEN THEY LIVED, AND WHAT STORIES THEY TOLD. NY: Scribner, Armstrong, 1878.

13966. BOUND TOGETHER: A SHEAF OF PAPERS. NY: Scribner's Sons, 1884.
Anon.

13971. ENGLISH LANDS LETTERS AND KINGS FROM CELT TO TUDOR. NY: Scribner's Sons, 1889.

13974. ENGLISH LANDS LETTERS AND KINGS FROM ELIZABETH TO ANNE. NY: Scribner, 1890.

13978. ENGLISH LANDS LETTERS AND KINGS QUEEN ANNE AND THE GEORGES. NY: Scribner's Sons, 1895.

*13980. AMERICAN LANDS AND LETTERS THE MAYFLOWER TO RIP-VAN-WINKLE. NY: Scribner's Sons, 1897.

13981. ENGLISH LANDS LETTERS AND KINGS THE LATER GEORGES TO VICTORIA. NY: Scribner's Sons, 1897.

13984. AMERICAN LANDS AND LETTERS LEATHER-STOCKING TO POE'S "RAVEN." NY: Scribner's Sons, 1899.

13988. LOOKING BACKWARD AT BOYHOOD. By "Ik Marvel." <n.p.>: Academy PR, 1906.

13989. THE WORKS OF DONALD G. MITCHELL. NY: Scribner's Sons, 1907.
15v. *Edgewood Edition.*

Isaac Mitchell
1759–1812

14020A. THE ASYLUM; OR, ALONZO AND MELISSA. AN AMERICAN TALE. Poughkeepsie: J. Nelson, 1811.
2v. See also next entry; sequence not known.

*14020B. A SHORT ACCOUNT OF THE COURTSHIP OF ALONZO & MELISSA. Plattsburgh NY: Ptd for the Proprieter, 1811.
Anon, but some copies attributed (by hand stamp?) to *Daniel Jackson, Jun.* on the title-page. See also preceding entry; sequence not known.

John Ames Mitchell
1845–1918

14021. THE SUMMER SCHOOL OF PHILOSOPHY AT MT. DESERT. NY: Holt, 1881.

14025. THE ROMANCE OF THE MOON. NY: Holt, 1886.

*14030. THE LAST AMERICAN A FRAGMENT FROM THE JOURNAL OF KHAN-LI. Ed. J.A. Mitchell. NY: Stokes & Brother, 1889.
Revised "edition de luxe" published in 1902 (No. 14042).

14035. LIFE'S FAIRY TALES. NY: Stokes, 1892.

14038. AMOS JUDD. NY: Scribner's Sons, 1895.

*14039. THAT FIRST AFFAIR AND OTHER SKETCHES. NY: Scribner's Sons, 1896.

14040. GLORIA VICTIS. NY: Scribner's Sons, 1897.
Revised edition published in 1910 as *Dr. Thorne's Idea* (No. 14046).

*14041. THE PINES OF LORY. NY: Life Pub. Co., 1901.

14043. THE VILLA CLAUDIA. NY: Life Pub. Co., 1904.

14045. THE SILENT WAR. NY: Life Pub. Co., 1906.

14047. PANDORA'S BOX. NY: Stokes, <1911>.

*14049. DROWSY. NY: Stokes, <1917>.

Silas Weir Mitchell
(Edward Kearsley)
1829–1914

Note : Mitchell's numerous medical writings are here omitted, as are occasional addresses and privately printed separate editions of his poems.

14061. THE CHILDREN'S HOUR. By E.W.S. and S.W.M. Phila, 1864.
"Published for the benefit of the Sanitary Commission." With Elizabeth W. Stevenson.

*14065. THE WONDERFUL STORIES OF FUZ-BUZ THE FLY AND MOTHER GRABEM THE SPIDER. Phila: Lippincott, 1867.
Anon.

14101. HEPHZIBAH GUINNESS; THEE AND YOU; AND A DRAFT ON THE BANK OF SPAIN. Phila: Lippincott, 1880.
Slightly revised "third edition" published in 1897 (No. 14181).

*14105. THE HILL OF STONES AND OTHER POEMS. Bos & NY: Houghton, Mifflin, 1883.

14110. IN WAR TIME. Bos & NY: Houghton, Mifflin, 1885.

14120. ROLAND BLAKE. Bos & NY: Houghton, Mifflin, 1886.
Also privately printed in 1886 (No. 14118).

14124. A MASQUE AND OTHER POEMS. Bos & NY: Houghton, Mifflin, 1887.

S. WEIR MITCHELL (cont.)

*14130. PRINCE LITTLE BOY AND OTHER TALES OUT OF FAIRY-LAND. Phila: Lippincott, 1888.

14135. FAR IN THE FOREST. A STORY. Phila: Lippincott, 1889.
Revised & extended edition published in 1899 (No. 14188).

14136. THE CUP OF YOUTH AND OTHER POEMS. Bos & NY: Houghton, Mifflin, 1889.

14141. A PSALM OF DEATHS AND OTHER POEMS. Bos & NY: Houghton, Mifflin, 1890.

14148. CHARACTERISTICS. NY: Century Co., 1892.

14155. THE MOTHER AND OTHER POEMS. Bos & NY: Houghton, Mifflin, 1893.
Also privately printed in 1891 (No. 14147).

14156. FRANCIS DRAKE A TRAGEDY OF THE SEA. Bos & NY: Houghton, Mifflin, 1893.

*14157. MR. KRIS KRINGLE. A CHRISTMAS TALE. Phila: Jacobs, 1893.
Revised edition published in 1904 (No. 14221).

14160. WHEN ALL THE WOODS ARE GREEN A NOVEL. NY: Century Co., 1894.

14165. PHILIP VERNON A TALE IN PROSE AND VERSE. NY: Century Co., 1895.

14166. A MADEIRA PARTY. NY: Century Co., 1895.

*14178. HUGH WYNNE FREE QUAKER. NY: Century Co., 1897.
2v. A prepublication printing is dated 1896. Also a simultaneous (?) U.K. edition
(No. 14179). Revised edition published in 1908 (No.14250)

14184. THE ADVENTURES OF FRANÇOIS ... DURING THE FRENCH REVOLUTION. NY: Century Co., 1898.

14191. THE WAGER AND OTHER POEMS. NY: Century Co., 1900.

14192. THE AUTOBIOGRAPHY OF A QUACK AND THE CASE OF GEORGE DEDLOW. NY: Century Co., 1900.
Extended edition published in 1901 (No. 14205).

*14193. DR. NORTH AND HIS FRIENDS. NY: Century Co., 1900.

14202. CIRCUMSTANCE. NY: Century Co., 1901.

*14216. A COMEDY OF CONSCIENCE. NY: Century Co., 1903.

14217. LITTLE STORIES. NY: Century Co., 1903.

14222. NEW SAMARIA AND THE SUMMER OF ST. MARTIN. Phila & Lon: Lippincott, 1904.
"New Samaria" originally published as the Aug. 1902 issue of *Lippincott's Monthly Magazine* (No. 14208).

*14223. THE YOUTH OF WASHINGTON TOLD IN THE FORM OF AN AUTO-BIOGRAPHY. NY: Century Co., 1904.
Unpublished proof version produced in 1902 as *An Autobiography of George Washington* (No. 14209). Revised & published in 1910 as part of the *Author's Definitive Edition*, see No. 14235 below.

S. WEIR MITCHELL (cont.)

14228. CONSTANCE TRESCOT A NOVEL. NY: Century Co., 1905.

14235. AUTHOR'S DEFINITIVE EDITION. NY: Century Co., 1905–14.
16v. The *Author's Edition* published in 10v. in 1903 (No. 14292) presumably contains only reprinted material.

14236. PEARL RENDERED INTO MODERN ENGLISH VERSE. NY: Century Co., 1906.
Extended edition published in 1908 (No. 14246).

14237. A DIPLOMATIC ADVENTURE. NY: Century Co., 1906.

14247. A VENTURE IN 1777. Phila: Jacobs, <1908>.

*14249. THE RED CITY A NOVEL OF THE SECOND ADMINISTRATION OF GEORGE WASHINGTON. NY: Century Co., 1908.

14262. THE COMFORT OF THE HILLS AND OTHER POEMS. NY: Century Co., 1910.

14263. THE GUILLOTINE CLUB AND OTHER STORIES. NY: Century Co., 1910.

*14265. JOHN SHERWOOD, IRONMASTER. NY: Century Co., 1911.

14272. WESTWAYS A VILLAGE CHRONICLE. NY: Century Co., 1913.

14275. THE COMPLETE POEMS. NY: Century Co., 1914.
Also published as part of the *Author's Definitive Edition*, see No. 14235 above.

14279. WEIR MITCHELL HIS LIFE AND LETTERS. NY: Duffield, 1929.
By Anna Robeson Burr.

William Vaughn Stoy Moody
1869–1910

*14308. THE MASQUE OF JUDGMENT A MASQUE-DRAMA. Bos: Small, Maynard, 1900.
These sheets reissued in 1902 (No. 14326) by Houghton, Mifflin, Boston & New York.

*14310. POEMS. Bos & NY: Houghton, Mifflin, 1901.
Reprinted in 1909 as *Gloucester Moors and Other Poems* (No. 14327).

*14311. A HISTORY OF ENGLISH LITERATURE. NY: Scribner's Sons, 1902.
With Robert Morss Lovett. A school text version based on this work was published in 1905 as *A First View of English Literature* (No. 14313) & extended in 1909 as *A First View of English and American Literature* (No. 14318).

*14312. THE FIRE-BRINGER. Bos & NY: Houghton, Mifflin, 1904.

14316. THE FAITH HEALER A PLAY. Bos & NY: Houghton Mifflin, 1909.
Revised version published in 1910 (No. 14320).

14319. THE GREAT DIVIDE A PLAY. NY: Macmillan, 1909.
A typescript with title *A Sabine Woman* was deposited for copyright in 1906.

14322. THE POEMS AND PLAYS. Bos & NY: Houghton Mifflin, 1912.
2v.

WILLIAM VAUGHN MOODY (cont.)
14323. SOME LETTERS OF WILLIAM VAUGHN MOODY. Bos & NY: Houghton Mifflin, 1913.
Ed. Daniel Gregory Mason.

14325. LETTERS TO HARRIET. Bos & NY: Houghton Mifflin, 1935.
Ed. Percy Mackaye.

Clement Clarke Moore
1779–1863

14342. ACCOUNT OF A VISIT FROM ST. NICHOLAS. 1824.
Otherwise "A Visit from St. Nicholas" & "The Night before Christmas." First printed in *The Troy Sentinel*, 23 Dec. 1823. BAL lists 4 almanacs printed in 1824 containing the poem. For the earliest known separate printing see next entry.

14346. ACCOUNT OF A VISIT FROM ST. NICHOLAS, OR SANTA CLAUS. <Troy NY>: Ptd by N. Tuttle, Office of the Daily Troy Sentinel, <n.d., *ca.* 1830>.

14348. POEMS. NY: Bartlett & Welford, 1844.

George Pope Morris
1802–1864

14355. THE DESERTED BRIDE; AND OTHER POEMS. NY: Adlard & Saunders, 1838.
Contains 30 poems, including "The Oak" (later "Woodman, Spare that Tree"). For extended editions see Nos. 14363 & 14382 below.

14356. THE LITTLE FRENCHMAN AND HIS WATER LOTS, WITH OTHER SKETCHES OF THE TIMES. Phila: Lea & Blanchard, 1839.
Slightly revised edition published in 1844 (No. 14366).

14357. AMERICAN MELODIES; CONTAINING A SINGLE SELECTION FROM THE PRODUCTIONS OF TWO HUNDRED WRITERS. NY: Linen & Fennell, 1841.
Compiled by Morris; for full entry see BAL (No. 997). Reprinted in 1854 as *The Gift Book of American Melodies* (No. 14550).

14360. SONGS, DUETTS AND CHORUSSES IN THE NEW OPERA OF THE MAID OF SAXONY. NY: House, 1842.
Music by C.E. Horn. For publication of the full text see No. 14382 below.

*14363. THE DESERTED BRIDE; AND OTHER POEMS. NY: Appleton, 1843.
Contains 74 poems. "The Whip-Poor-Will," here collected, was also published separately in 1843 (No. 14364).

14365. THE SONGS AND BALLADS. NY: Morris, Willis, 1844.
New Mirror Extra, No. 4. Extended "first complete edition" published in 1846 (No. 14370).

GEORGE POPE MORRIS (cont.)

14369. A LIBRARY OF THE PROSE AND POETRY OF EUROPE AND AMERICA. NY: Paine & Burgess, 1846.
Compiled by Morris & N.P. Willis. Reprinted from *The Mirror Library*, 1843–44, see No. 22785 below. Reprinted in 1852 as *The Prose and Poetry of Europe and America* (No. 14548).

14382. THE DESERTED BRIDE, AND OTHER PRODUCTIONS. NY: Scribner, 1853.
Contains 114 poems and "The Maid of Saxony."

14390. POEMS ... WITH A MEMOIR OF THE AUTHOR. NY: Scribner, <1860>.

Sarah Wentworth Apthorp Morton
1759–1846

14554. OUÂBI: OR THE VIRTUES OF NATURE. AN INDIAN TALE. By Philenia, a Lady of Boston. Bos: Thomas & Andrews, 1790.

14558. BEACON HILL. A LOCAL POEM, HISTORIC AND DESCRIPTIVE. BOOK I. Bos: The Author, 1797.
Anon, but "Apology for the Poem" signed *S.M.* at end. All published.

14559. THE VIRTUES OF SOCIETY. A TALE, FOUNDED ON FACT. Bos: The Author, 1799.
Anon.

14565. MY MIND AND ITS THOUGHTS, IN SKETCHES, FRAGMENTS, AND ESSAYS. Bos: Wells & Lilly, 1823.
A slightly revised selection published in 1835 as part of an omnibus volume with binder's title *Cabinet of Literature* (No. 14567).

John Lothrop Motley
1814–1877

14568. MORTON OF MORTON'S HOPE; AN AUTOBIOGRAPHY. Lon: Colburn, 1839.
3v. Anon. For U.S. edition see next entry.

14569. MORTON'S HOPE: OR THE MEMOIRS OF A PROVINCIAL. NY: Harper & Bros., 1839.
2v. Anon. The text varies from the U.K. edition.

14573. MERRY-MOUNT; A ROMANCE OF THE MASSACHUSETTS COLONY. Bos & Cambridge: Munroe, 1849.
2v., or 2v. in one. Anon.

14574. THE RISE OF THE DUTCH REPUBLIC. A HISTORY. Lon: Chapman, 1856.
3v.

14575. THE RISE OF THE DUTCH REPUBLIC. A HISTORY. NY: Harper & Bros., 1856.
3v.

JOHN LOTHROP MOTLEY (cont.)

14576. HISTORY OF THE UNITED NETHERLANDS: FROM THE DEATH OF WILLIAM THE SILENT TO THE SYNOD OF DORT. Lon: Murray, 1860.
Vols. 1–2 of four.

14578. HISTORY OF THE UNITED NETHERLANDS: FROM THE DEATH OF WILLIAM THE SILENT TO THE SYNOD OF DORT. NY: Harper & Bros., 1861.
Vols. 1–2 of four.

14579. CAUSES OF THE CIVIL WAR IN AMERICA. Lon: Manwaring, 1861.
"Reprinted, with permission," from *The Times*. For U.S. editions see next entry.

*14580. THE CAUSES OF THE AMERICAN CIVIL WAR. NY: Appleton, 1861.
Two simultaneous (?) editions noted, the second as *Letters of John Lothrop Motley, and Joseph Holt* (NY: H.E. Tudor, Ptr, 1861).

14584. HISTORY OF THE UNITED NETHERLANDS: FROM THE DEATH OF WILLIAM THE SILENT TO THE TWELVE YEARS' TRUCE—1609. Lon: Murray, 1867.
Vols. 3–4 of four.

14585. HISTORY OF THE UNITED NETHERLANDS: FROM THE DEATH OF WILLIAM THE SILENT TO THE TWELVE YEARS' TRUCE–1609. NY: Harper & Bros., 1868.
Vols. 3–4 of four.

14586. FOUR QUESTIONS FOR THE PEOPLE, AT THE PRESIDENTIAL ELECTION. Bos: Ticknor & Fields, 1868.
Address before the Parker Fraternity, 20 Oct. 1868.

14587. HISTORIC PROGRESS AND AMERICAN DEMOCRACY: AN ADDRESS. NY: Scribner, 1869.
Delivered before the New-York Historical Society, 16 Dec. 1868. Reprinted in the U.K. as *Democracy: The Climax of Political Progress and the Destiny of Advanced Races* (No. 14603).

14590. THE LIFE AND DEATH OF JOHN OF BARNEVELD, ADVOCATE OF HOLLAND. Lon: Murray, 1874.
2v.

14591. THE LIFE AND DEATH OF JOHN OF BARNEVELD, ADVOCATE OF HOLLAND. NY: Harper & Bros., 1874.
2v.

14592. PETER THE GREAT. NY: Harper & Bros., 1877.
First published in the U.K. in 1846 in a collection of essays entitled *Characteristics of Men of Genius* (No. 14572).

14594. THE CORRESPONDENCE OF JOHN LOTHROP MOTLEY. Lon: Murray, 1889.
2v. Ed. George William Curtis.

14595. THE CORRESPONDENCE OF JOHN LOTHROP MOTLEY. NY: Harper & Bros., 1889.
2v. Ed. George William Curtis. Additional letters were published in *John Lothrop Motley and His Family*, 1910 (No. 14597).

JOHN LOTHROP MOTLEY (cont.)

*14605. THE WRITINGS OF JOHN LOTHROP MOTLEY. NY & Lon: Harper & Bros., 1900.
17v.

Ellen Louise Chandler Moulton
1835–1908

14606. THE WAVERLEY GARLAND, A PRESENT FOR ALL SEASONS. Ed. "Ellen Louise." Bos: Dow, 1853.
Edited, with contributions, by Moulton. Reprinted in 1853 (?) as *The Book of the Boudoir* (No. 14708).

14608. THIS, THAT, AND THE OTHER. By Ellen Louise Chandler. Bos: Phillips, Sampson, 1854.

14609. JUNO CLIFFORD. A TALE. By a Lady. NY: Appleton, 1856.

*14610. MY THIRD BOOK. A COLLECTION OF TALES. NY: Harper & Bros., 1859.

14616. BED-TIME STORIES. Bos: Roberts Bros., 1873.

14620. SOME WOMEN'S HEARTS. Bos: Roberts Bros., 1874.

*14622. MORE BED-TIME STORIES. Bos: Roberts Bros., 1875.

14632. JESSIE'S NEIGHBOR, AND OTHER STORIES. Bos: Lothrop, <1877>.
Not to be confused with No. 14698 below.

14633. POEMS. Bos: Roberts Bros., 1878.
Extended edition published in 1892 as *Swallow Flights* (No. 14674).

14635. NEW BED-TIME STORIES. Bos: Roberts Bros., 1880.

14638. RANDOM RAMBLES. Bos: Roberts Bros., 1881.

14644. FIRELIGHT STORIES. Bos: Roberts Bros., 1883.

*14656. OURSELVES AND OUR NEIGHBORS: SHORT CHATS ON SOCIAL TOPICS. Bos: Roberts Bros., 1887.

*14663. MISS EYRE FROM BOSTON, AND OTHERS. Bos: Roberts Bros., 1889.

14664. IN THE GARDEN OF DREAMS: LYRICS AND SONNETS. Bos: Roberts Bros., 1890.
The "fourth edition," with 1 additional piece, published in 1891 (No. 14673).

14668. STORIES TOLD AT TWILIGHT. Bos: Roberts Bros., 1890.

14689. LAZY TOURS IN SPAIN AND ELSEWHERE. Bos: Roberts Bros., 1896.

*14691. IN CHILDHOOD'S COUNTRY. Bos: Copeland & Day, 1896.
The Yellow Hair Library, No. 2.

14696. FOUR OF THEM. Bos: Little, Brown, <1899>.

14697. AT THE WIND'S WILL LYRICS AND SONNETS. Bos: Little, Brown, 1899.

14698. JESSIE'S NEIGHBOR. Bos: Little, Brown, <1900>.
Contains 2 stories in addition to the title story. Not to be confused with No. 14632 above.

14700. HER BABY BROTHER. Bos: Little, Brown, <1901>.

LOUISE CHANDLER MOULTON (cont.)

14706. THE POEMS AND SONNETS OF LOUISE CHANDLER MOULTON. Bos: Little, Brown, 1909.

John Muir
1838–1914

*14744. PICTURESQUE CALIFORNIA. SF & NY: Dewing, 1887–88.
10 parts, 32 parts, or 2v. Edited, with contributions, by Muir. Abbreviated edition published in 1894 (No. 14747).

14746. THE MOUNTAINS OF CALIFORNIA. NY: Century Co., 1894.
A "new and enlarged" edition published in 1911 (No. 14764).

*14752. OUR NATIONAL PARKS. Bos & NY: Houghton, Mifflin, 1901.
A "new and enlarged" edition published in 1909 (No. 14760).

14759. STICKEEN. Bos & NY: Houghton Mifflin, 1909.

14765. MY FIRST SUMMER IN THE SIERRA. Bos & NY: Houghton Mifflin, 1911.

14766. EDWARD HENRY HARRIMAN. Garden City NY: Doubleday, Page, 1911.

14767. THE YOSEMITE. NY: Century Co., 1912.

14768. THE STORY OF MY BOYHOOD AND YOUTH. Bos & NY: Houghton Mifflin, 1913.

14770. LETTERS TO A FRIEND WRITTEN TO MRS. EZRA S. CARR 1866–1879. Bos & NY: Houghton Mifflin, 1915.

*14771. TRAVELS IN ALASKA. Bos & NY: Houghton Mifflin, 1915.

*14773. A THOUSAND-MILE WALK TO THE GULF. Bos & NY: Houghton Mifflin, 1916.
Ed. William Frederic Badè

14774. THE WRITINGS OF JOHN MUIR. Bos & NY: Houghton Mifflin, 1916–24.
10v. Manuscript edition. Also published in 1917–24 as the "Sierra Edition" (No. 14776).

*14775. THE CRUISE OF THE CORWIN. Bos & NY: Houghton Mifflin, 1917.
Ed. William Frederic Badè. Also published as *The Writings,* Vol. 7.

*14777. STEEP TRAILS. Bos & NY: Houghton Mifflin, 1918.
Ed. William Frederic Badè. Also published as *The Writings,* Vol. 8.

14779. THE LIFE AND LETTERS OF JOHN MUIR. Bos & NY: Houghton Mifflin, 1924.
By William Frederic Badè. Also published as *The Writings,* Vols. 9–10.

14781. JOHN OF THE MOUNTAINS THE UNPUBLISHED JOURNALS OF JOHN MUIR. Bos: Houghton Mifflin, 1938.
Ed. Linnie Marsh Wolfe.

14786. JOHN MUIR'S STUDIES IN THE SIERRA. SF: Sierra Club, 1950.
Revised edition published in 1960 (No. 14788).

JOHN MUIR (cont.)

14789. SELECTED WRITINGS BY JOHN MUIR SOUTH OF YOSEMITE. Garden City NY: American Museum of Natural History, 1968.
Ed. Frederic R. Gunsky.

14790. THE TREASURES OF THE YOSEMITE. Ashland: L. Osborne, 1970.
Ed. L.W. Lane, Jr.

Mary Noailles Murfree
(Charles Egbert Craddock)
1850–1922

Note: All works listed here were published under Murfree's pseudonym *Charles Egbert Craddock.*

*14800. IN THE TENNESSEE MOUNTAINS. Bos & NY: Houghton, Mifflin, 1884.

14801. WHERE THE BATTLE WAS FOUGHT A NOVEL. Bos: Osgood, 1884.

*14802. DOWN THE RAVINE. Bos & NY: Houghton, Mifflin, 1885.

*14803. THE PROPHET OF THE GREAT SMOKY MOUNTAINS. Bos & NY: Houghton, Mifflin, 1885.

*14804. IN THE CLOUDS. Bos & NY: Houghton, Mifflin, 1887.

*14805. THE STORY OF KEEDON BLUFFS. Bos & NY: Houghton, Mifflin, 1888.

14806. THE DESPOT OF BROOMSEDGE COVE. Bos & NY: Houghton, Mifflin, 1889.

*14807. IN THE "STRANGER PEOPLE'S" COUNTRY A NOVEL. NY: Harper & Bros., 1891.

*14808. HIS VANISHED STAR. Bos & NY: Houghton, Mifflin, 1894.

14809. THE PHANTOMS OF THE FOOTBRIDGE AND OTHER STORIES. NY: Harper & Bros., 1895.

14810. THE MYSTERY OF WITCH-FACE MOUNTAIN AND OTHER STORIES. Bos & NY: Houghton, Mifflin, 1895.

14811. THE YOUNG MOUNTAINEERS SHORT STORIES. Bos & NY: Houghton, Mifflin, 1897.

14812. THE JUGGLER. Bos & NY: Houghton, Mifflin, 1897.

*14813. THE STORY OF OLD FORT LOUDON. NY: Macmillan, 1899.

14814. THE BUSHWHACKERS & OTHER STORIES. Chi & NY: Stone, 1899.

14815. THE CHAMPION. Bos & NY: Houghton, Mifflin, 1902.

14816. A SPECTRE OF POWER. Bos & NY: Houghton, Mifflin, 1903.

*14817. THE FRONTIERSMEN. Bos & NY: Houghton, Mifflin, 1904.

14818. THE STORM CENTRE A NOVEL. NY: Macmillan, 1905.

14819. THE AMULET A NOVEL. NY: Macmillan, 1906.

14820. THE WINDFALL A NOVEL. NY: Duffield, 1907.

14821. THE FAIR MISSISSIPPIAN A NOVEL. Bos & NY: Houghton Mifflin, 1908.

MARY N. MURFREE (cont.)
14822. THE RAID OF THE GUERILLA AND OTHER STORIES. Phila & Lon: Lippincott, 1912.
14823. THE ORDEAL A MOUNTAIN ROMANCE OF TENNESSEE. Phila & Lon: Lippincott, 1912.
14824. THE STORY OF DUCIEHURST A TALE OF THE MISSISSIPPI. NY: Macmillan, 1914.

Peter Hamilton Myers
1812–1878
14826. ENSENORE. A POEM. NY: Wiley & Putnam, 1840.
Anon. For revised edition see No. 14846 below.

14827. SCIENCE. A POEM. Geneva NY: Ptd by Stow & Frazee, 1841.
Delivered before the Euglossian Society of Geneva College, 4 Aug. 1841.

14828. THE FIRST OF THE KNICKERBOCKERS: A TALE OF 1673. NY: Putnam, 1848.
Anon. Revised edition published in 1849 (No. 14831).

14829. ELLEN WELLES: OR, THE SIEGE OF FORT STANWIX. A TALE OF THE REVOLUTION. Rome NY: W.O. M'Clure, 1848.
Reprinted in 1865 as *Fort Stanwix* (No. 14840) & in 1871 as *The Red Spy* (No. 14845). See also No. 14836 below.

14830. THE YOUNG PATROON; OR, CHRISTMAS IN 1690. A TALE OF NEW-YORK. NY: Putnam, 1849.
Anon.

14832. THE KING OF THE HURONS. NY: Putnam, 1850.
Anon.

*14833. BELL BRANDON; AND THE WITHERED FIG TREE. A PRIZE NOVEL. Phila: Peterson, <1851>.
Anon.

*14835. THE EMIGRANT SQUIRE. Phila: Peterson, <1853>.

14836. THE MISER'S HEIR; OR, THE THE <sic> YOUNG MILLIONAIRE. Phila: Peterson, <1854>.
Reprints "Ellen Welles," pp. 167–222; see No. 14829 above.

14838. THE PRISONER OF THE BORDER; A TALE OF 1838. NY: Derby & Jackson, 1857.
Reprinted in 1860 as *Thrilling Adventures of the Prisoner of the Border* (No. 14839).

14841. THE GOLD CRUSHERS. A TALE OF CALIFORNIA. NY: Irwin, <1866>.
Reprinted in 1870 as *Nick Doyle, the Gold-Hunter* (No. 14844).

14846. ENSENORE, AND OTHER POEMS. NY: Dodd & Mead, <1875>.

*14847. THE GREAT MOGUL. A NOVEL. NY: Street & Smith, 1878.

14848. THE TREASURE SHIP. A TALE OF NEW YORK. <NY: G. Munro, 1884>.
The Seaside Library, Vol. 110, No. 1813, 29 Mar. 1884.

PETER HAMILTON MYERS (cont.)

14849. ROXY HASTINGS; OR, A RAFFLE FOR LIFE. NY: Street & Smith, <1890>.
The Select Series, No. 55, 20 Aug. 1890.

14850. THE SKY TRAVELER. <NY: Street & Smith, 1890>.
Log Cabin Library, No. 93, 25 Dec. 1890.

John Neal
1793–1876

*14852. KEEP COOL, A NOVEL. WRITTEN IN HOT WEATHER. By Somebody,
M.D.C. Baltimore: Cushing, 1817.
2v.

*14853. BATTLE OF NIAGARA, A POEM ... AND GOLDAU, OR THE MANIAC
HARPER. By Jehu O'Cataract. Baltimore: N.G. Maxwell, 1818.
For an extended edition see next entry.

14856. THE BATTLE OF NIAGARA: SECOND EDITION—ENLARGED: WITH OTHER
POEMS. Baltimore: N.G. Maxwell, 1819.

14857. OTHO: A TRAGEDY. Bos: West, Richardson & Lord, 1819.

14858. LOGAN, A FAMILY HISTORY. Phila: Carey & Lea, 1822.
2v. Reprinted in 1840 as *Logan, the Mingo Chief* (No. 14894).

14859. SEVENTY-SIX. Baltimore: J. Robinson, 1823.
2v. Anon.

14860. RANDOLPH, A NOVEL. <n.p., Philadelphia: S. Simpson>, 1823.
2v. Anon. "Published for Whom It May Concern."

14861. ERRATA; OR, THE WORKS OF WILL. ADAMS. NY: The Proprietors, 1823.
2v. Anon.

14862. BROTHER JONATHAN: OR, THE NEW ENGLANDERS. Edinburgh:
Blackwood, 1825.
3v. Anon.

14863. RACHEL DYER: A NORTH AMERICAN STORY. Portland ME: Shirley &
Hyde, 1828.

14874. AUTHORSHIP, A TALE. By a New Englander Over-Sea. Bos: Gray &
Bowen, 1830.

14880. THE DOWN-EASTERS. NY: Harper & Bros., 1833.
2v.

*14906. ONE WORD MORE: INTENDED FOR THE REASONING AND THOUGHT-
FUL AMONG UNBELIEVERS. Portland ME: The Author, 1854.
Extended "second edition" published in 1856 (No. 14907).

14910. TRUE WOMANHOOD: A TALE. Bos: Ticknor & Fields, 1859.

14913. THE WHITE-FACED PACER: OR, BEFORE AND AFTER THE BATTLE. NY:
Beadle, <1863>.
Beadle's Library of Choice Fiction, No. 1. Reprinted in 1890 as *Deacon Hale's Grit; or,
Ebenezer Day's Mad Ride* (No. 14929).

JOHN NEAL (cont.)

*14916. THE MOOSE-HUNTER; OR, LIFE IN THE MAINE WOODS. NY: Beadle, <1864>.
Beadle's Dime Novel, No. 72. Reprinted in 1889 as Uncle Jerry, the Quaker; or, the Schoolmaster's Trial (No. 14928).

14919. LITTLE MOCCASIN; OR, ALONG THE MADAWASKA. NY: Beadle, <1866>.
Beadle's Dime Novel, No. 96. Reprinted in 1889 as Bob Gage's Crew; or, the Boys of Logger-Camp (No. 14927).

14921. WANDERING RECOLLECTIONS OF A SOMEWHAT BUSY LIFE. AN AUTOBIOGRAPHY. Bos: Roberts Bros., 1869.

14922. GREAT MYSTERIES AND LITTLE PLAGUES. Bos: Roberts Bros., 1870.

14924. PORTLAND ILLUSTRATED. Portland ME: W.S. Jones, 1874.

14933. AMERICAN WRITERS. Durham NC: Duke U PR, 1937.
Ed. Fred Lewis Pattee. Reprinted from Blackwood's Magazine, 1824–25.

14935. OBSERVATIONS ON AMERICAN ART. State College PA: Pennsylvania State College, <1943>.
The Pennsylvania State College Studies, No. 12.

Joseph Clay Neal
1807–1847

14936. CHARCOAL SKETCHES; OR, SCENES IN A METROPOLIS. Phila: Carey & Hart, 1838.
Reprinted in the U.K. in 1841 as Vol. 2 of The Pic Nic Papers, ed. Charles Dickens (No. 14948).

14938. IN TOWN & ABOUT OR PENCILLINGS & PENNINGS. Phila: Godey & McMichael, <1843>.
Illustrated by Felix O.C. Darley.

14939. PETER PLODDY, AND OTHER ODDITIES. Phila: Carey & Hart, 1844.

14941. CHARCOAL SKETCHES. SECOND SERIES. NY: Burgess, Stringer, 1848.
Ed. Alice B. Neal. Reprinted in 1855 as "Boots:" or, The Misfortunes of Peter Faber, and Other Sketches (No. 14958) & in 1856 as The Misfortunes of Peter Faber, and Other Sketches (No. 14959).

Robert Henry Newell
(Orpheus C. Kerr)
1836–1901

14961. THE ORPHEUS C. KERR PAPERS. NY: Blakeman & Mason, 1862.

*14962. THE ORPHEUS C. KERR PAPERS. SECOND SERIES. NY: Carleton, 1863.

*14965. THE PALACE BEAUTIFUL, AND OTHER POEMS. By Orpheus C. Kerr. NY: Carleton, 1865.

ROBERT HENRY NEWELL (cont.)
14966. THE MARTYR PRESIDENT. NY: Carleton, 1865.
Anon.

*14967. THE ORPHEUS C. KERR PAPERS. THIRD SERIES. NY: Carleton, 1865.
A U.K. edition of material from the 3 series published in 1866 (No. 14968) with 2 pieces not in the U.S. editions. Revised edition of the 3 series published in 1871 (No. 14976).

14969. RECONSTRUCTION. By Orpheus C. Kerr. NY: American News Co., <n.d., 1866–67?>.
This piece was also printed in *Comicalities. By Orpheus C. Kerr, and Other Funny Fellows,* <n.d., 1866–67?> (No. 14970); no sequence established.

14971. AVERY GLIBUN; OR, BETWEEN TWO FIRES. A ROMANCE. By Orpheus C. Kerr. NY: Carleton, 1867.

14972. SMOKED GLASS. By Orpheus C. Kerr. NY: Carleton, 1868.

14974. THE CLOVEN FOOT. By Orpheus C. Kerr. NY: Carleton, 1870.
Adaptation of Dickens's *The Mystery of Edwin Drood* to "American Scenes, Characters, Customs, and Nomenclature." Published in the U.K. in 1871 as *The Mystery of Mr. E. Drood* (No. 14988).

14975. VERSATILITIES. Bos: Lee & Shepard, 1871.

14977. THE WALKING DOLL; OR, THE ASTERS AND DISASTERS OF SOCIETY. NY: Felt, 1872.

14980. STUDIES IN STANZAS. By Orpheus C. Kerr. NY: Useful Knowledge Pub. Co., 1882.

14981. THERE WAS ONCE A MAN. A STORY. NY: Our Continent Pub. Co., 1884.
"Our Continent" Library.

Mordecai Manuel Noah
1785–1851

14989. THE FORTRESS OF SORRENTO: A PETIT HISTORICAL DRAMA. NY: D. Longworth, 1808.
Anon.

14994. TRAVELS IN ENGLAND, FRANCE, SPAIN, AND THE BARBARY STATES, IN THE YEARS 1813–14 AND 15. NY: Kirk & Mercein, 1819.

14995. SHE WOULD BE A SOLDIER, OR THE PLAINS OF CHIPPEWA; AN HISTORICAL DRAMA. NY: Longworth's Dramatic Repository, 1819.

14997. ESSAYS OF HOWARD, ON DOMESTIC ECONOMY. NY: Birch, 1820.
Anon. "Originally published in the New-York National Advocate." Revised edition published in 1845 as *Gleanings from a Gathered Harvest* (No. 15012).

M. M. NOAH (cont.)

14998. THE WANDERING BOYS: OR, THE CASTLE OF OLIVAL. A MELO DRAMA.
Bos: Richardson & Lord, 1821.
Anon. Adaptation of Pixeré court's *Le Pèlerin Blanc ou les Orphelins du Hameau*.
Originally staged as *Paul and Alexis, or the Orphans of the Rhine*.

15000. MARION; OR, THE HERO OF LAKE GEORGE: A DRAMA ... FOUNDED ON
EVENTS OF THE REVOLUTIONARY WAR. NY: Murden, 1822.

15001. THE GRECIAN CAPTIVE, OR THE FALL OF ATHENS. NY: Murden, 1822.

Benjamin Franklin (Frank) Norris
1870–1902

15024. YVERNELLE A LEGEND OF FEUDAL FRANCE. Phila: Lippincott, 1892.

15029. MORAN OF THE LADY LETTY A STORY OF ADVENTURE OFF THE CALI-
FORNIA COAST. NY: Doubleday & McClure, 1898.
The U.K. edition published in 1899 as *Shanghaied A Story of Adventure off the
California Coast* (No. 15060).

*15031. McTEAGUE A STORY OF SAN FRANCISCO. NY: Doubleday & McClure,
1899.
Revised edition also published in 1899 (No. 15032).

15033. BLIX. NY: Doubleday & McClure, 1899.

*15034. A MAN'S WOMAN. NY: Doubleday & McClure, 1900.

*15036. THE OCTOPUS A STORY OF CALIFORNIA. NY: Doubleday, Page, 1901.

*15038. THE PIT A STORY OF CHICAGO. NY: Doubleday, Page, 1903.

*15039. A DEAL IN WHEAT AND OTHER STORIES OF THE NEW AND OLD WEST.
NY: Doubleday, Page, 1903.
Also published as Vol. 2 of the "Golden Gate Edition" of Norris's *Complete Works*,
1903 (No. 15061).

15040. THE RESPONSIBILITIES OF THE NOVELIST AND OTHER LITERARY
ESSAYS. NY: Doubleday, Page, 1903.
Also (simultaneously?) published as Vol. 7 of the "Golden Gate Edition" of Norris's
Complete Works, 1903 (No. 15061).

*15042. THE JOYOUS MIRACLE. NY: Doubleday, Page, 1906.
These sheets were issued simultaneously (?) in U.K. by Harper & Bros. (No.
15043).

15045. THE THIRD CIRCLE. NY: Lane, 1909.

15046. VANDOVER AND THE BRUTE. Garden City NY: Doubleday, Page,
1914.
Ed. Charles G. Norris.

15047. THE SURRENDER OF SANTIAGO. SF: Elder, 1917.
"Published for the benefit of the Red Cross."

15048. COLLECTED WRITINGS HITHERTO UNPUBLISHED IN BOOK FORM.
Garden City NY: Doubleday, Doran, 1928.
Complete Works, Vol. 10.

FRANK NORRIS (cont.)

*15049. COMPLETE WORKS OF FRANK NORRIS. Garden City NY: Doubleday, Doran, 1928.
10v. The "Golden Gate Edition" of Norris's *Complete Works* in 7v. was published in 1903 (No. 15061); another edition in 4v. in 1905 (No. 15063).

15052. FRANK NORRIS OF "THE WAVE." STORIES & SKETCHES FROM THE SAN FRANCISCO WEEKLY, 1893 TO 1897. SF: Westgate PR, 1931.
One gathering, containing "Unequally Yoked," was suppressed before publication (No. 15051).

15055. THE LETTERS OF FRANK NORRIS. SF: Book Club of California, 1956.
Ed. Franklin Walker.

15057. THE LITERARY CRITICISM OF FRANK NORRIS. Austin: U of Texas PR, <1964>.
Ed. Donald Pizer.

15059. A NOVELIST IN THE MAKING A COLLECTION OF STUDENT THEMES AND THE NOVELS BLIX AND VANDOVER AND THE BRUTE. Cambridge: Harvard U PR, 1970.
Ed. James D. Hart.

Edgar Wilson (Bill) Nye
1850–1896

15066. A HOWL IN ROME. <n.p., Chi?>: Chicago Milwaukee & St Paul Ry. <n.d., *ca.* 1880>.
Revised & collected as "Speech of Spartacus" in *Bill Nye and Boomerang,* see next entry.

*15069. BILL NYE AND BOOMERANG; OR, THE TALE OF A MEEK-EYED MULE, AND SOME OTHER LITERARY GEMS. Chi: Belford, Clarke, 1881.

*15073. FORTY LIARS, AND OTHER LIES. Chi: Belford, Clarke, 1882.
Extended edition also published in 1882 (No. 15074).

15079. BALED HAY. A DRIER BOOK THAN WALT WHITMAN'S "LEAVES O' GRASS." NY & Chi: Belford, Clarke, 1884.

15080. BOOMERANG SHOTS. Lon & NY: Ward, Lock, <n.d., 1884>.

15081. HITS AND SKITS. Lon & NY: Ward, Lock, <n.d., 1884>.

*15088. REMARKS. Chi: A.E. Davis, 1887.
Published by subscription.

15090. BILL NYE'S CORDWOOD. Chi: Rhodes & McClure, 1887.

15094. BILL NYE'S CHESTNUTS OLD AND NEW. LATEST GATHERING. Chi & NY: Belford, Clarke, 1888.

15096. AN ARISTOCRAT IN AMERICA: EXTRACTS FROM THE DIARY OF THE RIGHT HONORABLE LORD WILLIAM HENRY CAVENDISH-BENTINCK-PELHAM-CLINTON-ST. MAUR-BEAUCHAMP-DEVERE, K.G. NY: Ivers, <1888>.
American Series, No. 71, 25 Mar. 1888.

BILL NYE (cont.)

*15097. NYE AND RILEY'S RAILWAY GUIDE. Chi, NY, &c.: Dearborn, 1888.
With James Whitcomb Riley, see No. 16553 below.

15098. BILL NYE'S THINKS PREPARED AT THE INSTIGATION OF THE AUTHOR. Chi, NY, &c.: Dearborn Pub. Co., 1888.

*15113. BILL NYE'S HISTORY OF THE UNITED STATES. Phila: Lippincott, <1894>.

15114. BILL NYE'S HISTORY OF ENGLAND FROM THE DRUIDS TO THE REIGN OF HENRY VIII. Phila: Lippincott, 1896.

15116. A GUEST AT THE LUDLOW AND OTHER STORIES. Indianapolis & Kansas City: Bowen-Merrill, 1897.

15120. THE FUNNY FELLOWS GRAB-BAG. By Bill Nye and Other Funny Men. NY: Ogilvie, 1903.

15121. BILL NYE HIS OWN LIFE STORY. NY & Lon: Century Co., <1926>.
"Continuity by Frank Wilson Nye."

15122. LETTERS OF EDGAR WILSON NYE NOW IN THE UNIVERSITY OF WYOMING LIBRARY. Laramie: U of Wyoming Library, 1950.
Ed. Nixon Orwin Rush.

Fitz-James O'Brien
1828–1862

15162. SIR BRASIL'S FALCON, A POEM. <n.p., n.d.; 1853>
"Published in September No. of the United States Review. 1853."

15168. A GENTLEMAN FROM IRELAND. A COMEDY. NY: French, 1858.
The Minor Drama, No. 156.

15183. THE POEMS AND STORIES OF FITZ-JAMES O'BRIEN. Bos: Osgood, 1881.
Ed. William Winter.

John Boyle O'Reilly
1844–1890

15195. SONGS FROM THE SOUTHERN SEAS, AND OTHER POEMS. Bos: Roberts Bros., 1873.

15201. SONGS, LEGENDS, AND BALLADS. Bos: Pilot Pub. Co., 1878.

15202. MOONDYNE: A STORY FROM THE UNDER-WORLD. Bos: Pilot Pub. Co., 1879.
Revised "third edition" also published in 1879 (No. 15203).

15205. THE STATUES IN THE BLOCK, AND OTHER POEMS. Bos: Roberts Bros., 1881.

15218. IN BOHEMIA. Bos: Pilot Pub. Co., <1886>.

JOHN BOYLE O'REILLY (cont.)

*15221. THE POETRY AND SONG OF IRELAND. WITH BIOGRAPHICAL SKETCHES OF HER POETS. NY: Gay Bros., <1887>.
Compiled, with contributions (all reprints), by O'Reilly. The "second edition" published in 1889 (No. 15230) has a supplement, not compiled by O'Reilly.

15226. ETHICS OF BOXING AND MANLY SPORT. Bos: Ticknor, 1888.
Extended edition published in 1890 as *Athletics and Manly Sport* (No. 15232).

*15239. LIFE OF JOHN BOYLE O'REILLY ... TOGETHER WITH HIS COMPLETE POEMS AND SPEECHES. NY: Cassell, <1891>.
Ed. Mrs. John Boyle O'Reilly; "Life" by James Jeffrey Roche.

Frances Sargent Locke Osgood
1811–1850

15264. SKETCHES FOR THE FAIR. <n.p., n.d.; Bos, 1833>.
Anon. For the benefit of the Perkins Institute Fair, 1833.

*15274. A WREATH OF WILD FLOWERS FROM NEW ENGLAND. Lon: Churton, 1838.
These sheets also issued in the U.S.

15275. THE CASKET OF FATE. Lon, 1839.

15278. THE CASKET OF FATE ... SECOND EDITION. Bos: Weeks, Jordan, 1840.
Presumably the first U.S. edition.

*15281. THE POETRY OF FLOWERS AND FLOWERS OF POETRY. NY: Riker, 1841.
Edited, with contributions, by Osgood. Republished as *Flower Gift* (No. 15338).

15286. THE SNOW-DROP; A NEW-YEAR'S GIFT FOR CHILDREN. Providence: Fuller, 1842.

15290. PUSS IN BOOTS, AND THE MARQUIS OF CARABAS, RENDERED INTO VERSE. NY: Benjamin & Young, 1844.

15294. THE FLOWER ALPHABET, IN GOLD AND COLORS. Bos: Colman, <1845>.

*15299. POEMS. NY: Clark & Austin, 1846.

15301. THE CRIES OF NEW-YORK. NY: Doggett, 1846.

15309. THE FLORAL OFFERING, A TOKEN OF FRIENDSHIP. Phila: Carey & Hart, 1847.
Edited, with contributions, by Osgood.

15319. A LETTER ABOUT THE LIONS. NY: Putnam, 1849.

15326. POEMS. Phila: Carey & Hart, 1850.
Ed. Rufus Wilmot Griswold.

Thomas Nelson Page
1853–1922

*15361. IN OLE VIRGINIA OR MARSE CHAN AND OTHER STORIES. NY: Scribner's Sons, 1887.

15362. BEFO' DE WAR ECHOES IN NEGRO DIALECT. NY: Scribner's Sons, 1888.
With Armistead Churchill Gordon.

*15364. TWO LITTLE CONFEDERATES. NY: Scribner's Sons, 1888.

15366. ON NEWFOUND RIVER. NY: Scribner's Sons, 1891.
Extended edition published in 1906 (No. 15396).

15368. ELSKET AND OTHER STORIES. NY: Scribner's Sons, 1891.

15369. AMONG THE CAMPS OR YOUNG PEOPLE'S STORIES OF THE WAR. NY: Scribner's Sons, 1891.

15370. THE OLD SOUTH ESSAYS SOCIAL AND POLITICAL. NY: Scribner's Sons, 1892.
"Social Life in Old Virginia before the War," here collected, was published separately in 1897 (No. 15378).

15374. PASTIME STORIES. NY: Harper & Bros., 1894.

*15375. THE BURIAL OF THE GUNS. NY: Scribner's Sons, 1894.

15377. THE OLD GENTLEMAN OF THE BLACK STOCK. NY: Scribner's Sons, 1897.
The Ivory Series. Extended edition published in 1900 (No. 15387).

*15380. TWO PRISONERS. NY: Russell, 1898.
Revised edition published in 1903 (No. 15392).

*15381. RED ROCK A CHRONICLE OF RECONSTRUCTION. NY: Scribner's Sons, 1898.

*15383. SANTA CLAUS'S PARTNER. NY: Scribner's Sons, 1899.

15391. GORDON KEITH. NY: Scribner's Sons, 1903.

15393. BRED IN THE BONE. NY: Scribner's Sons, 1904.

*15394. THE NEGRO: THE SOUTHERNER'S PROBLEM. NY: Scribner's Sons, 1904.

*15397. PLANTATION EDITION OF THE WORKS OF THOMAS NELSON PAGE. NY: Scribner's Sons, 1906–12.
18v.

15399. THE COAST OF BOHEMIA. NY: Scribner's Sons, 1906.

*15401. UNDER THE CRUST. NY: Scribner's Sons, 1907.

15404. THE OLD DOMINION HER MAKING AND HER MANNERS. NY: Scribner's Sons, 1908.

15405. TOMMY TROT'S VISIT TO SANTA CLAUS. NY: Scribner's Sons, 1908.

15406. ROBERT E. LEE THE SOUTHERNER. NY: Scribner's Sons, 1908.

*15407. JOHN MARVEL ASSISTANT. NY: Scribner's Sons, 1909.

15414. ROBERT E. LEE MAN AND SOLDIER. NY: Scribner's Sons, 1911.

224 Epitome of Bibliography of American Literature

THOMAS NELSON PAGE (cont.)

15415. THE LAND OF THE SPIRIT. NY: Scribner's Sons, 1913.
"The Shepherd Who Watched by Night," here collected, was also published separately in 1913 (No. 15416).

15418. TOMMASO JEFFERSON APOSTOLO DELLA LIBERTÀ (1743–1826). Firenze, Milano, &c.: Bemporad & Figlio, <n.d., 1918>.
At head of title: *Americani Illustri Raccolta Biografica Diretta da H. Nelson Gay No. 1–2*

15423. ITALY AND THE WORLD WAR. NY: Scribner's Sons, 1920.

15425. DANTE AND HIS INFLUENCE STUDIES. NY: Scribner's Sons, 1922.
At head of title: *University of Virginia Florence Lathrop Page-Barbour Foundation*

15426. WASHINGTON AND ITS ROMANCE. NY: Doubleday, Page, 1923.

15428. THE RED RIDERS. NY: Scribner's Sons, 1924.

Francis Parkman
1823–1893

*15446. THE CALIFORNIA AND OREGON TRAIL: BEING SKETCHES OF PRAIRIE AND ROCKY MOUNTAIN LIFE. NY: Putnam, 1849.
The "third edition" published in 1852 as *Prairie and Rocky Mountain Life* (No. 15449); the revised "fourth edition" in 1872 as *The Oregon Trail* (No. 15461). The latter title was used for later editions, including the illustrated edition in 1892 (No. 15484) & the newly edited *Limited Editions Club* edition in 1943 (No. 15490).

15447. HISTORY OF THE CONSPIRACY OF PONTIAC. Lon: Bentley, 1851.
2v.

15448. HISTORY OF THE CONSPIRACY OF PONTIAC. Bos: Little & Brown, 1851.
Revised & extended editions published in 1855 (No. 15450), as the "fourth edition" in 1868 (No. 15457) & as the "sixth edition" in 1870 in 2v. as *The Conspiracy of Pontiac and the Indian War* (No. 15459).

15451. VASSALL MORTON. A NOVEL. Bos: Phillips, Sampson, 1856.

*15452. PIONEERS OF FRANCE IN THE NEW WORLD. Bos: Little, Brown, 1865.
France and England in North America, part 1. Revised "twenty-fifth edition" published in 1886 (No. 15473).

15453. THE BOOK OF ROSES. Bos: Tilton, 1866.

*15455. THE JESUITS IN NORTH AMERICA IN THE SEVENTEENTH CENTURY. Bos: Little, Brown, 1867.
France and England in North America, part 2.

*15458. THE DISCOVERY OF THE GREAT WEST. Bos: Little, Brown, 1869.
France and England in North America, part 3. Revised & extended "eleventh edition" published in 1879 as *La Salle and the Discovery of the Great West* (No. 15465).

*15462. THE OLD RÉGIME IN CANADA. Bos: Little, Brown, 1874.
France and England in North America, part 4. Revised edition published in 1894 (No. 15485).

FRANCIS PARKMAN (cont.)

*15463. COUNT FRONTENAC AND FRANCE UNDER LOUIS XIV. Bos: Little, Brown, 1877.
France and England in North America, part 5.

*15469. MONTCALM AND WOLFE. Bos: Little, Brown, 1884.
2v. *France and England in North America*, part 7.

*15483. A HALF-CENTURY OF CONFLICT. Bos: Little, Brown, 1892.
2v. *France and England in North America*, part 6.

*15486. THE WORKS OF FRANCIS PARKMAN. Bos: Little Brown, 1897–98.
20v.

15491. THE JOURNALS OF FRANCIS PARKMAN. NY & Lon: Harper & Bros., 1947.
2v. Ed. Mason Wade.

15494. LETTERS OF FRANCIS PARKMAN. Norman: U of Oklahoma PR, <1960>.
2v. Ed. Wilbur R. Jacobs. "Published in co-operation with the Massachusetts Historical Society."

Thomas William Parsons
1819–1892

*15521. POEMS. Bos: Ticknor & Fields, 1854.

*15530. THE ROSARY. Cambridge: Wilson & Sons, 1865.
"Eighty copies printed."

15531. THE MAGNOLIA. Cambridge: Wilson & Son, 1866.

*15534. THE OLD HOUSE AT SUDBURY. Cambridge: Wilson & Son, 1870.

*15536. THE SHADOW OF THE OBELISK AND OTHER POEMS. Lon: Hatchards, 1872.

*15539. THE WILLEY HOUSE AND SONNETS. Cambridge: Wilson & Son, 1875.
These sheets reissued in 1875 with 2 additional pieces (No. 15541).

15554. CIRCUM PRAECORDIA. Bos: Cupples, <1892>.
Binder's title: *The Collects of the Church.*

15556. DIVINE COMEDY OF DANTE ALIGHIERI. Bos & NY: Houghton, Mifflin, 1893.
Translation. Parsons's translations of portions of the *Divine Comedy* were earlier published in 1843 (No. 15518), 1867 (No. 15532), 1875 (No. 15540) & 1886 (Nos. 15545 & 15546).

15557. POEMS. Bos & NY: Houghton, Mifflin, 1893.

15561. LETTERS BY T.W. PARSONS. Bos: Trustees of the Public Library, <1940>.
Ed. Zoltán Haraszti.

James Kirke Paulding
1783–1859

*15685. SALMAGUNDI; OR, THE WHIM-WHAMS AND OPINIONS OF LAUNCELOT LANGSTAFF, ESQ. AND OTHERS. NY: D. Longworth, 1807–08.
2v. in 20 parts. Anon. Joint production with Washington Irving & his brother William Irving; see No. 10097 above. Revised by Paulding in 1835 (No. 10147) & published as his *Works*, Vols. 1–2, see No. 15722 below. Critical edition published in 1977 (No. 15757). For the *Second Series*, written by Paulding alone, see No. 15695 below.

15686. THE DIVERTING HISTORY OF JOHN BULL AND BROTHER JONATHAN. By Hector Bull-Us. NY: Inskeep & Bradford, 1812.
Published in London in 1814 as *A Brief and Humorous History of the Political Peculiarities of England and America* (No. 15690). Revised "second edition" published in 1813 (No. 15689). Revised & extended edition published in 1835 as Paulding's *Works*, Vol. 9, see No. 15722 below. Further revised & published in 1867 with *John Bull in America* as *The Bulls and the Jonathans* (No. 15749).

15688. THE LAY OF THE SCOTTISH FIDDLE: A TALE OF HAVRE DE GRACE. NY: Inskeep & Bradford, 1813.
Anon. "Supposed to be written by Walter Scott, Esq. First American, from the Fourth Edinburgh Edition."

*15692. THE UNITED STATES AND ENGLAND. NY: Inskeep; Phila: Bradford & Inskeep, 1815.
Anon. "A reply to the criticism on Inchiquin's Letters. Contained in the Quarterly Review for January, 1814."

15693. LETTERS FROM THE SOUTH, WRITTEN DURING AN EXCURSION IN THE SUMMER OF 1816. NY: Eastburn, 1817.
2v. Anon. Revised & extended edition published in 1835 (No. 15725) as Paulding's *Works*, Vols. 5–6, see No. 15722 below.

*15694. THE BACKWOODSMAN. A POEM. Phila: M. Thomas, 1818.

*15695. SALMAGUNDI. SECOND SERIES. By Launcelot Langstaff, Esq. Phila: M. Thomas, 1819–20.
3v. in 15 parts. Revised edition published in 1835 as Paulding's *Works*, Vols. 3–4, see No. 15722 below.

15696. A SKETCH OF OLD ENGLAND. By a New-England Man. NY: Wiley, 1822.
2v.

15697. KONINGSMARKE, THE LONG FINNE, A STORY OF THE NEW WORLD. NY: Wiley, 1823.
2v. Anon. Revised edition published in 1834–35 as Paulding's *Works*, Vols. 7–8, see No. 15722 below.

JAMES KIRKE PAULDING (cont.)

15699. JOHN BULL IN AMERICA; OR, THE NEW MUNCHAUSEN. NY: Wiley, 1825.
   Anon. Extended "second edition" also published in 1825 (No. 15700). Revised & published in 1867 with *The Diverting History of John Bull and Brother Jonathan* as *The Bulls and the Jonathans* (No. 15749).

15702. THE MERRY TALES OF THE THREE WISE MEN OF GOTHAM. NY: G. & C. Carvill, 1826.
   Anon. Slightly revised edition published in 1839 as Paulding's *Works,* Vol. 15, see No. 15722 below.

15706. THE NEW MIRROR FOR TRAVELLERS; AND GUIDE TO THE SPRINGS. By an Amateur. NY: G. & C. Carvill, 1828.
   See also No. 15751 below.

15709. TALES OF THE GOOD WOMAN. By a Doubtful Gentleman. NY: G. & C. & H. Carvill, 1829.
   Revised & published in 1836 with *Chronicles of the City of Gotham* as Paulding's *Works,* Vols. 10–11, see No. 15722 below.

15712. CHRONICLES OF THE CITY OF GOTHAM ... CONTAINING THE AZURE HOSE. THE POLITICIAN. THE DUMB GIRL. NY: G. & C. & H. Carvill, 1830.
   Anon. Revised & published in 1836 with *Tales of the Good Woman* as Paulding's *Works,* Vols. 10–11, see No. 15722 below.

15714. THE DUTCHMAN'S FIRESIDE. NY: J. & J. Harper, 1831.
   2v. Reprinted in 1837 as Paulding's *Works,* Vols. 12–13, see No. 15722 below.

*15715. WESTWARD HO! A TALE. NY: J. & J. Harper, 1832.
   2v. Anon. Some copies issued as *Library of Select Novels,* Nos. 25–26.

*15722. THE WORKS OF JAMES K. PAULDING. NY: Harper & Bros., 1834–39.
   15v.

*15727. A LIFE OF WASHINGTON. NY: Harper & Bros., 1835.
   2v. Issued as both Harper's *Family Library,* Nos. 75–76, & *The Common School Library,* 2nd Series, Nos. 1–2.

*15729. SLAVERY IN THE UNITED STATES. NY: Harper & Bros., 1836.

15730. THE BOOK OF SAINT NICHOLAS. NY: Harper & Bros., 1836.
   "Translated from the original Dutch of Dominie Nicholas Ægidius Oudenarde." Paulding's *Works,* Vol. 14.

15733. A CHRISTMAS GIFT FROM FAIRY LAND. NY: Appleton, <1838>.
   Anon. Reprinted, not before 1839, as *A Gift from Fairy Land.*

15738. THE OLD CONTINENTAL; OR, THE PRICE OF LIBERTY. NY: Paine & Burgess, 1846.
   2v. Anon.

15739. AMERICAN COMEDIES. Phila: Carey & Hart, 1847.
   With William I. Paulding. "The Bucktails; or, Americans in England," pp. <17>–100, by J.K. Paulding.

JAMES KIRKE PAULDING (cont.)

*15740. THE PURITAN AND HIS DAUGHTER. NY: Baker & Scribner, 1849.
2v. in one.

15748. LITERARY LIFE OF JAMES K. PAULDING. NY: Scribner, 1867.
Ed. William I. Paulding.

*15751. A BOOK OF VAGARIES; COMPRISING THE NEW MIRROR FOR TRAVEL-
LERS AND OTHER WHIM-WHAMS. NY: Scribner, 1868.
Ed. William I. Paulding.

15755. THE LION OF THE WEST RETITLED THE KENTUCKIAN, OR A TRIP TO
NEW YORK A FARCE. Stanford: Stanford U PR, 1954.
"Revised by John Augustus Stone and William Bayle Bernard." Ed. James N.
Tidwell.

15756. THE LETTERS OF JAMES KIRKE PAULDING. Madison: U of Wisconsin
PR, 1962.
Ed. Ralph M. Aderman.

John Howard Payne
1791–1852

Note: Many of Payne's dramatic works are adaptations of French works,
some prepared in collaboration with Washington Irving. Only the first
publication of these adaptations has been listed here, with reference to
the first U.S. edition if the work was first published in the U.K.

15759. JULIA, OR THE WANDERER; A COMEDY. NY: D. Longworth, 1806.
Anon.

15765. JUVENILE POEMS, PRINCIPALLY WRITTEN BEWEEN THE AGE OF THIR-
TEEN AND SEVENTEEN YEARS. Baltimore: E.J. Coale, 1813.
Offprint from *The Literary Visitor or Entertaining Miscellany*, Baltimore, 1813 (No.
15764). Revised & extended edition published in 1815 as *Lispings of the Muse*
(No. 15767).

15768. THE MAGPIE OR THE MAID? A MELO DRAME. Lon: J. Miller, 1815.
"Translated and altered from the French, by I. Pocock, Esq." Payne apparently
provided the original translation of *La Pie Voleuse, or la Servante de Palaiseau* by
Louis Charles Caigniez & J. Baudouin d'Aubigny. First U.S. edition published in
1816 (No. 15769).

*15770. ACCUSATION; OR, THE FAMILY D'ANGLADE: A PLAY. Lon: C. Chapple,
1817.
Adapatation with James Kenney of *Le Vol, ou la Famille d'Anglade* by Frédéric
Dupetit-Méré. First U.S. edition published in 1818 (No. 15771).

*15772. BRUTUS; OR, THE FALL OF TARQUIN. AN HISTORICAL TRAGEDY.
Lon: R. White, 1818.

JOHN HOWARD PAYNE (cont.)

15773. BRUTUS; OR, THE FALL OF TARQUIN. AN HISTORICAL TRAGEDY. NY: D. Longworth, 1819.
See also next entry, no sequence established.

15774. BRUTUS; OR, THE FALL OF TARQUIN. AN HISTORICAL TRAGEDY. Baltimore: J. Robinson, 1819.
See also preceding entry, no sequence established.

*15775. THÉRÈSE, THE ORPHAN OF GENEVA. A DRAMA. Lon: Theatre Royal, 1821.
Adapataion of *Thérèse, ou, l'Orpheline de Genève* by Victor Henri Joseph Brahain Ducange. Two U.S. editions also published in 1821 (Nos.15776 & 15777).

15778. ADELINE, THE VICTIM OF SEDUCTION: A MELO-DRAMATIC SERIOUS DRAMA. Lon: Theatre Royal, 1822.
Adaptation of *Valentine, ou la Séduction* by René Charles Guilbert de Pixeré court. First U.S. edition also published in 1822 (No. 15779).

15780. ALI PACHA; OR, THE SIGNET RING. A MELO-DRAMA. NY: Murden, 1823.

15781. CLARI; OR, THE MAID OF MILAN; AN OPERA. Lon: J. Miller, 1823.
Contains the first publication of "Home, Sweet Home." A sheet music edition of the songs from this opera was also published in London in 1823 (No. 15782).

15784. CLARI; OR, THE MAID OF MILAN, AN OPERA. NY: Circulating Library & Dramatic Repository, 1823.

15785. CHARLES THE SECOND, OR, THE MERRY MONARCH. A COMEDY. Lon: Longman, Hurst, et al, 1824.
Adaptation with Washington Irving of *La Jeunesse de Henri V* by Alexandre Duval. First U.S. edition published in 1829 (No. 15793).

15787. THE FALL OF ALGIERS, A NEW OPERA. Lon: Dolby, <n.d., 1825>.
Anon.

15788. LOVE IN HUMBLE LIFE; A PETITE COMEDY. Lon: Dolby, 1825.
Adaptation of *Michel et Christine* by Eugène Scribe & Jean Henri Dupin. First U.S. edition published *ca.* 1836 (No. 15801).

*15789. THE TWO GALLEY SLAVES; A MELODRAMA. Lon: Dolby, 1825.

15790. RICHELIEU; A DOMESTIC TRAGEDY FOUNDED ON FACT. NY: Murden, 1826.
Adaptation with Washington Irving of *La Jeunesse du Duc Richelieu ou le Lovelace Français* by Alexandre Duval.

*15791. 'TWAS I, OR THE TRUTH A LIE. A FARCE. NY: Murden, 1827.

15792. THE LANCERS: AN INTERLUDE. Lon: Cumberland, <n.d., *ca.* 1827–29>.
Cumberland's British Theatre, Vol 19, No. 129.

15797. SONGS, DUETS, CONCERTED PIECES, AND CHORUSES, IN THE WHITE LADY,—OR—SPIRIT OF AVENEL, A ROMANTIC OPERA. Bos: Dutton & Wentworth, Ptrs, 1833.
Anon. Translation of the libretto of *La Dame Blanche* by Eugène Scribe.

JOHN HOWARD PAYNE (cont.)

15804. MRS. SMITH: OR, THE WIFE AND THE WIDOW. A FARCE. Lon: Lacy, <n.d., not before 1857>.
First performed 18 June 1823. *Earliest located publication.*

15805. PETER SMINK; OR, THE ARMISTICE. A COMIC DRAMA. Lon: Lacy, <n.d., not before 1866>.
Lacy's Acting Edition, No. 125 or No. 1125. Adaptation with Washington Irving from the French. First performed July 1822. *Earliest located publication.*

15807. THE LIFE AND WRITINGS OF JOHN HOWARD PAYNE. Albany: Munsell, 1875.
By Gabriel Harrison. Revised edition published in 1885 as *John Howard Payne, Dramatist, Poet, Actor* (No. 15808).

15809. INDIAN JUSTICE A CHEROKEE MURDER TRIAL AT TAHLEQUAH IN 1840. Oklahoma City: Harlow Pub. Co., 1934.

15810. TRIAL WITHOUT JURY & OTHER PLAYS. Princeton: Princeton U PR, 1940.
Ed. Codman Hislop & W.R. Richardson. *America's Lost Plays,* Vol. 5.

15811. THE LAST DUEL IN SPAIN & OTHER PLAYS. Princeton: Princeton U PR, 1940.
Ed. Codman Hislop & W.R. Richardson. *America's Lost Plays,* Vol. 6.

15812. JOHN HOWARD PAYNE TO HIS COUNTRYMEN. Athens: U of Georgia PR, 1961.
Ed. Clemens de Baillou. *University of Georgia Libraries Miscellanea Publications,* No. 2.

James Gates Percival
1795–1856

15886. POEMS. New-Haven: The Author, 1821.

15888. CLIO ... NO. I. Charleston: Babcock, 1822.

15889. CLIO ... NO. II. New-Haven: Converse, 1822.

15891. ORATION ... ON SOME OF THE MORAL AND POLITICAL TRUTHS DERIVABLE FROM THE STUDY OF HISTORY. New-Haven: Maltby, 1822.
Delivered before the Phi Beta Kappa Society, 10 Sept. 1822.

15892. PROMETHEUS PART II WITH OTHER POEMS. New-Haven: Maltby, 1822.

15895. POEMS. NY: Wiley, 1823.

15901. POEM DELIVERED BEFORE THE CONNECTICUT ALPHA OF THE PHI BETA KAPPA SOCIETY, SEPTEMBER 13, 1825. Bos: Richardson & Lord, 1826.

15908. CLIO ... NO. III. NY: G. & C. Carvill, 1827.

15934. THE DREAM OF A DAY, AND OTHER POEMS. New Haven: Babcock, 1843.

15948. THE POETICAL WORKS OF JAMES GATES PERCIVAL. Bos: Ticknor & Fields, 1859.
2v.

JAMES GATES PERCIVAL (cont.)

15950. THE LIFE AND LETTERS OF JAMES GATES PERCIVAL. Bos: Ticknor & Fields, 1866.
By Julius H. Ward.

15953. UNCOLLECTED LETTERS. Gainesville: U of Florida PR, 1959.
Ed. Harry R Warfel. *University of Florida Monographs Humanities*, No. 1.

David Graham Phillips
1867–1911

15954. THE GREAT GOD SUCCESS A NOVEL. By John Graham. NY: Stokes, <1901>.

15955. HER SERENE HIGHNESS A NOVEL. NY & Lon: Harper & Bros., 1902.

15956. A WOMAN VENTURES A NOVEL. NY: Stokes, <1902>.

15957. GOLDEN FLEECE THE AMERICAN ADVENTURES OF A FORTUNE HUNTING EARL. NY: McClure, Phillips, 1903.

*15958. THE MASTER-ROGUE THE CONFESSIONS OF A CROESUS. NY: McClure, Phillips, 1903.

*15959. THE COST. Indianapolis: Bobbs-Merrill, <1904>.

15960. THE MOTHER-LIGHT A NOVEL. NY: Appleton, 1905.
Anon.

*15961. THE PLUM TREE. Indianapolis: Bobbs-Merrill, <1905>.

*15962. THE SOCIAL SECRETARY. Indianapolis: Bobbs-Merrill, <1905>.

15963. THE REIGN OF GILT. NY: Pott, 1905.

*15964. THE DELUGE. Indianapolis: Bobbs-Merrill, <1905>.

15965. THE FORTUNE HUNTER. Indianapolis: Bobbs-Merrill, <1906>.

15967. THE SECOND GENERATION. NY: Appleton, 1907.

15968. LIGHT-FINGERED GENTRY. NY: Appleton, 1907.

15969. OLD WIVES FOR NEW A NOVEL. NY: Appleton, 1908.

15970. THE WORTH OF A WOMAN A PLAY ... FOLLOWED BY A POINT OF LAW A DRAMATIC INCIDENT. NY: Appleton, 1908.

15971. THE FASHIONABLE ADVENTURES OF JOSHUA CRAIG A NOVEL. NY: Appleton, 1909.

15972. THE HUNGRY HEART A NOVEL. NY & Lon: Appleton, 1909.

15973. WHITE MAGIC A NOVEL. NY & Lon: Appleton, 1910.

15974. THE HUSBAND'S STORY A NOVEL. NY & Lon: Appleton, 1910.

15975. THE GRAIN OF DUST A NOVEL. NY & Lon: Appleton, 1911.

15976. THE CONFLICT A NOVEL. NY & Lon: Appleton, 1911.

15977. THE PRICE SHE PAID A NOVEL. NY & Lon: Appleton, 1912.

15978. GEORGE HELM. NY & Lon: Appleton, 1912.

15979. DEGARMO'S WIFE AND OTHER STORIES. NY & Lon: Appleton, 1913.

DAVID GRAHAM PHILLIPS (cont.)
15980. SUSAN LENOX HER FALL AND RISE. NY & Lon: Appleton, 1917.
2v.

*15981. THE TREASON OF THE SENATE. NY: Monthly Review PR, 1953.

John James Piatt
1835–1917

Note: Many of the works listed here (Nos. 15989, 16007, 16016, 16017 & 16022) are made up of reprinted material with only a very few new pieces.

15983. POEMS OF TWO FRIENDS. Columbus: Follett, Foster, 1860.
With William Dean Howells, see No. 9537 above.

15988. THE NESTS AT WASHINGTON, AND OTHER POEMS. NY: W. Low, 1864.
With Sarah M. Bryan Piatt.

15989. POEMS OF SUNSHINE AND FIRELIGHT. Cincinnati: Carroll, 1866.
Reissued (?) in 1871 as *The Pioneer's Chimney* (No. 15993).

15991. POEMS OF JOHN JAMES PIATT. Cincinnati: Carroll, 1868.
Reprinted in 1869 as *Western Windows and Other Poems* (No. 15992).

15994. LANDMARKS AND OTHER POEMS. NY: Hurd & Houghton, 1872.

16002. POEMS OF HOUSE AND HOME. Bos: Houghton, Osgood, 1879.
Slightly "revised edition" published in 1888 (No. 16015) with *A Dream of Church-Windows, etc.* at head of title.

16004. PENCILLED FLY-LEAVES: A BOOK OF ESSAYS IN TOWN AND COUNTRY. Cincinnati: Clarke, 1880.

16006. THE UNION OF AMERICAN POETRY AND ART A CHOICE COLLECTION OF POEMS BY AMERICAN POETS. Cincinnati: Dibble, 1880.
1v. in 20 parts. Edited, with contributions (all reprints), by Piatt.

16007. IDYLS AND LYRICS OF THE OHIO VALLEY. Cincinnati: Dibble, 1881.
Reprinted, with 1 new piece, in 1888 (No. 16014).

16010. THE CHILDREN OUT-OF-DOORS A BOOK OF VERSES. By Two in One House. Edinburgh: Douglas, 1884.
With Sarah M.B. Piatt.

16011. THE CHILDREN OUT-OF-DOORS A BOOK OF VERSES. By Two in One House. Cincinnati: Clarke, 1885.
With Sarah M.B Piatt.

16013. AT THE HOLY WELL WITH A HANDFUL OF NEW VERSES. Dublin: Gill & Son, 1887.

16016. A BOOK OF GOLD, AND OTHER SONNETS. Lon: Stock, 1889.

16017. A RETURN TO PARADISE, AND OTHER FLY-LEAF ESSAYS IN TOWN AND COUNTRY. Lon: Stock, 1891.

JOHN JAMES PIATT (cont.)

16019. LITTLE NEW-WORLD IDYLS AND OTHER POEMS. Lon & NY: Longmans, Green, 1893.
At head of title: *The Lost Hunting-Ground, etc.*

16021. THE GHOST'S ENTRY AND OTHER POEMS. Westminster: Constable, 1895.

16022. ODES IN OHIO, AND OTHER POEMS. Cincinnati: Clarke, 1897.

16027. HOW THE BISHOP BUILT HIS COLLEGE IN THE WOODS. Cincinnati: Western Literary PR, <1906>.

Albert Pike
1809–1891

16031. PROSE SKETCHES AND POEMS, WRITTEN IN THE WESTERN COUNTRY. Bos: Light & Horton, 1834.
Reprinted, with additional material collected from periodicals, in 1967 (No. 16096).

16033. LAYS OF THE HUMBUGGERS, &C. By Sam. Barnacle. Little Rock: Pike, 1836.

16044. NUGÆ. Phila: Sherman, 1854.
"Printed for private distribution."

16058. HYMNS TO THE GODS AND OTHER POEMS. <n.p., n.d.; Wash DC: Macoy, 1872>.
"Privately printed." For an extended edition see next entry.

16075. HYMNS TO THE GODS, AND OTHER POEMS. <n.p., Wash DC?> 1873–82 <i.e. 1882>.
2 parts in 1v. "Privately printed." Part 1, dated 1873, is a reprint of the undated 1872 edition, see preceding entry.

16087. GEN. ALBERT PIKE'S POEMS. Little Rock: Allsopp, 1900.

16091. LYRICS AND LOVE SONGS. Little Rock: Allsopp, 1916.
Ed. Lilian Pike Roome.

16093. ALBERT PIKE A BIOGRAPHY. Little Rock: Parke-Harper, 1928.
By Fred W. Allsopp. Contains numerous extracts from Pike's periodical articles, unpublished autobiography & diary.

Edward Coote Pinkney
1802–1828

16114. RODOLPH. A FRAGMENT. Baltimore: J. Robinson, 1823.
Anon.

16115. POEMS. Baltimore: J. Robinson, 1825.
Slightly revised "second edition" published in 1838 (No. 16117). A later collection of Pinkney's poems, all reprints, was published in 1844 as *The Rococo: Number Two* (No. 16118).

EDWARD COOTE PINKNEY (cont.)
16122. THE LIFE AND WORKS OF EDWARD COOTE PINKNEY A MEMOIR AND
COMPLETE TEXT OF HIS POEMS AND LITERARY PROSE. NY: Macmillan,
1926.
Ed. Thomas Ollive Mabbott & Frank Lester Pleadwell.

Edgar Allan Poe
1809–1849

16123. TAMERLANE AND OTHER POEMS. By a Bostonian. Bos: Calvin F.S.
Thomas, 1827.

16124. AL AARAAF, TAMERLANE, AND MINOR POEMS. Baltimore: Hatch &
Dunning, 1829.

*16125. POEMS ... SECOND EDITION. NY: Bliss, 1831.

16128. THE NARRATIVE OF ARTHUR GORDON PYM. OF NANTUCKET. NY:
Harper & Bros., 1838.
Anon.

*16131. THE CONCHOLOGIST'S FIRST BOOK. Phila: The Author, 1839.
Adaptation of Captain Thomas Brown's *The Conchologist's Text-Book*, Glasgow, 1833.
Revised "second edition" published in 1840 (No. 16132).

16133. TALES OF THE GROTESQUE AND ARABESQUE. Phila: Lea & Blanchard,
1840.
2v.

16138. THE PROSE ROMANCES ... NO. I. CONTAINING THE MURDERS IN THE
RUE MORGUE, AND THE MAN THAT WAS USED UP. Phila: Graham,
1843.

*16146. TALES. NY: Wiley & Putnam, 1845.
Library of American Books, No. 2. These sheets issued in London in 1845 & 1846,
reissued in New York in 1849.

*16147. THE RAVEN AND OTHER POEMS. NY: Wiley & Putnam, 1845.
Library of American Books, No 8. These sheets issued in London in 1846.

16151. MESMERISM "IN ARTICULO MORTIS." Lon: Short, 1846.

16153. EUREKA: A PROSE POEM. NY: Putnam, 1848.

*16158. THE WORKS OF THE LATE EDGAR ALLAN POE. NY: Redfield, 1850.
Vols. 1–2 of four. A later collected *Works* in 4v., ed. John H. Ingram, was published in 1874–75 (No. 16162) containing a few new pieces. See also Nos. 16172,
16199 & 16200 below.

*16159. THE LITERATI ... TOGETHER WITH MARGINALIA, SUGGESTIONS, AND
ESSAYS. NY: Redfield, 1850.
The Works, Vol. 3 of four.

16161. THE WORKS OF THE LATE EDGAR ALLAN POE ... ARTHUR GORDON
PYM &C. NY: Redfield, 1856.
Vol. 4. of four.

EDGAR ALLAN POE (cont.)

*16172. THE COMPLETE WORKS OF EDGAR ALLAN POE. NY: Crowell, 1902.
17v. Ed. James A. Harrison. Earlier collected editions of Poe's works in 10v. were published in 1894–95, ed. Edmund Clarence Stedman & George Edward Woodberry (No. 16168) & in 1902, ed. Charles F. Richardson; both contain a few new pieces. See also Nos. 16199 & 16200 below.

16187. POE'S CONTRIBUTIONS TO THE COLUMBIA SPY DOINGS OF GOTHAM. Pottsville PA: Spannuth, 1929.
Ed. Jacob E. Spannuth & Thomas Ollive Mabbott. "Together with various editorial comments and criticisms ... also a poem."

16195. THE LETTERS OF EDGAR ALLAN POE. Cambridge: Harvard U PR, 1948.
2v. Ed. John Ward Ostrom. Extended edition published in 1966 (No. 16197). Earlier collections of Poe's letters were published in 1898 (No. 16169); in 1902 as Vol. 17 of *The Complete Works*, see No. 16172 above; in 1909 (No. 16174); & in 1925 (No. 16184).

16199. COLLECTED WORKS OF EDGAR ALLAN POE ... POEMS. Cambridge: Harvard U PR, 1969.
Ed. Thomas Ollive Mabbott. An earlier *Complete Poems*, ed. J. H. Whitty, was published in 1911 (No. 16176); revised & extended editions appeared in 1917 (No. 16178) & 1918 (No. 16181).

16200. COLLECTED WORKS OF EDGAR ALLAN POE TALES AND SKETCHES. Cambridge: Harvard U PR, 1978.
2v. Ed. Thomas Ollive Mabbott, with Eleanor D. Kewer & Maureen C. Mabbott.

William Sydney Porter
(O. Henry)
1862–1910

Note: All works listed here were published under Porter's pseudonym *O. Henry*.

16270. CABBAGES AND KINGS. NY: McClure, Phillips, 1904.

16271. THE FOUR MILLION. NY: McClure, Phillips, 1906.

16273. THE TRIMMED LAMP AND OTHER STORIES OF THE FOUR MILLION. NY: McClure, Phillips, 1907.

16274. HEART OF THE WEST. NY: McClure, 1907.

*16275. THE VOICE OF THE CITY FURTHER STORIES OF THE FOUR MILLION. NY: McClure, 1908.

*16276. THE GENTLE GRAFTER. NY: McClure, 1908.

16277. ROADS OF DESTINY. NY: Doubleday, Page, 1909.

16292. OPTIONS. NY & Lon: Harper & Bros., 1909.

16294. STRICTLY BUSINESS MORE STORIES OF THE FOUR MILLION. NY: Doubleday, Page, 1910.

W. S. PORTER (O. Henry) (cont.)
  16295. WHIRLIGIGS. NY: Doubleday, Page, 1910.
  16296. LET ME FEEL YOUR PULSE. NY: Doubleday, Page, 1910.
  16297. THE TWO WOMEN THE ONE: A FOG IN SANTONE THE OTHER: A MEDLEY OF MOODS. Bos: Small, Maynard, <1910>.
  16298. SIXES AND SEVENS. Garden City NY: Doubleday, Page, 1911.
*16299. ROLLING STONES. Garden City NY: Doubleday, Page, 1912.
  16301. WAIFS AND STRAYS TWELVE STORIES. Garden City NY: Doubleday, Page, 1917.
  16302. O. HENRYANA SEVEN ODDS AND ENDS. Garden City NY: Doubleday, Page, 1920.
  16303. LETTERS TO LITHOPOLIS FROM O. HENRY TO MABEL WAGNALLS. Garden City NY & Toronto: Doubleday, Page, 1922.
  16304. POSTSCRIPTS. NY & Lon: Harper & Bros., 1923.
  16307. O. HENRY ENCORE STORIES AND ILLUSTRATIONS. NY: Doubleday, Doran, 1939.
     Ed. Mary Sunlocks Harrell. A copyright printing was produced in 1936 (No. 16305).

William Hickling Prescott
1796–1859

  16334. HISTORY OF THE REIGN OF FERDINAND AND ISABELLA, THE CATHOLIC. Bos: American Stationers' Co., 1838.
     3v. Revised editions published in 1842 (No. 16337), 1843 (No. 16341) & 1873, see No. 16372 below.

  16339. HISTORY OF THE CONQUEST OF MEXICO. Lon: Bentley, 1843.
     3v.

*16340. HISTORY OF THE CONQUEST OF MEXICO. NY: Harper & Bros., 1843.
     3v. Revised edition published in 1874, see No. 16372 below.

  16343. BIOGRAPHICAL AND CRITICAL MISCELLANIES. Lon: Bentley, 1845.
     A "second edition," with 1 additional essay, published in 1850 as *Critical and Historical Essays* (No. 16349).

  16344. BIOGRAPHICAL AND CRITICAL MISCELLANIES. NY: Harper & Bros., 1845.
     A "new edition," with 1 additional essay, published in 1855 (No. 16355).

  16345. HISTORY OF THE CONQUEST OF PERU. Lon: Bentley, 1847.
     2v.

*16346. HISTORY OF THE CONQUEST OF PERU. NY: Harper & Bros., 1847.
     2v. Revised edition published in 1874, see No. 16372 below.

  16353. HISTORY OF THE REIGN OF PHILIP THE SECOND, KING OF SPAIN. Lon: Bentley, 1855.
     Vols. 1–2 of three.

WILLIAM HICKLING PRESCOTT (cont.)

*16354. HISTORY OF THE REIGN OF PHILIP THE SECOND, KING OF SPAIN.
Bos: Phillips, Sampson, 1855.
Vols. 1–2 of three. Revised edition published in 1874, see No. 16372 below.

*16361. HISTORY OF THE REIGN OF CHARLES THE FIFTH. Lon: Routledge,
1857.
2v. By William Robertson. Prescott contributed "The Life of Charles the Fifth
after His Abdication," Vol. 2, pp. <327>–418.

 16362. THE HISTORY OF THE REIGN OF THE EMPEROR CHARLES THE FIFTH.
Bos: Phillips, Sampson, 1857.
3v. By William Robertson. Prescott contributed "The Life of Charles the Fifth
after His Abdication," Vol. 3, p. <325>–510.

 16365. HISTORY OF THE REIGN OF PHILIP THE SECOND, KING OF SPAIN. Bos:
Phillips, Sampson, 1858.
Vol. 3 of three. Revised edition published in 1874, see No. 16372 below.

*16372. PRESCOTT'S WORKS. Phila: Lippincott, 1873–75.
15v. Ed. John Foster Kirk.

*16373. THE CORRESPONDENCE OF WILLIAM HICKLING PRESCOTT 1833–1847.
Bos & NY: Houghton Mifflin, 1925.
Ed. Roger Wolcott.

 16374. PRESCOTT UNPUBLISHED LETTERS TO GAYANGOS IN THE LIBRARY OF
THE HISPANIC SOCIETY OF AMERICA. NY: Hispanic Soc'y of America,
1927.
Ed. Clara Louisa Penney.

 16375. THE LITERARY MEMORANDA OF WILLIAM HICKLING PRESCOTT.
Norman: U of Oklahoma PR, <1961>.
2v. Ed. C. Harvey Gardiner.

 16376. THE PAPERS OF WILLIAM HICKLING PRESCOTT. Urbana: U of Illinois
PR, 1964.
Ed. C. Harvey Gardiner.

Howard Pyle
1853–1911

 16378. THE MERRY ADVENTURES OF ROBIN HOOD OF GREAT RENOWN, IN
NOTTINGHAMSHIRE. NY: Scribner's Sons, 1883.

 16380. WITHIN THE CAPES. NY: Scribner's Sons, 1885.

 16381. PEPPER & SALT, OR SEASONING FOR YOUNG FOLK. NY: Harper & Bros.,
1886.

 16382. THE ROSE OF PARADISE. NY: Harper & Bros., 1888.

 16383. THE WONDER CLOCK OR FOUR & TWENTY MARVELLOUS TALES. NY:
Harper & Bros., 1888.

 16384. OTTO OF THE SILVER HAND. NY: Scribner's Sons, 1888.

HOWARD PYLE (cont.)

16388. MEN OF IRON. NY: Harper & Bros., 1892.

16389. A MODERN ALADDIN OR, THE WONDERFUL ADVENTURES OF OLIVER MUNIER AN EXTRAVAGANZA. NY: Harper & Bros., 1892.

16390. TWILIGHT LAND. NY: Harper & Bros., 1895.

16391. THE STORY OF JACK BALLISTER'S FORTUNES. NY: Century Co., 1895.

16392. THE GARDEN BEHIND THE MOON. NY: Scribner's Sons, 1895.

16393. THE GHOST OF CAPTAIN BRAND. Wilmington DE: Ptd by J.M. Rogers, 1896.

16398. THE PRICE OF BLOOD AN EXTRAVAGANZA OF NEW YORK LIFE IN 1807. Bos: Badger, 1899.

16403. REJECTED OF MEN A STORY OF TO-DAY. NY & Lon: Harper & Bros., 1903.

16405. THE STORY OF KING ARTHUR AND HIS KNIGHTS. NY: Scribner's Sons, 1903.

16406. THE STORY OF THE CHAMPIONS OF THE ROUND TABLE. NY: Scribner's Sons, 1905.

16408. STOLEN TREASURE. NY & Lon: Harper & Bros., 1907.

16410. THE STORY OF SIR LAUNCELOT AND HIS COMPANIONS. NY: Scribner's Sons, 1907.

16412. THE RUBY OF KISHMOOR. NY & Lon: Harper & Bros., 1908.

16413. THE STORY OF THE GRAIL AND THE PASSING OF ARTHUR. NY: Scribner's Sons, 1910.

Thomas Buchanan Read
1822–1872

16424. PAUL REDDING: A TALE OF THE BRANDYWINE. Bos: Tompkins & Mussey, 1845.

16429. POEMS. Bos: Ticknor, 1847.

*16434. THE FEMALE POETS OF AMERICA. WITH PORTRAITS, BIOGRAPHICAL NOTICES, AND SPECIMENS OF THEIR WRITINGS. Phila: Butler, 1849.
Compiled by Read.

*16435. LAYS AND BALLADS. Phila: G.S. Appleton, 1849.

16438. POEMS. Lon: Delf & Trübner, 1852.

16439. THE ONWARD AGE; AN ANNIVERSARY POEM. RECITED BEFORE THE YOUNG MEN'S MERCANTILE LIBRARY ASSOCIATION OF CINCINNATI. Cincinnati: The Association, 1852.
Recited in honor of the Association's 18th anniversary.

16441. POEMS ... A NEW AND ENLARGED EDITION. Phila: Hart, 1853.
Another "new and enlarged edition" of Read's *Poems* in 2v. published in 1860 (No. 16448) containing 5 new pieces.

T. BUCHANAN READ (cont.)

16442. THE NEW PASTORAL. Phila: Parry & M'Millan, 1855.
Revised edition published in 1856 (No. 16444).

16443. THE HOUSE BY THE SEA. A POEM. Phila: Parry & McMillan, 1855.

*16445. SYLVIA; OR THE LAST SHEPHERD. AN ECLOGUE. AND OTHER POEMS. Phila: Parry & McMillan, 1857.

16455. THE WAGONER OF THE ALLEGHANIES. A POEM OF THE DAYS OF SEVENTY-SIX. Phila: Lippincott, 1862.

*16464. A SUMMER STORY, SHERIDAN'S RIDE AND OTHER POEMS. Phila: Lippincott, 1865.
"Sheridan's Ride" was also printed in 1864–65 in a number of ephemeral forms (Nos. 16461 & 16462).

16469. GOOD SAMARITANS. A POEM. Cincinnati: Clarke, 1867.

16470. A LAY OF MODERN ROME. A VISION. <Rome: Tip Romana, 1870>.

16472. ROGERS' STATUE OF LINCOLN FOR PHILADELPHIA AN ODE. Roma: F. Martelli, 1871.
Also published as an undated broadside with title "The Lincoln Statue."

16473. THE POETICAL WORKS ... NEW REVISED EDITION. Phila & Lon: Lippincott, 1883.

Frederic Sackrider Remington
1861–1909

16489. PONY TRACKS. NY: Harper & Bros., 1895.

16491. CROOKED TRAILS. NY & Lon: Harper & Bros., 1898.

16492. SUNDOWN LEFLARE. NY & Lon: Harper & Bros., 1899.

16495. MEN WITH THE BARK ON. NY & Lon: Harper & Bros., 1900.

16497. JOHN ERMINE OF THE YELLOWSTONE. NY: Macmillan, 1902.

16498. THE WAY OF AN INDIAN. NY: Fox Duffield, 1906.

16502. FREDERIC REMINGTON'S OWN WEST. NY: Dial PR, 1960.
Ed. Harold McCracken.

16504. FREDERIC REMINGTON AND THE SPANISH-AMERICAN WAR. NY: Crown, <1971>.
By Douglas Allen.

16506. THE COLLECTED WRITINGS OF FREDERIC REMINGTON. Garden City NY: Doubleday, 1979.
Ed. Peggy & Harold Samuels.

James Whitcomb Riley
1849–1916

*16525. "THE OLD SWIMMIN'-HOLE," AND 'LEVEN MORE POEMS. By Benj. F. Johnson, of Boone. Indianapolis: Hitt, 1883.
Republished, with additional material, as *Neghborly Poems*, see No. 16576 below.

*16535. CHARACTER SKETCHES THE BOSS GIRL A CHRISTMAS STORY AND OTHER SKETCHES. Indianapolis: Bowen-Merrill, 1886.
"Little Orphan Annie" here collected (as "Little Orphant Allie").

*16548. AFTERWHILES. Indianapolis: Bowen-Merrill, 1888.
Extended edition published in 1898 as Vol. 3 of the "Homestead Edition" (No. 16633). "Old Aunt Mary's" here collected; later extended& published separately in 1904 as *Out to Old Aunt Mary's* (No. 16667).

 16551. OLD-FASHIONED ROSES. Lon: Longmans, Green, 1888.

*16553. NYE AND RILEY'S RAILWAY GUIDE. Chi, NY &c.: Dearborn, 1888.
With Edgar W. (Bill) Nye, see No. 15097 above.

*16558. PIPES O' PAN AT ZEKESBURY. Indianapolis: Bowen-Merrill, 1889.
Extended edition published in 1898 as Vol. 4. of the "Homestead Edition" (No. 16634).

 16559. OLD-FASHIONED ROSES. Indianapolis: Bowen-Merrill, 1889.
"An Old Sweetheart of Mine" here collected; later extended & published separately in 1902 (No. 16657).

*16572. RHYMES OF CHILDHOOD. Indianapolis: Bowen-Merrill, 1891.
Extended edition published in 1898 as Vol. 5 of the "Homestead Edition" (No. 16636). "The Raggedy Man" here collected; later extended & published as the title poem of *The Raggedy Man*, 1907 (No. 16682).

*16576. NEGHBORLY POEMS ON FRIENDSHIP GRIEF AND FARM-LIFE. By Benj. F. Johnson, of Boone. Indianapolis: Bowen-Merrill, 1891.
At head of title: *"The Old Swimmin'-Hole" and 'Leven More Poems* Extended editions published in 1895 (No. 16611) & in 1898 as Vol. 1 of the "Homestead Edition" (No. 16627).

*16587. THE FLYING ISLANDS OF THE NIGHT. Indianapolis: Bowen-Merrill, 1892.
Extended edition published in 1898 as Vol. 6 of the "Homestead Edition" (No. 16637).

*16594. GREEN FIELDS AND RUNNING BROOKS. Indianapolis: Bowen-Merrill, 1893.

 16599. POEMS HERE AT HOME. Lon: Longmans, Green, 1893.

*16600. POEMS HERE AT HOME. NY: Century Co., 1893.

*16602. ARMAZINDY. Indianapolis: Bowen-Merrill, 1894.

 16606. THE DAYS GONE BY AND OTHER POEMS. Chi: Weeks, <1895>.
Unauthorized edition.

JAMES WHITCOMB RILEY (cont.)

16607. A TINKLE OF BELLS AND OTHER POEMS. Chi: Weeks, <1895>.
Unauthorized edition.

16616. A CHILD-WORLD. Lon & Bombay: Longmans, Green, 1896.

*16622. A CHILD-WORLD. Indianapolis & Kansas City: Bowen-Merrill, 1897.

*16625. RUBÀIYÀT OF DOC SIFERS. NY: Century Co., 1897.
Extended edition published in 1902 as Vol. 11 of the "Homestead Edition" (No. 16658).

*16647. HOME-FOLKS. Indianapolis: Bowen-Merrill, <1900>.
Extended edition published in 1902 as Vol. 11 of the "Homestead Edition" (No. 16658).

16656. THE BOOK OF JOYOUS CHILDREN. NY: Scribner's Sons, 1902.
Extended edition published in 1902 as Vol. 12 of the "Homestead Edition" (No. 16659).

16666. HIS PA'S ROMANCE. Indianapolis: Bobbs-Merrill, <1903>.
Extended edition published in 1908 as Vol. 13 of the "Homestead Edition" (No. 16689).

16668. A DEFECTIVE SANTA CLAUS. Indianapolis: Bobbs-Merrill, <1904>.

*16681. MORNING. Indianapolis: Bobbs-Merrill, <1907>.

16683. THE BOYS OF THE OLD GLEE CLVB. Indianapolis: Bobbs-Merrill, <1907>.

16700. THE RILEY BABY BOOK. Indianapolis: Bobbs-Merrill, <1913>.
"Autograph verses reproduced in facsimile."

*16701. THE COMPLETE WORKS ... BIOGRAPHICAL EDITION. Indianapolis: Bobbs-Merrill, <1913>.
6v. Ed. Edmund Henry Eitel. Reprinted as "The Elizabeth Marine Riley Edition" in 1915 (No. 16843). Other collected editions with new Riley material are the "Homestead Edition" in 16v. of Riley's *Poems and Prose Sketches*, 1897-1914. (see No. 16627) & the "Memorial Edition" in 10v. of his *Complete Works*, 1916 (No. 16716).

16734. LETTERS OF JAMES WHITCOMB RILEY. Indianapolis: Bobbs-Merrill, <1930>.
Ed. William Lyon Phelps. Riley's letters to Elizabeth Kahle were published in 1902 as *Love Letters of the Bachelor Poet* (No. 16726).

Rowland Evans Robinson
1833–1900

16876. FOREST & STREAM FABLES. NY: Forest & Stream Pub. Co., <1886>.
Anon, but signed "Awahsoose the Bear" on p. <2>.

16877. UNCLE LISHA'S SHOP. LIFE IN A CORNER OF YANKEELAND. NY: Forest & Stream Pub. Co., 1887.

ROWLAND EVANS ROBINSON (cont.)
16878. SAM LOVEL'S CAMPS. UNCLE LISHA'S FRIENDS UNDER BARK AND
CANVAS. NY: Forest & Stream Pub. Co., 1889.
Sequel to *Uncle Lisha's Shop.*

*16881. VERMONT A STUDY OF INDEPENDENCE. Bos & NY: Houghton,
Mifflin, 1892.
American Commonwealths series.

16883. DANVIS FOLKS. Bos & NY: Houghton, Mifflin, 1894.

*16885. IN NEW ENGLAND FIELDS AND WOODS. Bos & NY: Houghton, Mifflin,
1896.

16886. UNCLE LISHA'S OUTING. Bos & NY: Houghton, Mifflin, 1897.

*16887. A HERO OF TICONDEROGA. Burlington VT: Shanley, 1898.

16888. IN THE GREEN WOOD. Burlington VT: Shanley, 1899.

16889. A DANVIS PIONEER A STORY OF ONE OF ETHAN ALLEN'S GREEN
MOUNTAIN BOYS. Bos & NY: Houghton, Mifflin, 1900.

*16890. SAM LOVEL'S BOY. Bos & NY: Houghton, Mifflin, 1901.

*16891. OUT OF BONDAGE AND OTHER STORIES. Bos & NY: Houghton,
Mifflin, 1905.

16892. HUNTING WITHOUT A GUN AND OTHER PAPERS. NY: Forest & Stream
Pub. Co., 1905.

16893. SILVER FIELDS AND OTHER SKETCHES OF A FARMER-SPORTSMAN. Bos
& NY: Houghton Mifflin, 1921.

*16894. CENTENNIAL EDITION ROWLAND E. ROBINSON. Rutland VT: Tuttle,
<1933–37>.
7v. Ed. Llewellyn R. Perkins.

Edward Payson Roe
1838–1888

16895. BARRIERS BURNED AWAY. NY: Dodd & Mead, 1872.
Revised edition published in 1885 (No. 16917).

16897. WHAT CAN SHE DO? NY: Dodd & Mead, <1873>.

*16898. OPENING A CHESTNUT BURR. NY: Dodd & Mead, <1874>.
Revised editions published in 1884. (No. 16912) & 1885 (No. 16916).

*16899. GENTLE WOMAN ROUSED. A STORY OF THE TEMPERANCE MOVEMENT
IN THE WEST. NY: National Temperance Soc'y, 1874.

*16900. FROM JEST TO EARNEST. NY: Dodd & Mead, <1875>.

*16902. NEAR TO NATURE'S HEART. NY: Dodd, Mead, <1876>.

16903. A KNIGHT OF THE NINETEENTH CENTURY. NY: Dodd, Mead, 1877.

*16904. A FACE ILLUMINED. NY: Dodd, Mead, <1878>.

*16907. A DAY OF FATE. NY: Dodd, Mead, <1880>.

*16908. WITHOUT A HOME. NY: Dodd, Mead, <1881>.
Slightly revised illustrated edition published in 1885 (No. 16915).

E. P. ROE (cont.)

16910. AN UNEXPECTED RESULT AND OTHER STORIES. NY: Dodd, Mead, <1883>.
First edition contains 3 stories; extended editions with 4.or 5 stories are reprints (Nos. 16973 & 16974).

*16911. HIS SOMBRE RIVALS. NY: Dodd, Mead, <1883>.

*16913. A YOUNG GIRL'S WOOING. NY: Dodd, Mead, <1884>.

16914. NATURE'S SERIAL STORY. NY: Harper & Bros., 1885.

*16918. AN ORIGINAL BELLE. NY: Dodd, Mead, <1885>.

*16919. DRIVEN BACK TO EDEN. NY: Dodd, Mead, 1885.

*16923. HE FELL IN LOVE WITH HIS WIFE. NY: Dodd, Mead, <1886>.

16926. THE HORNETS' NEST. A STORY OF LOVE AND WAR. NY: Dodd, Mead, 1887.

16928. THE EARTH TREMBLED. Lon & NY: Ward, Lock, <1887>.

16929. THE EARTH TREMBLED. NY: Dodd, Mead, 1887.

16931. FOUND, YET LOST. NY: Dodd, Mead, <1888>.

*16932. "MISS LOU." NY: Dodd, Mead, 1888.

*16936. THE HOME ACRE. NY: Dodd, Mead, 1889.
Roe's other gardening books are *Play and Profit in My Garden,* 1873 (No. 16896), *A Manual on the Culture of Small Fruits,* 1876 (No. 16901) & *Success with Small Fruits,* 1880 (No. 16906).

16938. TAKEN ALIVE AND OTHER STORIES WITH AN AUTOBIOGRAPHY. NY: Dodd, Mead, <1889>.

16941. E.P. ROE REMINISCENCES OF HIS LIFE. NY: Dodd, Mead, 1899.
By Mary A. Roe.

Susanna Haswell Rowson
1762–1824

16981. VICTORIA. A NOVEL. By Susannah Haswell. Lon: The Author, 1786.
2v.

16982. A TRIP TO PARNASSUS; OR, THE JUDGMENT OF APOLLO ON DRAMATIC AUTHORS AND PERFORMERS. A POEM. Lon: Abraham, 1788.
Anon.

16983. THE INQUISITOR; OR, INVISIBLE RAMBLER. <Lon>: G.G.J. & J. Robinson, 1788.
3v.

16984. POEMS ON VARIOUS SUBJECTS. <Lon>: G.G.J. & J. Robinson, 1788.
No copy located. Entry based on trade listings.

16985. THE TEST OF HONOUR, A NOVEL. By a Young Lady. Lon: Abraham, 1789.
2v.

SUSANNA ROWSON (cont.)

16988. CHARLOTTE. A TALE OF TRUTH. Lon: Lane, 1791.
2v. Anon.

*16989. MENTORIA; OR THE YOUNG LADY'S FRIEND. Lon: Lane, <n.d., 1791>.
2v. Dublin edition also published in 1791 (No. 16990).

16993. THE FILLE DE CHAMBRE, A NOVEL. Lon: Lane, 1792.
3v. Anon. Dublin edition published in 1793 (No. 16995).

16996. THE INQUISITOR; OR, INVISIBLE RAMBLER. Phila: Gibbons, 1793.
3v. in one.

*16997. CHARLOTTE. A TALE OF TRUTH. Phila: Carey, 1794.
2v. in one. Later editions published as *Charlotte Temple*.

16998. THE FILLE DE CHAMBRE, A NOVEL. Phila: H. & P. Rice, 1794.
Revised edition published in 1814 as *Rebecca; or the Fille de Chambre* (No. 17014).

16999. MENTORIA; OR THE YOUNG LADY'S FRIEND. Phila: Campbell, 1794.
2v. in one.

*17000. SLAVE IN ALGIERS; OR, A STRUGGLE FOR FREEDOM: A PLAY. Phila: The Author, 1794.

17002. TRIALS OF THE HUMAN HEART, A NOVEL. Phila: The Author, 1795.
4v. in two.

17003. REUBEN AND RACHEL; OR, TALES OF OLD TIMES. A NOVEL. Bos: D. West, 1798.
2v. in one.

17008. MISCELLANEOUS POEMS. Bos: The Author, 1804.

17012. A PRESENT FOR YOUNG LADIES. Bos: J. West, 1811.
"Poems, dialogues, addresses ... recited by the pupils of Mrs. Rowson's Academy, at the annual exhibitions."

17013. SARAH, OR THE EXEMPLARY WIFE. Bos: C. Williams, 1813.

17024. CHARLOTTE'S DAUGHTER: OR, THE THREE ORPHANS. Bos: Richardson & Lord, 1828.
Sequel to *Charlotte*. Later editions published as *Lucy Temple*.

Anne Newport Royall
1769–1854

17067. SKETCHES OF HISTORY, LIFE, AND MANNERS, IN THE UNITED STATES. By a Traveller. New-Haven: The Author, 1826.

*17068. THE TENNESSEAN; A NOVEL, FOUNDED ON FACTS. New-Haven: The Author, 1827.

17069. THE BLACK BOOK; OR, A CONTINUATION OF TRAVELS, IN THE UNITED STATES. Wash DC: The Author, 1828–29.
3v. Originally planned as 2v.

17070. MRS. ROYALL'S PENNSYLVANIA, OR TRAVELS CONTINUED IN THE UNITED STATES. Wash DC: The Author, 1829.
2v.

ANNE ROYALL (cont.)

17071. LETTERS FROM ALABAMA ON VARIOUS SUBJECTS. Wash DC, 1830.

17072. MRS. ROYALL'S SOUTHERN TOUR, OR SECOND SERIES OF THE BLACK BOOK. Wash DC, 1830–31.
3v.

Irwin Russell
1853–1879

*17090. POEMS. NY: Century Co., <1888>.
"Christmas-Night in the Quarters" here collected: extracts were first printed in 1878 in a number of publications (Nos. 17077–80); the original manuscript published in facsimile in 1970 (No. 17096).

17093. CHRISTMAS-NIGHT IN THE QUARTERS AND OTHER POEMS. NY: Century Co., 1917.

Abram Joseph Ryan
1838–1886

17098. ORATION DELIVERED BEFORE THE MEMBERS OF ST. MARY'S ORPHAN ASSOCIATION, JULY 4TH, 1866 ... THE CONQUERED BANNER ... THE SWORD OF LEE. Nashville: The Association, 1866.
BAL (No. 17097) also lists 5 other printings of "The Conquered Banner" dated 1865–66.

*17107. FATHER RYAN'S POEMS. Mobile: Rapier, 1879.

*17109. POEMS: PATRIOTIC, RELIGIOUS, MISCELLANEOUS. Baltimore: Piet, 1880.
Extended editions published in 1888 (No. 17115), 1894 (No. 17119), 1895 (Nos. 17120 & 17121) & 1897 (No. 17122).

17111. A CROWN FOR OUR QUEEN. Baltimore: Piet, 1882.

17114. A CATHOLIC CONVENTION OF ONE VERSUS THE CINCINNATI PRESBYTERIAN CONVENTION. NY: D. & J. Sadlier, <1886, i.e. 1888>.

Edgar Evertson Saltus
1855–1921

17128. BALZAC. Bos & NY: Houghton, Mifflin, 1884.

17129. THE PHILOSOPHY OF DISENCHANTMENT. Bos & NY: Houghton, Mifflin, 1885.

17131. THE ANATOMY OF NEGATION. Lon & Edinburgh: Williams & Norgate, 1886.

17132. THE ANATOMY OF NEGATION. NY: Scribner & Welford, 1886.
Revised edition published in 1889 (No. 17138).

EDGAR SALTUS (cont.)

*17134. MR. INCOUL'S MISADVENTURE A NOVEL. NY: Benjamin & Bell, 1887.

*17135. THE TRUTH ABOUT TRISTREM VARICK A NOVEL. Chi & NY: Belford, Clarke, <1888>.

*17136. EDEN AN EPISODE. Chi, NY, &c.: Belford, Clarke, <1888>.

17139. A TRANSACTION IN HEARTS AN EPISODE. Chi, NY, &c.: Belford, Clarke, <1889>.
Cloth; and paper wrapper of *The Household Library,* Vol. 4, No. 18, 15 Nov. 1888. Also published as the Feb. 1889 issue of *Lippincott's Monthly Magazine* (No. 17137).

*17141. THE PACE THAT KILLS A CHRONICLE. Chi, NY, &c.: Belford, Clarke, <1889>.
Cloth; and paper wrapper of *The Household Library,* Vol. 4, No. 38, 15 Nov. 1888.

*17142. A TRANSIENT GUEST AND OTHER EPISODES. Chi, NY, &c.: Belford, Clarke, <1889>.

17143. LOVE AND LORE. NY: Belford, <1890>.
The Belford American Novel Series, Vol. 2, No. 9, 28 July 1890.

17145. MARY MAGDALEN A CHRONICLE. NY: Belford, <1891>.
Cloth; and paper wrapper of *The Belford American Novel Series,* Vol. 3, No. 5, 17 Nov. 1890. These sheets also issued in the U.K. in 1891, presumably for copyright purposes (No. 17144).

*17147. IMPERIAL PURPLE. Chi: Morrill Higgins, 1892.

17148. THE FACTS IN THE CURIOUS CASE OF H. HYRTL ESQ. NY: Collier, 1892.
Once a Week Library, Vol. 9, No. 5, 17 May 1892.

17150. MADAM SAPPHIRA A FIFTH AVENUE STORY. NY: Neely, <1893>.
Cloth; and paper wrapper of *Neely's Library of Choice Literature,* Vol. 2, No. 6, Feb. 1893.

*17153. ENTHRALLED A STORY OF INTERNATIONAL LIFE. Lon, Paris, &c.: Tudor PR, 1894.

*17154. WHEN DREAMS COME TRUE A STORY OF EMOTIONAL LIFE. <NY: Collier, 1894?>.
Once a Week Semi-Monthly Library, Vol. 12, No. 13, 27 Dec. 1894. Also published with imprint "NY & Lon: Transatlantic Pub. Co., 1895" in cloth, and paper wrapper of the *Marshall Series,* Vol. 1, No. 1, Jan. 1895.

17162. PURPLE AND FINE WOMEN. NY & Lon: Ainslee, 1903.

17163. THE POMPS OF SATAN. Lon: Greening, 1904.

17164. A PERFUME OF EROS A FIFTH AVENUE INCIDENT. NY: Wessels, 1905.

*17165. VANITY SQUARE A STORY OF FIFTH AVENUE LIFE. Phila & Lon: Lippincott, 1906.

17166. HISTORIA AMORIS A HISTORY OF LOVE ANCIENT AND MODERN. NY: Kennerley, 1906.
Reprinted as *Love Throughout the Ages.*

17167. THE POMPS OF SATAN. NY: Kennerley, 1906.

EDGAR SALTUS (cont.)

*17168. THE LORDS OF THE GHOSTLAND A HISTORY OF THE IDEAL. NY: Kennerley, 1907.

17169. DAUGHTERS OF THE RICH. NY: Kennerley, <1909>.

*17170. THE MONSTER. NY: Pulitzer Pub. Co., 1912 <i.e. 1913>.

*17172. OSCAR WILDE AN IDLER'S IMPRESSION. Chi: Brothers of the Book, 1917.

17174. THE PALISER CASE. NY: Boni & Liveright, 1919.

17178. THE GARDENS OF APHRODITE. Phila: Pennell Club, 1920.

17179. THE IMPERIAL ORGY AN ACCOUNT OF THE TSARS FROM THE FIRST TO THE LAST. NY: Boni & Liveright, 1920.

17180. THE GHOST GIRL. NY: Boni & Liveright, <1922>.

17182. PARNASSIANS PERSONALLY ENCOUNTERED. Cedar Rapids IA: Torch PR, 1923.

17184. THE UPLANDS OF DREAM. Chi: Covici, 1925.
Ed. Charles Honce.

17185. VICTOR HUGO AND GOLGOTHA TWO ESSAYS. Chi: Covici, 1925.

*17186. POPPIES AND MANDRAGORA POEMS. NY: Vinal, 1926.
"With twenty-three additional poems by Marie Saltus."

Epes Sargent
1813–1880

17201. VELASCO; A TRAGEDY. NY: Harper & Bros., 1839.
Also privately printed in 1837 (No. 17198)

17206. WEALTH AND WORTH; OR, WHICH MAKES THE MAN? NY: Harper & Bros., 1842.
Anon.

17207. AMERICAN ADVENTURE BY LAND AND SEA. NY: Harper & Bros., 1842.
2v. Anon. *Harper & Brothers School District Library*, No. 153–54.

17209. WHAT'S TO BE DONE? OR, THE WILL AND THE WAY. NY: Harper & Bros., 1842.
Anon.

17210. LIFE AND PUBLIC SERVICES OF HENRY CLAY. <NY: J. Winchester, 1842>.
Anon. *Books for the People* series (*New World* extra). Revised & extended editions published in 1844. (No. 17218) & 1848 (No. 17224).

17213. PHILIP IN SEARCH OF A WIFE. By a Gentleman Butterfly. <NY: J. Winchester, 1843>.
New World Extra Series, No. 90, Aug. 1843.

17216. THE LIGHT OF THE LIGHTHOUSE, AND OTHER POEMS. NY: Mowatt, 1844.
The Drawing-Room Library, No. 1. This series edited by Sargent (No. 17217).

EPES SARGENT (cont.)

17219. FLEETWOOD, OR THE STAIN OF BIRTH. A NOVEL OF AMERICAN LIFE. NY: Burgess, Stringer, 1845.
Anon.

17223. SONGS OF THE SEA, WITH OTHER POEMS. Bos: Munroe, 1847.

17239. THE PRIESTESS: A TRAGEDY. Bos: Dutton & Wentworth, 1854.
"Only twenty copies printed." At head of title: [Not Published.]

17251. PECULIAR A TALE OF THE GREAT TRANSITION. NY: Carleton, 1864.

17262. THE WOMAN WHO DARED. Bos: Roberts Bros., 1870.

17273. HARPER'S CYCLOPÆDIA OF BRITISH AND AMERICAN POETRY. NY: Harper & Bros., 1881.
Edited, with contributions, by Sargent. For full entry see BAL (No. 4336).

John Godfrey Saxe
1816–1887

17276. PROGRESS: A SATIRICAL POEM. NY: J. Allen, 1846.
Reprinted, with a new preface, in 1847 (No. 17277).

17280. POEMS. Bos: Ticknor, Reed, & Fields, 1850.
Extended "second edition" published in 1850 (No. 17281), "third edition" in 1851 (No. 17283) & "new edition" in 1852 (No. 17385).

17291. THE MONEY-KING AND OTHER POEMS. Bos: Ticknor & Fields, 1860.

17292. POEMS ... COMPLETE IN ONE VOLUME. Bos: Ticknor & Fields, 1861.

17293. THE FLY-ING DUTCHMAN; OR, THE WRATH OF HERR VONSTOPPELNOZE. NY: Carleton, 1862.

17301. CLEVER STORIES OF MANY NATIONS. RENDERED IN RHYME. Bos: Ticknor & Fields, 1865.

17304. THE MASQUERADE AND OTHER POEMS. Bos: Ticknor & Fields, 1866.

*17306. THE POEMS ... COMPLETE IN ONE VOLUME. Bos: Ticknor & Fields, 1868.
Later collected editions of Saxe's poems with new material published in 1871 (No. 17310), 1873 (No. 17315) & 1889 (No. 17239).

17313. FABLES AND LEGENDS OF MANY COUNTRIES. RENDERED IN RHYME. Bos: Osgood, 1872.

17318. LEISURE-DAY RHYMES. Bos: Osgood, 1875.

Catharine Maria Sedgwick
1789–1867

17334. A NEW-ENGLAND TALE; OR, SKETCHES OF NEW-ENGLAND CHARACTER AND MANNERS. NY: Bliss & White, 1822.
Anon. Reprinted with additional material in 1852 as A New-England Tale, and Miscellanies (No. 17407).

CATHARINE M. SEDGWICK (cont.)

17335. MARY HOLLIS. AN ORIGINAL TALE. NY: NY Unitarian Book Soc'y, 1822.
Anon.

17337. REDWOOD; A TALE. NY: Bliss & White, 1824.
2v. Anon. Revised edition published in 1850 (No. 17400).

17338. THE TRAVELLERS. A TALE. DESIGNED FOR YOUNG PEOPLE. NY: Bliss & White, 1825.
Anon.

17340. THE DEFORMED BOY. Brookfield: E. & G. Merriam, Ptrs, 1826.
Anon.

17342. HOPE LESLIE; OR EARLY TIMES IN THE MASSACHUSETTS. NY: White, Gallaher, & White, 1827.
2v. Anon. Revised edition published in 1842 (No. 17387).

*17345. A SHORT ESSAY TO DO GOOD. Stockbridge: Webster & Stanley, 1828.
Anon. "Republished from the Christian Teacher's Manual."

*17349. CLARENCE; OR, A TALE OF OUR OWN TIMES. Phila: Carey & Lea, 1830.
2v. Anon. Revised edition published in 1849 (No. 17399).

*17361. HOME. Bos & Cambridge: Munroe, 1835.
Anon. *Scenes and Characters Illustrating Christian Truth*, No. 3.

*17362. THE LINWOODS; OR, "SIXTY YEARS SINCE" IN AMERICA. NY: Harper & Bros., 1835.
2v. Anon.

17365. TALES AND SKETCHES. Phila: Carey, Lea, & Blanchard, 1835.

17367. THE POOR RICH MAN, AND THE RICH POOR MAN. NY: Harper & Bros., 1836.
Anon.

*17373. LIVE AND LET LIVE; OR, DOMESTIC SERVICE ILLUSTRATED. NY: Harper & Bros., 1837.
Anon.

*17375. A LOVE TOKEN FOR CHILDREN. NY: Harper & Bros., 1838.
Anon.

17378. MEANS AND ENDS, OR SELF-TRAINING. Bos: Marsh, Capen, et al, 1839.
Anon. *Juvenile Series School Library*, Vol. 3.

17381. STORIES FOR YOUNG PERSONS. NY: Harper & Bros., 1840.
Anon. *Harper & Brothers School District Library*, No. 140.

17383. LETTERS FROM ABROAD TO KINDRED AT HOME. Lon: Moxon, 1841.
2v. Slightly revised 1v. edition also published in 1841 (No. 17386).

*17384. LETTERS FROM ABROAD TO KINDRED AT HOME. NY: Harper & Bros., 1841.
2v. Anon.

17390. TALES AND SKETCHES. SECOND SERIES. NY: Harper & Bros., 1844.
Anon. Binder's title: *Wilton Harvey and Other Tales*.

CATHARINE M. SEDGWICK (cont.)
17394. MORALS OF MANNERS; OR, HINTS FOR OUR YOUNG PEOPLE. NY:
Wiley & Putnam, 1846.
Revised edition published in 1854. (No. 17414).

17396. FACTS AND FANCIES FOR SCHOOL-DAY READING. NY & Lon: Wiley
& Putnam, 1848.
Sequel to *Morals of Manners.*

*17397. THE BOY OF MOUNT RHIGI. Bos: Peirce, 1848.
Anon.

17402. TALES OF CITY LIFE. I. THE CITY CLERK. II. "LIFE IS SWEET." Phila:
Hazard & Mitchell, 1850.
Reprinted in 1851 as *The City Clerk and His Sister* (No. 17405).

17418. MARRIED OR SINGLE? Lon: Knight & Son, <n.d., 1857>.

17419. MARRIED OR SINGLE? NY: Harper & Bros., 1857.
2v. Anon.

17421. MEMOIR OF JOSEPH CURTIS, A MODEL MAN. NY: Harper & Bros.,
1858.
Anon.

17428. LIFE AND LETTERS. NY: Harper & Bros., 1871.
By Mary E. Dewey.

Alan Seeger
1888–1916

17433. POEMS. NY: Scribner's Sons, 1916.
17435. LETTERS AND DIARY. NY: Scribner's Sons, 1917.

Henry Wheeler Shaw
(Josh Billings)
1818–1885

17439. JOSH BILLINGS, HIZ SAYINGS. NY: Carleton, 1866.
17441. JOSH BILLINGS ON ICE, AND OTHER THINGS. NY: Carleton, 1868.
*17443. JOSH BILLINGS' FARMER'S ALLMINAX FOR THE YEAR 1870. NY:
Carleton, 1870.
17444. JOSH BILLINGS' FARMER'S ALLMINAX FOR THE YEAR 1871. NY:
Carleton, 1871.
17448. JOSH BILLINGS' FARMER'S ALLMINAX FOR THE YEAR OF OUR LORD
1872. NY: Carleton, 1872.
17450. JOSH BILLINGS' FARMER'S ALLMINAX FOR THE YEAR OF OUR LORD
1873. NY: Carleton, 1873.
17453. JOSH BILLINGS' FARMER'S ALLMINAX FOR THE YEAR OF OUR LORD
1874. NY: Carleton, 1874.

H. W. SHAW (Josh Billings) (cont.)

17454. JOSH BILLINGS' WIT AND HUMOR. Lon: Routledge & Sons, 1874.
For U.S. edition see next entry.

17455. EVERYBODY'S FRIEND, OR; JOSH BILLING'S ENCYCLOPEDIA AND PROVERBIAL PHILOSOPHY OF WIT AND HUMOR. Hartford: American Pub. Co., 1874.

17458. JOSH BILLINGS' FARMER'S ALLMINAX FOR THE YEAR OF OUR LORD 1875. NY: Carleton, 1875.

17459. JOSH BILLINGS' (SENTENIAL) FARMER'S ALLMINAX FOR THE YEAR OF OUR LORD 1876. NY: Carleton, 1876.

17461. JOSH BILLINGS' FARMER'S ALLMINAX FOR THE YEAR OF OUR LORD 1877. NY: Carleton, 1877.

17462. JOSH BILLINGS' TRUMP KARDS. BLUE GLASS PHILOSOPHY. NY: Carleton, 1877.

17464. JOSH BILLINGS' FARMER'S ALLMINAX FOR THE YEAR OF OUR LORD 1878. NY: Carleton, 1878.

17465. JOSH BILLINGS' FARMER'S ALLMINAX FOR THE YEAR OF OUR LORD 1879. NY: Carleton, 1878.
The *Allminax* for 1870–79, with considerable additional material, published in 1879 as *Old Probability Perhaps Rain—Perhaps Not* (No. 17466) & reprinted in 1902 as *Josh Billings' Old Farmer's Allminax* 1870 1879 (No. 17481).

17467. JOSH BILLINGS COOK BOOK AND PICKTORIAL PROVERBS. NY: Carleton, 1880.
Slightly revised edition published in 1881 as *Josh Billings Struggling with Things* (No. 17470).

17469. JOSH BILLINGS' SPICE-BOX, CRAMMED WITH DROLL YARNS. NY: Ogilvie, 1881.
No copy located. Earliest located edition published not before 1883 (No. 17474).

17471. LIFE AND ADVENTURES OF JOSH BILLINGS. NY: Carleton, 1883.

Frank Dempster Sherman
1860–1916

17503. MADRIGALS AND CATCHES. NY: White, Stokes, & Allen, 1887.

17505. NEW WAGGINGS OF OLD TALES. By Two Wags. Bos: Ticknor, 1888.
With John Kendrick Bangs, see No. 697 above.

17507. LYRICS FOR A LUTE. Bos & NY: Houghton, Mifflin, 1890.

*17510. LITTLE-FOLK LYRICS. Bos & NY: Houghton Mifflin, 1892.
Extended edition published in 1897 (No. 17517).

*17522. LYRICS OF JOY. Bos & NY: Houghton, Mifflin, 1904.

17523. A SOUTHERN FLIGHT. <n.p., Clinton NY>: G. W. Browning, 1905.
With Clinton Scollard.

FRANK DEMPSTER SHERMAN (cont.)
17529. THE POEMS. Bos & NY: Houghton Mifflin, <1917>.
Ed. Clinton Scollard.

Benjamin Penhallow Shillaber
(Mrs. Ruth Partington)
1814–1890

17536. RHYMES WITH REASON AND WITHOUT. Bos: Tompkins & Mussey, 1853.

17538. MRS. PARTINGTON'S CARPET BAG OF FUN. NY: Garrett, 1854.
Ed. S.P. Avery.

*17540. LIFE AND SAYINGS OF MRS. PARTINGTON, AND OTHERS OF THE FAMILY. NY: J.C. Derby, 1854.

17556. KNITTING-WORK: A WEB OF MANY TEXTURES, WROUGHT BY RUTH PARTINGTON. Bos: Brown, Taggard & Chase, 1859.

17573. MRS. PARTINGTON'S RIDICULE. A COLLECTION OF WIT AND HUMOR. Bos: Thomes & Talbot, <1863, i.e. *ca.* 1870>.
Ten Cent Novelettes, No. 80.

*17578. PARTINGTONIAN PATCHWORK. Bos: Lee & Shepard, 1873.

*17581. LINES IN PLEASANT PLACES. RHYTHMICS OF MANY MOODS AND QUANTITIES. Chelsea: The Author, 1874.
Reprinted, with a new preface, in 1882 as *Wide-Swath* (No. 17599).

*17587. IKE PARTINGTON; OR, THE ADVENTURES OF A HUMAN BOY AND HIS FRIENDS. Bos: Lee & Shepard, 1879.

17591. IKE PARTINGTON AND HIS FRIENDS. CRUISES WITH CAPTAIN BOB ON SEA AND LAND. Bos: Lee & Shepard, 1880.

17598. THE DOUBLE-RUNNER CLUB OR THE LIVELY BOYS OF RIVERTOWN. Bos: Lee & Shepard, 1882.
At head of title: *Ike Partington Series.*

17607. A MIDNIGHT RACE. Bos: Ticknor, 1888.
"Privately printed."

17610. MRS. PARTINGTON'S NEW GRIP-SACK, FILLED WITH FRESH THINGS. NY: Ogilvie, <1890>.
The Red Cover Series, No. 85, April 1890. Reprinted in 1893 as *Mrs. Partington's Grab Bag* (No. 17613).

Lydia Huntley Sigourney
1791–1865

17615. MORAL PIECES, IN PROSE AND VERSE. By Lydia Huntley. Hartford: Sheldon & Goodwin, 1815.

17618. THE SQUARE TABLE. Hartford: Goodrich, 1819.
Anon. See next entry.

17619. NO. II. THE SQUARE TABLE, OR THE MEDITATIONS OF FOUR SECLUDED MAIDENS SEATED AROUND IT. <Hartford, 1819?>.
Anon.

17620. TRAITS OF THE ABORIGINES OF AMERICA. A POEM. Cambridge: University PR, 1822.
Anon.

17622. SKETCH OF CONNECTICUT, FORTY YEARS SINCE. Hartford: Cooke & Sons, 1824.
Anon.

17625. POEMS. Bos: Goodrich, 1827.
Anon.

17634. FEMALE BIOGRAPHY; CONTAINING SKETCHES OF THE LIFE AND CHARACTER OF TWELVE AMERICAN WOMEN. Phila: American Sunday-School Union, 1829.
Anon.

17654. EVENING READINGS IN HISTORY. Springfield: G. & C. Merriam, 1833.
Anon.

17655. MEMOIR OF PHEBE P. HAMMOND, A PUPIL IN THE AMERICAN ASYLUM AT HARTFORD. By Mrs. L.H.S. NY: Sleight & Van Norden, Ptrs, 1833.

17656. LETTERS TO YOUNG LADIES. By a Lady. Hartford: Ptd by Canfield, 1833.
Revised & extended editions published in 1835 (No. 17681), 1837 (No. 17702), 1841 (No. 17752) & 1842 (No. 17766).

*17657. HOW TO BE HAPPY. WRITTEN FOR THE CHILDREN OF SOME DEAR FRIENDS. By a Lady. Hartford: D.F. Robinson, 1833.
Published in the U.K. in 1835 as *The Way to Be Happy* (No. 17971).

17659. BIOGRAPHY OF PIOUS PERSONS; ABRIDGED FOR YOUTH. Springfield: G. & C. Merriam, 1833.
2v. Anon.

17660. THE FARMER AND SOLDIER. A TALE. Hartford: J.H. Wells, Ptr, 1833.
"Published with the Approbation of the Connecticut Peace Society." Anon, but signed *L.H.S.* at end.

17661. THE INTEMPERATE, AND THE REFORMED. Bos: Bliss, 1833.
"The Intemperate" by Sigourney; "The Reformed" by Gerrit Smith.

LYDIA HUNTLEY SIGOURNEY (cont.)

*17667. SKETCHES. Phila: Key & Biddle, 1834.

17669. POETRY FOR CHILDREN. Hartford: Robinson & Pratt, 1834.
Anon. Extended edition published in 1836 as *Poems for Children* (No. 17697).

17671. POEMS. Phila: Key & Biddle, 1834.
Extended "second edition" published in 1836 (No. 17693).

17672. LAYS FROM THE WEST. Lon: Ward, 1834.
Ed. Joseph Belcher.

17679. TALES AND ESSAYS FOR CHILDREN. Hartford: Huntington, 1835.

17680. MEMOIR OF MARGARET AND HENRIETTA FLOWER. Bos: Perkins, Marvin, 1835.
Anon. Reprinted in 1845 as *The Lovely Sisters* (No. 17976) & in 1852 as *Margaret and Henrietta* (No. 17984).

17683. ZINZENDORFF, AND OTHER POEMS. NY: Leavitt, Lord, 1835.

17688. HISTORY OF MARCUS AURELIUS, EMPEROR OF ROME. Hartford: Belknap & Hamersley, 1836.

17689. OLIVE BUDS. Hartford: Watson, 1836.

*17711. THE GIRL'S READING-BOOK; IN PROSE AND POETRY. NY: J.O. Taylor, 1838.
Revised & extended "ninth edition" published in 1839 (No. 17732); reprinted in 1844 as *The Book for Girls* (No. 17974) & in 1851 as *The Girl's Book* (No. 17983).

17715. LETTERS TO MOTHERS. Hartford: Hudson & Skinner, 1838.
Extended "second edition" published in 1839 (No. 17733).

17719. SELECT POEMS ... THIRD EDITION. Phila: Greenough, 1838.
Extended "fourth edition" published in 1842 (No. 17769), "fifth edition" in 1845 (No. 17806) & "tenth edition" in 1851 (No. 17878).

17729. THE BOY'S READING-BOOK; IN PROSE AND POETRY. NY: J.O. Taylor, 1839.
Revised & extended edition published in 1843 as *The Boy's Book* (No. 17772) & reprinted in 1845 as *A Book for Boys* (No. 17975).

17745. MEMOIR OF MARY ANNE HOOKER. Phila: American Sunday-School Union, <1840>.
Anon. "Revised by the Committee of Publication."

17751. POCAHONTAS, AND OTHER POEMS. Lon: Tyas, 1841.

*17753. POEMS, RELIGIOUS AND ELEGAIC. Lon: Tyas, 1841.

17758. POCAHONTAS, AND OTHER POEMS. NY: Harper & Bros., 1841.
A different selection from the U.K. edition.

17762. PLEASANT MEMORIES OF PLEASANT LANDS. Bos: Munroe, 1842.
Revised & extended "second edition" published in 1844 (No. 17782) & "third edition" in 1856 (No. 17914).

17768. POEMS. Phila: Locken, 1842.

17784. THE PICTORIAL READER. NY: Turner & Hayden, 1844.
Reprinted in 1844 as *The Child's Book* (No. 17973).

LYDIA HUNTLEY SIGOURNEY (cont.)

17795. SCENES IN MY NATIVE LAND. Bos: Munroe, 1845.

17796. POETRY FOR SEAMEN. Bos: Munroe, 1845.
Extended edition published in 1850 as *Poems for the Sea* (No. 17857); reprinted in 1852 as *Voices of Home* (No. 17887) & 1857 as *The Sea and the Sailor* (No. 17922).

17811. THE VOICE OF FLOWERS. Hartford: Parsons, 1846.

*17813. MYRTIS, WITH OTHER ETCHINGS AND SKETCHINGS. NY: Harper & Bros., <1846>.

17824. THE WEEPING WILLOW. Hartford: Parsons, 1847.

17830. WATER-DROPS. NY & Pittsburgh: Carter, 1848.

17846. ILLUSTRATED POEMS. Phila: Carey & Hart, 1849.
Published in the U.K. in 1850 as *The Poetical Works* (Nos. 17981 & 17982).

17856. WHISPER TO A BRIDE. Hartford: Parsons, 1850.
Extended "second edition" published in 1851 (17867).

17870. LETTERS TO MY PUPILS: WITH NARRATIVE AND BIOGRAPHICAL SKETCHES. NY: Carter & Bros., 1851.

17873. EXAMPLES OF LIFE AND DEATH. NY: Scribner, 1851.

17881. OLIVE LEAVES. NY: Carter & Bros., 1852.

17889. THE FADED HOPE. NY: Carter & Bros., 1853.

17890. MEMOIR OF MRS. HARRIET NEWELL COOK. NY: Carter & Bros., 1853.

17901. THE WESTERN HOME, AND OTHER POEMS. Phila: Parry & McMillan, 1854.

17903. PAST MERIDIAN. NY: Appleton, 1854.
Revised & extended "second edition" published in 1856 (No. 17917) & "fifth edition" in 1864 (No. 17952).

17907. SAYINGS FOR THE LITTLE ONES, AND POEMS FOR THEIR MOTHERS. Buffalo: Phinney, 1855.

*17918. EXAMPLES FROM THE EIGHTEENTH AND NINETEENTH CENTURIES ... FIRST SERIES. NY: Scribner, 1857.

17923. LUCY HOWARD'S JOURNAL. NY: Harper & Bros., 1858.

17926. THE DAILY COUNSELLOR. Hartford: Brown & Gross, 1859.

17936. GLEANINGS. Hartford: Brown & Gross, 1860.

17941. THE MAN OF UZ, AND OTHER POEMS. Hartford: Williams, Wiley & Waterman, 1862.

17958. THE TRANSPLANTED DAISY: A MEMOIR OF FRANCES RACILLIA HACKLEY. NY: Ptd by Sanford, Harroun, 1865.

*17960. LETTERS OF LIFE. NY: Appleton, 1866.

Edward Rowland Sill
1841–1887

*17999.   THE HERMITAGE AND OTHER POEMS. NY: Leypoldt & Holt, 1868.

*18013.   THE VENUS OF MILO AND OTHER POEMS. Berkeley, 1883.

*18017.   POEMS. Bos & NY: Houghton, Mifflin, 1888.

*18019.   THE HERMITAGE AND LATER POEMS. Bos & NY: Houghton, Mifflin, 1889.

18024.   HERMIONE AND OTHER POEMS. Bos & NY: Houghton, Mifflin, 1899.

18025.   THE PROSE OF EDWARD ROWLAND SILL. Bos & NY: Houghton, Mifflin, 1900.

18029.   THE POETICAL WORKS ... HOUSEHOLD EDITION. Bos & NY: Houghton, Mifflin, 1906.

18035.   AROUND THE HORN. New Haven: Yale U PR, 1944.
Ed. Stanley T. Williams & Barbara D. Simison. A journal, 10 Dec. 1861 to 25 Mar. 1862.

William Gilmore Simms
1806–1870

18037.   MONODY, ON THE DEATH OF GEN. CHARLES COTESWORTH PINCKNEY. By a South-Carolinian. Charleston: Ptd by Gray & Ellis, 1825.

18038.   LYRICAL AND OTHER POEMS. Charleston: Ellis & Neufville, 1827.

18039.   EARLY LAYS. Charleston: A.E. Miller, 1827.

18040.   THE VISION OF CORTES, CAIN, AND OTHER POEMS. Charleston: Burges, 1829.

18041.   THE TRI-COLOR; OR THE THREE DAYS OF BLOOD, IN PARIS. WITH SOME OTHER PIECES. Lon: Wigfall & Davis, 1830.
Anon.

18043.   ATALANTIS. A STORY OF THE SEA: IN THREE PARTS. NY: J. & J. Harper, 1832.
Anon. For revised edition see No. 18111 below.

18044.   MARTIN FABER; THE STORY OF A CRIMINAL. NY: J. & J. Harper, 1833.
Anon. For revised edition see No. 18059 below.

*18045.   THE BOOK OF MY LADY. A MELANGE. By a Bachelor Knight. Phila: Key & Biddle, 1833.
See No. 18059 below.

18050.   GUY RIVERS: A TALE OF GEORGIA. NY: Harper & Bros., 1834.
2v. Anon. Revised editions published in 1835 (No. 18055) & 1855 (No. 18153).

*18051.   THE YEMASSEE. A ROMANCE OF CAROLINA. NY: Harper & Bros., 1835.
2v. Anon. Revised editions published in 1853 (No. 18140) & 1854. (No. 18152).

18053.   THE PARTISAN: A TALE OF THE REVOLUTION. NY: Harper & Bros., 1835.
2v. Anon. Revised edition published in 1854 (No. 18145).

WILLIAM GILMORE SIMMS (cont.)

18057. MELLICHAMPE. A LEGEND OF THE SANTEE. NY: Harper & Bros., 1836.
2v. Anon. Revised edition published in 1854 (No. 18146).

18059. MARTIN FABER, THE STORY OF A CRIMINAL; AND OTHER TALES. NY: Harper & Bros., 1837.
2v. Anon. Revised & extended texts of *Martin Faber*, 1833, and stories from *The Book of My Lady*, 1833, with 1 new piece.

18060. SLAVERY IN AMERICA, BEING A BRIEF REVIEW OF MISS MARTINEAU ON THAT SUBJECT. By a South Carolinian. Richmond: T. White, 1838.

18061. RICHARD HURDIS; OR, THE AVENGER OF BLOOD. A TALE OF ALABAMA. Phila: Carey & Hart, 1838.
2v. Anon. Revised edition published in 1855 (No. 18154).

18062. CARL WERNER, AN IMAGINATIVE STORY; WITH OTHER TALES OF IMAGINATION. NY: Adlard, 1838.
2v. Anon. Also noted 2v. in one, with binder's title: *Young Ladies Book of Romantic Tales.* The title story reprinted in 1846 as *Matilda: or, the Spectre of the Castle* (No. 18195).

18063. PELAYO: A STORY OF THE GOTH. NY: Harper & Bros., 1838.
2v. Anon.

18064. SOUTHERN PASSAGES AND PICTURES. NY: Adlard, 1839.
Anon.

18065. THE DAMSEL OF DARIEN. Phila: Lea & Blanchard, 1839.
2v. Anon.

18068. BORDER BEAGLES; A TALE OF MISSISSIPPI. Phila: Carey & Hart, 1840.
2v. Anon.

*18069. THE HISTORY OF SOUTH CAROLINA. Charleston: Babcock, 1840.
Slightly revised "second edition" published in 1842 (No. 18080); revised & extended edition in 1860 (No. 18169).

18071. THE KINSMEN: OR THE BLACK RIDERS OF CONGAREE. Phila: Lea & Blanchard, 1841.
2v. Anon. Revised edition published in 1854 as *The Scout or the Black Riders of Congaree* (No. 18148).

18072. CONFESSION; OR, THE BLIND HEART. A DOMESTIC STORY. Phila: Lea & Blanchard, 1841.
2v. Anon. Revised edition published in 1856 (No. 18160).

18075. BEAUCHAMPE, OR THE KENTUCKY TRAGEDY. A TALE OF PASSION. Phila: Lea & Blanchard, 1842.
2v. Anon. Revised edition published in 1856: Vol. 1 as *Charlemont or the Pride of the Village* (No. 18158) & Vol. 2 with the original title (No. 18159).

18082. DONNA FLORIDA. A TALE. Charleston: Burges & James, 1843.
Anon.

18083. THE GEOGRAPHY OF SOUTH CAROLINA. Charleston: Babcock, 1843.
Companion to *The History of South Carolina*, 1840.

WILLIAM GILMORE SIMMS (cont.)

18085. THE PRIMA DONNA: A PASSAGE FROM CITY LIFE. Phila: Godey, 1844.
Lady's Book Extra, No. 1.

*18086. THE LIFE OF FRANCIS MARION. NY: H.G. Langley, 1844.

18087. CASTLE DISMAL: OR, THE BACHELOR'S CHRISTMAS. NY: Burgess, Stringer, 1844.
Anon.

18090. HELEN HALSEY: OR, THE SWAMP STATE OF CONELACHITA. NY: Burgess, Stringer, 1845.

*18093. THE WIGWAM AND THE CABIN ... FIRST SERIES. NY: Wiley & Putnam, 1845.
Anon. *Library of American Books,* No. 4. These sheets also issued in the U.K. in 1845. Reprinted in the U.K., with additional material (by Simms?), in 1848 as *Life in America; or, the Wigwam and the Cabin* (No. 18114). Revised edition published in 1856 (No. 18163).

18094. THE WIGWAM AND THE CABIN ... SECOND SERIES. NY: Wiley & Putnam, 1845.
Anon. *Library of American Books,* No. 12. These sheets reissued in the U.K. in 1846. Revised edition published in 1856 (No. 18163).

18095. VIEWS AND REVIEWS IN AMERICAN LITERATURE, HISTORY AND FICTION ... FIRST SERIES. NY: Wiley & Putnam, 1845.
Anon. *Library of American Books,* No 9.

18096. COUNT JULIAN; OR, THE LAST DAYS OF THE GOTH. Baltimore: W. Taylor, 1845.
Anon.

18097. GROUPED THOUGHTS AND SCATTERED FANCIES. A COLLECTION OF SONNETS. Richmond: MacFarlane, 1845.
Anon.

18100. AREYTOS: OR, SONGS OF THE SOUTH. Charleston: Russell, 1846.

18101. THE LIFE OF CAPTAIN JOHN SMITH. THE FOUNDER OF VIRGINIA. NY: Cooledge & Bro., <1846>.

18104. VIEWS AND REVIEWS IN AMERICAN LITERATURE, HISTORY AND FICTION ... SECOND SERIES. NY: Wiley & Putnam, 1845 <i.e. 1847>.
Anon. Originally planned as part of the *Library of American Books.*

18106. SELF-DEVELOPMENT. AN ORATION. Milledgeville: Thalian Society, 1847.
Delivered before the literary societies of Oglethorpe U, Georgia, 10 Nov. 1847.

18107. THE LIFE OF THE CHEVALIER BAYARD; "THE GOOD KNIGHT." NY: Harper & Bros., 1847.

18111. ATALANTIS; A STORY OF THE SEA. Phila: Carey & Hart, 1848.
Anon. Revised edition of *Atalantis,* 1832, with additional pieces.

18112. CHARLESTON, AND HER SATIRISTS; A SCRIBBLEMENT. By a City Bachelor. Charleston: Burges, 1848.
2 parts.

WILLIAM GILMORE SIMMS (cont.)

18113. LAYS OF THE PALMETTO. Charleston: Russell, 1848.
"A tribute to the South Carolina regiment, in the war with Mexico."

*18116. THE CASSIQUE OF ACCABEE. A TALE OF ASHLEY RIVER. WITH OTHER PIECES. NY: Putnam, 1849.

18117. FATHER ABBOT, OR, THE HOME TOURIST; A MEDLEY. Charleston: Miller & Browne, 1849.

18118. THE LIFE OF NATHANAEL GREENE, MAJOR-GENERAL IN THE ARMY OF THE REVOLUTION. Ed. W. Gilmore Simms. NY: Cooledge & Bro., <1849>.

18120. SABBATH LYRICS; OR, SONGS FROM SCRIPTURE. A CHRISTMAS GIFT OF LOVE. Charleston: Walker & James, 1849.

18121. THE LILY AND THE TOTEM, OR, THE HUGUENOTS IN FLORIDA. NY: Baker & Scribner, 1850.
Anon. Reprinted in 1853 as *The Huguenots in Florida* (No. 18197).

18122. THE CITY OF THE SILENT: A POEM. Charleston: Walker & James, 1850.
Delivered at the consecration of Magnolia Cemetery, 19 Nov. 1850.

18123. FLIRTATION AT THE MOULTRIE HOUSE: IN A SERIES OF LETTERS, FROM MISS GEORGIANA APPLEBY, TO HER FRIENDS IN GEORGIA. Charleston: Councell, 1850.
Anon. Presumed to be by Simms.

18127. KATHARINE WALTON: OR, THE REBEL OF DORCHESTER. Phila: Hart, 1851.
Anon. Revised edition published in 1854(No. 18147).

18128. NORMAN MAURICE; OR, THE MAN OF THE PEOPLE. AN AMERICAN DRAMA. Richmond: J.R. Thompson, 1851.
Revised & extended edition published in 1852 (No. 18135).

18129. THE GOLDEN CHRISTMAS: A CHRONICLE OF ST. JOHN'S, BERKELEY. Charleston: Walker, Richards, 1852.
Anon. "Compiled from the notes of a briefless barrister."

18130. AS GOOD AS A COMEDY: OR, THE TENNESSEEAN'S STORY. By an Editor. Phila: Hart, 1852.
For a critical edition see No. 18191 below.

*18133. THE SWORD AND THE DISTAFF; OR, "FAIR, FAT AND FORTY," A STORY OF THE SOUTH, AT THE CLOSE OF THE REVOLUTION ... SECOND EDITION. Charleston: Walker, Richards, 1852.
Anon. *Earliest located edition.* Reprinted (revised?) edition published in 1854 as *Woodcraft or Hawks about the Dovecote* (No. 18149).

18134. MICHAEL BONHAM: OR, THE FALL OF BEXAR. A TALE OF TEXAS. By a Southron. Richmond: J.R. Thompson, 1852.

WILLIAM GILMORE SIMMS (cont.)

18138. MARIE DE BERNIERE: A TALE OF THE CRESCENT CITY. Phila: Lippincott, 1853.
Reprinted in 1855 as *The Maroon* (No. 18198). The title story published separately in 1866 as *The Ghost of My Husband* (No. 18203).

18139. EGERIA: OR, VOICES OF THOUGHT AND COUNSEL. Phila: Butler, 1853.

18142. SOUTH-CAROLINA IN THE REVOLUTIONARY WAR. By a Southron. Charleston: Walker & James, 1853.

18143. VASCONSELOS A ROMANCE OF THE NEW WORLD. By Frank Cooper. NY: Redfield, 1853.

*18144. POEMS DESCRIPTIVE, DRAMATIC, LEGENDARY AND CONTEMPLATIVE. NY: Redfield, 1853.
2v.

18150. SOUTHWARD HO! A SPELL OF SUNSHINE. NY: Redfield, 1854.

18155. THE FORAYERS OR THE RAID OF THE DOG-DAYS. NY: Redfield, 1855.

18161. EUTAW ... A TALE OF THE REVOLUTION. NY: Redfield, 1856.
Sequel to *The Forayers*.

18166. THE CASSIQUE OF KIAWAH A COLONIAL ROMANCE. NY: Redfield, 1859.

18170. SIMMS'S POEMS AREYTOS OR SONGS AND BALLADS OF THE SOUTH WITH OTHER POEMS. Charleston: Russell & Jones, 1860.

18173. SACK AND DESTRUCTION OF THE CITY OF COLUMBIA, S.C. Columbia: Daily Phoenix Power PR, 1865.
Anon.

18174. WAR POETRY OF THE SOUTH. NY: Richardson, 1866.
Edited, with contributions, by Simms. For full entry see BAL (No. 3723).

18189. THE LETTERS OF WILLIAM GILMORE SIMMS. Columbia SC: U of South Carolina PR, 1952–56.
5v. Ed. Mary C. Simms Oliphant, Alfred Taylor Odell & T.C. Duncan Eaves.

18190. VOLTMEIER OR THE MOUNTAIN MEN. Columbia: U of South Carolina PR, <1969>.
Ed. Donald Davidson & Mary C. Simms Oliphant. *The Writings of William Gilmore Simms, Centennial Edition*, Vol. 1.

18191. AS GOOD AS A COMEDY: OR THE TENNESSEEAN'S STORY. AND PADDY McGANN: OR THE DEMON OF THE STUMP. Columbia: U of South Carolina PR, <1972>.
Ed. Robert Bush. *The Writings of William Gilmore Simms, Centennial Edition*, Vol. 3.

18192. STORIES AND TALES. Columbia: U of South Carolina PR, <1974>.
The Writings of William Gilmore Simms, Centennial Edition, Vol. 5.

18193. JOSCELYN A TALE OF THE REVOLUTION. Columbia: U of South Carolina PR, <1975>.
The Writings of William Gilmore Simms, Centennial Edition, Vol. 16.

Francis Hopkinson Smith
1838–1915

*18206. A BOOK OF THE TILE CLVB. Bos & NY: Houghton Mifflin, 1886.
With Edward Strahan <i.e. Earl Shinn>.

*18207. WELL-WORN ROADS OF SPAIN, HOLLAND, AND ITALY TRAVELED BY A PAINTER IN SEARCH OF THE PICTURESQUE. Bos & NY: Houghton, Mifflin, 1887.
Extended edition published in 1898 (No. 18228).

18209. A WHITE UMBRELLA IN MEXICO. Bos & NY: Houghton, Mifflin, 1889.

*18211. COLONEL CARTER OF CARTERSVILLE. Bos & NY: Houghton, Mifflin, 1891.

*18212. A DAY AT LAGUERRE'S AND OTHER DAYS. Bos & NY: Houghton Mifflin, 1892.

*18213. AMERICAN ILLUSTRATORS. NY: Scribner's Sons, 1892.
5 parts.

*18218. A GENTLEMAN VAGABOND AND SOME OTHERS. Bos & NY: Houghton, Mifflin, 1895.

18220. VENICE OF TO-DAY. NY: H.T. Thomas, 1895.
20 parts. Reprinted in 1897 as *Gondola Days* (No. 18225).

*18221. TOM GROGAN. Bos & NY: Houghton, Mifflin, 1896.

*18227. CALEB WEST MASTER DIVER. Bos & NY: Houghton, Mifflin, 1898.
A copyright printing produced in 1897 (No. 18226).

*18229. THE OTHER FELLOW. Bos & NY: Houghton, Mifflin, 1899.

*18233. THE NOVELS, STORIES AND SKETCHES OF F. HOPKINSON SMITH. NY: Scribner's Sons, 1902–15.
23v. *Beacon Edition.*

*18234. THE FORTUNES OF OLIVER HORN. NY: Scribner's Sons, 1902.

18235. THE UNDER DOG. NY: Scribner's Sons, 1903.

*18236. COLONEL CARTER'S CHRISTMAS. NY: Scribner's Sons, 1903.

18238. AT CLOSE RANGE. NY: Scribner's Sons, 1905.

*18239. THE WOOD FIRE IN NO. 3. NY: Scribner's Sons, 1905.

18242. THE TIDES OF BARNEGAT. NY: Scribner's Sons, 1906.
Originally in *Scribner's Magazine* in 1905–06; the magazine sheets were also issued "for private distribution only" (No. 18241).

18244. THE VEILED LADY AND OTHER MEN AND WOMEN. NY: Scribner's Sons, 1907.

18245. OLD FASHIONED FOLK. Bos, 1907.
Privately printed.

*18246. THE ROMANCE OF AN OLD-FASHIONED GENTLEMAN. NY: Scribner's Sons, 1907.

F. HOPKINSON SMITH (cont.)

18247. PETER A NOVEL OF WHICH HE IS NOT THE HERO. NY: Scribner's Sons, 1908.

18248. CAPTAIN THOMAS A. SCOTT MASTER DIVER. Bos: American Unitarian Assn., 1908.
True American Types, Vol. 5.

18249. FORTY MINUTES LATE AND OTHER STORIES. NY: Scribner's Sons, 1909.

18250. KENNEDY SQUARE. NY: Scribner's Sons, 1911.

18251. THE ARM-CHAIR AT THE INN. NY: Scribner's Sons, 1912.

*18252. CHARCOALS OF NEW AND OLD NEW YORK. Garden City NY: Doubleday, Page, 1912.

*18255. IN THACKERAY'S LONDON. Garden City NY: Doubleday, Page, 1913.

*18258. IN DICKENS'S LONDON. NY: Scribner's Sons, 1914.

18260. OUTDOOR SKETCHING. NY: Scribner's Sons, 1915.
"Four talks given before the Art Institue of Chicago The Scammon Lectures, 1914."

*18261. FELIX O'DAY. NY: Scribner's Sons, 1915.

18263. ENOCH CRANE A NOVEL. NY: Scribner's Sons, 1916.
Completed by F. Berkeley Smith.

Richard Penn Smith
1799–1854

18267. THE EIGHTH OF JANUARY, A DRAMA. Phila: Neal & MacKenzie, 1829.
Adaptation of *Le Maréchal de Luxembourg* by Frédéric Dupetit-Méré & Eugène Cantiran de Boirie.

18271. THE DISOWNED; OR, THE PRODIGALS, A PLAY. Phila: C. Alexander, Ptr, 1830.
Based on *Le Cassier* by Armand Jouslin de la Salle.

18272. THE DEFORMED, OR, WOMAN'S TRIAL, A PLAY. Phila: C. Alexander, Ptr, 1830.
Based on the second part of *The Honest Whore* by Thomas Dekker.

18275. THE FORSAKEN. A TALE. Phila: Grigg, 1831.
2v. Anon.

18277. THE ACTRESS OF PADUA, AND OTHER TALES. Phila: Carey & Hart, 1836.
2v. Anon.

18278. COL. CROCKETT'S EXPLOITS AND ADVENTURES IN TEXAS. By an Eye-Witness. Phila: T.K. & P.G. Collins, 1836.
Almost certainly by Smith.

18283. THE MISCELLANEOUS WORKS OF THE LATE RICHARD PENN SMITH. Phila: H.W. Smith, 1856.
Ed. Horace W. Smith.

RICHARD PENN SMITH (cont.)

18286. THE SENTINELS & OTHER PLAYS. Princeton: Princeton U PR, 1941.
Ed. Ralph H. Ware & H.W. Schoenberger. *America's Lost Plays*, Vol. 13.

18287. CAIUS MARIUS A TRAGEDY. Phila: U of Pennsylvania PR, <1968>.
Ed. Neda McFadden Westlake.

Samuel Francis Smith
1808–1895

18289. CELEBRATION OF AMERICAN INDEPENDENCE BY THE BOSTON
SABBATH SCHOOL UNION ... JULY 4, 1831. <Bos, 1831>.
First publication of "America," here untitled, as the 5th feature of the program.
This hymn was published later in 1831 in sheet music form as "My Country! 'Tis
of Thee" (No. 18291).

18300. LYRIC GEMS: A COLLECTION OF ORIGINAL AND SELECT SACRED
POETRY. Bos: Gould, Kendall & Lincoln, 1844.
Edited, with contributions, by Smith.

18302. LIFE OF THE REV. JOSEPH GRAFTON. Bos: Putnam, 1849.

18328. ROCK OF AGES. ORIGINAL AND SELECTED POEMS. Bos: Lothrop,
<1870>.
Edited, with contributions, by Smith.

18332. MYTHS AND HEROES; OR, THE CHILDHOOD OF THE WORLD. Bos:
Lothrop, <1873>.

18334. KNIGHTS AND SEA-KINGS; OR, THE MIDDLE AGES. Bos: Lothrop, <n.d.,
1874?>.

18343. MISSIONARY SKETCHES: A CONCISE HISTORY OF THE WORK OF THE
AMERICAN BAPTIST MISSIONARY UNION. Bos: Corthell, 1879.
Extended edition published in 1881 (No. 18351). The "fourth edition" of 1885
(No. 18355) was "brought up to date" by E.F. Merriam.

18346. HISTORY OF NEWTON, MASSACHUSETTS. Bos: American Logotype
Co., 1880.

18352. RAMBLES IN MISSION-FIELDS. Bos: Corthell, 1883.

18353. AMERICA. OUR NATIONAL HYMN. Bos: Lothrop, <1884>.
Contains 12 poems in addition to "America." The latter was published separately in this form in 1879 (No. 18342).

18360. DISCOURSE IN MEMORY OF WILLIAM HAGUE. Bos: Lee & Shepard,
1889.

*18371. POEMS OF HOME AND COUNTRY. ALSO, SACRED AND MISCELLANEOUS
VERSE. NY, Bos, &c.: Silver, Burdett, 1895.
Ed. Gen. Henry B. Carrington.

Seba Smith
(Major Jack Downing, John Smith)
1792–1868

18377. THE LIFE AND WRITINGS OF THE MAJOR JACK DOWNING, OF DOWNINGVILLE ... WRITTEN BY HIMSELF. Bos: Lilly, Wait, et al, 1833.
The "third edition" published in 1834 (No. 18378) contains 1 additional letter. A pirated edition of some of this & other material was published in 1833 as *Letters Written during the President's Tour* (Nos. 18376 & 4491); another unauthorized edition published in 1834 as *Select Letters of Major Jack Downing* (Nos. 18379 & 4502).

*18382. JOHN SMITH'S LETTERS. NY: Colman, 1839.

18385. POWHATAN; A METRICAL ROMANCE. NY: Harper & Bros., 1841.

18392. MAY-DAY IN NEW-YORK ... EXPLAINED IN LETTERS TO AUNT KEZIAH. By Major Jack Downing. NY: Burgess, Stringer, 1845.
Reprinted *ca.* 1859 as *Jack Downing's Letters* (No. 18406).

*18400. NEW ELEMENTS OF GEOMETRY. NY: Putnam, 1850.

18402. 'WAY DOWN EAST; OR, PORTRAITURES OF YANKEE LIFE. NY: J.C. Derby, 1854.

18405. MY THIRTY YEARS OUT OF THE SENATE. By Major Jack Downing. NY: Oaksmith, 1859.
Reprints letters from *The Life and Writings*, 1833, and adds new ones.

18407. SPEECH OF JOHN SMITH, ESQUIRE, NOT DELIVERED AT SMITHVILLE SEPT. 15TH, 1864. NY: Bryant, 1864.

William Joseph Snelling
1804–1848

18410. TALES OF THE NORTHWEST; OR, SKETCHES OF INDIAN LIFE AND CHARACTER. By a Resident beyond the Frontier. Bos: Hilliard, Gray, et al, 1830.
Extended edition published in 1936 (No. 18440).

18411. TALES OF TRAVELS WEST OF THE MISSISSIPPI. By Solomon Bell. Bos: Gray & Bowen, 1830.
Tales of Travels, No. 1.

18413. TRUTH: A NEW YEAR'S GIFT FOR SCRIBBLERS. Bos: Ptd by S. Foster, 1831.
Anon. Revised & extended "second edition" published in 1831 (No. 18414) & with further revisions in 1832 (No. 18419).

*18415. THE POLAR REGIONS OF THE WESTERN CONTINENT EXPLORED. Bos: W.W. Reed, 1831.

*18416. TALES OF TRAVELS IN CENTRAL AFRICA. By Solomon Bell. Bos: Gray & Bowen, 1831.
Tales of Travels, No. 2.

WILLIAM J. SNELLING (cont.)

*18417. TALES OF TRAVELS IN THE NORTH OF EUROPE. By Solomon Bell. Bos: Gray & Bowen, 1831.
Tales of Travels, No. 3.

*18418. A BRIEF AND IMPARTIAL HISTORY OF THE LIFE AND ACTIONS OF ANDREW JACKSON. By a Freeman. Bos: Stimpson & Clapp, 1831.

18422. EXPOSÉ OF THE VICE OF GAMING, AS IT LATELY EXISTED IN MASSACHUSETTS. Bos: Snelling, 1833.

18430. THE RAT-TRAP; OR COGITATIONS OF A CONVICT IN THE HOUSE OF CORRECTION. Bos: G.N. Thomson, 1837.
Anon. Slightly revised "second edition" also published in 1837 (No. 18431).

Harriet Prescott Spofford
1835–1921

18441. SIR ROHAN'S GHOST. A ROMANCE. Bos: Tilton, 1860.
Anon.

18442. THE AMBER GODS AND OTHER STORIES. By Harriet Elizabeth Prescott. Bos: Ticknor & Fields, 1863.

18443. AZARIAN: AN EPISODE. By Harriet Elizabeth Prescott. Bos: Ticknor & Fields, 1864.

18452. NEW-ENGLAND LEGENDS. Bos: Osgood, 1871.

*18455. THE THIEF IN THE NIGHT. Bos: Roberts Bros., 1872.

18467. ART DECORATION APPLIED TO FURNITURE. NY: Harper & Bros., 1878.

18472. THE SERVANT GIRL QUESTION. Bos: Houghton, Mifflin, 1881.

18475. POEMS. Bos & NY: Houghton, Mifflin, 1882.

18477. THE MARQUIS OF CARABAS. Bos: Roberts Bros., 1882.

18478. HESTER STANLEY AT ST. MARKS. Bos: Roberts Bros., 1882.

*18486. BALLADS ABOUT AUTHORS. Bos: Lothrop, <1887>.

18501. A LOST JEWEL. Bos: Lee & Shepard, 1891.

18502. HOUSE AND HEARTH. NY: Dodd, Mead, 1891.

18511. A SCARLET POPPY AND OTHER STORIES. NY: Harper Bros., 1894.

*18512. THREE HEROINES OF NEW ENGLAND ROMANCE. Bos: Little Brown, 1894.
With Louise Imogen Guiney & Alice Brown; see No. 6729 above.

18516. A MASTER SPIRIT. NY: Scribner's Sons, 1896.

18519. AN INHERITANCE. NY: Scribner's Sons, 1897.

18520. IN TITIAN'S GARDEN AND OTHER POEMS. Bos: Copeland & Day, 1897.

18522. STEPPING-STONES TO HAPPINESS. NY: Christian Herald, 1897.

18524. PRISCILLA'S LOVE-STORY. Chi & NY: Stone, 1898.

18529. HESTER STANLEY'S FRIENDS. Bos: Little, Brown, 1898.

18531. THE MAID HE MARRIED. Chi & NY: Stone, 1899.

HARRIET PRESCOTT SPOFFORD (cont.)

18534. OLD MADAME & OTHER TRAGEDIES. Bos: Badger, 1900.

*18539. THE CHILDREN OF THE VALLEY. NY: Crowell, <1901>.

18540. THE GREAT PROCESSION AND OTHER VERSES FOR AND ABOUT CHILDREN. Bos: Badger, 1902.
    Arcadian Library, No. 2.

18542. THAT BETTY. NY, Chi, &c.: Revell, <1903>.

18546. FOUR DAYS OF GOD. Bos: Badger, 1905.

18547. OLD WASHINGTON. Bos: Little, Brown, 1906.

18554. THE FAIRY CHANGELING A FLOWER AND FAIRY PLAY. Bos: Badger, 1911.

18555. THE MAKING OF A FORTUNE A ROMANCE. NY & Lon: Harper & Bros., 1911.

18560. A LITTLE BOOK OF FRIENDS. Bos: Little, Brown, 1916.

18561. THE ELDER'S PEOPLE. Bos & NY: Houghton Mifflin, 1920.

Edmund Clarence Stedman
1833–1908

18566. POEMS, LYRICAL AND IDYLLIC. NY: Scribner, 1860.

18567. THE PRINCE'S BALL. A BROCHURE. FROM "VANITY FAIR." NY: Rudd & Carleton, 1860.

18571. THE BATTLE OF BULL RUN. NY: Rudd & Carleton, 1861.

18573. ALICE OF MONMOUTH AN IDYL ... WITH OTHER POEMS. NY: Carleton, 1864.

*18578. A RECONSTRUCTION LETTER. NY, 1866.
    Anon. "Privately printed."

18581. THE BLAMELESS PRINCE, AND OTHER POEMS. Bos: Fields, Osgood, 1869.

18582. RIP VAN WINKLE AND HIS WONDERFUL NAP. Bos: Fields, Osgood, 1870.
    Uncle Sam Series for American Children; the series also issued bound in 1v. as *Brave Ballads for American Children.*

18589. THE POETICAL WORKS ... COMPLETE EDITION. Bos: Osgood, 1873.

18594. VICTORIAN POETS. Bos: Osgood, 1876.
    Revised & extended edition published in 1887 (No. 18636).

18595. OCTAVIUS BROOKS FROTHINGHAM AND THE NEW FAITH. NY: Putnam's Sons, 1876.

18597. HAWTHORNE AND OTHER POEMS. Bos: Osgood, 1877.

18616. EDGAR ALLAN POE. Bos: Houghton, Mifflin, 1881.

*18630. POETS OF AMERICA. Bos & NY: Houghton, Mifflin, 1885.
    1v. or 2v.

EDMUND CLARENCE STEDMAN (cont.)

18638. A LIBRARY OF AMERICAN LITERATURE FROM THE EARLIEST SETTLE-
MENT TO THE PRESENT TIME. NY: Webster, 1888–90.
11v. Edited by Stedman & Ellen Mackay Hutchinson. Vol. 1 was first printed in
1884 (No. 18627), possibly for copyright purposes. A "new edition" published in
1894 (No. 18671).

18658. THE NATURE AND ELEMENTS OF POETRY. Bos & NY: Houghton,
Mifflin, 1892.

*18674. A VICTORIAN ANTHOLOGY 1837–1895. Bos & NY: Houghton, Mifflin,
1895.
Edited by Stedman.

18682. POEMS NOW FIRST COLLECTED. Bos & NY: Houghton, Mifflin, 1897.

*18690. AN AMERICAN ANTHOLOGY 1787–1899. Bos & NY: Houghton, Mifflin,
1900.
Edited by Stedman.

18694. MATER CORONATA. Bos & NY: Houghton, Mifflin, 1901.
Recited at the bicentennial celebration of Yale University, 23 Oct. 1901.

*18716. THE POEMS OF EDMUND CLARENCE STEDMAN. Bos & NY: Houghton
Mifflin, 1908.

18719. LIFE AND LETTERS OF EDMUND CLARENCE STEDMAN. NY: Moffat,
Yard, 1910.
2v. By Laura Stedman & George M. Gould.

18720. GENIUS AND OTHER ESSAYS. NY: Moffat, Yard, 1911.

George Sterling
1869–1926

18744. THE TESTIMONY OF THE SUNS AND OTHER POEMS. SF: W.E. Wood,
1903.
Slightly revised edition published in 1907 (No. 18748). The typescript of the
title poem was published in facsimile in 1927 (No. 18839).

18749. THE TRIUMPH OF BOHEMIA A FOREST PLAY. <n.p. n.d.; SF, 1907?>.
Enacted at the Bohemian Grove, 27 July 1907.

18751. A WINE OF WIZARDRY AND OTHER POEMS. SF: Robertson, 1909.

18756. THE HOUSE OF ORCHIDS AND OTHER POEMS. SF: Robertson, 1911.

18760. BEYOND THE BREAKERS AND OTHER POEMS. SF: Robertson, 1914.

18762. ODE ON THE OPENING OF THE PANAMA-PACIFIC INTERNATIONAL EX-
POSITION SAN FRANCISCO FEBRUARY 1915. SF: Robertson, 1915.

18763. THE EVANESCENT CITY. SF: Robertson, 1915.

18765. YOSEMITE AN ODE. SF: Robertson, 1916.

18767. THE CAGED EAGLE AND OTHER POEMS. SF: Robertson, 1916.

18771. SONGS. SF: Sherman, Clay, <1916>.
With Lawrence Zenda. "Lovingly Dedicated to Nellie Holbrook." Extended edition published in 1928 (No. 18847).

GEORGE STERLING (cont.)

*18772. THE PLAY OF EVERYMAN. SF: Robertson, 1917.
Translation, with Richard Ordynski. "Based on the old English morality play
New version by Hugo von Hofmannstal."

18774. THIRTY-FIVE SONNETS. <n.p., SF>: Book Club of California, <n.d.,
1917>.

18776. THE BINDING OF THE BEAST AND OTHER WAR VERSE. SF: Robertson,
1917.

18788. LILITH A DRAMATIC POEM. SF: Robertson, 1910.
Slightly revised edition published in 1926 (No. 18825).

18790. ROSAMUND A DRAMATIC POEM. SF: Robertson, 1920.

18795. TO A GIRL DANCING. <SF: Ptd by E. & R. Grabhorn>, 1921.

18797. SAILS AND MIRAGE AND OTHER POEMS. SF: Robertson, 1921.
Two pieces from this collection were also printed separately in 1821: "To a Girl
Dancing" (see preceding entry) & "The Cool, Grey City of Love" (No. 18798).

18807. SELECTED POEMS. NY: Holt, 1923.

18809. TRUTH. Chi: The Bookfellows, 1923.
Revised acting version published in 1926 (No. 18826).

18827. STRANGE WATERS. <n.p., n.d.; SF, 1926?>.

18834. ROBINSON JEFFERS THE MAN AND THE ARTIST. NY: Boni & Liveright,
1926.

18840. FIVE POEMS. <n.p., SF?>: Windsor PR, 1927.
"Privately printed."

*18845. SONNETS TO CRAIG. NY: A. & C. Boni, 1928.
Also published with the imprint of Upton Sinclair, Long Beach, CA.

18857. POEMS TO VERA. NY: Oxford U PR, 1938.

*18858. AFTER SUNSET. <SF, 1939>.

18863. GEORGE STERLING A CENTENARY MEMOIR-ANTHOLOGY. South
Brunswick & NY: Barnes, <1969>.
"For the Poetry Society of America." Ed. Charles Angoff.

Frank Richard Stockton
1834–1902

18864. A NORTHERN VOICE FOR THE DISSOLUTION OF THE UNION.
<n.p.>, 1860.
Anon.

18866. TING A LING. NY: Hurd & Houghton, 1870.

18867. ROUND-ABOUT RAMBLES IN LANDS OF FACT AND FANCY. NY: Scribner,
Armstrong, <1872>.

*18868. THE HOME: WHERE IT SHOULD BE AND WHAT TO PUT IN IT. NY:
Putnam & Sons, 1873.
With Marian Stockton. *Putnam's Handy-Book Series.*

FRANK STOCKTON (cont.)

*18869. WHAT MIGHT HAVE BEEN EXPECTED. NY: Dodd & Mead, <1874>.

18870. TALES OUT OF SCHOOL. NY: Scribner, Armstrong, 1876.

*18874. RUDDER GRANGE. NY: Scribner's Sons, 1879.

> Chaps. 1–5 were published in 1878 as part of an "extra" by *Scribner's Monthly* (No. 18872). Extended edition published in 1880 (No. 18875). Reprinted in 1886 with *Stockton's Stories First Series* at head of title (No. 18951).

18876. A JOLLY FELLOWSHIP. NY: Scribner's Sons, 1880.

18877. THE FLOATING PRINCE AND OTHER FAIRYTALES. NY: Scribner's Sons, 1881.

18880. THE LADY, OR THE TIGER? AND OTHER STORIES. NY: Scribner's Sons, 1884.

> The U.K. edition published in 1884 (No. 18882) contains 3 stories not in the U.S. edition.

18881. THE STORY OF VITEAU. NY: Scribner's Sons, 1884.

*18884. THE LATE MRS NULL. NY: Scribner's Sons, 1886.

18885. THE CHRISTMAS WRECK AND OTHER STORIES. NY: Scribner's Sons, 1886.

> At head of title: *Stockton's Stories Second Series*.

*18887. THE CASTING AWAY OF MRS. LECKS AND MRS. ALESHINE. NY: Century Co., <1886>.

*18888. THE BEE-MAN OF ORN AND OTHER FANCIFUL TALES. NY: Scribner's Sons, 1887.

> An earlier version of the title story & "Prince Hassak's March" were first published in 1883 in the "holiday issue" of *St. Nicholas* (No. 18878).

*18889. THE HUNDREDTH MAN. NY: Century Co., <1887>.

18891. THE DUSANTES. NY: Century Co., <1888>.

> Sequel to *The Casting Away of Mrs. Lecks and Mrs. Aleshine*.

*18892. AMOS KILBRIGHT HIS ADSCITITIOUS EXPERIENCES WITH OTHER STORIES. NY: Scribner's Sons, 1888.

18894. THE GREAT WAR SYNDICATE. Lon: Longmans, Green, 1889.

18895. THE GREAT WAR SYNDICATE. NY: Collier, 1889.

*18896. PERSONALLY CONDUCTED. NY: Scribner's Sons, 1889.

*18898. THE STORIES OF THE THREE BURGLARS. NY: Dodd, Mead, <1889>.

*18900. THE MERRY CHANTER. NY: Century Co., <1890>.

> *The Century Series*.

*18902. ARDIS CLAVERDEN. NY: Dodd, Mead, <1890>.

18903. THE COSMIC BEAN; OR, THE GREAT SHOW IN KOBOL-LAND. Lon: Black & White Pub. Co., 1891.

> Later London edition also published in 1891 as *The Great Show in Kobol-Land* (No. 18953).

*18904. THE RUDDER GRANGERS ABROAD AND OTHER STORIES. NY: Scribner's Sons, 1891.

FRANK STOCKTON (cont.)

*18906. THE SQUIRREL INN. NY: Century Co., 1891.

18907. THE HOUSE OF MARTHA. Bos & NY: Houghton, Mifflin, 1891.

18908. MY TERMINAL MORAINE. NY: Collier, 1892.
   Once a Week Library, Vol. 9, No. 2, 26 April 1892.

*18910. THE CLOCKS OF RONDAINE AND OTHER STORIES. NY: Scribner's Sons, 1892.

18912. THE WATCHMAKER'S WIFE AND OTHER STORIES. NY: Scribner's Sons, 1893.

*18917. POMONA'S TRAVELS. <NY>: Scribner's Sons, <1894>.

*18920. THE ADVENTURES OF CAPTAIN HORN. NY: Scribner's Sons, 1895.

18922. STORIES OF NEW JERSEY. NY, Cincinnati, &c.: American Book Co., 1896.
   Republished in 1896 as *Stories from American History New Jersey* (No. 18957).

18923. MRS. CLIFF'S YACHT. NY: Scribner's Sons, 1896.

18925. CAPTAIN CHAP OR THE ROLLING STONES. Phila: Lippincott, 1897.

*18926. A STORY-TELLER'S PACK. NY: Scribner's Sons, 1897.

18929. THE GREAT STONE OF SARDIS A NOVEL. NY & Lon: Harper & Bros., 1898.

*18930. THE GIRL AT COBHURST. NY: Scribner's Sons, 1898.

*18931. BUCCANEERS AND PIRATES OF OUR COASTS. NY: Macmillan, 1898.

*18933. THE ASSOCIATE HERMITS. NY & Lon: Harper & Bros., 1899.

*18934. THE VIZIER OF THE TWO-HORNED ALEXANDER. NY: Century Co., 1899.

*18936. THE NOVELS AND STORIES OF FRANK R. STOCKTON. NY: Scribner's Sons, 1899–1904.
   23v. *Shenandoah Edition.*

18937. THE YOUNG MASTER OF HYSON HALL. Phila: Lippincott, 1900.

18938. AFIELD AND AFLOAT. NY: Scribner's Sons, 1900.

18939. A BICYCLE OF CATHAY A NOVEL. NY & Lon: Harper & Bros., 1900.

*18943. KATE BONNET THE ROMANCE OF A PIRATE'S DAUGHTER. NY: Appleton, 1902.

18944. JOHN GAYTHER'S GARDEN AND THE STORIES TOLD THEREIN. NY: Scribner's Sons, 1902.

*18945. THE CAPTAIN'S TOLL-GATE. NY: Appleton, 1903.
   "With a memorial sketch by Mrs. Stockton and a bibliography."

18948. THE LOST DRYAD. Riverside CT: United Workers of Greenwich, 1912.

18950. THE POOR COUNT'S CHRISTMAS. NY: Stokes, 1927.

Charles Warren Stoddard
1843–1909

18971. POEMS. SF: Roman, 1867.

18979. SOUTH-SEA IDYLS. Bos: Osgood, 1873.
The U.K. edition, with new preface and 1 additional piece, published in 1874 as *Summer Cruising in the South Seas* (No. 18980). Further extended edition published in 1892 (No. 18999).

18987. MASHALLAH! A FLIGHT INTO EGYPT. NY: Appleton, 1881.
Appletons' New Handy-Volume Series.

18992. A TRIP TO HAWAII. <SF: Oceanic Steamship Co., 1885>.

18993. A TROUBLED HEART AND HOW IT WAS COMFORTED AT LAST. Notre Dame: Lyons, 1885.
Anon.

*18994. THE LEPERS OF MOLOKAI. Notre Dame: Ave Maria PR, <1885, i.e. 1886>.
Extended edition published in 1909 (No. 19018).

19002. HAWAIIAN LIFE BEING LAZY LETTERS FROM LOW LATITUDES. Chi & NY: Neely, 1894.
Neely's Library of Choice Literature, No. 31, April 1894.

*19004. THE WONDER-WORKER OF PADUA. Notre Dame: Ave Maria <PR>, <1896>.

19006. A CRUISE UNDER THE CRESCENT FROM SUEZ TO SAN MARCO. Chi & NY: Rand, McNally, <1898>.

19007. OVER THE ROCKY MOUNTAINS TO ALASKA. St. Louis: Herder, 1899.

19010. FATHER DAMIEN THE MARTYR OF MOLOKAI. SF: Catholic Truth Soc'y, 1901.

19011. IN THE FOOTPRINTS OF THE PADRES. SF: Robertson, 1902.
Extended edition published in 1912 (No. 19022).

19012. EXITS AND ENTRANCES A BOOK OF ESSAYS AND SKETCHES. Bos: Lothrop, <1903>.

19013. FOR THE PLEASURE OF HIS COMPANY. SF: Robertson, 1903.

19014. THE ISLAND OF TRANQUIL DELIGHTS A SOUTH SEA IDYL AND OTHERS. Bos: Turner, 1904.

19019. THE PASSION PLAY AT BRIXLEG. Notre Dame: Ave Maria PR, <n.d., 1909>.

19024. POEMS. NY: Lane, 1917.
Ed. Ina Coolbrith.

19027. CHARLES WARREN STODDARD'S DIARY OF A VISIT TO MOLOKAI IN 1884. SF: Book Club of California, 1933.

Elizabeth Drew Barstow Stoddard
1823–1902

*19028. THE MORGESONS. NY: Carleton, 1862.
Revised edition published in 1889 (No. 19039). See also No. 19049 below.

 19030. TWO MEN. A NOVEL. NY: Bunce & Huntington, 1865.
Revised edition published in 1888 (No. 19037).

 19031. TEMPLE HOUSE. A NOVEL. NY: Carleton, <1867>.
Revised edition published in 1888 (No. 19038).

*19034. LOLLY DINKS'S DOINGS. By his Mother, Old Mrs. Dinks. Bos: Gill, 1874.
Little Folk Life Series.

 19043. POEMS. Bos & NY: Houghton, Mifflin, 1895.

 19049. THE MORGESONS AND OTHER WRITINGS, PUBLISHED AND UNPUBLISHED. Phila: U of Pennsylvania PR, 1984.
Ed. Lawrence Buell & Sandra A. Zagarell.

Richard Henry Stoddard
1825–1903

 19050. FOOT-PRINTS. NY: Spalding & Shepard, 1849.

 19057. POEMS. Bos: Ticknor, Reed, & Fields, 1852.

 19060. ADVENTURES IN FAIRY-LAND. Bos: Ticknor, Reed, & Fields, 1853.

 19069. TOWN AND COUNTRY, AND THE VOICES IN THE SHELLS. NY: Dix, Edwards, 1857.

 19070. SONGS OF SUMMER. Bos: Ticknor & Fields, 1857.

*19072. THE LIFE TRAVELS AND BOOKS OF ALEXANDER VON HUMBOLDT. NY: Rudd & Carleton, 1859.
Anon, but signed *R.H.S.* at end of text. These sheets also issued in the U.K.

*19081. THE KING'S BELL. NY: Carleton, 1863.

*19087. THE STORY OF LITTLE RED RIDING HOOD, TOLD IN VERSE. NY: Gregory, <1864>.

 19091. ABRAHAM LINCOLN. AN HORATIAN ODE. NY: Bunce & Huntington, <1865>.

 19095. THE CHILDREN IN THE WOOD TOLD IN VERSE. NY: Hurd & Houghton, 1866.

*19106. THE STORY OF PUTNAM THE BRAVE. Bos: Fields, Osgood, 1870.
Uncle Sam Series for American Children; the series also issued bound in 1v. as *Brave Ballads for American Children.*

 19109. THE BOOK OF THE EAST, AND OTHER POEMS. Bos: Osgood, 1871.

 19167. THE POEMS...COMPLETE EDITION. NY: Scribner's Sons, 1880.

 19180. HENRY WADSWORTH LONGFELLOW. A MEDLEY IN PROSE AND VERSE. NY: Harlan, 1882.

RICHARD HENRY STODDARD (cont.)

19183. THE LIFE OF WASHINGTON IRVING. NY: Alden, <1883>.
The Elzevir Library, Vol. 1, No. 4, 12 Jan. 1883. Originally published in 1879 as part of the unauthorized *Kaaterskill Edition* of Washington Irving's works (No. 19162).

19213. THE LION'S CUB WITH OTHER VERSE. NY: Scribner's Sons, 1890.

19219. UNDER THE EVENING LAMP. NY: Scribner's Sons, 1892.

*19237. RECOLLECTIONS PERSONAL AND LITERARY. NY: Barnes, 1903.
Ed. Ripley Hitchcock.

William Wetmore Story
1819–1895

19243. ADDRESS DELIVERED BEFORE THE HARVARD MUSICAL ASSOCIATION... CAMBRIDGE, AUGUST 24TH, 1842. Bos: Ptd by S.N. Dickinson, 1842.
"Printed at the request of The Society."

*19245. NATURE AND ART; A POEM. Bos: Little & Brown, 1844.
Delivered before the Phi Beta Kappa Society, Harvard University, 29 Aug. 1844.

19249. POEMS. Bos: Little & Brown, 1847.

19253. POEMS. Bos: Little, Brown, 1856.
These sheets reissued in London in 1863.

19255. THE AMERICAN QUESTION. Lon: Manwaring, 1862.
"Reprinted, by permission," from *The Daily News.*

19257. ROBA DI ROMA. Lon: Chapman & Hall, 1863.
2v. Revised & extended editions are the "third edition" published in 1864 (19260), "fifth edition" in 1866 (Nos. 19266 & 19267), "sixth edition" in 1871 (No. 19274) & "eighth edition" in 1887 (No. 19313). For U.S. edition see next entry.

19261. ROBA DI ROMA...FOURTH EDITION. Lon: Chapman & Hall; NY: Appleton, 1864.
2v. First U.S. edition.

19262. THE PROPORTIONS OF THE HUMAN FIGURE. Lon: Chapman & Hall, 1864.
Extended edition published in 1866 (No. 19265)

*19268. GRAFFITI D'ITALIA. Edinburgh & Lon: Blackwood & Sons, 1868.

*19269. GRAFFITI D'ITALIA. NY: Scribner, 1868.

*19272. A ROMAN LAWYER IN JERUSALEM. FIRST CENTURY. Bos: Loring, <n.d., 1870>.
"Reprinted from Blackwood."

19277. NERO. Edinburgh & Lon: Blackwood & Sons, 1875.

19278. NERO AN HISTORICAL PLAY. Edinburgh & Lon: Blackwood & Sons; NY: Scribner, Welford & Armstrong, 1875.

19284. STEPHANIA A TRAGEDY. Edinburgh & Lon: Blackwood & Sons, <n.d., 1876>.
"For private circulation only."

WILLIAM WETMORE STORY (cont.)

19286. CASTLE ST. ANGELO AND THE EVIL EYE. Lon: Chapman & Hall, 1877.
Additional chapters to *Roba di Roma*.

19287. CASTLE ST. ANGELO AND THE EVIL EYE. Lon: Chapman & Hall; Phila:
Lippincott, 1877.

19288. ODE ON THE ANNIVERSARY ... OF THE LANDING OF GOV. JOHN
ENDICOTT. Salem: Salem PR, 1878.
Delivered at the Essex Institute, 18 Sept. 1878. Revised & extended text pub-
lished in *The Fifth Half Century of the Landing of John Endicott*, 1879 (No. 19297).

19292. SECOND THOUGHTS. A COMEDY. NY, 1878.

19293. "STALE MATE." By W.W.S. NY, 1878.

19303. VALLOMBROSA. Edinburgh & Lon: Blackwood & Sons, 1881.

19307. HE AND SHE OR A POET'S PORTFOLIO. Bos & NY: Houghton, Mifflin,
1884.

19308. POEMS. Bos & NY: Houghton, Mifflin, 1886.
2v.: *Parchments and Portraits* and *Monologues and Lyrics*. These sheets also issued in
the U.K. with title-page dated 1885.

19309. FIAMMETTA A SUMMER IDYL. Edinburgh & Lon: Blackwood & Sons,
1886.

*19310. FIAMMETTA A SUMMER IDYL. Bos & NY: Houghton, Mifflin, 1886.

*19315. CONVERSATIONS IN A STUDIO. Bos & NY: Houghton, Mifflin, 1890.
2v.

19316. EXCURSIONS IN ART AND LETTERS. Bos & NY: Houghton, Mifflin,
1891.

19318. A POET'S PORTFOLIO LATER READINGS. Bos & NY: Houghton,
Mifflin, 1894.

*19320. WILLIAM WETMORE STORY AND HIS FRIENDS FROM LETTERS, DIARIES,
AND RECOLLECTIONS. Bos: Houghton, Mifflin, 1903.
By Henry James, see No. 10655 above.
2v.

Harriet Beecher Stowe
1811–1896

19323. PRIMARY GEOGRAPHY FOR CHILDREN. By C. & H. Beecher.
Cincinnati: Corey & Fairbank, 1833.
With Catharine E. Beecher. See also No. 19377 below.

19324. A NEW ENGLAND SKETCH. Lowell: A. Gilman, 1834.
At head of title: *Prize Tale.*

19335. THE MAYFLOWER; OR, SKETCHES OF SCENES AND CHARACTERS
AMONG THE DESCENDANTS OF THE PILGRIMS. NY: Harper & Bros.,
1843.
For extended edition see No. 19378 below.

HARRIET BEECHER STOWE (cont.)

19343. UNCLE TOM'S CABIN; OR, LIFE AMONG THE LOWLY. Bos: Jewett, 1852.
2v. For comment on early U.K. editions see BAL (No. 19518). For dramatization by Stowe see No. 19383 below.

*19345. EARTHLY CARE, A HEAVENLY DISCIPLINE. Bos: Jewett, 1853 <i.e. 1852>.

19346. THE TWO ALTARS; OR, TWO PICTURES IN ONE. <Bos: Jewett, 1852>.
Liberty Tracts, No. 1.

*19356. A KEY TO UNCLE TOM'S CABIN. Lon: Low, Son; Clarke, Beeton; Bosworth, 1853.
Published simultaneously in the U.K. in 3 editions (see also Nos. 19357 & 19358).

*19359. A KEY TO UNCLE TOM'S CABIN. Bos: Jewett, 1853.
These sheets reissued anonymously with undated title-page: *Facts for the People. Southern Life: or, Inside Views of Slavery.*

19360. UNCLE SAM'S EMANCIPATION; EARTHLY CARE, A HEAVENLY DISCIPLINE; AND OTHER SKETCHES. Phila: Hazard, 1853.
The U.K. edition, with additional material, also published in 1853 (No. 19363).

19374. SUNNY MEMORIES OF FOREIGN LANDS. Lon: Low, Son, 1854.
2v.

19375. SUNNY MEMORIES OF FOREIGN LANDS. Bos: Phillips, Sampson, 1854.
2v.

*19377. FIRST GEOGRAPHY FOR CHILDREN. Bos: Phillips, Sampson, 1855.
Ed. Catharine E. Beecher. Based in part on No. 19323 above.

19378. THE MAY FLOWER, AND MISCELLANEOUS WRITINGS. Bos: Phillips, Sampson, 1855.
The U.K. edition published as *Tales and Sketches of New England Life* (No. 19539).

*19383. THE CHRISTIAN SLAVE. A DRAMA. Bos: Phillips, Sampson, 1855.
Based on *Uncle Tom's Cabin.* Dramatized by Stowe for Mary E. Webb.

*19387. DRED; A TALE OF THE GREAT DISMAL SWAMP. Lon: Low, Son, 1856.
2v. Also published simultaneously in 1v. (No. 19388).

*19389. DRED; A TALE OF THE GREAT DISMAL SWAMP. Bos: Phillips, Sampson, 1856.
2v.

19401. OUR CHARLEY, AND WHAT TO DO WITH HIM. Bos: Phillips, Sampson, 1858.
The title story also published in 1859 as *What Is to Be Done with Our Charlie?* (No. 19408).

*19405. THE MINISTER'S WOOING. Lon: Low, Son, 1859.
Unillustrated, 16 Nos. in eleven. Also published simultaneously in an illustrated edition, 14 parts in ten (No 19406). Both editions also issued in 1v.

*19407. THE MINISTER'S WOOING. NY: Derby & Jackson, 1859.

19416. AGNES OF SORRENTO. Lon: Smith, Elder, 1862.

HARRIET BEECHER STOWE (cont.)

*19417. THE PEARL OF ORR'S ISLAND: A STORY OF THE COAST OF MAINE. Lon: Low, Son, 1862.
1v. Also published in 2 parts: Part 1 in 1861 (No. 19412), Part 2 in 1862 (No. 19419).

19418. AGNES OF SORRENTO. Bos: Ticknor & Fields, 1862.

19420. THE PEARL OF ORR'S ISLAND: A STORY OF THE COAST OF MAINE. Bos: Ticknor & Fields, 1862.

*19423. A REPLY TO "THE AFFECTIONATE AND CHRISTIAN ADDRESS OF MANY THOUSANDS OF WOMEN ... " Lon: Low, Son, 1863.
63 pp. Also published (simultaneously?) in 24pp. (No. 19424).

19433. HOUSE AND HOME PAPERS. By Christopher Crowfield. Bos: Ticknor & Fields, 1865.

19434. STORIES ABOUT OUR DOGS. Edinburgh: Nimmo, <n.d., 1865>.
Nimmo's Sixpenny NY Juvenile Series. "Anecdotes of Dogs," pp. <59>–70, presumably not by Stowe.

*19439. LITTLE FOXES. Lon: Bell & Daldy, 1866.
Published simultaneously in 2 editions: 188pp. (No. 19439) & 133pp. (No. 19440).

19441. LITTLE FOXES. By Christopher Crowfield. Bos: Ticknor & Fields, 1866.

19443. RELIGIOUS POEMS. Bos: Ticknor & Fields, 1867.

19444. THE DAISY'S FIRST WINTER, AND OTHER STORIES. Edinburgh: Nimmo, <n.d., 1867>.
Nimmo's One Shilling Juvenile Books, No. 11.

19445. QUEER LITTLE PEOPLE. Bos: Ticknor & Fields, 1867.
Extended edition published in 1881 (No. 19498).

19447. THE CHIMNEY-CORNER. Lon: Low, Son, & Marston, 1868.

19448. THE CHIMNEY-CORNER. By Christopher Crowfield. Bos: Ticknor & Fields, 1868.

*19449. MEN OF OUR TIMES; OR LEADING PATRIOTS OF THE DAY. Hartford: Hartford Pub. Co., 1868.
"Published by subscription only." Extended edition published in 1872 as *The Lives and Deeds of Our Self-Made Men* (No. 19473).

19451. OLDTOWN FOLKS. Lon: Low, Son, & Marston, 1869.
3v.

*19452. OLDTOWN FOLKS. Bos: Fields, Osgood, 1869.

*19453. THE AMERICAN WOMAN'S HOME: OR, PRINCIPLES OF DOMESTIC SCIENCE. NY: Ford, 1869.
With Catharine E. Beecher. Abridged edition published in 1870 as *Principles of Domestic Science* (No. 19458); revised edition in 1873 as *The New Housekeeper's Manual* (No. 19477).

*19456. LADY BYRON VINDICATED. A HISTORY OF THE BYRON CONTROVERSY. Bos: Fields, Osgood, 1870.

HARRIET BEECHER STOWE (cont.)

19459. LITTLE PUSSY WILLOW. Bos: Fields, Osgood, 1870.
Extended edition published in 1880 (No. 19496).

19460. PINK AND WHITE TYRANNY. Lon: Low, Son, & Marston, 1871.

*19461. PINK AND WHITE TYRANNY. A SOCIETY NOVEL. Bos: Roberts Bros., 1871.

19462. MY WIFE AND I: OR, HARRY HENDERSON'S HISTORY. NY: Ford, 1871.
Slightly revised edition published in 1872 (No. 19474).

*19463. OLDTOWN FIRESIDE STORIES. Lon: Low, Marston, et al, 1871.

19467. OLDTOWN FIRESIDE STORIES. Bos: Osgood, 1872.
Extended editions, with title *Sam Lawson's Oldtown Fireside Stories,* published in 1872 (No. 19469) & 1881 (No. 19497).

19476. PALMETTO-LEAVES. Bos: Osgood, 1873.

19478. WOMAN IN SACRED HISTORY. Lon: Low, Marston, et al, 1874.
Contains 19 sketches.

*19479. WOMAN IN SACRED HISTORY. NY: Ford, 1874.
Contains 19 sketches. Also (later?) published in an extended edition with 25 sketches (No. 19480). The shorter version reprinted in 1878 as *Bible Heroines* (No. 19562).

19482. WE AND OUR NEIGHBORS OR THE RECORDS OF AN UNFASHIONABLE STREET. Lon: Low, Marston, et al, 1875.

*19483. WE AND OUR NEIGHBORS: OR, THE RECORDS OF AN UNFASHIONABLE STREET. NY: Ford, <1875>.
Sequel to *My Wife and I.*

*19484. BETTY'S BRIGHT IDEA. ALSO, DEACON PITKIN'S FARM, AND THE FIRST CHRISTMAS OF NEW ENGLAND. NY: Ford, 1876.

19486. FOOTSTEPS OF THE MASTER. NY: Ford, 1877.

*19488. POGANUC PEOPLE: THEIR LOVES AND LIVES. NY: Fords, Howard, & Hulbert, <1878>.

19495. A DOG'S MISSION ... AND OTHER STORIES. NY: Fords, Howard, & Hulbert, <1880>.
These sheets reissued in 1885 by Houghton, Mifflin, Boston & New York.

19506. LIFE OF HARRIET BEECHER STOWE. Bos & NY: Houghton, Mifflin, 1889.
Ed. Charles Edward Stowe & Kirk Munroe.

*19508. THE WRITINGS OF HARRIET BEECHER STOWE. Bos & NY: Houghton, Mifflin, 1896.
16v.

*19509. LIFE AND LETTERS OF HARRIET BEECHER STOWE. Bos & NY: Houghton, Mifflin, 1897.
Ed. Annie Fields.

HARRIET BEECHER STOWE (cont.)
19513. COLLECTED POEMS. Hartford: Transcendental Book Drawer, <1967>.
Ed. John Michael Moran, Jr.

John Banister Tabb
1845–1909

19583. POEMS. <n.p., n.d.; Baltimore, 1882>.

19587. AN OCTAVE TO MARY. Baltimore: Murphy, 1893.

*19589. POEMS. Bos: Copeland & Day, 1894.

*19591. LYRICS. Bos: Copeland & Day, 1897.

19592. BONE RULES; OR, SKELETON OF ENGLISH GRAMMAR. NY, Cinc, &c: Benziger Bros., 1897.
Revised edition published in 1901 (No. 19597).

19593. CHILD VERSE POEMS GRAVE & GAY. Bos: Small, Maynard, 1899.

*19596. TWO LYRICS. <Bos, 1900>.

19598. LATER LYRICS. Lon & NY: Lane, 1902.

19599. THE ROSARY IN RHYME. <Bos: Small, Maynard>, 1904.

19601. A SELECTION FROM THE VERSES OF JOHN B. TABB. Lon: Burns & Oates, <n.d., 1906>.
Ed. Alice Meynell. Extended edition published in 1910 (No. 19608).

*19603. A SELECTION FROM THE VERSES OF JOHN B. TABB. NY: Longmans, Green, 1907.
Ed. Alice Meynell.

19604. QUIPS AND QUIDDITS QUES FOR THE <Q>URIOUS. Bos: Small Maynard, 1907.

19609. LATER POEMS. Lon: Burns & Oates, 1910.

19610. LATER POEMS. NY: Kennerley, 1910.

19613. FATHER TABB HIS LIFE AND WORK A MEMORIAL. Bos: Stratford, 1921.
By Jennie Masters Tabb.

19615. FATHER TABB A STUDY OF HIS LIFE AND WORKS. Balt: Johns Hopkins PR, 1923.
By Francis A. Litz.

19617. THE POETRY OF FATHER TABB. NY: Dodd, Mead, 1928.
Ed. Francis A. Litz.

19622. LETTERS—GRAVE AND GAY AND OTHER PROSE. Wash DC: Catholic U of America PR, 1950.
Ed. Francis E. Litz.

Bayard Taylor
1825–1878

Note: Copies of many of Taylor's works published by Putnam were issued in the 1850s and 1860s in uniform bindings to form sets of *Bayard Taylor's Travels* or *Bayard Taylor's Prose Writings.*

19625. XIMENA; OR THE BATTLE OF THE SIERRA MORENA, AND OTHER POEMS. By James Bayard Taylor. Phila: Hooker, 1844.

*19626. VIEWS A-FOOT; OR EUROPE SEEN WITH KNAPSACK AND STAFF. By J. Bayard Taylor. NY: Wiley & Putnam, 1846.
2 parts or 1v. *Library of American Books,* Nos. 23–24. Revised & extended editions published in 1848 (No. 19631), 1855 (No. 19652) & 1869 (No. 19708).

19634. RHYMES OF TRAVEL, BALLADS AND POEMS. NY: Putnam, 1849.

*19638. ELDORADO, OR, ADVENTURES IN THE PATH OF EMPIRE. NY: Putnam, 1850.
2v. These sheets reissued in the U.K. in 1852 as *Adventures and Life in San Francisco* (No. 19798).

19639. THE AMERICAN LEGEND. A POEM. Cambridge: Bartlett, 1850.
Delivered at the Phi Beta Kappa Society, Harvard University, 18 July 1850.

19643. A BOOK OF ROMANCES, LYRICS, AND SONGS. Bos: Ticknor, Reed, & Fields, 1852.

19646. A JOURNEY TO CENTRAL AFRICA. NY: Putnam, 1854.
The U.K. edition published as *Life and Landscapes from Egypt to the Negro Kingdoms of the White Nile* (No. 19799).

19647. POEMS OF THE ORIENT. Bos: Ticknor & Fields, 1855.

*19648. THE LANDS OF THE SARACEN. NY: Putnam, 1855.
The U.K. edition published as *Pictures of Palestine.*

19650. A VISIT TO INDIA, CHINA, AND JAPAN, IN THE YEAR 1853. NY: Putnam, 1855.

19651. POEMS OF HOME AND TRAVEL. Bos: Ticknor & Fields, 1855.

19661. NORTHERN TRAVEL. SUMMER AND WINTER PICTURES OF SWEDEN, LAPLAND, AND NORWAY. Lon: Low, Son, 1858.

*19662. NORTHERN TRAVEL: SUMMER AND WINTER PICTURES OF SWEDEN, DENMARK AND LAPLAND. NY: Putnam, 1858.

19663. TRAVELS IN GREECE AND RUSSIA, WITH AN EXCURSION TO CRETE. NY: Putnam, 1859.

*19666. AT HOME AND ABROAD: A SKETCH-BOOK OF LIFE, SCENERY, AND MEN. NY: Putnam, 1860.

*19679. AT HOME AND ABROAD: A SKETCH-BOOK OF LIFE, SCENERY AND MEN ... SECOND SERIES. NY: Putnam, 1862.

19682. THE POET'S JOURNAL. Bos: Ticknor & Fields, 1863.

19684. HANNAH THURSTON: A STORY OF AMERICAN LIFE. NY: Putnam, 1863.

BAYARD TAYLOR (cont.)

19691. JOHN GODFREY'S FORTUNES; RELATED BY HIMSELF. Lon: Low, Son, & Marston, 1864.
3v.

19692. JOHN GODFREY'S FORTUNES; RELATED BY HIMSELF. A STORY OF AMERICAN LIFE. NY: Putnam, 1864.

19695. THE POEMS OF BAYARD TAYLOR. Bos: Ticknor & Fields, 1865.

*19698. THE STORY OF KENNETT. NY: Putnam, 1866.

19699. THE PICTURE OF ST. JOHN. Bos: Ticknor & Fields, 1866.

19702. COLORADO: A SUMMER TRIP. NY: Putnam & Son, 1867.

19705. BYEWAYS OF EUROPE. Lon: Low, Son, & Marston, 1869.
2v.

19706. BY-WAYS OF EUROPE. NY: Putnam & Son, 1869.

19712. THE BALLAD OF ABRAHAM LINCOLN. Bos: Fields, Osgood, 1870.
Uncle Sam Series for American Children; the series also issued bound in 1v. as *Brave Ballads for American Children.*

*19713. JOSEPH AND HIS FRIEND: A STORY OF PENNSYLVANIA. NY: Putnam & Sons, 1870.

*19720. FAUST A TRAGEDY BY JOHANN WOLFGANG VON GOETHE THE FIRST PART. Bos: Fields, Osgood, 1871.
"Translated, in the original metres." Extracts were also published in 1871 to accompany Paul Konewka's illustrations (No. 19721).

*19722. FAUST A TRAGEDY BY JOHANN WOLFGANG VON GOETHE THE SECOND PART. Bos: Osgood, 1871.
"Translated, in the original metres."

*19727. BEAUTY AND THE BEAST: AND TALES OF HOME. NY: Putnam & Sons, 1872.
Some copies issued in *Putnams' Library of Choice Reading.*

19728. THE MASQUE OF THE GODS. Bos: Osgood, 1872.

*19732. DIVERSIONS OF THE ECHO CLUB. Lon: Hotten, <n.d., 1872?>.
Anon. For U.S. edition, containing additional material, see No. 19758 below.

19736. LARS A PASTORAL OF NORWAY. Lon: Strahan, 1873.

19737. LARS: A PASTORAL OF NORWAY. Bos: Osgood, 1873.

19746. THE PROPHET: A TRAGEDY. Bos: Osgood, 1874.

*19748. EGYPT AND ICELAND IN THE YEAR 1874. NY: Putnam's Sons, 1874.

19749. A SCHOOL HISTORY OF GERMANY: FROM THE EARLIEST PERIOD TO ... 1871. NY: Appleton, 1874.
Reprinted, with an additional chapter by Marie Hansen-Taylor, in 1894 (No. 19824).

19753. HOME PASTORALS, BALLADS AND LYRICS. Bos: Osgood, 1875.

19758. THE ECHO CLUB, AND OTHER LITERARY DIVERSIONS. Bos: Osgood, 1876.
Extended edition published in 1895 (No. 19785).

BAYARD TAYLOR (cont.)

*19761. BOYS OF OTHER COUNTRIES STORIES FOR AMERICAN BOYS. NY: Putnam's Sons, 1876.
Extended edition published in 1901 (No. 19789).

19762. THE NATIONAL ODE. JULY 4, 1876. <Bos: Osgood, 1876>.
First separate edition. BAL lists 5 other printings of this piece in 1876 (No. 19757).

19767. PRINCE DEUKALION. Bos: Houghton, Osgood, 1878.

*19774. STUDIES IN GERMAN LITERATURE. NY: Putnam's Sons, 1879.

19776. THE POETICAL WORKS OF BAYARD TAYLOR. HOUSEHOLD EDITION. Bos: Houghton, Osgood, 1880.

19777. CRITICAL ESSAYS AND LITERARY NOTES. NY: Putnam's Sons, 1880.

19780. LIFE AND LETTERS OF BAYARD TAYLOR. Bos & NY: Houghton, Mifflin, 1884.
2v. Ed. Marie Hansen-Taylor & Horace E. Scudder.

19796. THE UNPUBLISHED LETTERS OF BAYARD TAYLOR IN THE HUNTINGTON LIBRARY. San Marino, 1937.
Ed. John Richie Schultz.

19797. THE CORRESPONDENCE OF BAYARD TAYLOR AND PAUL HAMILTON HAYNE. Baton Rouge: Louisiana State U PR, 1945.
Ed. Charles Duffy. See No. 7908 above.

Celia Laighton Thaxter
1835–1894

19847. POEMS. NY: Hurd & Houghton, 1872.
For extended edition see No. 19850 below.

*19848. AMONG THE ISLES OF SHOALS. Bos: Osgood, 1873.

19850. POEMS. NY: Hurd & Houghton, 1874.

19871. DRIFT-WEED. Bos: Houghton, Osgood, 1879.

19891. POEMS FOR CHILDREN. Bos & NY: Houghton, Mifflin, 1884.

19895. THE CRUISE OF THE MYSTERY AND OTHER POEMS. Bos & NY: Houghton, Mifflin, 1886.

*19896. IDYLS AND PASTORALS … A HOME GALLERY OF POETRY AND ART. Bos: Lothrop, <1886>.
Published in 2 editions: *Edition de Luxe* with 24 poems; & *Popular Edition* with 12 poems (No.19897). The *Edition de Luxe* reprinted in 1891 as *Verses* (No. 19915).

19904. THE YULE-LOG. Bos: Prang, <1889>.

19910. MY LIGHTHOUSE, AND OTHER POEMS. Bos: Prang, <1890>.

19923. AN ISLAND GARDEN. Bos & NY: Houghton, Mifflin, 1894.

19924. LETTERS OF CELIA THAXTER. Bos & NY: Houghton, Mifflin, 1895.
Ed. Annie Fields & Rose Lamb.

CELIA THAXTER (cont.)

19927. STORIES AND POEMS FOR CHILDREN. Bos & NY: Houghton, Mifflin, 1895.
Ed. Sarah Orne Jewett (No. 10907).

19928. THE POEMS OF CELIA THAXTER. Bos & NY: Houghton, Mifflin, 1896.
Ed. Sarah Orne Jewett (No. 10909).

19932. THE HEAVENLY GUEST WITH OTHER UNPUBLISHED WRITINGS.
<Andover, 1935>.
Ed. Oscar Laighton.

Frederick William Thomas
1806–1866

*19935. THE EMIGRANT, OR REFLECTIONS WHILE DESCENDING THE OHIO. A POEM. Cincinnati: Flash, 1833.
Anon.

19938. CLINTON BRADSHAW; OR, THE ADVENTURES OF A LAWYER. Phila: Carey, Lea & Blanchard, 1835.
2v. Anon.

19939. EAST AND WEST. A NOVEL. Phila: Carey, Lea & Blanchard, 1836.
2v. Anon.

19942. HOWARD PINCKNEY. A NOVEL. Phila: Lea & Blanchard, 1840.
2v. Anon.

19947. THE BEECHEN TREE. A TALE: TOLD IN RHYME. NY: Harper & Bros., 1844.

19949. SKETCHES OF CHARACTER, AND TALES FOUNDED ON FACT. Louisville: Office of the Chronicle of Western Literature & Art, 1849.

19950. AN AUTOBIOGRAPHY OF WILLIAM RUSSELL. Balt: Gobright, Thorne, 1852.
Anon.

*19952. JOHN RANDOLPH, OF ROANOKE, AND OTHER SKETCHES OF CHARACTER ... TOGETHER WITH TALES OF REAL LIFE. Phila: Hart, 1853.

Daniel Pierce Thompson
1795–1868

19956. THE ADVENTURES OF TIMOTHY PEACOCK, ESQUIRE. By a Member of the Vermont Bar. Middlebury: Knapp & Jewett, Ptrs, 1835.

19958. MAY MARTIN: OR THE MONEY DIGGERS. A GREEN MOUNTAIN TALE. Montpelier: Walton & Son, 1835.
Revised editions published in 1848 (No. 19965) & 1852 (No. 19971).

*19959. THE GREEN MOUNTAIN BOYS: A HISTORICAL TALE OF THE EARLY SETTLEMENT OF VERMONT. Montpelier: Walton & Sons, 1839.
2v. Anon. Revised edition published in 1848 (No. 19963).

D. P. THOMPSON (cont.)

19962. LOCKE AMSDEN, OR THE SCHOOLMASTER: A TALE.. Bos: Mussey, 1847.
Anon.

*19964. LUCY HOSMER, OR THE GUARDIAN AND THE GHOST. Burlington: Goodrich & Nichols, 1848.
Revised & published as part of *May Martin, and Other Tales*, 1852 (No. 19971).

19966. THE SHAKER LOVERS, AND OTHER TALES. Burlington: Goodrich & Nichols, 1848.
Revised & published as part of *May Martin, and Other Tales*, 1852 (No. 19971).

*19969. THE RANGERS; OR, THE TORY'S DAUGHTER. Bos: Mussey, 1851.
2v. Anon.

*19973. GAUT GURLEY; OR, THE TRAPPERS OF UMBAGOG. Bos: Jewett, 1857.
Reprinted in 1890 as *The Demon Trapper of Umbagog* (No. 19978).

*19974. THE DOOMED CHIEF; OR, TWO HUNDRED YEARS AGO. Phila: Bradley, 1860.
Anon.

*19975. HISTORY OF THE TOWN OF MONTPELIER. Montpelier: Walton, Ptr, 1860.

19976. CENTEOLA; AND OTHER TALES. NY: Carleton, 1864.
Anon.

19980. THE NOVELIST OF VERMONT A BIOGRAPHICAL AND CRITICAL STUDY OF DANIEL PIERCE THOMPSON. Cambridge: Harvard U PR, 1929.
By John E. Flitcroft.

19981. GREEN MOUNTAIN BOY AT MONTICELLO A TALK WITH JEFFERSON IN 1822. Brattleboro: Book Cellar, 1962.

James Maurice Thompson
1844–1901

19984. HOOSIER MOSAICS. NY: Hale & Son, 1875.

19985. THE WITCHERY OF ARCHERY: A COMPLETE MANUAL. NY: Scribner's Sons, 1878.
Extended edition published in 1879 (No. 19988).

*19989. HOW TO TRAIN IN ARCHERY. NY: Horsman, <1879>.
With Will H. Thompson. Extended "second edition" published in 1880 (No. 19993).

19998. A TALLAHASSEE GIRL. Bos: Osgood, 1882.
Anon. *Round-Robin Series.*

20000. HIS SECOND CAMPAIGN. Bos: Osgood, 1883.
Anon. *Round-Robin Series.*

20001. SONGS OF FAIR WEATHER. Bos: Osgood, 1883.

20004. A RED-HEADED FAMILY. NY: Alden, <1885>.
The Elzevir Library, Vol. 4, No. 149, 2 April 1885. Collected in No. 20006 below.

MAURICE THOMPSON (cont.)
20005. AT LOVE'S EXTREMES. NY: Cassell, 1885.
Reprinted in 1901 as *Millie: At Love's Extremes* (No. 20057).

20006. BY-WAYS AND BIRD NOTES. NY: Alden, 1885.
Much of this material was apparently republished in 1887 as *The Elzevir Library,*
Vol. 6, Nos. 298–302 (Nos. 20013–17); see also No. 20004 above.

20008. THE BOYS' BOOK OF SPORTS AND OUTDOOR LIFE. NY: Century Co.,
1886.
Edited by Thompson.

20009. A BANKER OF BANKERSVILLE A NOVEL. NY: Cassell, <1886>.

20018. SOME HYOID HINTS. NY: Alden, <1887>.
The Elzevir Library, Vol. 6, No. 305, 15 Oct. 1887. Also in *Sylvan Secrets,* see next
entry.

*20019. SYLVAN SECRETS, IN BIRD-SONGS AND BOOKS. NY: Alden, 1887.

*20022. A FORTNIGHT OF FOLLY. NY: Alden, 1888.

20023. THE STORY OF LOUISIANA. Bos: Lothrop, <1888>.
The Story of the States series.

20032. POEMS. Bos & NY: Houghton, Mifflin, 1892.

*20036. THE KING OF HONEY ISLAND. A NOVEL. NY: Bonner's Sons, 1893.
Cloth; and paper wrappers of *The Ledger Library* or *The Choice Series.*

20037. THE ETHICS OF LITERARY ART. Hartford: Hartford Seminary PR,
1893.
"The Carew Lectures for 1893 Hartford Theological Seminary."

*20038. LINCOLN'S GRAVE. Cambridge & Chi: Stone & Kimball, 1894.

20042. THE OCALA BOY A STORY OF FLORIDA TOWN AND FOREST. Bos:
Lothrop, 1895.

20046. STORIES OF INDIANA. NY, Cinc, &c: American Book Co., 1898.

20047. STORIES OF THE CHEROKEE HILLS. Bos & NY: Houghton, Mifflin,
1898.

*20052. ALICE OF OLD VINCENNES. Indianapolis: Bowen-Merrill, <1900>.

20054. MY WINTER GARDEN A NATURE-LOVER UNDER SOUTHERN SKIES. NY:
Century Co., 1900.

20056. SWEETHEART MANETTE. Phila & Lon: Lippincott, 1901.
Originally published as the Aug. 1894 issue of *Lippincott's Monthly Magazine* (No.
20039).

*20058. ROSALYNDE'S LOVERS. Indianapolis: Bowen-Merrill, <1901>.

William Tappan Thompson
(Major Joseph Jones)
1812–1882

20070. MAJOR JONES' COURTSHIP ... TO WHICH IS ADDED, THE "GREAT ATTRACTION!" Madison GA: Ptd by C.R. Hanleiter, 1843.
Contains 16 letters and 1 sketch. See next entry.

20071. MAJOR JONES'S COURTSHIP ... SECOND EDITION, GREATLY ENLARGED. Phila: Carey & Hart, 1844.
Contains 26 letters. The "eighth edition" of 1847 (No. 20075) contains 2 additional letters; for a revised & extended edition see No. 20083 below. For a drama based on this material see No. 20078 below.

20072. CHRONICLES OF PINEVILLE. Phila: Carey & Hart, 1845.
Anon. Reprinted in 1880 as *Major Jones's Georgia Scenes* (No. 20086).

20074. JOHN'S ALIVE; OR, THE BRIDE OF A GHOST. Balt: Taylor, Wilde, 1846.
Anon.

20077. MAJOR JONES'S SKETCHES OF TRAVEL. Phila: Carey & Hart, 1848.
Carey & Hart's Humorous Library, Vol. 15. Reprinted in 1880 as *Major Jones's Travels* (No. 20087).

20078. MAJOR JONES' COURTSHIP ... A DOMESTIC COMEDY, IN TWO ACTS. By Major Joseph Jones. Savannah: E.J. Purse, Ptr, 1850.

20083. MAJOR JONES'S COURTSHIP ... REVISED AND ENLARGED. TO WHICH ARE ADDED THIRTEEN HUMOROUS SKETCHES. NY: Appleton, 1872.
The 13 sketches, with one additional piece, published in 1879 as *Rancy Cottem's Courtship ... with Other Humorous Sketches* (No. 20085).

20088. JOHN'S ALIVE; OR, THE BRIDE OF A GHOST, AND OTHER SKETCHES. By Major Joseph Jones. Phila: McKay, 1883.

Mortimer Neal Thomson
(Q.K. Philander Doesticks, P.B.)
1831–1875

20089. DOESTICKS. A POETICAL LETTER FROM Q.K. PHILANDER DOESTICKS, P.B., TO HIS YOUNGER BROTHER. Detroit: E.A. Wales, 1854.
"Printed for Private Circulation."

20091. DOESTICKS WHAT HE SAYS. By Q.K. Philander Doesticks, P.B. NY: Livermore, 1855.
Reprinted *ca.* 1859 as *Doesticks' Letters: and What He Says* (No. 20097).

20092. PLU-RI-BUS-TAH. A SONG THAT'S-BY-NO-AUTHOR. By Q.K. Philander Doesticks, P.B. NY: Livermore & Rudd, 1856.

MORTIMER N. THOMSON (cont.)

*20093. THE HISTORY AND RECORDS OF THE ELEPHANT CLUB; COMPILED
FROM AUTHENTIC DOCUMENTS. By Knight Russ Ockside, M.D.,
and Q.K. Philander Doesticks, P.B. NY: Livermore & Rudd, 1856.
With Edward Fitch Underhill ("Knight Russ Ockside, M.D.")

20094. NOTHING TO SAY: A SLIGHT SLAP AT MOBOCRATIC SNOBBERY. By
Q.K. Philander Doesticks, P.B. NY: Rudd & Carleton, 1857.

20095. GREAT AUCTION SALE OF SLAVES, AT SAVANNAH, GEORGIA, MARCH
2D AND 3D, 1859. NY: American Anti-Slavery Soc'y, <n.d., 1859>.
Anon. Reprinted in 1863 as *What Became of the Slaves on a Georgia Plantation?* (No.
20099).

*20096. THE WITCHES OF NEW YORK. By Q.K. Philander Doesticks, P.B.
NY: Rudd & Carleton, 1859.

20098. THE LADY OF THE LAKE. A TRAVESTIE IN ONE ACT. NY: French,
<1860>.
The Minor Drama, No. 176.

20102. THE ADVENTURES OF SNOOZER, A SLEEPWALKER. By Philander
Doesticks, Esq. <n.p., NY?>: J.L. Winchell, <1877>.

20103. "PLUCK." A LECTURE. NY, 1883.
"For private circulation only."

Henry David Thoreau
1817–1862

20104. A WEEK ON THE CONCORD AND MERRIMACK RIVERS. Bos &
Cambridge: Munroe, 1849.
These sheets also issued in the U.K. by J. Chapman & reissued in 1862 by Ticknor
& Fields, Boston. Revised edition published in 1868 (No. 20118). Critical edi-
tion published in 1980 (No. 20180).

20106. WALDEN; OR, LIFE IN THE WOODS. Bos: Ticknor & Fields, 1854.
New editions based on Thoreau's early manuscripts published in 1909 (No.
20147) & as *The Making of Walden* in 1957 (No. 20162). Critical edition published in 1971 (No. 20175).

20111. EXCURSIONS. Bos: Ticknor & Fields, 1863.
Ed. R.W. Emerson.

20113. THE MAINE WOODS. Bos: Ticknor & Fields, 1864.
Ed. William Ellery Channing & Sophia Thoreau. Critical edition published in
1971 (No. 20176).

20115. CAPE COD. Bos: Ticknor & Fields, 1865.
Ed. William Ellery Channing & Sophia Thoreau.

20116. LETTERS TO VARIOUS PERSONS. Bos: Ticknor & Fields, 1865.
Ed. R.W. Emerson.

HENRY DAVID THOREAU (cont.)

20117. A YANKEE IN CANADA, WITH ANTI-SLAVERY AND REFORM PAPERS. Bos: Ticknor & Fields, 1866.
Ed. William Ellery Channing & Sophia Thoreau. Critical edition of *Reform Papers*, with 1 additional piece, published in 1973 (No. 20177).

20123. EARLY SPRING IN MASSACHUSETTS. Bos: Houghton, Mifflin, 1881.
Journal extracts, ed. H.G.O. Blake.

20127. SUMMER. Bos & NY: Houghton, Mifflin, 1884.
Journal extracts, ed. H.G.O. Blake.

20129. WINTER. Bos & NY: Houghton, Mifflin, 1888.
Journal extracts, ed. H.G.O. Blake.

*20130. AUTUMN. Bos & NY: Houghton, Mifflin, 1892.
Journal extracts, ed. H.G.O. Blake.

*20132. THE WRITINGS OF HENRY DAVID THOREAU. Bos & NY: Houghton, Mifflin, 1894.
10v. *Riverside Edition.*

*20133. FAMILIAR LETTERS. Bos & NY: Houghton, Mifflin, 1894.
Ed. F.B. Sanborn. Uniform with *The Writings*, 1894.

20134. POEMS OF NATURE. Lon: Lane, 1895.
Ed. Henry S. Salt & Frank B. Sanborn.

20135. POEMS OF NATURE. Bos & NY: Houghton Mifflin, 1895.
Ed. Henry S. Salt & Frank B. Sanborn. Sheets of the U.K. edition, see preceding entry.

*20138. THE SERVICE. Bos: Goodspeed, 1902.
Ed. F.B. Sanborn.

*20142. SIR WALTER RALEIGH. Bos: Bibliophile Soc'y, 1905.
Ed. Henry Aiken Metcalf.

*20143. THE FIRST AND LAST JOURNEYS OF THOREAU. Bos: Bibliophile Soc'y, 1905.
2v. Ed. F.B. Sanborn. Some of this material newly edited & published in 1962 as *Thoreau's Minnesota Journey* (No. 20167).

*20145. THE WRITINGS OF HENRY DAVID THOREAU. Bos & NY: Houghton Mifflin, 1906.
20v. Vols. 7–20 publish Thoreau's journals; see also No. 20163 below. Critical editions of the journals for 1837–44 published in 1981 (No. 20181) and for 1842–48 in 1984 (No. 20182).

20153. THE MOON. Bos & NY: Houghton Mifflin, 1927.

*20155. THE TRANSMIGRATION OF THE SEVEN BRAHMANS. NY: Rudge, 1931.
"A translation from the Harivansa of Langlois." Ed. Arthur Christy.

*20159. COLLECTED POEMS. Chi: Packard, 1943.
Ed. Carl Bode. Extended edition published in 1964 (No. 20168).

HENRY DAVID THOREAU (cont.)

20163. CONSCIOUSNESS IN CONCORD THE TEXT OF THOREAU'S HITHERTO "LOST JOURNAL" (1840–1841). Bos: Houghton Mifflin, 1958.
Ed. Perry Miller.

20164. THE CORRESPONDENCE OF HENRY DAVID THOREAU. <NY>: New York U PR, 1958.
Ed. Walter Harding & Carl Bode.

20179. EARLY ESSAYS AND MISCELLANIES. Princeton: Princeton U PR, 1975.
Ed. Joseph J. Moldenhauer & Edwin Moser, with Alexander C. Kern.

Thomas Bangs Thorpe
1815–1878

*20302. THE MYSTERIES OF THE BACKWOODS; OR, SKETCHES OF THE SOUTH-WEST. Phila: Carey & Hart, 1846.

*20303. OUR ARMY ON THE RIO GRANDE. Phila: Carey & Hart, 1846.

*20306. OUR ARMY AT MONTEREY. Phila: Carey & Hart, 1847.

20307. THE TAYLOR ANECDOTE BOOK. By Tom Owen, the Bee-Hunter. NY: Appleton, 1848.

20308. THE HIVE OF "THE BEE-HUNTER," A REPOSITORY OF SKETCHES. NY & Lon: Appleton, 1854.
"The Big Bear of Arkansas," here collected, was first published in book form in 1845 in *The Big Bear of Arkansas, and Other Sketches*, ed. William T. Porter (No. 20301).

*20309. THE MASTER'S HOUSE; A TALE OF SOUTHERN LIFE. By Logan. NY: McElrath, 1854.
Sheets of printing 2 reissued in 1855 as the "third edition."

20311. A VOICE TO AMERICA; OR, THE MODEL REPUBLIC, ITS GLORY, OR ITS FALL. NY: Walker, 1855.
Anon. With Frederick Saunders. These sheets reissued in an undated "new edition" as *The Progress and Prospects of America* (No. 20312).

Henry Timrod
1828–1867

20320. POEMS. Bos: Ticknor & Fields, 1860.

20321. ODE ON THE MEETING OF THE SOUTHERN CONGRESS. <n.p., n.d.; 1861?>.
Broadside. Revised & collected in *Poems*, 1873, as "Ethnogenesis."

*20327. THE POEMS. NY: Hale & Son, 1873.
Ed. Paul H. Hayne. Extended "new revised edition" also published in 1873 (No. 20328).

HENRY TIMROD (cont.)

20331. POEMS. Bos & NY: Houghton, Mifflin, 1899.
Memorial Edition.

20336. THE LAST YEARS OF HENRY TIMROD 1864–1867. Durham NC: Duke U PR, 1941.
Ed. Jay B. Hubbell.

20337. THE UNCOLLECTED POEMS. Athens: U of Georgia PR, 1942.
Ed. Guy A. Cardwell, Jr.

20338. THE ESSAYS. Athens: U of Georgia PR, 1942.
Ed. Edd Winfield Parks.

20339. THE COLLECTED POEMS ... A VARIORUM EDITION. Athens: U of Georgia PR, <1965>.
Ed. Edd Winfield Parks & Aileen Wells Parks.

Albion Winegar Tourgée
1838–1905

*20341. TOINETTE. A NOVEL. By Henry Churton. NY: Ford, 1874.
Revised editions published in 1879 (No. 20345) & with an additional story ("'Zouri's Christmas") in 1881 as *A Royal Gentleman* (No. 20351).

20342. THE "C" LETTERS. AS PUBLISHED IN "THE NORTH STATE." Greensboro NC: "The North State" Book & Job Ptg Office, 1878.
Anon.

20344. FIGS AND THISTLES: A WESTERN STORY. NY: Fords, Howard, & Hulbert, <1879>.

*20346. A FOOL'S ERRAND. By One of the Fools. NY: Fords, Howard, & Hulbert, 1879.
Anon. Revised edition with additional material published in 1880 as *The Invisible Empire* (No. 20347). For dramatization see No. 20388 below.

*20349. BRICKS WITHOUT STRAW A NOVEL. NY: Fords, Howard, & Hulbert, <1880>.

*20353. JOHN EAX AND MAMELON OR THE SOUTH WITHOUT THE SHADOW. NY: Fords, Howard, & Hulbert, <1882>.

*20355. HOT PLOWSHARES. A NOVEL. NY: Fords, Howard, & Hulbert, 1883.

*20358. AN APPEAL TO CAESER. NY: Fords, Howard, & Hulbert, 1884.

*20359. A MAN OF DESTINY. By Siva. Chi & NY: Belford, Clarke, 1885.
Ed. William Penn Nixon.

20360. THE VETERAN AND HIS PIPE. Chi & NY: Belford, Clarke, 1886.
Anon.

20361. BUTTON'S INN. Bos: Roberts Bros., 1887.

20362. BLACK ICE. NY: Fords, Howard, & Hulbert, 1888.

20363. "89. NY, Lon, &c.: Cassell, 1891 <i.e. 1888>.
Anon. "Edited from the original manuscript by Edgar Henry <i.e. Tourgée>."

ALBION W. TOURGÉE (cont.)

*20364. LETTERS TO A KING. Cincinnati: Cranston & Stowe, 1888.

20366. WITH GAUGE & SWALLOW, ATTORNEYS. Phila: Lippincott, 1889.

20368. PACTOLUS PRIME. NY: Cassell, <1890>.

*20369. MURVALE EASTMAN CHRISTIAN SOCIALIST. NY: Fords, Howard, & Hulbert, <1890>.

*20371. A SON OF OLD HARRY A NOVEL. NY: Bonner's Sons, 1891.

20373. OUT OF THE SUNSET SEA. NY: Merrill & Baker, <1893>.

20376. AN OUTING WITH THE QUEEN OF HEARTS. NY: Merrill & Baker, 1894.

20381. THE STORY OF A THOUSAND. Buffalo: McGerald & Son, 1896.
History of the 105th Ohio Volunteer Infantry in the Civil War, 21 Aug. 1862 to 6 June 1865.

20382. THE WAR OF THE STANDARDS COIN AND CREDIT VERSUS COIN WITHOUT CREDIT. NY & Lon: Putnam's Sons, 1896.
Questions of the Day, No. 88.

20383. THE MORTGAGE ON THE HIP-ROOF HOUSE. Cincinnati: Curts & Jennings, 1896.

20386. THE MAN WHO OUTLIVED HIMSELF. NY: Fords, Howard, & Hulbert, 1898.

20388. A FOOL'S ERRAND. Metuchen NJ: Scarecrow PR, 1969.
Dramatization, with Steele MacKaye. Ed. Dean H. Keller.

John Townsend Trowbridge
(Paul Creyton)
1827–1916

20391. KATE, THE ACCOMPLICE, OR THE PREACHER AND BURGLAR. By Paul Creyton. Bos: 'Star Spangled Banner' Office, 1849.

20394. LUCY DAWSON; OR THE BANDITS OF THE PRAIRIE. By Paul Creyton. Bos: G.H. Williams, 1850.

20398. FATHER BRIGHTHOPES; OR, AN OLD CLERGYMAN'S VACATION. By Paul Creyton. Bos: Phillips, Sampson, 1853.
Revised & extended edition published in 1892 (No. 20501).

20399. HEARTS AND FACES; OR HOME-LIFE UNVEILED. By Paul Creyton. Bos: Phillips, Sampson, 1853.

20400. THE DESERTED FAMILY; OR, WANDERINGS OF AN OUTCAST. By Paul Creyton. Bos: Crown, 1853.

20401. BURRCLIFF: ITS SUNSHINE AND ITS CLOUDS. By Paul Creyton. Bos: Phillips, Sampson, 1854.

*20402. MARTIN MERRIVALE: HIS X MARK. By Paul Creyton. Bos: Phillips, Sampson, 1854.
15 parts or 1v.

JOHN T. TROWBRIDGE (cont.)

20404. IRONTHORPE: THE PIONEER PREACHER. By Paul Creyton. Bos: Phillips, Sampson, 1855.

*20406. NEIGHBOR JACKWOOD. By Paul Creyton. Bos: Phillips, Sampson, 1857.
Revised & extended edition published in 1895 (No. 20507). For dramatization see next entry.

*20407. NEIGHBOR JACKWOOD. A DOMESTIC DRAMA, IN FIVE ACTS. Bos: Phillips, Sampson, 1857.

20408. THE OLD BATTLE-GROUND. NY: Sheldon, 1860.

20411. THE DRUMMER BOY. A STORY OF BURNSIDE'S EXPEDITION. Bos: Tilton, 1863.
Anon. Reprinted in 1876 as *Frank Manly* (No. 20444).

20412. THE VAGABONDS. NY: Gregory, 1863.
"Re-printed from the Atlantic Monthly."

*20413. CUDJO'S CAVE. Bos: Tilton, 1864.

20415. THE FERRY-BOY AND THE FINANCIER. By a Contributor to the "Atlantic." Bos: Walker, Wise, 1864.
All copies examined have the statement *Tenth Thousand* on the title-page.

20416. THE LITTLE REBEL. Bos: Tilton, 1864.
Anon.

20417. THE THREE SCOUTS. Bos: Tilton, 1865.
These sheets reissued in 1874 by Gill, Boston.

20418. COUPON BONDS. Bos: Ticknor & Fields, 1866.
For dramatization see No. 20443 below.

20419. LUCY ARLYN. Bos: Ticknor & Fields, 1866.

20421. THE SOUTH: A TOUR OF ITS BATTLE-FIELDS AND RUINED CITIES. Hartford: Stebbins, 1866.
Reprinted in 1868, with additional material not by Trowbridge, as *A Picture of the Desolated States* (No. 20425); condensed version published in 1956 as *The Desolate South* (No. 20528).

20423. NEIGHBORS' WIVES. Bos: Lee & Shepard, 1867.

20426. THE VAGABONDS, AND OTHER POEMS. Bos: Fields, Osgood, 1869.

20427. THE STORY OF COLUMBUS. Bos: Fields, Osgood, 1870.
Uncle Sam Series for American Children; the series also issued bound in 1v. as *Brave Ballads for American Children.*

20430. LAWRENCE'S ADVENTURES AMONG THE ICE-CUTTERS, GLASS-MAKERS, COAL-MINERS, IRON-MEN, AND SHIP-BUILDERS. Bos: Fields, Osgood, 1871.

20431. JACK HAZARD AND HIS FORTUNES. Bos: Osgood, 1871.
Later published in the U.K. with *Doing His Best,* 1873: in 1875 as *How to Rise in the World* (No. 20441) & again, not before 1883, as *Who Won at Last* (No. 20475).

20434. A CHANCE FOR HIMSELF; OR, JACK HAZARD AND HIS TREASURE. Bos: Osgood, 1872.

JOHN T. TROWBRIDGE (cont.)

20435. COUPON BONDS, AND OTHER STORIES. Bos: Osgood, 1873.

20436. DOING HIS BEST. Bos: Osgood, 1873.
For comment see No. 20431 above.

20437. FAST FRIENDS. Bos: Osgood, 1875.

20438. THE EMIGRANT'S STORY, AND OTHER POEMS. Bos: Osgood, 1875.

*20439. THE YOUNG SURVEYOR. Lon: Low, Marston, et al, 1875.

20440. THE YOUNG SURVEYOR; OR, JACK ON THE PRAIRIES. Bos: Osgood, 1875.

*20443. COUPON BONDS: A PLAY. Bos: Baker, 1876.

20445. THE GREAT MATCH, AND OTHER MATCHES. Bos: Roberts Bros., 1877.
Anon. *No Name Series.*

*20446. THE BOOK OF GOLD AND OTHER POEMS. NY: Harper & Bros., 1878.

*20447. HIS OWN MASTER. Bos: Lee & Shepard, 1878.

20448. BOUND IN HONOR; OR, A HARVEST OF WILD OATS. Bos: Lee & Shepard, 1878.

20457. YOUNG JOE AND OTHER BOYS. Bos: Lee & Shepard, 1880.

*20463. THE SILVER MEDAL. Bos: Lee & Shepard, 1881.

20466. A HOME IDYL AND OTHER POEMS. Bos: Houghton, Mifflin, 1881.

20468. THE POCKET-RIFLE. Bos: Lee & Shepard, 1882.

20473. THE JOLLY ROVER. Bos: Lee & Shepard, 1883.

20476. PHIL AND HIS FRIENDS. Bos: Lee & Shepard, 1884.
Published in the U.K. as *Philip Farlow and His Friends.*

20477. THE TINKHAM BROTHERS' TIDE-MILL. Bos: Lee & Shepard, 1884.

20480. FARNELL'S FOLLY. Bos: Lee & Shepard, 1885.

20482. THE SATIN-WOOD BOX. Bos: Lee & Shepard, 1886.

20485. THE LITTLE MASTER. Bos: Lee & Shepard, 1887.

*20486. HIS ONE FAULT. Bos: Lee & Shepard, 1887.

*20488. PETER BUDSTONE THE BOY WHO WAS HAZED. Bos: Lee & Shepard, 1888.

20490. THE LOST EARL WITH OTHER POEMS AND TALES IN VERSE. Bos: Lothrop, <1888>.

20492. A START IN LIFE A STORY OF THE GENESEE COUNTRY. Bos: Lee & Shepard, 1889.

20493. BIDING HIS TIME OR ANDREW HAPNELL'S FORTUNE. Bos: Lee & Shepard, 1889.

20495. THE ADVENTURES OF DAVID VANE AND DAVID CRANE. Bos: Lothrop, <1889>.

*20499. THE KELP-GATHERERS A STORY OF THE MAINE COAST. Bos: Lee & Shepard, 1891.

20500. THE SCARLET TANAGER AND OTHER BIPEDS. Bos: Lee & Shepard, 1892.

JOHN T. TROWBRIDGE (cont.)

20502. THE FORTUNES OF TOBY TRAFFORD. Bos: Lee & Shepard, 1893.

20503. WOODIE THORPE'S PILGRIMAGE AND OTHER STORIES. Bos: Lee & Shepard, 1893.

20508. THE PRIZE CUP. NY: Century Co., 1896.

20509. THE LOTTERY TICKET. Bos: Lee & Shepard, 1896.

20510. A QUESTION OF DAMAGES. Bos: Lee & Shepard, 1897.

20513. TWO BIDDICUT BOYS AND THEIR ADVENTURES WITH A WONDERFUL TRICK-DOG. NY: Century Co., 1898.

*20515. MY OWN STORY WITH RECOLLECTIONS OF NOTED PERSONS. Bos & NY: Houghton, Mifflin, 1903.

*20516. THE POETICAL WORKS. Bos & NY: Houghton, Mifflin, 1903.

20522. A PAIR OF MADCAPS. Bos: Lothrop, Lee & Shepard, <1909>.

John Trumbull
1750–1831

20530. AN ESSAY ON THE USE AND ADVANTAGES OF THE FINE ARTS. New Haven: Ptd by T. & S. Green, <1770?>.
Anon. Delivered at the Public Commencement, New Haven, 12 Sept. 1770.

*20532. THE PROGRESS OF DULNESS, PART FIRST: OR THE RARE ADVENTURES OF TOM BRAINLESS. <New Haven>, 1772.
Anon. Revised & corrected edition published in 1773 (No. 20535).

20533. THE PROGRESS OF DULNESS, PART SECOND: OR AN ESSAY ON THE LIFE AND CHARACTER OF DICK HAIRBRAIN. <New Haven>, 1773.
Anon.

20534. THE PROGRESS OF DULNESS, PART THIRD, AND LAST: SOMETIMES CALLED, THE PROGRESS OF COQUETRY, OR THE ADVENTURES OF MISS HARRIET SIMPER. New Haven: Ptd by T. & S. Green, 1773.
Anon.

20536. AN ELEGY OF THE TIMES. New Haven: Ptd by T. & S. Green, 1775.
Anon. "First Printed at Boston, September 20th, A.D. 1774."

20537. M'FINGAL: A MODERN EPIC POEM. CANTO FIRST, OR THE TOWN-MEETING. Phila: W. & T. Bradford, 1775.
Anon.

20539. M'FINGAL: A MODERN EPIC POEM, IN FOUR CANTOS. Hartford: Ptd by Hudson & Goodwin, 1782.
Anon.

20547. THE POETICAL WORKS. Hartford: Goodrich, 1820.
2v. Vol. 2 also issued separately as *Miscellaneous Poems*.

20552. THE ANARCHIAD: A NEW ENGLAND POEM. New Haven: Pease, 1861.
With David Humphreys, Joel Barlow & Dr. Lemuel Hopkins. Ed. Luther G. Riggs.
See also No. 915 above.

Nathaniel Beverley Tucker
1784–1851

20586. THE PARTISAN LEADER; A TALE OF THE FUTURE. By Edward William Sidney. <n.p.>: Ptd by J. Caxton, 1856 <i.e. Wash DC: Duff Green, 1836>.
2v. Republished in 1861 (No. 20601) & 1862 (No. 20602).

20587. GEORGE BALCOMBE. A NOVEL. NY: Harper & Bros., 1836.
Anon. 2v.

20596. A SERIES OF LECTURES ON THE SCIENCE OF GOVERNMENT. Phila: Carey & Hart, 1845.
Many of these lectures were first published separately (Nos. 20589, 20590, 20592 & 20594).

20597. THE PRINCIPLES OF PLEADING. Bos: Little & Brown, 1846.
A supplement was also produced *ca.* 1846 (No. 20598).

Henry Theodore Tuckerman
1813–1871

20606. THE ITALIAN SKETCH BOOK. By an American. Phila: Key & Biddle, 1835.
Extended "second edition" published in 1837 (No. 10612); for the "third edition" see No. 20653 below.

20616. ISABEL: OR, SICILY. A PILGRIMAGE. Phila: Lea & Blanchard, 1839.
Reprinted in 1852 as *Sicily: a Pilgrimage* (No. 20719).

20621. RAMBLES AND REVERIES. NY: Giffing, 1841.

*20641. THOUGHTS ON THE POETS. NY: C.S. Francis, 1846.

20647. ARTIST-LIFE: OR SKETCHES OF AMERICAN PAINTERS. NY: Appleton, 1847.
Reprinted in 1849 as *Sketches of Eminent American Painters* (No. 20716). For revised & extended edition see No. 20704 below.

*20653. THE ITALIAN SKETCH BOOK. NY: Riker, 1848.
2 parts or 1v. "Third edition, revised and enlarged."

20656. CHARACTERISTICS OF LITERATURE. Phila: Lindsay & Blakiston, 1849.

20657. THE OPTIMIST. NY & Lon: Putnam, 1850.
These sheets reissued in 1852 (No. 20720).

20658. THE LIFE OF SILAS TALBOT. NY: Riker, 1850.

20660. POEMS. Bos: Ticknor, Reed, & Fields, 1851.

20661. CHARACTERISTICS OF LITERATURE ... SECOND SERIES. Phila: Lindsay & Blakiston, 1851.

20666. MENTAL PORTRAITS; OR, STUDIES OF CHARACTER. Lon: Bentley, 1853.
For U.S. publication of all but 2 of these pieces see No. 20675 below.

HENRY T. TUCKERMAN (cont.)

20668. LEAVES FROM THE DIARY OF A DREAMER. FOUND AMONG HIS PAPERS. Lon: Pickering, 1853.
Anon.

20669. A MONTH IN ENGLAND. NY: Redfield, 1853.

*20675. BIOGRAPHICAL ESSAYS. ESSAYS, BIOGRAPHICAL AND CRITICAL; OR, STUDIES OF CHARACTER. Bos: Phillips, Sampson, 1857.

20676. ART IN AMERICA. ITS HISTORY, CONDITION, AND PROSPECTS. Macao: <Gideon Nye, Jr.>, 1858.
"For private circulation." Reprinted from the *Cosmopolitan Art Journal.*

20685. THE REBELLION: ITS LATENT CAUSES AND TRUE SIGNIFICANCE. NY: Gregory, 1861.

20690. A SHEAF OF VERSE BOUND FOR THE FAIR. NY: Alvord, 1864.
Prepared for the U.S. Sanitary Commission fair, New York, April 1864.

*20691. AMERICA AND HER COMMENTATORS. WITH A CRITICAL SKETCH OF TRAVEL IN THE UNITED STATES. NY: Scribner, 1864.

20700. JOHN W. FRANCIS, M.D., LL.D. A BIOGRAPHICAL ESSAY. <n.p., n.d.; NY: Widdleton, 1866>.
Separate issue of sheets from Francis's *Old New York,* 1866 (see No. 20699).

20701. THE CRITERION ... A SERIES OF ESSAYS. NY: Hurd & Houghton, 1866.
The U.K. edition published in 1868 as *The Collector* (No. 20722).

20703. MAGA PAPERS ABOUT PARIS. NY: Putnam & Son, 1867.
Putnam's Railway Classics.

*20704. BOOK OF THE ARTISTS. AMERICAN ARTIST LIFE. NY: Putnam & Son, 1867.

*20708. THE LIFE OF JOHN PENDLETON KENNEDY. NY: Putnam & Sons, 1871.
Issued as part of Kennedy's *Collected Works,* see No. 11076 above.

20711. SELECTIONS FROM THE WRITINGS OF HENRY THEODORE TUCKERMAN. <n.p., n.d; not before 1872>.
"For private circulation." Ed. Lucy K. Tuckerman.

Royall Tyler
1757–1826

20725. SONGS IN THE COMIC OPERA ... MAY DAY IN TOWN. NY: Ptd by H. Gaine, 1787.
Anon.

20726. THE CONTRAST, A COMEDY. By a Citizen of the United States. Phila: Prichard & Hall, 1790.
Anon.

20727. THE ORIGIN OF EVIL. AN ELEGY. <n.p.>, 1793.
Anon.

ROYALL TYLER (cont.)

20728. THE ALGERINE CAPTIVE; OR, THE LIFE AND ADVENTURES OF DOCTOR
UPDIKE UNDERHILL. Walpole NH: Carlisle, 1797.
2v. Anon. The U.K. edition revised & published in 1802 (No. 20732) & reprinted
in the U.S. in 1816 (No. 20738).

20735. THE YANKEY IN LONDON, BEING THE FIRST PART OF A SERIES OF
LETTERS ... VOLUME I. By an American Youth. NY: I. Riley, 1809.
Anon. All published.

20752. THE CHESTNUT TREE OR A SKETCH OF BRATTLEBOROUGH ... AT
THE CLOSE OF THE TWENTIETH CENTURY ... WRITTEN 1824.
<N. Montpelier VT>: Driftwind PR, 1931.

20754. FOUR PLAYS. Princeton: Princeton U PR, 1941.
Ed. Arthur Wallace Peach & George Floyd Newbrough. *America's Lost Plays*, Vol.
15.

20756. THE VERSE OF ROYALL TYLER. Charlottesville: U PR of Virginia,
<1968>.
Ed. Marius B. Péladeau.

20757. THE PROSE OF ROYALL TYLER. Montpelier: Vermont Historical
Soc'y; Rutland VT: Tuttle, <1972>.
Ed. Marius B. Péladeau.

Jones Very
1813–1880

20763. ESSAYS AND POEMS. Bos: Little & Brown, 1839.
Ed. Ralph Waldo Emerson.

20786. POEMS. Bos & NY: Houghton, Mifflin, 1883.

20787. POEMS AND ESSAYS ... COMPLETE AND REVISED EDITION. Bos & NY:
Houghton, Mifflin, 1886.

20788. JONES VERY EMERSON'S "BRAVE SAINT." Durham NC: Duke U PR,
1942.
By William Irving Bartlett.

Lewis Wallace
1827–1905

*20795. THE FAIR GOD; OR, THE LAST OF THE 'TZINS. Bos: Osgood, 1873.

20796. COMMODUS AN HISTORICAL PLAY. <n.p., Crawfordsville; 1876>.
Revised edition printed in 1877 (No. 20797). See also No. 20825 below.

*20798. BEN-HUR A TALE OF CHRIST. NY: Harper & Bros., 1880.

*20805. LIFE OF GEN. BEN HARRISON. Phila, Chi, &c.: Hubbard Bros.,
<1888>.
Also published with George Alfred Townsend's life of Levi P. Morton (No. 20804).
Later revised & republished for the 1892 presidential campaign (No. 20850).

LEW. WALLACE (cont.)

20808. THE BOYHOOD OF CHRIST. NY: Harper & Bros., 1889.

*20819. THE PRINCE OF INDIA OR WHY CONSTANTINOPLE FELL. NY: Harper & Bros., 1893.
2v.

20825. THE WOOING OF MALKATOON COMMODUS. NY & Lon: Harper & Bros., 1898.

*20838. LEW WALLACE AN AUTOBIOGRAPHY. NY & Lon: Harper & Bros., 1906.
2v.

Elizabeth Stuart Phelps Ward
1844–1911

*20854. ELLEN'S IDOL. Bos: Mass. Sabbath School Soc'y, <1864>.
Anon.

20855. UP HILL; OR, LIFE IN THE FACTORY. Bos: Hoyt, <1865>.
Anon.

20856. MERCY GLIDDON'S WORK. Bos: Hoyt, <1865>.

20857. TINY. Bos: Mass. S<abbath>. S<chool>. Soc'y, 1866.

20858. GYPSY BREYNTON. Bos: Graves & Young, 1866.

20859. GYPSY'S COUSIN JOY. Bos: Graves & Young, 1866.

20860. GYPSY'S SOWING AND REAPING. Bos: Graves & Young, 1866.

*20861. TINY'S SUNDAY NIGHTS. Bos: Mass. S<abbath>. S<chool>. Soc'y, 1866.

20862. GYPSY'S YEAR AT THE GOLDEN CRESCENT. Bos: Graves & Young, 1867.

20864. I DON'T KNOW HOW. Bos: Mass. Sabbath School Soc'y, 1868.

*20865. THE GATES AJAR. Bos: Fields, Osgood, 1869.

20866. MEN, WOMEN, AND GHOSTS. Bos: Fields, Osgood, 1869.

20869. THE TROTTY BOOK. Bos: Fields, Osgood, 1870.

20870. HEDGED IN. Bos: Fields, Osgood, 1870.

20872. THE SILENT PARTNER. Bos: Osgood, 1871.

20874. WHAT TO WEAR? Bos: Osgood, 1873.

20875. TROTTY'S WEDDING TOUR AND STORY-BOOK. Lon: Low, Marston, et al, 1873.

20876. TROTTY'S WEDDING TOUR, AND STORY-BOOK. Bos: Osgood, 1874.

20880. POETIC STUDIES. Bos: Osgood, 1875.

20887. THE STORY OF AVIS. Bos: Osgood, 1877.

20895. MY COUSIN AND I. A STORY IN TWO PARTS. Lon: Sunday School Union, <n.d., 1879>.

20896. OLD MAIDS' PARADISE. Lon: J. Clarke, 1879.
The Family Circle Library.

ELIZABETH STUART PHELPS WARD (cont.)
  20897. SEALED ORDERS. Bos: Houghton, Osgood, 1879.
  20903. FRIENDS: A DUET. Bos: Houghton, Mifflin, 1881.
  20912. DOCTOR ZAY. Bos & NY: Houghton, Mifflin, 1882.
  20916. BEYOND THE GATES. Lon: Chatto & Windus, 1883.
 *20917. BEYOND THE GATES. Bos & NY: Houghton, Mifflin, 1883.
  20921. SONGS OF THE SILENT WORLD AND OTHER POEMS. Bos & NY:
         Houghton, Mifflin, 1885.
  20922. AN OLD MAID'S PARADISE. Bos & NY: Houghton, Mifflin, 1885.
         The Riverside Paper Series, No. 9, 1 Aug. 1885. Republished with *Burglars in Para-
         dise* in 1887 as *Old Maids, and Burglars in Paradise* (No. 20929).
  20924. BURGLARS IN PARADISE. Bos & NY: Houghton, Mifflin, 1886.
         The Riverside Paper Series, No. 14, 15 May 1886. For comment see preceding en-
         try.
  20925. THE MADONNA OF THE TUBS. Bos & NY: Houghton, Mifflin, 1887.
         Collected in *Fourteen to One,* 1891.
  20926. THE GATES BETWEEN. Lon & NY: Ward, Lock, <n.d., 1887>.
  20927. THE GATES BETWEEN. Bos & NY: Houghton, Mifflin, 1887.
         For dramatization see No. 29073 below.
  20928. JACK THE FISHERMAN. Bos & NY: Houghton, Mifflin, 1887.
         Collected in *Fourteen to One,* 1891.
  20937. THE STRUGGLE FOR IMMORTALITY. Bos & NY: Houghton, Mifflin,
         1889.
 *20941. THE MASTER OF THE MAGICIANS. Bos & NY: Houghton, Mifflin,
         1890.
         With Herbert D. Ward.
  20944. COME FORTH! Lon: Heinemann, 1890.
         With Herbert D. Ward. A copyright printing was also produced in 1890 (No.
         20940).
 *20948. COME FORTH. Bos & NY: Houghton, Mifflin, 1891.
         With Herbert D. Ward.
 *20949. FOURTEEN TO ONE. Bos & NY: Houghton, Mifflin, 1891.
  20950. AUSTIN PHELPS A MEMOIR. NY: Scribner's Sons, 1891.
  20951. A LOST HERO. Bos: Roberts Bros., 1891.
         With Herbert D. Ward.
 *20955. DONALD MARCY. Bos & NY: Houghton, Mifflin, 1893.
 *20959. A SINGULAR LIFE. Bos & NY: Houghton, Mifflin, 1895.
  20962. THE SUPPLY AT SAINT AGATHA'S. Bos & NY: Houghton, Mifflin,
         1896.
  20963. CHAPTERS FROM A LIFE. Bos & NY: Houghton, Mifflin, 1896.
 *20965. THE STORY OF JESUS CHRIST AN INTERPRETATION. Bos & NY:
         Houghton, Mifflin, 1897.
 *20968. LOVELINESS A STORY. Bos & NY: Houghton, Mifflin, 1899.

ELIZABETH STUART PHELPS WARD (cont.)

*20971. THE SUCCESSORS OF MARY THE FIRST. Bos & NY: Houghton, Mifflin, 1901.

*20973. WITHIN THE GATES. Bos & NY: Houghton, Mifflin, 1901.
Dramatization of *The Gates Between*, 1887.

20980. AVERY. Bos & NY: Houghton, Mifflin, 1902.

20982. CONFESSIONS OF A WIFE. By Mary Adams. NY: Century Co., 1902.

20986. TRIXY. Bos & NY: Houghton, Mifflin, 1904.

*20991. THE MAN IN THE CASE. Bos & NY: Houghton, Mifflin, 1906.

20993. WALLED IN A NOVEL. NY & Lon: Harper & Bros., 1907.
Advance copies "for private distribution" from sheets of *Harper's Bazar* also produced in 1907 (No. 20992).

20994. THOUGH LIFE US DO PART. Bos & NY: Houghton Mifflin, 1908.

*20998. JONATHAN AND DAVID. NY & Lon: Harper & Bros., 1909.

20999. THE OATH OF ALLEGIANCE AND OTHER STORIES. Bos & NY: Houghton Mifflin, 1909.

*21002. THE EMPTY HOUSE AND OTHER STORIES. Bos & NY: Houghton Mifflin, 1910.

*21003. COMRADES. NY & Lon: Harper & Bros., 1911.

William Ware
1797–1852

21017. LETTERS OF LUCIUS M. PISO, FROM PALMYRA, TO HIS FRIEND MARCUS CURTIUS, AT ROME. NY: C.S. Francis, 1837.
2v. Anon. "Now first translated and published." Reprinted in 1838 as *Zenobia* (Nos. 21019 & 21020), in 1839 as *Palmyra* (No. 21022) & in 1851 as *Letters from Palmyra* (No. 21032).

21018. PROBUS: OR ROME IN THE THIRD CENTURY. NY: C.S. Francis, 1838.
2v. Anon. "In letters of Lucius M. Piso from Rome, to Fausta the daughter of Gracchus, at Palmyra." The U.K. edition published in 1838 as *The Last Days of Aurelian* (No. 21021). Reprinted in 1840 as *Rome and the Early Christians* (No. 21023) & in 1848 as *Aurelian* (No. 21030).

21024. JULIAN: OR SCENES IN JUDEA. NY: C.S. Francis, 1841.
2v. Anon.

21033. SKETCHES OF EUROPEAN CAPITALS. Bos: Phillips, Sampson, 1851.
An extract was also published anonymously in 1851 as *An American Habit* (No. 21034).

21035. LECTURES ON THE WORKS AND GENIUS OF WASHINGTON ALLSTON. Bos: Phillips, Sampson, 1852.

Anna Bartlett Warner
(Amy Lothrop)
1824–1915

21037. ROBINSON CRUSOE'S FARMYARD. NY & Lon: Putnam, 1849.
Anon. "Designed to accompany the game of natural history for children."

21039. DOLLARS AND CENTS. By Amy Lothrop. NY: Putnam, 1852.
2v. First U.K. edition published in 1852 as *Glen Luna;* later reprinted frequently in the U.K., often with changed title.

21042. MR. RUTHERFORD'S CHILDREN. Lon: Nisbet, <n.d., 1853>.
Anon. With Susan Warner. At head of title: *Ellen Montgomery's Bookcase.*

21043. MR. RUTHERFORD'S CHILDREN. NY: Putnam, 1853.
Anon. With Susan Warner. At head of title: *Ellen Montgomery's Bookcase.*

21045. MR. RUTHERFORD'S CHILDREN. SECOND VOLUME. NY: Putnam, 1855.
Anon. *Ellen Mongomery's Book Shelf* series. Later published as *Sybil and Chryssa.*

21046. MY BROTHER'S KEEPER. Lon: Nisbet, 1855.
Anon. Reprinted from *Excelsior.*

21047. MY BROTHER'S KEEPER. NY & Lon: Appleton, 1855.

21048. CASPER. By Amy Lothrop. NY: Putnam, 1856.
Ellen Montgomery's Book Shelf series. Later published as *Casper and His Friends.*

*21049. POND LILY STORIES. Phila & NY: American Sunday-School Union, <1857>.
Anon.

21051. SUNDAY ALL THE WEEK. Phila & NY: American Sunday-School Union, <1859>.
Anon.

21052. HARD MAPLE. Bos: Shepard, Clark, & Brown, 1859.
Anon. *Ellen Mongomery's Book Shelf* series.

21053. SAY AND SEAL. Lon: Bentley, 1860.
Anon. With Susan Warner.

21054. SAY AND SEAL. Phila: Lippincott, 1860.
2v. Anon. With Susan Warner.

21055. THE GOLDEN LADDER: STORIES ILLUSTRATIVE OF THE EIGHT BEATITUDES. Lon: Nisbet, 1863.
Anon. With Susan Warner. For U.S. publication as a set in 8v., see following entries.

21056. THE TWO SCHOOL GIRLS. NY: Carlton & Porter, <1862, i.e. 1863>.
Anon. Part of a series written with Susan Warner. This tale by Susan Warner.

21057. ALTHEA. NY: Carlton & Porter, <1862, i.e. 1863>.
Anon. Part of a series written with Susan Warner.

21058. GERTRUDE AND HER CAT. NY: Carlton & Porter, <1862, i.e. 1863>.
Anon. Part of a series written with Susan Warner. This tale by Susan Warner.

ANNA B. WARNER (cont.)

21059. THE ROSE IN THE DESERT. NY: Carlton & Porter, <1862, i.e. 1863>.
Anon. Part of a series written with Susan Warner.

21060. THE LITTLE BLACK HEN. NY: Carlton & Porter, <1862, i.e. 1863>.
Anon. Part of a series written with Susan Warner.

21061. MARTHA'S HYMN. NY: Carlton & Porter, <1862, i.e. 1863>.
Anon. Part of a series written with Susan Warner.

*21062. THE CARPENTER'S HOUSE. NY: Carlton & Porter, <1862, i.e. 1863>.
Anon. Part of a series written with Susan Warner. This tale by Susan Warner.

21063. THE PRINCE IN DISGUISE. NY: Carlton & Porter, <1862, i.e. 1863>.
Anon. Part of a series written with Susan Warner. This tale by Anna Warner.

*21064. THE CHILDREN OF BLACKBERRY HOLLOW. Phila & NY: American
Sunday-School Union, <1861–63>.
6v., each printing a separate story. Anon.

*21066. THE LITTLE NURSE OF CAPE COD. Phila & NY: American Sunday-
School Union, <1863>.
Anon.

21068. MISS MUFF AND LITTLE HUNGRY. Phila: Presbyterian Publication
Committee, <1866>.
Anon.

21070. THE THREE LITTLE SPADES. Lon: Nisbet, 1868.
Anon. *Golden Ladder Series.*

21071. THREE LITTLE SPADES. NY: Harper & Bros., 1868.
Anon.

21072. THE STAR OUT OF JACOB. NY: Carter & Bros., 1868.
Anon. *The Word* series. All other works in the series by Susan Warner.

21073. LITTLE JACK'S FOUR LESSONS. NY: American Tract Soc'y, <1869>.
Anon.

*21075. THE MELODY OF THE TWENTY-THIRD PSALM. NY: Randolph, 1869.

*21076. WAYFARING HYMNS, ORIGINAL AND TRANSLATED. NY: Randolph,
1869.

21077. STORIES OF VINEGAR HILL. Lon: Nisbet, 1871.
Anon. *Golden Ladder Series.* For simultaneous U.S. publication in 6v., see following entries.

21078. THE FOWLS OF THE AIR. NY: Carter & Bros., 1872.
Anon. *Stories of Vinegar Hill* series.

21079. GOLDEN THORNS. NY: Carter & Bros., 1872.
Anon. *Stories of Vinegar Hill* series.

21080. AN HUNDREDFOLD. NY: Carter & Bros., 1872.
Anon. *Stories of Vinegar Hill* series.

21081. THE OLD CHURCH DOOR. NY: Carter & Bros., 1872.
Anon. *Stories of Vinegar Hill* series.

ANNA B. WARNER (cont.)

21082. PLANTS WITHOUT ROOT. NY: Carter & Bros., 1872.
Anon. *Stories of Vinegar Hill* series.

21083. SPRING WORK. NY: Carter & Bros., 1872.
Anon. *Stories of Vinegar Hill* series.

21084. GARDENING BY MYSELF. NY: Randolph, 1872.

21085. THE OTHER SHORE. Lon: Nisbet, 1873 <i.e. 1872>.
2 parts or 1v.

*21086. THE OTHER SHORE. NY: Randolph, <n.d., 1872>.

21087. MISS TILLER'S VEGETABLE GARDEN AND THE MONEY SHE MADE BY IT. NY: Randolph, <1873>.

21088. THE FOURTH WATCH. NY: Randolph, <1874>.

*21090. WYCH HAZEL. Lon: Nisbet, 1876.
Anon. With Susan Warner.

21091. WYCH HAZEL. NY: Putnam's Sons, 1876.
With Susan Warner.

21092. THE GOLD OF CHICKAREE. NY: Putnam's Sons, 1876.
With Susan Warner.

21093. BLUE FLAG AND CLOTH OF GOLD. NY: Carter & Bros., 1880.

21094. WHAT AILETH THEE? Lon: Nisbet, 1881.
Anon.

21095. WHAT AILETH THEE? NY: Randolph, <1880, i.e. 1881>.
Anon. Reprinted in 1887 as *The Question to Hagar* (No. 21103).

21096. TIRED CHURCH MEMBERS. NY: Carter & Bros., 1881.

21097. THE LIGHT OF THE MORNING: CLEAR SHINING AFTER RAIN. NY: Randolph, <1882>.

21098. A BAG OF STORIES. NY: Carter & Bros., 1883.

21099. THE SHOES OF PEACE. NY: Carter & Bros., <1884>.

21102. CROSS CORNERS. NY: Carter & Bros., <1887>.

21104. YOURS AND MINE. NY: Carter & Bros., <1888>.

21105. A SERVANT OF THE KING. INCIDENTS IN THE LIFE OF THE REV. GEORGE AINSLIE. NY: Ireland, 1889.

21106. OAK BEND; OR, PATIENCE AND HER SCHOOLING. Lon: Nisbet, 1891.
Golden Ladder Series. For U.S. publication see next entry.

*21107. PATIENCE. Phila: Lippincott, 1891.

21108. UP AND DOWN THE HOUSE. NY: Randolph, <1892>.

21110. FRESH AIR. NY: American Tract Soc'y, <1899>.

21111. WEST POINT COLORS. NY, Chi, &c.: Revell, <1903>.

21112. SUSAN WARNER ("ELIZABETH WETHERELL"). NY & Lon: Putnam's Sons, 1909.

21114. LETTERS AND MEMORIES OF SUSAN WARNER & ANNA BARTLETT WARNER. NY & Lon: Putnam's Sons, 1925.
By Olivia Egleston Phelps Stokes.

Charles Dudley Warner
1829–1900

21122. MY SUMMER IN A GARDEN. Bos: Fields, Osgood, 1871.
Extended edition published in 1885 (No. 21161).

*21124. SAUNTERINGS. Bos: Osgood, 1872.

*21125. BACKLOG STUDIES. Bos: Osgood, 1873.
Published simultaneously (?) in the U.K. with title-page dated 1872. Unauthorized U.K. edition published in 1873 with a slightly different selection of material (No. 21126).

21127. THE GILDED AGE A TALE OF TO-DAY. Hartford: American Pub. Co.,
1873.
With Mark Twain, see No. 3357 above.

*21128. BADDECK, AND THAT SORT OF THING. Bos: Osgood, 1874.

21133. MUMMIES AND MOSLEMS. Hartford: American Pub. Co., 1876.
"Issued by subscription only." Reprinted in 1876 as *My Winter on the Nile* (No.
21232); revised edition with the latter title published in 1881 (No. 21152).

*21134. IN THE LEVANT. Bos: Osgood, 1877.

*21135. BEING A BOY. Bos: Osgood, 1878.

21136. IN THE WILDERNESS. Bos: Houghton, Osgood, 1878.
Extended edition published in 1881 (No. 21147).

21148. THE AMERICAN NEWSPAPER AN ESSAY. Bos: Osgood, 1881.
Read before the Social Science Association, Saratoga Springs, 6 Sept.1881.

21149. CAPTAIN JOHN SMITH (1579–1631) ... A STUDY OF HIS LIFE AND
WRITINGS. NY: Holt, 1881.
Lives of American Worthies.

21150. WASHINGTON IRVING. Bos: Houghton, Mifflin, 1881.
American Men of Letters series. An earlier biographical & critical study by Warner
was published in 1880 in the *Geoffrey Crayon Edition* of Irving's works (No. 21141).
See also No. 21187 below.

*21159. A ROUNDABOUT JOURNEY. Bos & NY: Houghton, Mifflin, 1884.

21165. THEIR PILGRIMAGE. NY: Harper & Bros., 1887.

21168. ON HORSEBACK A TOUR IN VIRGINA, NORTH CAROLINA, AND
TENNESSEE WITH NOTES OF TRAVEL IN MEXICO AND CALIFORNIA.
Bos & NY: Houghton, Mifflin, 1888.

21172. STUDIES IN THE SOUTH AND WEST WITH COMMENTS ON CANADA.
NY: Harper & Bros., 1889.

21173. A LITTLE JOURNEY IN THE WORLD. A NOVEL. NY: Harper &
Bros., 1889.

21179. OUR ITALY. NY: Harper & Bros., 1891.

21180. AS WE WERE SAYING. NY: Harper & Bros., 1891.

21187. THE WORK OF WASHINGTON IRVING. NY: Harper & Bros., 1893.
Harper's Black & White Series.

CHARLES DUDLEY WARNER (cont.)

*21190. AS WE GO. NY: Harper & Bros., 1894.

 21196. THE GOLDEN HOUSE. A NOVEL. NY: Harper & Bros., 1895.

 21205. THE RELATION OF LITERATURE TO LIFE. NY: Harper & Bros., 1897.

*21206. THE PEOPLE FOR WHOM SHAKESPEARE WROTE. NY: Harper & Bros., 1897.

 21210. THAT FORTUNE. A NOVEL. NY & Lon: Harper & Bros., 1899.

 21222. FASHIONS IN LITERATURE AND OTHER LITERARY AND SOCIAL ESSAYS & ADDRESSES. NY: Dodd, Mead, 1902.
Several of these addresses were first published separately.

 21223. CHARLES DUDLEY WARNER. NY: McClure, Phillips, 1904.
By Mrs. James T. Fields. *Contemporary Men of Letters Series.*

*21224. THE COMPLETE WRITINGS OF CHARLES DUDLEY WARNER. Hartford: American Pub. Co., 1904.
15v.

Susan Bogert Warner
(Elizabeth Wetherell)
1819–1885

*21253. THE WIDE, WIDE WORLD. By Elizabeth Wetherell. NY: Putnam, 1851.
2v. The original final chapter, here omitted, first published in 1978 in Mabel Baker's *Light in the Morning* (Nos. 21119 & 21310).

 21254. AMERICAN FEMALE PATRIOTISM. A PRIZE ESSAY. By Elizabeth Wetherell. NY: Fletcher, 1852.

*21255. QUEECHY. By Elizabeth Wetherell. NY: Putnam, 1852.
2v. Published simultaneously (?) in the U.K. (No. 21256).

 21260. CARL KRINKEN: HIS CHRISTMAS STOCKING. NY: Putnam, 1854.
Anon. *Ellen Montgomery's Book Shelf* series. The series was largely written by Anna Warner, though this work is probably by Susan Warner.

*21261. THE HILLS OF THE SHATEMUC. Lon: Low, Son, 1856.
These sheets also issued in Paris in 1856 & reissued in London in 1857 as *Rufus & Winthrop* in the *Run and Read Library.* A Tauchnitz edition was also published in 1856 (No. 21262).

*21263. THE HILLS OF THE SHATEMUC. NY: Appleton, 1856.
Anon.

 21264. SAY AND SEAL. Lon: Bentley, 1860.
Anon. With Anna Warner, see No. 21053 above.

 21265. SAY AND SEAL. Phila: Lippincott, 1860.
Anon. With Anna Warner, see No. 21054 above.

SUSAN B. WARNER (cont.)

21266. THE GOLDEN LADDER: STORIES ILLUSTRATIVE OF THE EIGHT BEATITUDES. Lon: Nisbet, 1863.
Anon. With Anna Warner, see No. 21055 above. For U.S. publication as a set in 8v., see the following entries.

21267. THE TWO SCHOOL GIRLS. NY: Carlton & Porter, <1862, i.e. 1863>.
Anon. Part of a series written with Anna Warner, see No. 21056 above. This tale by Susan Warner.

21268. ALTHEA. NY: Carlton & Porter, <1862, i.e. 1863>.
Anon. Part of a series written with Anna Warner, see No. 21057 above.

21269. GERTRUDE AND HER CAT. NY: Carlton & Porter, <1862, i.e. 1863>.
Anon. Part of a series written with Anna Warner, see No. 21058 above. This tale by Susan Warner.

21270. THE ROSE IN THE DESERT. NY: Carlton & Porter, <1862, i.e. 1863>.
Anon. Part of a series written with Anna Warner, see No. 21059 above.

21271. THE LITTLE BLACK HEN. NY: Carlton & Porter, <1862, i.e. 1863>.
Anon. Part of a series written with Anna Warner, see No. 21060 above.

21272. MARTHA'S HYMN. NY: Carlton & Porter, <1862, i.e. 1863>.
Anon. Part of a series written with Anna Warner, see No. 21061 above.

21273. THE CARPENTER'S HOUSE. NY: Carlton & Porter, <1862, i.e. 1863>.
Anon. Part of a series written with Anna Warner, see No. 21062 above. This tale by Susan Warner.

21274. THE PRINCE IN DISGUISE. NY: Carlton & Porter, <1862, i.e. 1863>.
Anon. Part of a series written with Anna Warner, see No. 21063 above. This tale by Anna Warner.

*21275. THE OLD HELMET. NY: Carter & Bros., 1864.
2v. Anon.

21276. MELBOURNE HOUSE. NY: Carter & Bros., 1864.
2v. Anon.

*21277. WALKS FROM EDEN. NY: Carter & Bros., 1866.
Anon. *The Word* series.

21278. THE HOUSE OF ISRAEL. NY: Carter & Bros., 1867.
Anon. *The Word* series.

21279. DAISY. Phila: Lippincott, 1868.
Anon. Continued from *Melbourne House.*

*21280. DAISY IN THE FIELD. Lon: Nisbet, 1869.
Anon. *Golden Ladder Series.* For U.S. edition see next entry.

21281. DAISY ... SECOND SERIES. Phila: Lippincott, 1869.
Anon. Continued from *Melbourne House.*

*21282. "WHAT SHE COULD." NY: Carter & Bros., 1871.
Anon.

*21283. OPPORTUNITIES. NY: Carter & Bros., 1871.
Anon. Sequel to *"What She Could".*

SUSAN B. WARNER (cont.)

*21284. THE HOUSE IN TOWN. NY: Carter & Bros., 1872.
   Anon. Sequel to *Opportunities.*

 21285. LESSONS ON THE STANDARD BEARERS OF THE OLD TESTAMENT.
   NY: Randolph, <1872>.
   "Third grade for older classes." At head of title: *Oldest Grade.*

*21286. TRADING. NY: Carter & Bros., 1873.
   Anon. Finishing the story of *The House in Town.*

 21287. THE LITTLE CAMP ON EAGLE HILL. NY: Carter & Bros., 1874.
   Anon.

 21288. WILLOW BROOK. NY: Carter & Bros., 1874.
   Anon.

 21289. SCEPTRES AND CROWNS. NY: Carter & Bros., 1875.
   Anon.

 21290. THE FLAG OF TRUCE. NY: Carter & Bros., 1875.
   Anon.

 21291. GIVING TRUST. I. BREAD AND ORANGES. II. RAPIDS OF NIAGARA. Lon:
   Nisbet, 1875.
   Anon. "Tales illustrating the Lord's prayer." *Golden Ladder Series.*

 21292. BREAD AND ORANGES. NY: Carter & Bros., 1875.
   Anon.

*21293. THE RAPIDS OF NIAGARA. NY: Carter & Bros., 1876.
   Anon.

 21294. WYCH HAZEL. Lon: Nisbet, 1876.
   Anon. With Anna Warner, see No. 21090 above.

 21295. WYCH HAZEL. NY: Putnam's Sons, 1876.
   With Anna Warner, see No. 21091 above.

 21296. THE GOLD OF CHICKAREE. NY: Putnam's Sons, 1876.
   With Anna Warner, see No. 21092 above..

 21297. PINE NEEDLES. Lon: Nisbet, 1877.
   Anon. *Golden Ladder Series.*

 21298. PINE NEEDLES. NY: Carter & Bros., 1877.
   Anon.

 21299. DIANA. NY: Putnam's Sons, 1877.

 21300. THE KINGDOM OF JUDAH. NY: Carter & Bros., 1878.
   Anon.

 21301. THE BROKEN WALLS OF JERUSALEM AND THE REBUILDING OF
   THEM. NY: Carter & Bros., 1879.
   Anon.

 21302. MY DESIRE. NY: Carter & Bros., 1879.
   Anon.

 21303. THE END OF A COIL. NY: Carter & Bros., 1880.
   Anon.

SUSAN B. WARNER (cont.)

*21304. THE LETTER OF CREDIT. NY: Carter & Bros., 1882.
Anon.

21305. NOBODY. NY: Carter & Bros., 1883.
Anon.

*21306. STEPHEN, M.D. NY: Carter & Bros., 1883.
Anon.

21307. A RED WALLFLOWER. NY: Carter & Bros., 1884.
Anon.

*21308. DAISY PLAINS. NY: Carter & Bros., <1885>.
Anon. Completed by Anna Warner after Susan Warner's death.

21309. LETTERS AND MEMORIES OF SUSAN & ANNA BARTLETT WARNER.
NY & Lon: Putnam's Sons, 1925.
By Olivia Egleston Phelps Stokes. See No. 21114.

Edward Noyes Westcott
1847–1898

21313. DAVID HARUM A STORY OF AMERICAN LIFE. NY: Appleton, 1898.

21316. THE TELLER A STORY...WITH THE LETTERS OF EDWARD NOYES
WESTCOTT. NY: Appleton, 1901.
Ed. Margaret Westcott Muzzey. An undated Canadian edition of *The Teller* was
also published (No. 21317), presumably a reprint.

James Abbott McNeill Whistler
1834–1903

Note: The title-pages of many of these works are signed only with
Whistler's butterfly device.

21319. WHISTLER V. RUSKIN ART & ART CRITICS. Lon: Chatto & Windus,
<1878>.

21323. CORRESPONDENCE. PADDON PAPERS. THE OWL AND THE CABINET.
<n.p., n.d.; Lon, 1882>.

21330. MR. WHISTLER'S "TEN O'CLOCK." Lon, 1888.
First published privately in 1885 (No. 21328).

21331. "TEN O'CLOCK." Bos & NY: Houghton, Mifflin, 1888.

21332. THE GENTLE ART OF MAKING ENEMIES. Paris: Delabrosse, 1890.
Anon. Ed. Sheridan Ford. Unauthorized edition, containing material not in the
London 1890 edition.

21333. THE GENTLE ART OF MAKING ENEMIES. NY: Stokes & Bro., 1890.
Anon. Ed. Sheridan Ford. Sheets of the Paris edition, see preceding entry.

*21334. THE GENTLE ART OF MAKING ENEMIES. Lon: Heinemann, 1890.
Authorized edition. Slightly extended edition published in 1892 (No. 21337).

JAMES McNEILL WHISTLER (cont.)

*21335. THE GENTLE ART OF MAKING ENEMIES. NY: Lovell, 1890.
Sheets of the London edition, see preceding entry.

*21342. EDEN VERSUS WHISTLER THE BARONET & THE BUTTERFLY A VALEN-
TINE WITH A VERDICT. Paris: May, <1899>.

*21343. EDEN VERSUS WHISTLER THE BARONET & THE BUTTERFLY A VALEN-
TINE WITH A VERDICT. NY: Russell, 1899.

*21346. WILDE V WHISTLER BEING AN ACRIMONIOUS CORRESPONDENCE ON
ART. Lon, 1906.
"Privately printed." All Whistler material here reprinted from No. 21334 above.

 21347. NINE LETTERS TO TH. WATTS-DUNTON. Chelsea: <Ehrman>, 1922.
"Printed for private distribution."

 21348. CORRESPONDANCE MALLARMÉ-WHISTLER HISTOIRE DE LA GRANDE
AMITIÉ DE LEURS DERNIÈRES ANNÉES. Paris: Nizet, 1964.
Ed. Carl Paul Barbier.

Sarah Helen Power Whitman
1803–1878

 21366. HOURS OF LIFE, AND OTHER POEMS. Providence: Whitney, 1853.

*21368. EDGAR POE AND HIS CRITICS. NY: Rudd & Carleton, 1860.

 21370. CINDERELLA. By Miss Power. Providence: Hammond, Angell, Ptrs,
1867.
With Susan Anna Power, Whitman's sister.

 21371. THE SLEEPING BEAUTY. By Miss Power. Providence: Hammond,
Angell, Ptrs, 1868.
With Susan Anna Power, Whitman's sister.

 21383. POEMS. Bos: Houghton, Osgood, 1879.

 21387. POE'S HELEN. NY: Scribner's Sons, 1916.
By Caroline Ticknor.

 21392. POE'S HELEN REMEMBERS. Charlottesville: U PR of Virginia,
<1979>.
Ed. John Carl Miller.

Walt Whitman
1819–1892

Note: The many reissues and corrected printings of Whitman's works
have not been listed or noted here, for full details see BAL. Whitman's
name is not present on the title-page of many of these works.

*21393. FRANKLIN EVANS; OR THE INEBRIATE. <NY: J. Winchester, 1842>.
New World, Extra Series, No. 34 (Vol. 2, No. 10), Nov. 1842. Reissued in 1843 with
cover-title *The Merchant's Clerk, in New York.*

WALT WHITMAN (cont.)

*21395. LEAVES OF GRASS. Brooklyn, 1855.

21396. LEAVES OF GRASS. Brooklyn, 1856.
Whitman's manuscript notes for this edition published in 1959 as *An 1855–56 Notebook toward the Second Edition of Leaves of Grass*, (No. 21485).

*21397. LEAVES OF GRASS. Bos: Thayer & Eldridge, 1860–61.
Whitman's copy, containing manuscript additions & revisions, reproduced in facsimile in 1968 as *Walt Whitman's Blue Book* (No. 21495). Critical edition of the manuscripts for this edition by Fredson Bowers published in 1955 (No. 21483).

*21398. WALT WHITMAN'S DRUM-TAPS. NY, 1865.
Reissued in 1865 with a *Sequel.*

*21399. LEAVES OF GRASS. NY, 1867.
Issued in 2 forms.

21401. POEMS. Lon: Hotten, 1868.
Ed. William Michael Rossetti. Contains revisions by Whitman.

21402. DEMOCRATIC VISTAS. Wash DC, 1871.

*21403. LEAVES OF GRASS. Wash DC, 1871.

*21404. PASSAGE TO INDIA. Wash DC, 1871.
The title poem was also distributed in proof from a different setting of type (No. 21574).

21405. AFTER ALL, NOT TO CREATE ONLY. Bos: Roberts Bros., 1871.
Recited at the American Institute Annual Exhibition, New York, 7 Sept. 1871. Also distributed in proof from a different setting of type (No. 21513).

21408. AS A STRONG BIRD ON PINIONS FREE. AND OTHER POEMS. Wash DC, 1872.

*21409. MEMORANDA DURING THE WAR. Camden NJ, 1875–76.
"Author's publication."

*21410. LEAVES OF GRASS. Camden NJ, 1876.
"Author's edition, with portraits and intercalations." On spine: *Centennial Edition.* Printed from the altered plates of No. 21403. Reprinted in 1876 (No. 21412) as the "Author's edition, with portraits from life."

*21411. TWO RIVULETS. Camden NJ: The Author, 1876.
"Author's edition." On spine: *Centennial Edition.* Reprinted & reissued in 1876 (No. 21413).

*21418. LEAVES OF GRASS. Bos: Osgood, 1881–82.
These sheets also issued in the U.K. dated 1881 & reissued in Camden NJ as the "Author's edition" dated 1882.

21422. SPECIMEN DAYS & COLLECT. Phila: Rees Welsh, 1882–83.
Revised edition of "Specimen Days" published in the U.K. in 1887 as *Specimen Days in America* (No. 21428).

21429. DEMOCRATIC VISTAS, AND OTHER PAPERS. Lon: Scott, 1888.
"Published by arrangement with the author."

WALT WHITMAN (cont.)

*21430. NOVEMBER BOUGHS. Phila: McKay, 1888.
These sheets also issued in the U.K. dated 1889.

21431. COMPLETE POEMS & PROSE ... 1855 ... 1888. <Camden NJ, 1888>.
Printed from the altered plates of Nos. 21418, 21422 & 21430.

21435. LEAVES OF GRASS WITH SANDS AT SEVENTY & A BACKWARD GLANCE
O'ER TRAVEL'D ROADS. <Camden NJ, 1889>.
Printed from the altered plates of Nos. 21418 & 21430.

*21440. GOOD-BYE MY FANCY 2D ANNEX TO LEAVES OF GRASS. Phila: McKay,
1891.

*21441. LEAVES OF GRASS INCLUDING SANDS AT SEVENTY ... 1ST ANNEX,
GOOD-BYE MY FANCY ... 2D ANNEX, A BACKWARD GLANCE O'ER
TRAVEL'D ROADS. Phila: McKay, 1891–92.
Printed from the altered plates of Nos. 21418, 21430 & 21440. Reprinted in
1897 with 13 additional poems (No. 21447).

*21446. CALAMUS. Bos: Maynard, 1897.
Ed. Richard Maurice Bucke. Letters to Peter Doyle, 1868–80.

*21448. THE WOUND DRESSER. Bos: Small, Maynard, 1898.
Ed. Richard Maurice Bucke. Letters written during the Civil War.

21451. NOTES AND FRAGMENTS: LEFT BY WALT WHITMAN. <London,
Ontario>, 1899.
"Printed for private distribution only." Ed. Richard Maurice Bucke.

*21454. THE COMPLETE WRITINGS. NY & Lon: Putnam's Sons, <1902>.
10v. Ed. Richard Maurice Bucke, Thomas B. Harned & Horace L. Traubel, with
additional material by Oscar Lovell Triggs. Material from Vol. 8 was also issued
separately for copyright purposes as *Letters Written by Walt Whitman to His Mother
... Together with Certain Papers ... Now First Utilized* (No. 21455).

21456. AN AMERICAN PRIMER. Bos: Small, Maynard, 1904.
Ed. Horace Traubel.

21457. WALT WHITMAN'S DIARY IN CANADA WITH EXTRACTS FROM OTHER OF
HIS DIARIES AND LITERARY NOTE-BOOKS. Bos: Small, Maynard, 1904.
Ed. William Sloane Kennedy.

21464. THE GATHERING OF THE FORCES. NY & Lon: Putnam's Sons, 1920.
2v. Ed. Cleveland Rodgers & John Black. Material from the *Brooklyn Daily Eagle*,
1846–47.

21465. THE UNCOLLECTED POETRY AND PROSE. Garden City NY & Toronto:
Doubleday, Page, 1921.
2v. Ed. Emory Holloway.

21470. RIVULETS OF PROSE CRITICAL ESSAYS. NY: Greenberg, 1928.
Ed. Carolyn Wells & Alfred F. Goldsmith.

21471. WALT WHITMAN'S WORKSHOP. A COLLECTION OF UNPUBLISHED
MANUSCRIPTS. Cambridge: Harvard U PR, 1928.
Ed. Clifton Joseph Furness. "The Eighteenth Presidency," here collected, was
also published separately in 1928 (No. 21469).

WALT WHITMAN (cont.)

21472. A CHILD'S REMINISCENCE. Seattle: U of Washington Book Store, 1930.
Ed. Thomas O. Mabbott & Rollo G. Silver. Material from the New York *Saturday Press*.

21473. I SIT AND LOOK OUT. NY: Columbia U PR, 1932.
Ed. Emory Holloway & Vernolian Schwartz. Editorials from the *Brooklyn Daily Times*.

*21474. WALT <W>HITMAN AND THE CIVIL WAR. Phila: U of Pennsylvania PR, 1933.
Ed. Charles I. Glicksberg.

*21475. NEW YORK DISSECTED. NY: R.R. Wilson, 1936.
Ed. Emory Holloway & Ralph Adimari. Newspaper articles.

21478. FAINT CLEWS & INDIRECTIONS. Durham NC: Duke U PR, 1949.
Ed. Clarence Gohdes & Rollo G. Silver.

21479. WALT WHITMAN OF THE NEW YORK AURORA. State College PA: Bald Eagle PR, 1950.
Ed. Joseph Jay Rubin & Charles H. Brown.

21480. WALT WHITMAN LOOKS AT THE SCHOOLS. NY: King's Crown PR, 1950.
Ed. Florence Bernstein Freedman. Newspaper articles.

21489. THE CORRESPONDENCE. <NY>: New York U PR, 1961.
Vols. 1–2 of six. Ed. Edwin Haviland Miller. *The Collected Writings of Walt Whitman*.

21491. THE EARLY POEMS AND THE FICTION. <NY>: New York U PR, 1963.
Ed. Thomas L. Brasher. *The Collected Writings of Walt Whitman*.

21492. PROSE WORKS 1892. <NY>: New York U PR, 1963–64.
2v. Ed. Floyd Stovall. *The Collected Writings of Walt Whitman*.

21493. THE CORRESPONDENCE. <NY>: New York U PR, 1964.
Vol. 3 of six. Ed. Edwin Haviland Miller. *The Collected Writings of Walt Whitman*.

*21494. LEAVES OF GRASS COMPREHENSIVE READER'S EDITION. <NY>: New York U PR, 1965.
Ed. Harold W. Blodgett & Sculley Bradley. *The Collected Writings of Walt Whitman*.

21496. THE CORRESPONDENCE. <NY>: New York U PR, 1969.
Vols. 4–5 of six. Ed. Edwin Haviland Miller. *The Collected Writings of Walt Whitman*.

21499. THE CORRESPONDENCE. <NY>: New York U PR, 1977.
Vol. 6 of six. Ed. Edwin Haviland Miller. *The Collected Writings of Walt Whitman*.

21500. DAYBOOKS AND NOTEBOOKS. <NY>: New York U PR, 1978.
3v. Ed. William White. *The Collected Writings of Walt Whitman*.

21501. LEAVES OF GRASS A TEXTUAL VARIORUM. <NY>: New York U PR, 1980.
Ed. Sculley Bradley, Harold W. Blodgett, Arthur Golden, William White. *The Collected Writings of Walt Whitman*.

WALT WHITMAN (cont.)
21502. NOTEBOOKS AND UNPUBLISHED PROSE MANUSCRIPTS. <NY>: New York U PR, 1984.
6v. Ed. Edward F. Grier. *The Collected Writings of Walt Whitman.*

John Greenleaf Whittier
1807–1892

*21671. LEGENDS OF NEW-ENGLAND. Hartford: Hanmer & Phelps, 1831.

*21677. MOLL PITCHER, A POEM. Bos: Carter & Hendee, 1832.
Anon. Type facsimile of this edition published in 1887 (No. 22310).

21681. JUSTICE AND EXPEDIENCY; OR, SLAVERY CONSIDERED. Haverhill: Ptd by Thayer, 1833.

21687. OUR COUNTRYMEN IN CHAINS! NY: Anti-Slavery Office, <n.d., 1834>. Broadside.

21697. MOGG MEGONE, A POEM. Bos: Light & Stearns, 1836.

*21705. POEMS WRITTEN DURING THE PROGRESS OF THE ABOLITION QUESTION ... BETWEEN ... 1830 AND 1838. Bos: Knapp, 1837.

*21709. NARRATIVE OF JAMES WILLIAMS, AN AMERICAN SLAVE. NY: American Anti- Slavery Soc'y, 1838.
Anon.

21710. POEMS. Phila: Healy, 1838.

21727. LAYS OF MY HOME, AND OTHER POEMS. Bos: Ticknor, 1843.

21728. SONG OF THE VERMONTERS.* 1779. Windsor VT: Ptd by Bishop & Tracy, <n.d., 1843>.
Broadside.

21739. THE STRANGER IN LOWELL. Bos: Waite, Peirce <*sic*>, 1845.
Anon.

21747. VOICES OF FREEDOM ... FOURTH AND COMPLETE EDITION. Phila: Cavender, 1846.

21753. THE SUPERNATURALISM OF NEW ENGLAND. NY & Lon: Wiley & Putnam, 1847.
Anon. *Library of American Books,* No. 27. These sheets also issued in the U.K. in 1847.

*21765. POEMS. Bos: Mussey, 1849.

21766. LEAVES FROM MARGARET SMITH'S JOURNAL IN THE PROVINCE OF MASSACHUSETTS BAY. 1678-9. Bos: Ticknor, Reed, & Fields, 1849.
Anon.

21769. OLD PORTRAITS AND MODERN SKETCHES. Bos: Ticknor, Reed, & Fields, 1850.

21771. SONGS OF LABOR, AND OTHER POEMS. Bos: Ticknor, Reed, & Fields, 1850.

21780. THE CHAPEL OF THE HERMITS, AND OTHER POEMS. Bos: Ticknor, Reed, & Fields, 1853.

JOHN GREENLEAF WHITTIER (cont.)
21786. LITERARY RECREATIONS AND MISCELLANIES. Bos: Ticknor & Fields, 1854.

21792. THE PANORAMA, AND OTHER POEMS. Bos: Ticknor & Fields, 1856.
"Maud Muller," here collected, was also (earlier?) printed several times as a broadside (No. 21787) & first published separately in book form in 1867 (No. 22258).

21803. THE POETICAL WORKS. Bos: Ticknor & Fields, 1857.
2v. *Blue & Gold* edition.

21804. THE SYCAMORES. Nantucket <i.e. Hartford>, 1857.
Privately printed.

21819. HOME BALLADS AND POEMS. Bos: Ticknor & Fields, 1860.

21846. IN WAR TIME AND OTHER POEMS. Bos: Ticknor & Fields, 1864.
"Barbara Frietchie," here collected, was also (earlier?) printed several times as a broadside or leaflet (No. 21843).

*21862. SNOW-BOUND. A WINTER IDYL. Bos: Ticknor & Fields, 1866.

*21866. THE TENT ON THE BEACH AND OTHER POEMS. Bos: Ticknor & Fields, 1867.

21874. AMONG THE HILLS, AND OTHER POEMS. Bos: Fields, Osgood, 1869.

21889. MIRIAM AND OTHER POEMS. Bos: Fields, Osgood, 1871.

21901. CHILD LIFE: A COLLECTION OF POEMS. Bos: Osgood, 1872.
Edited, with contributions (all reprints), by Whittier with assistance from Lucy Larcom (see No. 11332).

*21904. THE PENNSYLVANIA PILGRIM, AND OTHER POEMS. Bos: Osgood, 1872.

21915. CHILD LIFE IN PROSE. Bos: Osgood, 1874.
Edited, with 1 contribution, by Whittier with assistance from Lucy Larcom (see No. 11334).

*21923. HAZEL-BLOSSOMS. Bos: Osgood, 1875.
Poems, pp. <103>–133, by Elizabeth H. Whittier.

*21932. MABEL MARTIN A HARVEST IDYL. Bos: Osgood, 1876.
Extended version of "The Witch's Daughter" from *Home Ballads*, 1860.

21933. SONGS OF THREE CENTURIES. Bos: Osgood, 1876.
Edited, with contributions (all reprints), by Whittier with assistance from Lucy Larcom (see No. 11341).

21958. THE VISION OF ECHARD AND OTHER POEMS. Bos: Houghton, Osgood, 1878.

21996. THE KING'S MISSIVE, AND OTHER POEMS. Bos: Houghton, Mifflin, 1881.

22025. THE BAY OF SEVEN ISLANDS, AND OTHER POEMS. Lon: Low, Marston, et al, 1883.

22026. THE BAY OF SEVEN ISLANDS, AND OTHER POEMS. Bos & NY: Houghton, Mifflin, 1883.

22072. SAINT GREGORY'S GUEST AND RECENT POEMS. Bos & NY: Houghton, Mifflin, 1886.

JOHN GREENLEAF WHITTIER (cont.)

*22102. THE WRITINGS OF JOHN GREENLEAF WHITTIER. Bos & NY: Houghton, Mifflin, 1888.
7v.

22137. AT SUNDOWN. Cambridge: Riverside PR, 1890.
"Privately printed." For published edition see next entry.

*22158. AT SUNDOWN. Bos & NY: Houghton, Mifflin, 1892.
These sheets also issued in the U.K. Contains a preface & 7 poems not in the 1890 privately printed edition.

*22172. LIFE AND LETTERS OF JOHN GREENLEAF WHITTIER. Bos & NY: Houghton, Mifflin, 1894.
2v. By Samuel T. Pickard.

22200. WHITTIER CORRESPONDENCE FROM THE OAK KNOLL COLLECTIONS 1830–1892. Salem: Essex Book & Print Club, 1911.
Ed. John Albree.

22214. WHITTIER ON WRITERS AND WRITING THE UNCOLLECTED CRITICAL WRITINGS. <Syracuse>: Syracuse U PR, <1950>.
Ed. Edwin Harrison Cady & Harry Hayden Clark.

22221. THE LETTERS OF JOHN GREENLEAF WHITTIER. Cambridge & Lon: Harvard U PR, 1975.
3v. Ed. John B. Pickard.

Kate Douglas Smith Wiggin
1856–1923

22571. THE STORY OF PATSY A REMINISCENCE. By Kate Douglas Smith. SF: Murdock, 1883.
See also No. 22588 below.

*22577. KINDERGARTEN CHIMES, A COLLECTION OF SONGS AND GAMES. Bos: O. Ditson, 1885.
Edited, with contributions, by Wiggin. Revised & extended edition published in 1887 (No. 22581).

22580. THE BIRDS' CHRISTMAS CAROL. SF: Murdock, 1887.
See also next entry.

22587. THE BIRDS' CHRISTMAS CAROL. Bos & NY: Houghton, Mifflin, 1889.
First trade publication. Slightly revised edition published in 1891 (No. 22598).
For a dramatization see No. 22670 below.

22588. THE STORY OF PATSY. Bos & NY: Houghton, Mifflin, 1889.
First trade publication. Considerably expanded from the 1883 edition.

22589. A SUMMER IN A CAÑON A CALIFORNIA STUDY. Bos & NY: Houghton, Mifflin, 1889.

22594. TIMOTHY'S QUEST. Bos & NY: Houghton, Mifflin, 1890.

KATE DOUGLAS WIGGIN (cont.)

22596. THE STORY HOUR A BOOK FOR THE HOME AND THE KINDERGARTEN. Bos & NY: Houghton, Mifflin, 1890.
With Nora A. Smith.

*22602. CHILDREN'S RIGHTS A BOOK OF NURSERY LOGIC. Bos & NY: Houghton, Mifflin, 1892.
With Nora A. Smith.

*22606. A CATHEDRAL COURTSHIP AND PENELOPE'S ENGLISH EXPERIENCES. Bos & NY: Houghton, Mifflin, 1893.
Revised & extended editions of the 2 works published separately in 1900 (Nos. 22623 & 22626).

*22607. POLLY OLIVER'S PROBLEM A STORY FOR GIRLS. Bos & NY: Houghton, Mifflin, 1893.

22611. THE VILLAGE WATCH-TOWER. Bos & NY: Houghton, Mifflin, 1895.

22612. FROEBEL'S GIFTS. Bos & NY: Houghton, Mifflin, 1895.
At head of title: *The Republic of Childhood*. With Nora A. Smith.

22613. FROEBEL'S OCCUPATIONS. Bos & NY: Houghton, Mifflin, 1896.
At head of title: *The Republic of Childhood*. With Nora A. Smith.

22616. KINDERGARTEN PRINCIPLES AND PRACTICE. Bos & NY: Houghton, Mifflin, 1896.
At head of title: *The Republic of Childhood*. With Nora A. Smith.

*22617. MARM LISA. Bos & NY: Houghton, Mifflin, 1896.
A U.K. copyright printing was also produced in 1896 (No. 22614).

*22620. PENELOPE'S PROGRESS ... EXPERIENCES IN SCOTLAND. Bos & NY: Houghton, Mifflin, 1898.
A U.K. copyright printing was also produced in 1897–98 (No. 22619). Slightly revised edition published in 1900 (No. 22624).

*22625. PENELOPE'S IRISH EXPERIENCES. Bos & NY: Houghton, Mifflin, 1901.

*22627. DIARY OF A GOOSE GIRL. Bos & NY: Houghton, Mifflin, 1902.

*22631. HALF-A-DOZEN HOUSEKEEPERS. Phila: Altemus, <1903>.

*22632. REBECCA OF SUNNYBROOK FARM. Bos & NY: Houghton, Mifflin, 1903.
For a dramatization see No. 22708 below.

*22636. ROSE O' THE RIVER. Bos & NY: Houghton Mifflin, 1905.

22642. NEW CHRONICLES OF REBECCA. Bos & NY: Houghton, Mifflin, 1907.

*22644. THE OLD PEABODY PEW A CHRISTMAS ROMANCE OF A COUNTRY CHURCH. Bos & NY: Houghton, Mifflin, 1907.
For a dramatization see No. 22677 below.

22652. SUSANNA AND SUE. Bos & NY: Houghton Mifflin, 1909.

22658. MOTHER CAREY'S CHICKENS. Bos & NY: Houghton Mifflin, 1911.
For a dramatization see No. 22702 below.

KATE DOUGLAS WIGGIN (cont.)

*22662. A CHILD'S JOURNEY WITH DICKENS. Bos & NY: Houghton Mifflin, 1912.

22668. THE STORY OF WAITSTILL BAXTER. Bos & NY: Houghton Mifflin, 1913.

*22669. BLUEBEARD A MUSICAL FANTASY. NY & Lon: Harper & Bros., 1914.

*22670. THE BIRDS' CHRISTMAS CAROL DRAMATIC VERSION. Bos & NY: Houghton Mifflin, 1914.
With Helen Ingersoll.

22672. PENELOPE'S POSTSCRIPTS SWITZERLAND: VENICE WALES: DEVON HOME. Bos & NY: Houghton Mifflin, 1915.

22675. THE ROMANCE OF A CHRISTMAS CARD. Bos & NY: Houghton Mifflin, 1916.

22677. THE OLD PEABODY PEW: DRAMATISED. NY: French, <1917>.

*22679. THE WRITINGS OF KATE DOUGLAS WIGGIN. Bos & NY: Houghton Mifflin, <1917>.
10v.

*22680. LADIES-IN-WAITING. Bos & NY: Houghton Mifflin, 1919.

22689. MY GARDEN OF MEMORY AN AUTOBIOGRAPHY. Bos & NY: Houghton Mifflin, 1923.

22695. THE QUILT OF HAPPINESS. Bos & NY: Houghton Mifflin, 1923.
The Evergreen Series.

22698. LOVE BY EXPRESS A NOVEL OF CALIFORNIA. Hollis & Buxton, ME: Dorcas Soc'y, 1924.

22699. CREEPING JENNY AND OTHER NEW ENGLAND STORIES. Bos & NY: Houghton Mifflin, 1924.

22701. KATE DOUGLAS WIGGIN AS HER SISTER KNEW HER. Bos & NY: Houghton Mifflin, 1925.
By Nora Archibald Smith.

*22702. MOTHER CAREY'S CHICKENS A LITTLE COMEDY OF HOME. NY: French, 1925.
With Rachel Crothers.

22703. A THORN IN THE FLESH A MONOLOGUE. NY: French, 1926.
"Freely adapted from the French of Ernest Legouvé."

22704. THE SPIRIT OF CHRISTMAS. Bos & NY: Houghton Mifflin, 1927.

22706. A THANKSGIVING RETROSPECT OR SIMPLICITY OF LIFE IN OLD NEW ENGLAND. Bos & NY: Houghton Mifflin, 1928.

22708. REBECCA OF SUNNYBROOK FARM A STATE O' MAINE PLAY. NY & LA: French, <1932>.
With Charlotte Thompson.

Nathaniel Parker Willis
1806–1867

Note: Many of the works listed here, especially those published after 1845, are largely made up of material reprinted from earlier books; for details see BAL.

22713. SKETCHES. Bos: Goodrich, 1827.
Binder's title: *Willis' Poems.*

*22722. FUGITIVE POETRY. Bos: Peirce< sic > & Williams, 1829.

22731. POEM DELIVERED BEFORE THE SOCIETY OF UNITED BROTHERS, AT BROWN UNIVERSITY ... SEPTEMBER 6, 1831. WITH OTHER POEMS. NY: J. & J. Harper, 1831.

22735. MELANIE AND OTHER POEMS. Lon: Saunders & Otley, 1835.
Ed. Barry Cornwall <i.e. Bryan Waller Procter>. For extended U.S. edition see No. 22748 below.

22737. PENCILLINGS BY THE WAY. Lon: Macrone, 1835.
3v. Extended U.K. editions published in 1836 (No. 22742) & 1842 (No. 22765).

22741. PENCILLINGS BY THE WAY. Phila: Carey, Lea, & Blanchard, 1836.
2v. For extended U.S. edition see No. 22782 below.

22743. INKLINGS OF ADVENTURE. Lon: Saunders & Otley, 1836.
3v. Anon.

22744. INKLINGS OF ADVENTURE. NY & Lon: Saunders & Otley, 1836.
2v. Anon.

22748. MELANIE AND OTHER POEMS. NY: Saunders & Otley, 1837.
Contains 10 poems not in the U.K. edition of 1835.

22750. BIANCA VISCONTI; OR THE HEART OVERTASKED. NY: Colman, 1839.
These sheets reissued not before 1840 by Giffing, New York, in a nonce collection entitled *American Dramatic Library* (No. 4594). For comment on the U.K. edition see next entry.

22751. TORTESA THE USURER. A PLAY. NY: Colman, 1839.
These sheets reissued not before 1840 by Giffing, New York, in a nonce collection entitled *American Dramatic Library* (No. 4594). Reprinted together with *Bianca Visconti* in the U.K. in 1839 as *Two Ways of Dying for a Husband* (No. 22753).

22752. AL'ABRI, OR THE TENT PITCH'D. NY: Colman, 1839.
Later published as *Letters from Under a Bridge:* in the U.K., with a selection of reprinted poems, in 1840 (No. 22759); in the U.S. in a slightly revised & extended "complete edition" in 1844 (No. 22776). Later collected in *Rural Letters,* 1849, see No. 22801 below.

*22755. AMERICAN SCENERY. Lon: Virtue, 1840.
30 parts or 2v. "From drawings by W.H. Bartlett."

22756. LOITERINGS OF TRAVEL. Lon: Longman, Orme, et al, 1840.
3v.

N. P. WILLIS (cont.)

22757. ROMANCE OF TRAVEL, COMPRISING TALES OF FIVE LANDS. NY: Colman, 1840.
Anon.

22764. CANADIAN SCENERY ILLUSTRATED. Lon: Virtue, 1842.
30 parts or 2v. "From drawings by W.H. Bartlett."

22766. THE SCENERY AND ANTIQUITIES OF IRELAND. Lon: Virtue, <n.d., 1842>.
30 parts or 2v. With J. Stirling Coyne. "From drawings by W.H. Bartlett."

22769. THE SACRED POEMS. NY: Morris, Willis, 1843.
"The only complete edition ever published." *New Mirror Extra* <No. 1>. Revised edition published in 1844 (No. 22784); later collections with this title published in 1847 (No. 22797), 1860 (No. 22844) & 1868 (No. 22951).

*22770. POEMS OF PASSION. NY: Morris, Willis, 1843.
New Mirror Extra, No. 2.

22775. THE LADY JANE, AND OTHER HUMOUROUS POEMS. NY: Morris, Willis, 1844.
New Mirror Extra, No. 3.

22781. THE POEMS, SACRED, PASSIONATE, AND HUMOROUS. NY: Clark & Austin, 1844.
Extended edition published in 1849 (No. 22802); later collections with this title published in 1861 (No. 22933) & 1869 (No. 22954).

22782. PENCILLINGS BY THE WAY. NY: Morris & Willis, 1844.
"The first complete edition." *Mirror Library*, No. 28.   See No. 22741 above.

22783. LECTURE ON FASHION. NY: Morris & Willis, <1844>.
Delivered before the New-York Lyceum, June 1844. *Mirror Library*, No. 32.

22785. THE MIRROR LIBRARY. NY: Morris, Willis, 1843–44.
32 Nos. Edited by Willis & George P. Morris. The series was reprinted in 1846 & published in 2v.: as part of Willis's *The Complete Works* (No. 22792) & *A Library of the Prose and Poetry of Europe and America* (No. 22793), see No. 14369 above.

*22788. DASHES AT LIFE WITH A FREE PENCIL. NY: Burgess, Stringer, 1845.
3v. in 5 parts. Reprinted with material from the *Mirror Library* in 1846 as *The Complete Works* (No. 22792). For U.K. edition see next entry.

*22789. DASHES AT LIFE WITH A FREE PENCIL. Lon: Longman, Brown, Green et al, 1845.
3v. in one. The contents vary from the U.S. edition.

22799. POEMS OF EARLY AND AFTER YEARS. Phila: Carey & Hart, 1848.

22801. RURAL LETTERS AND OTHER RECORDS OF THOUGHT AT LEISURE. NY: Baker & Scribner, 1849.

*22807. PEOPLE I HAVE MET. NY: Baker & Scribner, 1850.

22809. LIFE, HERE AND THERE. NY: Baker & Scribner, 1850.

22813. MEMORANDA OF THE LIFE OF JENNY LIND. Phila: R.E. Peterson, 1851.

N. P. WILLIS (cont.)

22814. HURRY-GRAPHS. NY: Scribner, 1851.

*22821. SUMMER CRUISE IN THE MEDITERRANEAN, ON BOARD AN AMERICAN FRIGATE. NY: Scribner, 1853.

*22822. FUN-JOTTINGS; OR LAUGHS I HAVE TAKEN A PEN TO. NY: Scribner, 1853.

22823. A HEALTH TRIP TO THE TROPICS. Lon: Low, 1854 <i.e. 1853>.

22824. HEALTH TRIP TO THE TROPICS. NY: Scribner, 1853.

*22826. FAMOUS PERSONS AND PLACES. NY: Scribner, 1854.

22827. OUT-DOORS AT IDLEWILD. NY: Scribner, 1855.

22829. THE RAG-BAG, A COLLECTION OF EPHEMERA. NY: Scribner, 1855.

*22833. PAUL FANE; OR, PARTS OF A LIFE ELSE UNTOLD. NY: Scribner, 1857.

22841. THE CONVALESCENT. NY: Scribner, 1859.

Augusta Jane Evans Wilson
1835–1909

22979. INEZ: A TALE OF THE ALAMO. NY: Harper & Bros., 1855.
Anon. These sheets reissued in 1864 by J. Bradburn, New York (No. 22982).

22980. BEULAH. NY: Derby & Jackson, 1859.

22981. MACARIA; OR, ALTARS OF SACRIFICE. Richmond: West & Johnston, 1864.
Anon. Also published in New York in 1864 (No. 22983).

22984. ST. ELMO. A NOVEL. NY: Carleton, 1867.

22985. VASHTI: OR, "UNTIL DEATH US DO PART." A NOVEL. NY: Carleton, 1869.

*22986. INFELICE: A NOVEL. NY: Carleton, 1876.

*22989. AT THE MERCY OF TIBERIUS A NOVEL. NY: G.W. Dillingham, 1887.

22991. A SPECKLED BIRD. NY: G.W. Dillingham, <1902>.

*22992. DEVOTA. NY: G.W. Dillingham, <1907>.

William Winter
1836–1917

22993. POEMS. Bos: Briggs, 1855.

22994. THE EMOTION OF SYMPATHY: A METRICAL ESSAY. Bos: H.W. Dutton & Son, 1856.
Read before the Cambridge High School Association, 26 July 1856.

22997. THE QUEEN'S DOMAIN; AND OTHER POEMS. Bos: Libby, 1859.

23005. "HUMPTY DUMPTY." A PLAYFUL PARAPHRASE. By Mark Vale. <NY, 1868>.

23008. WEE WILLIE WINKIE. HIS RUN. IN A RIVULET OF VERSE. By Mark Vale. <n.p., n.d.; NY, 1870–71>.

WILLIAM WINTER (cont.)

23009. MY WITNESS: A BOOK OF VERSE. Bos: Osgood, 1871.

23011. EDWIN BOOTH IN TWELVE DRAMATIC CHARACTERS. Bos: Osgood, 1872.

23024. THISTLE-DOWN: A BOOK OF LYRICS. Lon: Tinsley Bros., 1878.

23036. THE TRIP TO ENGLAND. Bos: Lee & Shepard, 1879.
Slightly revised & extended edition published in 1881 (No. 23042). In 1886 a further revised text was published together with *English Rambles,* 1884, as *Shakespeare's England* (Nos. 23058 & 23059), which was again revised & extended in 1892 (No. 23092), 1893 (No. 23099) & 1910 (No. 23139).

23041. THE POEMS ... COMPLETE EDITION. Bos: Osgood, 1881.

23045. THE JEFFERSONS. Bos: Osgood, 1881.
American Actor Series.

*23052. ENGLISH RAMBLES: AND OTHER FUGITIVE PIECES. Bos: Osgood, 1884.
For comment on revised editions see No. 23036 above.

*23054. HENRY IRVING. NY: Coombes, 1885.

*23057. THE STAGE LIFE OF MARY ANDERSON. NY: Coombes, 1886.

23069. WANDERERS. Edinburgh: Douglas, 1888.

23071. WANDERERS. Bos: Ticknor, 1889.
Extended edition published in 1892 (No. 23096).

23074. THE PRESS AND THE STAGE AN ORATION. NY: Lockwood & Coombes, 1889.
Delivered before the Goethe Society, New York, 28 Jan. 1889.

23075. BRIEF CHRONICLES. NY: Dunlap Soc'y, 1889.
3 parts.

23081. A SKETCH OF THE LIFE OF JOHN GILBERT. NY: Dunlap Soc'y, 1890.

23084. ADA REHAN: A STUDY. NY, 1891.
Revised & extended editions published in 1891 (No. 23090) & 1898 (No. 23113).

*23087. GRAY DAYS AND GOLD ... AUTHOR'S EDITION. Edinburgh: Douglas, 1891.
A copyright printing of Part 1 was produced in 1890 (No. 23080).

*23088. GRAY DAYS AND GOLD. NY: Macmillan, 1891.
Revised editions published in 1892 (No. 23095), 1896 (No. 23110) & 1911 (No. 23141).

23089. THE ACTOR AND OTHER SPEECHES CHIEFLY ON THEATRICAL SUBJECTS AND OCCASIONS. NY: Dunlap Soc'y, 1891.

*23093. SHADOWS OF THE STAGE. NY & Lon: Macmillan, 1892.

*23094. OLD SHRINES AND IVY. NY & Lon: Macmillan, 1892.

*23097. GEORGE WILLIAM CURTIS A EULOGY. NY & Lon: Macmillan, 1893.
Delivered at Staten Island, St. George, 24 Feb. 1893.

*23098. SHADOWS OF THE STAGE SECOND SERIES. NY & Lon: Macmillan, 1893.

WILLIAM WINTER (cont.)

*23100. LIFE AND ART OF EDWIN BOOTH. NY & Lon: Macmillan, 1893.
Revised edition published in 1894 (No. 23105).

*23106. LIFE AND ART OF JOSEPH JEFFERSON. NY & Lon: Macmillan, 1894.

23107. SHADOWS OF THE STAGE THIRD SERIES. NY & Lon: Macmillan, 1895.

23108. BROWN HEATH AND BLUE BELLS. NY & Lon: Macmillan, 1895.

23114. A WREATH OF LAUREL BEING SPEECHES ON DRAMATIC AND KINDRED OCCASIONS. NY: Dunlap Soc'y, 1898.
Winter's tribute to Joseph Jefferson, here collected, was also published separately in 1898, as *The Poet and the Actor* (No. 23116).

23126. MARY OF MAGDALA AN HISTORICAL AND ROMANTIC DRAMA. NY & Lon: Macmillan, 1903.
Verse translation from the German of Paul Heyse. An earlier prose translation by "Lionel Vale <i.e. Winter>" was printed (for copyright purposes?) in 1902 (No. 23123).

23130. OTHER DAYS BEING CHRONICLES AND MEMORIES OF THE STAGE. NY: Moffat, Yard, 1908.

23134. OLD FRIENDS BEING LITERARY RECOLLECTIONS OF OTHER DAYS. NY: Moffat, Yard, 1909.

23135. THE POEMS ... AUTHOR'S EDITION. NY: Moffat, Yard, 1909.
Also, a limited edition published earlier in 1909 (No. 23132).

23137. LIFE AND ART OF RICHARD MANSFIELD WITH SELECTIONS FROM HIS LETTERS. NY: Moffat, Yard, 1910.
2v.

23143. OVER THE BORDER. NY: Moffat, Yard, 1911.

23144. SHAKESPEARE ON THE STAGE. NY: Moffat, Yard, 1911.

23148. THE WALLET OF TIME CONTAINING PERSONAL, BIOGRAPHICAL, AND CRITICAL REMINISCENCE OF THE AMERICAN THEATRE. NY: Moffat, Yard, 1913.
2v.

23149. TYRONE POWER. NY: Moffat, Yard, 1913.
Lives of the Players series.

23153. SHAKESPEARE ON THE STAGE SECOND SERIES. NY: Moffat, Yard, 1915.

23155. VAGRANT MEMORIES BEING FURTHER RECOLLECTIONS OF OTHER DAYS. NY: Doran, 1915.

23158. SHAKESPEARE ON THE STAGE THIRD SERIES. NY: Moffat, Yard, 1916.

23161. THE LIFE OF DAVID BELASCO. NY: Moffat, Yard, 1918.
2v.

Theodore Winthrop
1828–1861

23164. A COMPANION TO THE HEART OF THE ANDES. NY: Appleton, 1859.

23165. CECIL DREEME. Bos: Ticknor & Fields, 1861.

23166. JOHN BRENT. Bos: Ticknor & Fields, 1862.

23167. EDWIN BROTHERTOFT. Bos: Ticknor & Fields, 1862.

23168. THE CANOE AND THE SADDLE, ADVENTURES AMONG THE NORTH-WESTERN RIVERS AND FORESTS; AND ISTHMIANA. Bos: Ticknor & Fields, 1863.
   Republished in 1913 with additional material (No. 23175).

23169. LIFE IN THE OPEN AIR, AND OTHER PAPERS. Bos: Ticknor & Fields, 1863.
   Ed. George William Curtis (No. 4283).

23172. THE LIFE AND POEMS. NY: Holt, 1884.
   Ed. Winthrop's sister.

23174. MR. WADDY'S RETURN. NY: Holt, 1904.
   Ed. Burton E. Stevenson.

George Edward Woodberry
1855–1930

Note: Many of Woodberry's works were first issued in small privately printed editions: these are here omitted save for the 7 volumes published by the Woodberry Society from 1912 to 1918.

23180. A HISTORY OF WOOD-ENGRAVING. NY: Harper & Bros., 1883.

23182. EDGAR ALLAN POE. Bos & NY: Houghton, Mifflin, 1885.
   American Men of Letters series.

23190. THE NORTH SHORE WATCH AND OTHER POEMS. Bos & NY: Houghton, Mifflin, 1890.
   The title poem was privately printed in 200 copies in 1883 (No. 21181).

23191. STUDIES IN LETTERS AND LIFE. Bos & NY: Houghton, Mifflin, 1890.

23210. HEART OF MAN. NY: Macmillan, 1899.

*23211. WILD EDEN. NY: Macmillan, 1899.

23214. MAKERS OF LITERATURE. NY: Macmillan, 1900.

*23219. NATHANIEL HAWTHORNE. Bos & NY: Houghton, Mifflin, 1902.
   American Men of Letters series. A "large paper edition" also published in 1902 (No. 23218).

23229. AMERICA IN LITERATURE. NY & Lon: Harper & Bros., 1903.

23230. POEMS. NY: Macmillan, 1903.

23240. THE TORCH EIGHT LECTURES ON RACE POWER IN LITERATURE. NY: McClure, Phillips, 1905.
   Delivered at the Lowell Institute of Boston, 1903.

GEORGE E. WOODBERRY (cont.)
23241. SWINBURNE. NY: McClure, Phillips, 1905.
Contemporary Men of Letters Series.

23242. RALPH WALDO EMERSON. NY & Lon: Macmillan, 1907.
English Men of Letters series.

23245. THE APPRECIATION OF LITERATURE. NY: Baker & Taylor, 1907.

23246. GREAT WRITERS. NY: McClure, 1907.

*23251. THE LIFE OF EDGAR ALLAN POE PERSONAL AND LITERARY. Bos & NY: Houghton Mifflin, 1909.
2v.

23253. THE INSPIRATION OF POETRY. NY: Macmillan, 1910.

*23257. WENDELL PHILLIPS THE FAITH OF AN AMERICAN. <n.p.>: Woodberry Soc'y, 1912.

23258. A DAY AT CASTROGIOVANNI. <n.p.>: Woodberry Soc'y, 1912.

23260. THE KINGDOM OF ALL-SOULS AND TWO OTHER POEMS FOR CHRISTMAS. <n.p.>: Woodberry Soc'y, 1912.

*23268. THE FLIGHT AND OTHER POEMS. NY: Macmillan, 1914.

23269. NORTH AFRICA AND THE DESERT SCENES AND MOODS. NY: Scribner's Sons, 1914.

23270. TWO PHASES OF CRITICISM HISTORICAL AND AESTHETIC LECTURES. <n.p.>: Woodberry Soc'y, 1914.
Delivered at Kenyon College, 7–8 May 1913.

23275. SHAKESPEARE AN ADDRESS. <n.p.>: Woodberry Soc'y, 1916.

23278. IDEAL PASSION SONNETS. <n.p.>: Woodberry Soc'y, 1917.

23281. AN EASTER ODE 1918. <n.p.>: Woodberry Soc'y, 1918.

23282. NATHANIEL HAWTHORNE HOW TO KNOW HIM. Indianapolis: Bobbs-Merrill, <1918>.

*23288. THE ROAMER AND OTHER POEMS. NY: Harcourt, Brace & Howe, 1920.

23292. STUDIES OF A LITTERATEUR. NY: Harcourt, Brace, 1921.
Collected Essays, Vol. 4; for comment see next entry.

23293. LITERARY MEMOIRS OF THE NINETEENTH CENTURY. NY: Harcourt, Brace, 1921.
Collected Essays, Vol. 5. The 6v. set is designated as the *Collected Essays* only on the dust wrapper: Vols. 1–3 & 6 contain only reprinted material, but collect a few fugitive pieces.

23310. SELECTED LETTERS. Bos & NY: Houghton Mifflin, 1933.

Samuel Woodworth
1785–1842

23313. NEW-HAVEN, A POEM. By Selim. NY: The Author, 1809.

23314. BEAST AT LAW, OR ZOOLOGIAN JURISPRUDENCE; A POEM. NY: Harmer, 1811.
These sheets reissued in 1814 in an omnibus volume with title *Bubble & Squeak* (No. 23323).

23315. THE FIRST ATTEMPT, OR SOMETHING NEW. NY: Woodworth, 1811.

23318. QUARTER-DAY, OR THE HORRORS OF THE FIRST OF MAY. A POEM. NY: Woodworth, 1812.
Anon.

23325. THE CHAMPIONS OF FREEDOM, OR THE MYSTERIOUS CHIEF. NY: Baldwin, 1816.
2v. These sheets reissued in 1818–19 (No. 23334).

23331. THE POEMS, ODES, SONGS, AND OTHER METRICAL EFFUSIONS. NY: Asten & Lopez, 1818.
These sheets reissued in 1821 as the "second edition" (No. 23338).

23342. THE DEED OF GIFT, A COMIC OPERA. NY: Baldwin, 1822.

23347. LA FAYETTE, OR THE CASTLE OF OLMUTZ. A DRAMA. NY: Circulating Library & Dramatic Repository, 1824.

*23349. THE FOREST ROSE, OR AMERICAN FARMERS. A PASTORAL OPERA. NY: Circulating Library & Dramatic Repository, 1825.

*23350. THE WIDOW'S SON, OR, WHICH IS THE TRAITOR. A MELO-DRAMA. NY: Circulating Library & Dramatic Repository, 1825.

23354. MELODIES, DUETS, TRIOS, SONGS, AND BALLADS. NY: Campbell, 1826.
Extended "second edition" published in 1830 (No. 23359). "The Bucket" (also "The Old Oaken Bucket") & "The Hunters of Kentucky" are here collected; BAL lists many early ephemeral printings of both poems. The earliest known book publication of "The Bucket" is in *The Post-Chaise Companion*, 1821 (No. 23339).

23377. THE POETICAL WORKS. NY: Scribner, 1861.
2v. Ed. Woodworth's son.

Constance Fenimore Woolson
1840–1894

*23446. THE OLD STONE HOUSE. By Anne March. Bos: Lothrop, <1873>.
The Thousand Dollar Prize Series.

23448. CASTLE NOWHERE: LAKE-COUNTRY SKETCHES. Bos: Osgood, 1875.
Some of these sketches were also published (reprinted?) in undated Canadian editions as *Castle Nowhere* (No. 23450) & *Solomon* (No. 23451).

23455. TWO WOMEN: 1862. A POEM. NY: Appleton, 1877.
"Reprinted from Appleton's Journal."

CONSTANCE FENIMORE WOOLSON (cont.)

23457. RODMAN THE KEEPER: SOUTHERN SKETCHES. NY: Appleton, 1880.

23458. ANNE A NOVEL. NY: Harper & Bros., 1882.

23460. FOR THE MAJOR A NOVELETTE. NY: Harper & Bros., 1883.

23465. EAST ANGELS A NOVEL. NY: Harper & Bros., 1886.

23468. JUPITER LIGHTS A NOVEL. NY: Harper & Bros., 1889.

*23471. HORACE CHASE A NOVEL. NY: Harper & Bros., 1894.

23472. THE FRONT YARD AND OTHER ITALIAN STORIES. NY: Harper & Bros., 1895.

23473. MENTONE, CAIRO, AND CORFU. NY: Harper & Bros., 1896.

23474. DOROTHY AND OTHER ITALIAN STORIES. NY: Harper & Bros., 1896.

23478. VOICES OUT OF THE PAST. Lon: Ellis, <n.d., 1930>.
Ed. Clare Benedict. *Five Generations (1785–1923)*, Part 1.

23479. CONSTANCE FENIMORE WOOLSON. Lon: Ellis, <n.d., 1930>.
Ed. Clare Benedict. *Five Generations (1785–1923)*, Part 2. Revised & extended edition published in 1932 (No. 23481).

23480. "THE BENEDICTS ABROAD." Lon: Ellis, <n.d., 1931>.
Ed. Clare Benedict. *Five Generations (1785–1923)*, Part 3.

Elinor Hoyt Wylie
1885–1928

23483. INCIDENTAL NUMBERS. Lon: Ptd by Clowes & Sons, 1912.
Anon.

*23484. NETS TO CATCH THE WIND. NY: Harcourt, Brace, 1921.

23491. BLACK ARMOUR A BOOK OF POEMS. NY: Doran, <1923>.

*23495. JENNIFER LORN: A SEDATE EXTAVAGANZA. NY: Doran, 1923.

*23505. THE VENETIAN GLASS NEPHEW. NY: Doran, 1925.

*23508. THE ORPHAN ANGEL. NY: Knopf, 1926.
Published in the U.K. in 1927 as *Mortal Image* (No. 23513).

*23517. MR. HODGE & MR. HAZARD. NY: Knopf, 1928.

*23518. TRIVIAL BREATH. NY & Lon: Knopf, 1928.

*23521. ANGELS AND EARTHLY CREATURES. NY & Lon: Knopf, 1929.
The first 19 sonnets were privately printed in the U.K. in 1928 (No. 23520).

23522. BIRTHDAY SONNET. NY: Random House, 1929.
One of *The Poetry Quartos.*

*23526. COLLECTED POEMS. NY: Knopf, 1932.

23527. COLLECTED PROSE. NY: Knopf, 1933.

23536. LAST POEMS OF ELINOR WYLIE ... WITH OTHER POEMS HITHERTO UNPUBLISHED IN BOOK FORM. NY: Knopf, 1943.
Ed. Jane D. Wise.